EVERY
CHILD
A LION

EVERY CHILD
A LION The Origins of

Maternal and Infant Health Policy in the

United States and France, 1890–1920

ALISA KLAUS

Cornell University Press

Ithaca and London

First published 1993 by Cornell University Press.

International Standard Book Number 0-8014-2447-X
Library of Congress Catalog Card Number 92-34682

Printed in the United States of America

Librarians: Library of Congress cataloging information appears on the last page of the book.

⊗ The paper in this book meets the minimum requirements of the American National Standard for Information Sciences— Permanence of Paper for Printed Library Materials, ANSI Z39.48–1984.

Contents

Preface

I first began to research this subject for seminar papers for Michael Katz and Charles Rosenberg in 1980 and 1981. I am grateful to them for pointing out the importance of the movement to prevent infant mortality, and encouraging me to pursue my interest in it. Carroll Smith-Rosenberg's repeated reminders to think broadly helped me to avoid drowning in my notecards and to keep my mind on the relationship of maternal and infant health to wider issues in women's history. Jack Reece straightened out my French history; he and Diana Long helped me to define the significance and context of my research.

I am grateful to those who saw enough value in my proposal to grant me the Bourse Chateaubriand and Penfield Scholarship that enabled me to pursue my research in France, though my formal background in French history was limited. Several people assisted me in my search for sources in various intimidating libraries and archives in Paris. Rachel Fuchs generously shared her knowledge of the available material on maternal and child welfare. Marion Hunt assisted me in tracking down elusive sources. The archivists and librarians at the Bibliothèque nationale, the Archives nationales, and the Assistance publique helped me to negotiate the complexities of their cataloging systems. The staff of the National Archives in Washington, D.C., greatly facilitated my work with the well-organized and cataloged Children's Bureau records.

I owe special thanks to Janet Golden, who read the entire manuscript with care and provided me with detailed and incisive suggestions, and Glenna Matthews, whose comments and encouragement were invaluable. Barry Bergen, Naomi Rogers, and Janna Dieckman took the time to read parts of the manuscript. Participants in the lunchtime seminars of the Wood Institute for Medical History, the Graduate History Workshop at the University of Pennsylvania, and the Women's History Cluster of the Feminist Studies Focused Research Activity at the University of California, Santa Cruz, provided friendly, insightful, and useful comments on various chapters.

My approach to maternal and child welfare policy has been shaped through discussions with many people. I learned a great deal from the clear and uncompromising thinking of other members of the Philadelphia Reproductive Rights Organization and the women's history group at the University of Pennsylvania. Discussions with Sybil Lipschutz and Molly Ladd-Taylor helped me to clarify my thinking on the history of women's movements of the Progressive Era. I am grateful to Rebecca Levy for expert word-processing assistance.

Pamela Roby's support and reminders that academic work is worthwhile helped to rekindle my confidence and enthusiasm at frustrating moments. Heather Trumbower and Kathi Jaramillo provided me with excellent companionship between the footnotes, and Gael Livingston with humor and unfailing encouragement. Finally, I thank my mother, who took such good care of her own five children *and* taught us how to think, and my father, who has, over the years, done his best to save many babies, while also taking the time to pay attention to their parents, and has learned to question the medical model in which he was trained.

ALISA KLAUS

Santa Cruz, California

EVERY
CHILD
A LION

Introduction: Infant Mortality and Social Reform

"It is a tragedy that there should live at the present day men who believe that organizations such as ours are running counter to the interests of mankind in attempting to save the lives of helpless infants, or, as they express it, to save the weak and decrepit to become a burden to the family and the state. . . . They do not realize . . . that to prevent death means to prevent disease; they do not appreciate the economic value of these lives to the state, a fact which is receiving the earnest consideration of nearly all of the great nations of the earth; . . . and they are immune to the appeal of the helpless bit of humanity suffering not as a result of any inherent weakness or any fault of its own, but rather as a result of the ignorance, avarice and selfishness of adult man."[1] Samuel McClintock Hammill, a Philadelphia physician, addressed these words to the members of the American Association for the Study and Prevention of Infant Mortality, assembled in Milwaukee in 1916 for their seventh annual meeting. The organization, over which Hamill presided in that year, was dedicated to arousing the indifferent public to its responsibility for the lives of the nation's children. As Hamill pointed out, the movement to prevent infant mortality in the early twentieth century was an international one. Physicians and public health officials in all the industrial nations

1. S. McC. Hamill, "The Presidential Address," *Transactions of the American Association for the Study and Prevention of Infant Mortality* 7 (1916): 23–24.

believed that they understood the causes of yearly summer epidemics of infant diarrhea well enough to prevent most of the deaths that resulted. They also sought to reduce the number of deaths in the first weeks of life—the most dangerous—from prematurity, congenital diseases, and malformations. At international medical and social welfare conferences professionals from all over the world shared their scientific findings, social analyses, and ideas for reform. Those who attended the meetings of the International Congress of *Gouttes de lait* (milk stations) held in 1905, 1907, and 1911 or the International Congress on Hygiene and Demography in 1912 learned about pure milk stations, infant health clinics, maternity insurance, prenatal care programs, propaganda to encourage breast-feeding, and instructive visiting nurses in countries as diverse as Rumania, the Philippines, the United States, France, Britain, and Germany.

Maternal and infant health movements in individual countries, particularly the United States and Great Britain, have been the subject of several excellent recent histories.[2] In focusing on the development of public programs to combat infant mortality in two countries, this book seeks to address larger isssues in the comparative history of maternal and child welfare policy. Until recently, maternal and child welfare has been neglected in histories of public policy. In the past several years, however, feminist historians have argued that addressing questions related to gender is essential to a full understanding of the history of the welfare state. These historians have focused on the development of programs to aid women and children; they have also brought to the fore the vital role that women, as volunteers, activists, and professionals, played in creating welfare-state structures. In the late nineteenth century bourgeois women demanded a voice in the world of politics and bureaucracy, transforming the dominant ideol-

2. See Richard A. Meckel, *Save the Babies: American Public Health Reform and the Prevention of Infant Mortality, 1850–1929* (Baltimore: Johns Hopkins University Press, 1990); Deborah Dwork, *War Is Good for Babies and Other Young Children: A History of the Infant and Child Welfare Movement in England, 1898–1918* (London: Tavistock, 1987); Anna Davin, "Imperialism and Motherhood," *History Workshop Journal* 5 (Spring 1978): 9–66; Jane Lewis, *The Politics of Motherhood: Child and Maternal Welfare in England, 1900–1939* (London: Croom Helm, 1980). On the history of motherhood and the pediatric profession, see Sydney A. Halpern, *American Pediatrics: The Social Dynamics of Professionalism, 1880–1980* (Berkeley: University of California Press, 1988), and Rima Apple, *Mothers and Medicine: A Social History of Infant Feeding, 1890–1950* (Madison: University of Wisconsin Press, 1987).

ogies of gender difference and separate spheres to justify their participation in public decisions that affected the home and the lives of women and children.[3]

While the maternal and infant health programs of the early twentieth century owed much to women's activism, social reform philosophies based on concepts of social interdependence also suggested that it was in the interest of the state to make an investment in the lives of its citizens. As one German bureaucrat put it, speaking at the International Congress on Hygiene and Demography in 1912, "The most valuable asset of a nation is the people themselves. This asset, in amount and quality, is the organic national capital, forming the virgin soil of civilization and economic productivity."[4] A declining birthrate and repeated preparation for war in western Europe also brought home the value of children's lives to their nations. Concern for the number and health of future mothers, soldiers, and workers transcended political divisions; fascists and Fabians alike advocated public programs to protect maternal and child life and to encourage childbearing. Underlying all European maternal and child welfare programs was the belief that motherhood was a patriotic duty and rearing children a social service. In no country was this more true than in France, the first to experience a decline in the birthrate; in view of the military threat posed by Germany, many observers warned that this demographic trend was a potential national catastrophe.

As Hamill's words illustrate, reformers in the United States also saw children's lives as a national asset. This view did not provide a rationale for pronatalist family policies, however. American social scientists could document a decline in the birthrate of native-born whites, but immigration and the higher birthrate among immigrants

3. For a summary of this work see Seth Koven and Sonya Michel, "Womanly Duties: Maternalist Politics and the Origins of Welfare States in France, Germany, Great Britain and the United States, 1880–1920," *American Historical Review* 95 (1990): 1076–1114; *Mothers of a New World: Maternalist Politics and the Origins of Welfare States*, ed. Seth Koven and Sonya Michel (London: Routledge; forthcoming); *Women, the State, and Welfare*, ed. Linda Gordon (Madison: University of Wisconsin Press, 1990); *Lady Bountiful Revisited: Women, Philanthropy, and Power*, ed. Kathleen D. McCarthy (New Brunswick, N.J.: Rutgers University Press, 1990).

4. Frederick Ahn, "Woman in Industrial Life of the Principal Civilized Nations— A Social, Demographic, Hygienic Study," *Transactions of the Fifteenth International Congress on Hygiene and Demography*, 1912, vol. 6, p. 321.

more than offset this trend. Rather than welcome the nation's new citizens, native-born social reformers disparaged the changing ethnic composition of the country's population. Furthermore, the United States did not face military threats to its national integrity during this period; politicians had no reason to fear a potential shortage of children. Progressive reformers saw internal social change, not external military force, as the greatest threat to the stability and prosperity of the nation. "Race suicide," a favorite concept of Progressive reformers, referred not to the rate of growth of the population as a whole but to the population's changing composition. Racism and a traditional mistrust of government intervention in public welfare combined to limit public commitment to maternal and child welfare; we see the legacy of this reluctance in the contemporary hostility toward public assistance to poor mothers and their children.

A central question of this book, therefore, concerns the effects of populationist ideologies and the associated politics of race, military mobilization, and nationalism on public and professional intervention in reproduction and childrearing. Clearly, the French population crisis stimulated an interest in infant mortality and a consensus in favor of maternal and child welfare programs which was not duplicated in the United States. American reformers were more concerned about the quality and the composition of the population than with the rate of population growth; thus a significant eugenic element found its way into the infant health movement. Also fundamental to understanding the different approaches to infant health in the two countries is that French policy making was far more centralized and was rooted in centuries-old traditions of government intervention in social life. The absence of a federal public welfare bureaucracy in the United States worked to the advantage of women: already far more unified and independent of male-dominated institutions than were their French counterparts, women's organizations and female physicians in the United States were able to influence public maternal and infant health programs on the local, state, and national levels. These women developed a distinctive approach to maternal and infant health care; as a result the organization and actions of municipal and state divisions of child hygiene and the U.S. Children's Bureau reflected the larger vision of the Progressive women's movement.[5] In France the high

5. See Kathryn Kish Sklar, "Explaining the Power of Women's Political Culture

level of official interest in infant health and the dominance of well-established bureaucracies in both public and private social welfare institutions contributed to the exclusion of women from policy making. Their role in maternal and infant welfare before the 1920s was confined essentially to fund raising and voluntary service.

Women's organizations were not the only interest group active in infant health campaigns. In both countries the movement to prevent infant mortality provided a significant opportunity for pediatricians and obstetricians in the process of establishing themselves as authorities on childbirth and child care. Historically the French medical profession had depended on the state in the development of its legal monopoly and social legitimacy, and Republican politicians' efforts to make French women the paid nurses of their own children, under medical supervision, enhanced physicians' authority. Physicians in the United States, without the benefits of a centralized system of medical education and licensing, had to rely more on their own powers of persuasion in convincing women to depend on their expert advice. Ultimately, while the French medical establishment supported public health and welfare programs, the mainstream of American physicians perceived their interests differently, and the American Medical Association waged a vigorous battle against federal maternal and infant health legislation.

Campaigns to prevent infant mortality must also be viewed in the context of the larger reform movements of which they were a part. The political groups most active in creating social welfare policies—Progressive reformers in the United States and the solidarist Radical Republicans in France—shared a philosophical perspective and had similar visions of social organization and the role of the state in society. Both groups sought to protect the working class from the worst excesses of industrial capitalism with the goal of restoring social harmony among the classes. Progressive reformers also aspired to restore

---

in the Creation of the American Welfare State," in *Mothers of a New World*, ed. Koven and Michel. On the Children's Bureau see Mary Madeleine Ladd-Taylor, "Mother-Work: Ideology, Public Policy, and the Mothers' Movement, 1890–1930," Ph.D. diss., Yale University, 1986; also, her article in *Mothers of a New World*, ed. Koven and Michel. On institutional-political factors influencing welfare-state formation in the United States generally, see Margaret Weir, Ann Shola Orloff, and Theda Skocpol, "Understanding American Social Politics," in *The Politics of Social Policy in the United States,* ed. Weir, Orloff, and Skocpol (Princeton, N.J.: Princeton University Press, 1988), pp. 3–27.

to cities transformed by immigration and industrialization something of the social and moral tone of a mythical past. Those who campaigned for infant health programs hoped that the education of mothers by public health nurses, baby health contests, and classes for schoolgirls in infant care would both save infant lives and serve the political purposes of Progressivism. While often sympathetic to the plight of the poor, they saw most forms of public assistance as demoralizing; "Education, not charity," was their motto.

French maternal and infant health policy was not free of moral objectives: the debate over depopulation was part of a larger discourse on national moral and physical degeneration. Both Radical Republicans and conservative Catholics attributed the population crisis at least partly to moral decadence, and legislators and physicians addressing the problem of infant mortality hoped at the same time to counter such trends as the purported decay of the maternal instinct in women and the increasing unwillingness of French men to take on the responsibilities of family life. At the same time, the urgency of the population crisis led politicians to sacrifice such moral imperatives as the punishment of women who bore illegitimate children. It also stimulated those who subscribed to liberal economic theory to soften their stance against government interference in the economy in the case of maternity leaves and maternity benefits.

Chapter 1 of this book compares the French discourse on depopulation with American writings on "race suicide" and examines how these ideas shaped the approach to infant mortality in each country. Chapter 2 traces the medical discourse on infant mortality and the development of the medical supervision of infant care in the United States and France, in the context of some of the larger questions in the comparative history of the medical profession. Chapters 3 and 4 address the roles of French female volunteers and charitable organizations in infant health institutions in contrast to the massive women's infant health movement in the United States and offer an explanation for the much greater influence of female reformers in the United States.

Chapter 5 traces the development of maternal welfare policy in France up to World War I, focusing on efforts to make it possible for women to fulfill their maternal functions without giving up their economic contributions to their families and the larger economy— in particular, the campaign for maternity leaves and crèches, or day nurseries. Chapter 6 describes the work of the U.S. Children's Bureau, created in 1912. The women who directed and staffed this agency developed a woman-centered perspective on maternal and child welfare policy. In the late 1910s this vision increasingly came into conflict with a medical model of maternity care that reflected the interests of obstetricians and pediatricians.

Chapter 7 explores the effect of World War I and its aftermath on maternal and infant health policy in both countries. To many, the war drove home the gruesome nature of the state's interest in reproduction. Throughout Europe maternal and child welfare received more attention than ever before, and for the first time advocates of infant health programs in the United States began to cite the need for infant lives to replace the adult lives lost on the battlefield. The war reinvigorated French pronatalism; the result was that in the 1920s and 1930s increasingly comprehensive maternal and child health programs were integrated into a pronatalist family policy that also included repressive legislation against birth control and abortion. In the United States the war provided the stimulus for the massive mobilization of women to protect infant health as part of the war effort. The great triumph of this movement came with the passage of the Sheppard-Towner Act in 1921, providing federal support to states for instruction to mothers in prenatal and infant care.

Exploring the approaches of two different societies to maternal and infant health illuminates the politics of public welfare on several levels. First, it reveals the importance of reproduction to political goals such as military strength, economic growth, social stability, and ethnic and racial homogeneity. Second, the movement to prevent infant mortality is a critical chapter in the history of medical professionalization; it suggests some of the ways in which physicians' search for monopoly and legitimacy interacted with larger processes in the development of social institutions. Finally, this book illustrates the many-faceted meaning of motherhood in modern capitalist society, as a symbol of social stability and moral purity, as the basis for women's claim to political power, as a social role in competition with wage labor for women's time and energy, and as the source of citizens, soldiers, and workers.

I

Pronatalism, Eugenics, and Infant Mortality

When S. Josephine Baker, head of the Child Hygiene Division of the New York City Department of Health, visited the Soviet Union in the 1930s she was impressed with the child welfare institutions she observed there. Though disappointed by the primitive facilities and the backward state of medical practice, she later wrote, "It was exciting for me who had spent twenty-three years fighting and intriguing to keep a huge municipality interested in babies, compromising here and there and gaining a little as years went by, to see a whole nation straining every nerve to give babies and little children the best available, even if it was not altogether the best possible." Baker suspected, however, that this effort was not simply due to the Soviet people's sentimentality toward children. The Soviet government, she thought, was aware of the need for a high birthrate and a vigorous population, especially with war in sight. "Now the Soviet Union," she wrote, "is certainly feeling the full effect of the demand for child welfare that always arises in any nation that is frantically preparing for war. It is just another example of the grisly connection between the need for life and preparation for wholesale death."[1]

1. S. Josephine Baker, *Fighting for Life* (New York: Macmillan, 1939), pp. 220–21. Ironically, though she reports a striking reduction in Soviet infant mortality of 50 percent between 1914 and 1925, Francine du Plessix Gray, visiting the Soviet Union some fifty years after Baker, was appalled by the "phenomenal backwardness

The Soviet government was not alone in making such calculations. The legislators and officials who developed child welfare policy in all European countries between 1870 and 1950 believed that a healthy and growing population was essential to national political and economic power; they saw the medical and financial assistance of mothers and children as a means of fostering their nations' human resources. It is true that European family policy had other goals as well: French family allowances, for example, had their origins in the 1890s in the efforts of industrialists to satisfy the most immediate demands for higher wages while keeping the general wage level down.[2] Similarly, in the 1940s British authorities hoped that family allowances would inhibit inflation.[3] Nazi pronatalist propaganda in the 1930s was designed not only to encourage "Aryan" women to have babies but also to keep them from competing with men for jobs.[4] Still, political leaders could not ignore the voracious appetite of modern warfare for human lives, and the declining birthrate contributed significantly to family policy debates.

In the United States, immigration more than compensated numerically for the declining birthrate in the late nineteenth century. Furthermore, the threat of war did not affect American politics as fundamentally as it did in Europe. Baker was consistently frustrated by the indifference of American politicians to child life—except during World War I. During the war she observed, somewhat bitterly, a sudden interest in child welfare—a result, she thought, of the realization that infant lives were valuable to the nation as replacements for the adult lives lost on the battlefield.[5] Like their European counterparts, American political leaders, physicians, and reformers considered human beings as a national resource; the difference lay in the overriding concern of Progressive reformers in the United States for the quality and composition of the population. They sought an increase in the birthrate only among the native-

---

on the issue of women's and children's health." Francine du Plessix Gray, *Soviet Women: Walking the Tightrope* (New York: Doubleday, 1989), p. 25.

2. David Glass, *Population Policies and Movements in Europe* (Oxford: Clarendon Press, 1940), p. 104.

3. John Macnicol, "Family Allowances and Less Eligibility," in *The Origins of British Social Policy*, ed. Pat Thane (London: Croom Helm, 1978), p. 193.

4. Tim Mason, "Women in Germany, 1917–1940: Family, Welfare and Work," *History Workshop Journal* 1 (Spring 1976): 91.

5. Baker, *Fighting for Life*, p. 165.

born white middle class, in the hopes that this would counteract the effects of immigration.

At the same time, late-nineteenth-century reformers in both France and the United States, as in Canada and other western European nations, shared fears about the physical and moral degeneration of the population. They turned to a medical model of national decline to explain both loss of national power and internal social problems such as crime, mental illness, alcoholism, and prostitution. Thus Jacques Donzelot points out the fundamental proximity of the superficially opposed populationist and Neo-Malthusian views of the family in twentieth-century France; both, he argues, implied an "interventionist, coercive pole that welded them to one another." It is especially revealing, Donzelot suggests, that both sides quoted from Hitler's *Mein Kampf.* Populationists liked Hitler's pronouncements on the family and his emphasis on the importance of children; Neo-Malthusians found attractive his call for measures to prevent venereal disease and his proposals for regulating marriage.[6]

In England the Boer War stimulated a campaign to improve infant health, not only because children constituted an important national asset in an era of imperialist expansion but also because the army rejected a large percentage of working-class recruits as physically unfit. British concerns about national decline—as manifested, for example, in the work of the Inter-Departmental Committee on Physical Deterioration in 1903—centered on fears about Britain's military weakness and the ability of British industry to maintain its international position.[7]

This chapter explores the ways in which the impulse to increase the rate of population growth and to influence the composition or quality of the population shaped and colored the discourse on infant mortality in the United States and France. For those concerned about

6. Robert A. Nye, *Crime, Madness, and Politics in Modern France: The Medical Concept of National Decline* (Princeton, N.J.: Princeton University Press, 1984), pp. 334–35, 331–33; Jacques Donzelot, *The Policing of Families* (New York: Pantheon, 1979), p. 187.

7. Anna Davin, "Imperialism and Motherhood," *History Workshop Journal* 5 (Spring 1978): 12; Deborah Dwork, *War Is Good for Babies and Other Young Children: A History of the Infant and Child Welfare Movement in England, 1898–1918* (London: Tavistock, 1987), pp. 9–10, 18–19; Nye, *Crime, Madness, and Politics,* p. 333.

population growth or national decline, infant mortality was a critical issue, because deaths of young children made up a large percentage of all deaths. Around the turn of the century, about 150 of every thousand children born in France died before the age of one year.[8] In both the United States and France infant mortality rates were higher in urban areas, especially in industrial cities and mining towns, than in small towns and rural areas. In a few southern American cities and New England industrial towns, as many as 30 percent of infants died.[9] In all communities poor children were far more likely to die than children of the well-to-do. Certain groups of children had particularly low chances of surviving their first year: in the United States African-American children had a mortality rate more than twice as high as that of whites, and infants in foundling homes might have only a 60 percent chance of living through their first year or two.[10] French children who were placed out to nurse in the country, especially those who were wards of the state or illegitimate, also died in large numbers.[11]

8. Michel Huber calculated an infant mortality rate of 158/1000 live births for all of France: *La population de la France pendant la guerre* (Paris: Presses Universitaires de France, 1931), p. 54. No national statistics are available for the United States, as reformers lamented, because of the lack of effective birth registration laws.

9. Wilbur C. Phillips, "A Plan for Reducing Infant Mortality in New York City," *Medical Record,* May 30, 1908: 890; R. Felhoen, *Etude statistique sur la mortalité infantile à Roubaix et dans ses cantons comparée avec celle de Lille et Tourcoing, 1871–1905* (Paris: Vigot Frères, 1906), p. 78; E. Ausset, "Rapport général sur la mortalité infantile et les consultations de nourissons dans la région du Nord," in Alliance d'hygiène sociale, *La lutte sociale contre la mortalité infantile dans le Pas-de-Calais et le Nord* (Bordeaux: Librairie de la Mutalité, 1904), pp. 6–8; Richard A. Meckel, *Save the Babies: American Public Health Reform and the Prevention of Infant Mortality, 1850–1929* (Baltimore: Johns Hopkins University Press, 1990), pp. 105–6.

10. The infant mortality rate was 143/1000 live births for white children in the registration area and 297/1000 live births for African-American children. U.S. Cong., Senate, 61st Cong., 2d Sess., Document No. 645, *Infant Mortality and Its Relation to the Employment of Mothers,* p. 20, vol. 13 of *Report on Condition of Woman and Child Wage-Earners in the United States, 1912.* A survey of twenty-two institutions in New York reported a mortality rate of 40.3 percent for children under age two. Hastings Hart, "Study of Infant Mortality by the Russell Sage Foundation," *Transactions of the American Association for the Study and Prevention of Infant Mortality* 1 (1910): 54; John W. Trask, "The Significance of the Mortality Rate of the Colored Population of the United States," *American Journal of Public Health* 6 (1916): 255.

11. Rachel Ginnis Fuchs, *Abandoned Children: Foundlings and Child Welfare in Nineteenth-Century France* (Albany: State University of New York Press, 1984), pp. 196–97.

*Population and Pronatalism in France and
the United States*

Pronatalism provided the perspective most obviously influencing French efforts to save infant lives and led to a broad political consensus in favor of maternal and child health programs. French population thought had another aspect to it, however, one that was also reflected in infant health policy. Because the mainstream of French political thought defined population growth as essential to the nation's integrity, the Neo-Malthusian argument that birth control would solve many social problems was by definition unpatriotic; only a handful of political radicals dared to express this view openly. Nonetheless, eugenics was not incompatible with pronatalism. Depopulation was only what Robert Nye has called the "master pathology" in the French model of national degeneration. [12] Both right- and left-wing politicians believed that moral and physical degeneration, manifested in alcoholism, tuberculosis, and a high infant mortality rate, were intimately related to the declining birthrate. It is therefore not surprising to find that some of the most ardent pronatalists actively advocated eugenic measures to counteract some of the causes of the perceived decline in the nation's physical health. The measures they proposed as solutions, among them the protection of maternal and infant health, addressed not only the question of the birthrate but the larger question of social disorder and degeneration as well. In particular, the Radical Republicans—the group most active in advocating maternal and infant health programs—focused their attention on women's wage labor as the most important cause of infant mortality and an important factor in the decline of the birthrate and the disordered state of working-class morality and family life.

French observers pointed to the declining birthrate as both cause and symptom of the nation's general physical and moral degeneration. They cited "depopulation" as the cause of economic stagnation, as a sign of rampant individualism and the denial of family and patriotic responsibility, and, most important, as the cause of France's military defeat at the hands of Germany. Because infant mortality was part and parcel of the population problem, they sought to discover its causes in the same social pathology that had caused

12. Nye, *Crime, Madness, and Politics*, p. 140.

the decline in the birthrate. Underlying the analyses of scientists and social scientists was a conviction that the source of the nation's problems was a moral one.

French debates over national degeneration reflected the political and social tensions within the Third Republic. Most obvious was the continuing struggle of Republicans to maintain their hold on the nation in the face of conservative opposition. Recently, however, historians have seen late-nineteenth- and early-twentieth-century social reforms such as social insurance and regulation of working conditions as a response to fears of working-class revolt. Mary Lynn Stewart has suggested that legislation to regulate women's working conditions was also an indirect way of reinforcing the working-class family, as a response to the social disorders resulting from economic depression. This search for "social peace" was intertwined with the quest for national power and prestige and thus, especially in the case of legislation affecting women and children, with depopulation.[13]

The proceedings of the Alliance d'hygiène sociale, founded in 1904 to coordinate the work of regional groups of entrepreneurs interested in improving the conditions of the working class, illustrate the relationship between social reform and degeneration. In this organization's debates, the various symptoms of degeneration—alcoholism, tuberculosis, infant mortality, syphilis, and crime—were all united into a single problem that was to be remedied through public health and education. The alliance and its local branches supported reforms that ranged from the improvement of workers' housing, assistance of mothers, and mutual aid to physical education and the teaching of child hygiene.[14]

13. Sanford Elwitt, *The Third Republic Defended: Bourgeois Reform in France, 1880–1914* (Baton Rouge: Louisiana State University Press, 1986), p. 7; Judith F. Stone, *The Search for Social Peace: Reform Legislation in France, 1890–1914* (Albany: State University of New York Press, 1985), p. 23; Mary Lynn Stewart, *Women, Work, and the French State* (Kingston, Ont.: McGill-Queen's University Press, 1989), p. 12. Angus McLaren argues that a close reading of the debates over depopulation suggests that legislators were more concerned to maintain controls over workers and women than to increase the birthrate. *Sexuality and Social Order* (New York: Holmes and Meier, 1983), pp. 181–82.

14. Elwitt, *Third Republic Defended*, pp. 143–45; Alliance d'hygiène sociale, Comité régional de Marseille, *Réunion constitutive* (Bordeaux: l'Avenir de la Mutualité, 1908), pp. 13–15; Alliance d'hygiène sociale, *La lutte sociale contre la mortalité infantile*; Henri de Rothschild, *La mortalité par gastro-entérite chez les enfants âgés de o à 1 an à Paris* (Paris: Progrès médical, 1900), pp. 9–10. On the social hygiene movement generally, see Nye, *Crime, Madness, and Politics*, p. 169.

Eugenics was a much more pervasive and explicit factor in discussions of infant health in the United States. Economic concentration, industrial growth, urbanization, and immigration were the
broad issues that defined American politics in the late nineteenth and
early twentieth centuries. "Race suicide," a concept widely accepted
among Progressive reformers of all varieties, reflected a concern with
the changing composition of the American population, as upper- and
middle-class whites bore fewer and fewer children while more prolific
immigrants from southern and eastern Europe filled the factories and
slums. The concept of race suicide colored all Progressive reform.
Those who were disturbed by militant labor organization and urban
poverty, crime and overcrowding, often blamed exploitative employers and corrupt landlords, but they also blamed the immigrants
themselves.

Urban public health officials in the United States traced the causes
of infant mortality partly to poverty and defective public hygiene,
but they placed the primary blame on the ignorance of immigrant
mothers. They organized infant health campaigns in part as a way of
reaching into the immigrant family and making its moral and social
life more "American." This is not to say that the campaigns did not
promote some scientifically valid policies. As in France, however, the
social visions of reformers and politicians and the political culture in
which they worked determined the institutional structures through
which scientific principles were put into practice.

It is important to point out that only racism and a particular social
vision made the decline of Anglo-Saxon predominance in the United
States alarming. Similarly, only from the vantage point of a particular
political outlook was the decline in the French birthrate a national
catastrophe and not a promising indicator of social progress. In Britain, the death rate began to decline in the eighteenth century; not
until the late nineteenth century did the birthrate begin to fall. The
result was an explosion in population growth.[15] In France, however,
the marital fertility rate seems to have been declining as early as the
late eighteenth century, so that industrialization was accompanied by
a decrease in the rate of population growth. It was in the nineteenth
century that the French situation became distinctive: after 1800 the

15. H. J. Habakkuk, *Population Growth and Economic Development since 1750* (Leicester, Eng.: Leicester University Press, 1972), chap. 2.

birthrate and the rate of population growth both declined rapidly in comparison with those of other European nations.[16] The birthrate per one thousand people declined from around 38 before 1789 to 32.4 in 1801–10, to 26.3 in 1851–60, and to 18.8 in the three years preceding World War I. In contrast, in England and Wales, the birthrate was an estimated 33.8 in 1801–10 and peaked in 1871–80 at 35.4. When it began to decline in the late 1870s it did so rapidly, reaching 24.1 just before World War I. Germany had a higher birthrate still: about 42.5 (for Prussia only) in 1811–20. It was still as high as 36.1 at the turn of the century, and decreased to 28.0 in 1911–13.[17]

French demographic thought and policy before the late eighteenth century was based essentially on the mercantilist theory that a growing population was both a sign of a prosperous nation and an essential factor in its prosperity, but Malthusianism came to dominate demographic thought in the early nineteenth century. The French population was growing, and the increasing concentration of working-class people in newly industrial cities probably seemed more threatening to intellectuals and the government than did any threat from outside. It was the consciousness of an external military threat in the form of Germany that brought the problem of "depopulation" into existence. Beginning in the five years before the Franco-Prussian War, sociologists, demographers, journalists, physicians, and politicians described depopulation as the source of France's military weakness, economic stagnation, and moral degeneration; for over fifty years they tirelessly debated the causes of the decline in the birthrate and proposed a host of measures—few of them ever actually implemented—to counteract the trend. Twice, in 1901 and 1912, the government acknowledged the gravity of the problem by appointing a special commission on depopulation.[18]

Though by 1900 demographers were aware that the demographic

16. Carlo M. Cipolla, *The Economic History of World Population* (Harmondsworth, Eng.: Penguin, 1978), pp. 103–4; J. Dupaquier and M. Lachiver, "Les débuts de la contraception en France ou les deux Malthusianismes," *Annales, E.S.C.* 24 (1969): 1401; Joseph J. Spengler, *France Faces Depopulation: Postlude Edition, 1936–1976* (Durham, N.C.: Duke University Press, 1979), p. 52; McLaren, *Sexuality and Social Order*, p. 26.

17. Spengler, *France Faces Depopulation*, p. 53.

18. Ibid., pp. 117, 225–27; McLaren, *Sexuality and Social Order*, pp. 9–11; Robert Talmy, *Histoire du mouvement familial en France (1896–1939)* (Aubenas: Union nationale des caisses d'allocations familiales, 1962), pp. 100, 128.

transition was a universal tendency in industrialized societies, they did not cease to worry. They continued to describe the situation in alarming terms, using statistics designed to fuel nationalistic alarm. One physician concluded in 1914, for example, that Germany's rate of population growth between 1866 and 1900 was ten times as high as that of France. Though the German birthrate in 1910 was only 31 per thousand compared with 24.4 in France, each year Germany gained nine hundred thousand to one million new citizens, while France acquired twenty to thirty thousand at most and sometimes none. Thus Germany could muster a military contingent at least one and one half times as strong as that of France.[19]

In comparison it is perhaps indicative that accurate fertility statistics were not even available for the United States in the early twentieth century. As late as 1916 and 1917 those who wrote to the U.S. Children's Bureau asking for information about birth and death rates in the United States were told that these statistics could only be estimated, because birth registration was far from complete. In 1914, Cressy Wilbur of the Census Bureau complained that even in Massachusetts, with the highest percentage of registered births in the country, city authorities could not claim registration "even as fairly complete as that of the ordinary European country." "Unless the American people wake up," he warned, "China and Turkey will have satisfactory data for infant mortality long before the United States."[20] Available evidence suggests that in the United States the birthrate began to decline around 1800 in rural areas where farmland became scarce. By 1905–9, however, the crude birthrate was 30 per thousand, much higher than in France and also somewhat higher than in the other countries of western Europe.[21]

19. B. Roussy, *Education domestique de la femme et rénovation sociale* (Paris: Delagrave, 1914), pp. 62–66.

20. Cressy Wilbur, "The Need for Thorough Birth Registration for Race Betterment," in Race Betterment Foundation, *Proceedings of the First National Conference on Race Betterment* (Battle Creek, Mich.: Gage Printing Co., 1914), pp. 75–77; Margaret Roche to U.S. Children's Bureau, 7/16/17 and reply, 7/25/17; J. Leypoldt to Director, U.S. Children's Bureau, 2/23/16 (U.S. Children's Bureau, 4–0–1–2); Edward Bunnell Phelps, "A Statistical Survey of Infant Mortality's Urgent Call for Action," *Transactions of the American Association for the Study and Prevention of Infant Mortality* 1 (1910): 165–89.

21. Robert V. Wells, "Family History and Demographic Transition," in *The American Family in Social-Historical Perspective,* ed. Michael Gordon (New York: St. Martin's Press, 1978), pp. 524–25; Richard A. Easterlin, "Factors in the Decline of Farm Family

A few militant nationalists pointed to the declining birthrate in alarm, especially around the time of the Spanish-American War, warning that American political ambitions required an ever-increasing population. More often, however, United States nationalism and patriotism were expressed as a desire to maintain the nation's racial purity. National population growth was not really threatened; the problem was that southern and eastern European working-class immigrants were increasing faster than the native-born white middle class. Racism also underlay the pronatalism of the militant imperialists, who described the expansion of the United States as the natural triumph of the fittest human stock over inferior races.[22]

Like French writers, scholars and journalists in the United States warned that such factors as moral decadence, a rising cost of living accompanied by rising expectations, and the education of women could lead to reduced fertility, but this concern extended only to the native-born white middle-class element of the population. One writer pointed out that the rate of reproduction of the entire native-born element of the population was even lower than the French birthrate, "which has long been known to be at the point of stagnation."[23] Census figures in 1910 showed that marriages of native-born white literate couples produced few children, especially in urban areas, while the families of the foreign-born were large.[24]

Progressive reformers found troubling the disparity between urban society in the late nineteenth century and the ideals of American democracy they had learned in school, from their parents, at Inde-

Fertility in the United States: Some Preliminary Research Results," in ibid., p. 533; Cipolla, *Economic History of World Population*, p. 92.

22. Richard Hofstadter, *Social Darwinism in American Thought, 1860–1915* (Philadelphia: University of Pennsylvania Press, 1945), pp. 154–55; Donald K. Pickens, *Eugenics and the Progressives* (Nashville, Tenn.: Vanderbilt University Press, 1968), pp. 16–17, 122, 129; Walter Willcox, "Differential Fecundity," in *Proceedings of the First National Conference on Race Betterment*, pp. 81–82, 84–85; Robert DeC. Ward, "Race Betterment and Our Immigration Laws," ibid., pp. 545–46; Cressy L. Wilbur, "Some of the Measures Most Urgently Needed for the Prevention of Infant Mortality in the United States," *Transactions of the American Association for the Study and Prevention of Infant Mortality* 3 (1912): 36.

23. George J. Engelmann, "Education not the Cause of Race Decline," *Popular Science Monthly* 63 (June 1903): 176.

24. *Sixteenth Census of the United States (1940), Differential Fertility 1940 and 1910* (Washington, D.C.: GPO, 1945), pp. 3–4; Edward P. Davis, "The Size of Families in Relation to Nationality, Occupation and Economic Conditions," *Transactions of the American Association for the Study and Prevention of Infant Mortality* 3 (1912): 113.

pendence Day celebrations, and their own childhood experiences.[25]One trend in nativist thought, Anglo-Saxonism, traced American and British democratic political forms to ancient Germanic tribes; most Progressive reformers agreed at least that American democracy appeared to be threatened by the influx of people who had centuries of habituation to autocratic political systems.[26] The eugenic concept that social characteristics could be inherited provided a scientific explanation for this phenomenon.

In contrast, French writers paid little attention to variations in the birthrate by class. For one thing, these variations were less marked in France than in the United States: because both employers and workers had larger families than did white-collar workers, politicians could hardly argue that the French intellectual or political elite was not reproducing itself.[27] In addition, given the slow rate of economic growth and the need for bodies to fill the army, the French state welcomed working-class children. French eugenists believed that alcoholism, tuberculosis, and venereal diseases were "race poisons," but the French Eugenics Society did not support such negative eugenic measures as sterilization and selective contraception. Instead, it advocated milder measures such as legislation requiring premarital physical examinations.[28] Pronatalism was such an integral part of French nationalism that only a few political radicals—anarchists and socialist feminists—openly advocated birth control and abortion in the late nineteenth and early twentieth centuries; they urged the working class not to bear children to support capitalist production and military enterprises. Not even the mainstream left supported birth control, and birth limitation was not part of the program of those who wished to control social problems and working-class unrest.[29]

Pronatalism and Neo-Malthusianism did not clearly represent two

25. See Linda Gordon, *Woman's Body, Woman's Right: A Social History of Birth Control in America* (New York: Penguin, 1976), p. 156.

26. See Barbara Miller Solomon, *Ancestors and Immigrants: A Changing New England Tradition* (Cambridge: Harvard University Press, 1956), chap. 4; Hofstadter, *Social Darwinism in American Thought*, p. 149; Pickens, *Eugenics and the Progressives*, pp. 17–18, 74, 116.

27. See Spengler, *France Faces Depopulation*, p. 71.

28. See William Schneider, "Toward the Improvement of the Human Race: The History of Eugenics in France," *Journal of Medical History* 54 (1982): 272, 274, 283.

29. Francis Ronsin, *La grève des ventres: Propagande Néo-Malthusienne et baisse de la natalité française, XIXe–XXe siècle* (n.p.: Editions Aubier Montaigne, 1980), p. 214; McLaren, *Sexuality and Social Order*, pp. 115–21.

poles of political thought. Though only a few on the far left of the political spectrum openly espoused Neo-Malthusianism, certain aspects of the theory appealed to both conservatives and Republicans. Among the members of both groups were those who were strongly influenced by hereditarian social thought and who sought to eliminate intractable social and public health problems, including some—like alcoholism and venereal disease—which represented moral decadence. Eugenics was compatible with both pronatalist and Neo-Malthusian politics. Writers on both sides saw it as a potential tool for the creation of the perfect society.

William Schneider argues that French eugenics is best understood as part of a larger movement to arrest moral and physical decline. The French eugenics movement avoided coming into conflict with pronatalist organizations by emphasizing "positive" eugenics—measures designed to improve the general health of the population and prevent diseases thought to be hereditary—alcoholism, tuberculosis, and epilepsy—rather than by preventing conception among the unfit. Though some members of the eugenics society—most notably, Charles Richet—called for sterilization of the unfit, French eugenics was profoundly influenced by Neo-Lamarckianism. The belief that the heredity of newborns could be altered by improving their parents' health and environment made eugenics compatible with the pronatalist and social hygiene movements.[30]

Among the founders of the French eugenics movement were Jacques Bertillon and Charles Richet, leaders of the Alliance nationale pour l'accroissement de la population française, an organization founded in 1896 to promote legislation designed to stimulate the birthrate, especially tax reforms.[31] Joining them was Adolphe Pinard, professor of obstetrics and gynecology at the Faculté de Médecine at the University of Paris, who served with Richet on the first Commission de dépopulation and was prominent in campaigns for measures to protect maternal and infant health. Pinard insisted that

30. See Schneider, "Toward the Improvement of the Human Race," p. 274, and "The Eugenics Movement in France 1890–1940," in *The Wellborn Science: Eugenics in Germany, France, Brazil, and Russia,* ed. Mark B. Adams (New York: Oxford University Press, 1990), p. 75; Linda L. Clark, *Social Darwinism in France* (Tuscaloosa: University of Alabama Press, 1984), p. 156; Jacques Léonard, *La médecine entre les savoirs et les pouvoirs: Histoire intellectuelle et politique de la médecine française au XIXe siècle* (Paris: Aubier Montaigne, 1981), p. 271.

31. Talmy, *Histoire du mouvement familial,* pp. 67–80.

educating girls in *puériculture,* the science of child raising, was one of
the most important solutions to the population problem and personally taught classes of girls in primary school. He not only advocated
teaching the rules of infant hygiene; he emphasized the importance
of inculcating into children of both sexes that they were "seed bearers"
who had a sacred duty to preserve their health for the benefit of their
descendants. Eugenics, Pinard believed, promised to eliminate some
of society's most pressing social and public health problems: alcoholism, tuberculosis, and crime. This concept of *puériculture,* Schneider argues, provided a unifying theme for French eugenics.[32]

The arguments of certain prominent Neo-Malthusian activists had
a similar eugenic content. Paul Robin, for example, advocated birth
control not only on libertarian grounds but also as a means of removing defective stock from the race.[33] More often, however, Neo-
Malthusians saw birth control as an instrument of class struggle. They
urged working-class people not to produce children who would only
fall victim to capitalist exploitation, and they pointed out that large
families were likely to fall into poverty and dependence on meager
public assistance.

G. Hardy, for example, writing in the Neo-Malthusian publication
Rénovation, argued that pronatalists like Bertillon, who urged people
who did not have the means to feed their children to bear more, were
criminals. The infant mortality rate among the children of the unfortunate who "had the stupidity to listen to Bertillon's advice,"
Hardy continued, was 25 percent, while the rest vegetated, destined
to the degradation that accompanied poverty.[34] Neo-Malthusian writers urged women to leave their cradles empty rather than bear children
condemned to suffer. Membra Jard wrote in 1911 that a poor woman
obliged to work in a servile job from seven or eight in the morning
until after dark could not spare the time and money to raise a child
she might love but could not bear to see made into a slave.[35]

A few feminists who openly advocated birth control, notably Nelly
Roussel and Madeleine Pelletier, argued that the state had an obli-

32. Commission de la dépopulation, Sous-commission de la mortalité, *Rapport
général sur les causes de la mortalité* (Melun: Imprimerie administrative, 1911), p. 68;
Schneider, *The Eugenics Movement in France,* p. 72.

33. McLaren, *Sexuality and Social Order,* pp. 99–100.

34. G. Hardy, "Criminels," *Rénovation,* July 14, 1913: 1.

35. Mme Membra Jard, "Autour des berceaux," *Rénovation,* June 15, 1911: 2.

gation to support motherhood. In the future, Roussel predicted, when liberty and equality prevailed, people would be painfully surprised to read about those days when the poor mother who, "until the last day is forced, in order to eat, to drag her heavy and painful belly into the factories and, returning to her wretched lodging, amidst her herd of weakly children already too numerous, is yet forced to serve a drunken husband, stupefied himself by work and utter poverty."[36]

Curiously, this image of working class motherhood was not unlike that invoked by the Radical Republicans, who constituted the primary force for measures to protect maternal and infant health within the government. Like Nelly Roussel, these men observed that bearing children was incompatible with the life that poverty forced working-class women to lead. Ultimately, it was their concern about the birth-rate which led the Radical Republicans to argue, along with such feminist anarchists as Pelletier and Roussel, that maternity deserved protection and remuneration as a service to the state.

Depopulation and Infant Mortality in France

Virtually all French authors writing about infant mortality intro-duced their subject with a discussion of the declining French birthrate and a comparison with other countries, especially Germany. As J. Marie, professor of law at Rennes concluded in 1892, "It is . . . of the greatest importance for the nation, to protect the lives of children, those factors in the national prosperity and power who are born in small numbers but, during the first years of their life, die in such large numbers."[37] The authors of a famous study of urban infant

36. Report of Meeting of March 13, *Rénovation*, April 5, 1912: 1. See Marilyn J. Boxer, "French Socialism, Feminism, and the Family," *Third Republic/Troisième République* 3–4 (1977): 128–67.
37. J. Marie, *De l'assistance publique relativement à l'enfance* (Paris: Berger-Levrault, 1892), p. 40. Other examples are found in J. Hideux, *Crèche des établissements A. Badin et Fils: Prime à l'allaitement maternel* (Barentin [Seine Inferieur], 1908), (Archives na-tionales, F^{22} 446); Charles Delplanque, *Assistance aux enfants du premier âge privés de ressources (avant et après la naissance): Fonctionnement des consultations du Bureau de bien-faisance de Lille* (Lille: Wilmot-Courtecuisse, 1910), p. 3; Claude Souquet, *Mortalité infantile de la première année à Toulouse, de 1900 à 1910* (Toulouse: Ch. Dirion, 1911), p. 7; Henri Bouquet, *La puériculture sociale* (Paris: Blond, 1911), pp. 2–3; G. Variot, *L'hygiène infantile: Allaitement maternel et artificiel; sèvrage* (Paris: Librairie Hachette, 1908), p. 1.

mortality published in 1901 introduced their subject with a similar warning. Each year, they wrote, 36,000 children died in the cities of France—this added up to a loss of about 15,000 soldiers twenty years in the future: "If the rest of the population yields the same deficit, then ignorance, neglect, and alcohol cost us an army corps every year! the expansive force of France is stifled and declines, it means gradual weakening, it means decadence, it means the fall of the *patrie*."[38]

Those French legislators, physicians, and social scientists who invoked depopulation as the rationale for measures to protect maternal and infant health argued that increasing the birthrate was no simple matter, since the decline in fertility was the result of such a complex set of factors and seemed so embedded in French society.[39] Nonetheless, they were optimistic about the prospects for French population growth. Infant mortality was so high, they argued, that reducing it to any significant extent would actually reverse the trend toward depopulation.[40]

When René Waldeck-Rousseau, the French minister of the interior and a Radical Republican, appointed a commission to study the population question in 1902, infant mortality figured prominently on the agenda as one of the most serious causes of depopulation.[41] The population crisis, the minister pointed out in his opening statement at the first meeting of the commission, was primarily the result of a low birthrate, but the problem was exacerbated by a high mortality rate. He admitted, however, that it seemed to be practically impossible to increase the birthrate; reducing the mortality rate, on the other hand, would be a comparatively simple undertaking. It was on this premise that the Ligue contre la mortalité infantile was created in 1913 to prevent infant mortality. Addressing the first national congress of the league, Paul Morel, an official at the Ministry of the

38. A. Balestre and A. Giletta de Saint-Joseph, *Etude sur la mortalité de la première enfance dans la population urbaine de la France de 1892 à 1897* (Paris: O. Doin, 1901), p. 42.

39. Victor Turquan, "Contribution à l'étude de la population et de la dépopulation," *Bulletin de la Société d'anthropologie de Lyon,* tome 21, fascicule 1 (1902): 80.

40. Rothschild, *La mortalité par gastro-entérite,* pp. 2–3; Bouquet, *Puériculture sociale,* pp. 2–3; Delplanque, *Assistance aux enfants du premier âge,* p. 3; Souquet, *Mortalité infantile de la première année,* p. 7; Turquan, "Contribution à l'étude de la population et de la dépopulation," p. 80.

41. Commission de la dépopulation, *Séance du 29 janvier 1902* (Melun: Imprimerie administrative, n.d.), p. 2.

Interior, urged his listeners to sound the alarm, to call forth national campaigns to protect the race and save the nation.[42]

Radical Republicans saw both the high infant mortality rate and the declining birthrate as consequences of the disintegration of family life and parental responsibility—the result of voluntary action in the case of the bourgeoisie, but the result of oppression in the working class. Economic pressure and bad housing conditions, they argued, made a healthy home life impossible for working-class families. That so many women had to work outside their homes was especially tragic. At the same time, members of the bourgeoisie were losing their sense of social responsibility; more and more they acted out of individualistic motives. Men delayed marriage to avoid family obligations; couples had only one or two children so they could provide both children and home with the expected social and material trappings; women neglected to breast-feed out of vanity or social ambition.

The mores of the bourgeoisie were hardly susceptible to legislation, though the government could require, for example, that schools teach girls the meaning of maternal duty. Making childbearing and infant care compatible with wage labor, though, was something that legislators could address; this was the primary object of much French maternal and child welfare legislation.[43] Thus, while the authors of such legislation offered it primarily as a means of preventing infant mortality, they also hoped that these measures would make maternity more attractive to working-class women.[44]

The proposition that social welfare and public health programs would provide at least a partial solution to the population crisis aroused controversy, however. While right- and left-wing politicians shared a sense of the gravity of the question and its implications, they

42. *Bulletin trimestriel de la Ligue contre la mortalité infantile* 12 (July 1913): 6.

43. Louis Marin and Paul Strauss, rapporteurs, "La Protection de la maternité ouvrière," *Association nationale française pour la protection légale des travailleurs, Compte rendu des discussions,* 7th sér., no. 2 (1912); André Goirand, *De la protection et de l'assistance légales des femmes salariées avant et après leur accouchement* (Paris: Imprimerie de la Gazette du Palais, 1906), p. 34; Félix Saporte, *Assistance et maternité* (Bordeaux: Imprimerie de l'Université, 1910), p. 30; Deborah Bernson, *Nécessité d'une loi protectrice pour la femme ouvrière avant et après ses couches* (Paris: Société d'éditions scientifiques, 1899), p. 107.

44. Jacques Mornet, *Les mutualités maternelles* (Paris: Blond et Cie., 1911), p. 3; Maurice Melin, *L'assurance maternelle* (Paris: Librairie de la Société du Recueil Sirey, 1911), pp. 8–11; Saporte, *Assistance et maternité,* pp. 30–31.

disagreed over its causes. Conservative Catholic writers pointed out
that the birthrate was highest in those regions where Catholicism was
strongest and argued that the decline in fertility elsewhere was the
result of the abandonment of religion and traditional morality, as well
as the effect of public policies such as equal inheritance, which weakened the family. In general, they denied that the decline in the birthrate
was a consequence of working-class poverty and blamed the rise of
individualism and materialism instead. They favored measures that
would strengthen the family, stimulate people's sense of social duty,
and promote a return to the land.[45] Liberal economists, following the
argument of the sociologist Frédéric LePlay, insisted that the rule of
equal inheritance introduced by the Revolution led couples to limit
their fertility in order to avoid having to divide their patrimony into
ever smaller portions.[46] Thus the Alliance nationale pour l'accroissement de la population française and right-wing populationist groups
such as the Action populaire did not include measures to protect
infants' lives in their programs. They focused instead on tax reforms
that would favor large families, the repression of abortion and of
Neo-Malthusian propaganda, and the revivial of religious belief and
a spirit of self-sacrifice.[47]

Jacques Bertillon, an influential demographer and pronatalist, denied that reducing the infant mortality rate would affect the rate of
population growth, since this reduction would conflict with one of
the constant laws of demography: the direct correlation between mortality and fertility. If the infant mortality rate declined, he insisted,
the birthrate would inevitably decline as well. Bertillon told the members of the Commission de dépopulation, "We have seen the complete
futility of measures proposed to limit mortality: were they effective,
they would not be effective, they would have no influence at all on
the population of France."[48] Arsène Dumont, a socialist and anticleric,

45. Alcide Leroux, "La question de la dépopulation devant l'Académie de médi-
cine," *Société académique de Nantes et du Départment de la Loire-Inférieure. Annales,* ser.
7, 2 (1891): 323–79; DeBlic, [Capitaine], *Nous les aurons. Mais après . . . ?* (Paris: L'alliance nationale pour l'accroissement de la population française, 1916).

46. See McLaren, *Sexuality and Social Order,* pp. 11, 171–73.

47. DeBlic, *Nous les aurons;* "La France qui meurt," *Peuple de France,* n.d. (Archives
nationales, F7 13955); Koenraad W. Swart, *The Sense of Decadence in Nineteenth-Century
France* (The Hague: Martinus Nijhoff, 1964), pp. 127–28; Talmy, *Histoire du mouvement
familial,* pp. 67–80, 106.

48. Commission de la dépopulation, Sous-commission de la mortalité, *Séances,*
1902–3, Séance du 17 décembre 1902, p. 4.

agreed with Bertillon. He argued, for example, that the law requiring the medical supervision of infants placed out to nurse was not an effective measure against depopulation, since if more children survived, then fewer were born.[49] Republican legislators, however, made the connection among depopulation, infant mortality, and the employment of women early in the life of the Third Republic.

Perhaps the most disturbing evidence of the failure of the French family to fill its social and reproductive functions was the widespread practice of placing children out to nurse. In 1873, when Théophile Roussel, physician and member of the Chamber of Deputies, proposed a law establishing a system of medical supervision of children placed out to nurse he addressed the larger question of why so many French mothers abandoned their children to the care of strangers. Depopulation and infant mortality, he wrote, were both measures of demoralization, because "the wiping out of the basic feelings of the family and the weakening of the most vital and the most essential of these sentiments, maternal love, are discovered at the head of the causes of the downward movement of our population."[50] The deputies assigned to report on Roussel's proposition agreed that the causes of infant mortality and the decline in the birthrate were closely related. Not only did the infant require its mother's breast milk for survival but the child's presence in the home "constitutes the domestic hearth . . . and gives birth to those feelings that lead to happiness through the carrying out of duty and sacrifice."[51] Happy homes, this argument implied, produced a plentiful supply of children.

Most late-nineteenth- and early twentieth-century legislative measures to protect maternal and infant health addressed the issue of women's employment more directly. In focusing on women's work, reformers hoped to affect both infant mortality and the declining birthrate. Not only did infants die because their mothers gave up breast-feeding to place them out to nurse or leave them with a neighbor during the day, but the physical drain and in many cases physical injuries made women reluctant to become pregnant. Writers of all political persuasions agreed that wage labor interfered with mater-

49. Arsène Dumont, *Dépopulation et civilisation: Etude démographique* (Paris: Lecrosnier et Babé, 1890), p. 510.

50. Chambre des Députés, *Proposition de Loi Roussel, ayant pour objet la protection des enfants du premier âge et en particulier des nourrissons*, March 24, 1873, p. 3.

51. Chambre des Députés, *Rapport au nom de la commission chargée d'examiner la proposition de Loi Roussel*, June 19, 1874, p. 7.

nity—women's fundamental social duty. Most saw women's employment as a necessary evil, however.[52] The most that legislators could do was to make it possible for women to take a temporary leave from work before and after childbirth and to keep their children at home with them and continue to breast-feed after they returned to work.

Socialists and Radical Republicans were often allied on this issue, as they frequently were around the turn of the century.[53] Socialists viewed women's participation in the labor force as more than simply an inconvenience; it was both indicator and symbol of the degeneration and decadence that resulted from individualism and capitalist barbarism. Furthermore, they attributed depopulation to capitalist oppression, which forced working-class women to limit their fertility and killed many of their children. If, the socialists pointed out, production were organized to meet the real needs of the whole population, there would be food for all and women would happily bear children.[54]

A group of deputies—several of them socialists, including the only three deputies to support the Neo-Malthusian position in the parliament—expressed a similar argument in their proposal for comprehensive legislation for maternity assistance. These men evoked a picture of working-class decadence and degeneration in which women's wage labor was a central factor. The deplorable hygienic conditions of workers' home and work lives made existence a hell and fostered a decadent morality associated with sterility: begging, vagabondage, theft, prostitution, crime, tuberculosis, and alcoholism were all endemic in working-class communities. More and more, the deputies argued, working-class children were orphans with living mothers, and already marked for death: "Large industry, by transforming women factory laborers and children into automatons or machines, has been the great criminal, the great and monstrous child-

52. See Stewart, *Women, Work, and the French State,* p. 23; Jane Jenson, "Gender and Reproduction; or, Babies and the State," *Studies in Political Economy* 20 (Summer 1986): 35.

53. See John A. Scott, *Republican Ideas and the Liberal Tradition in France, 1870–1914,* Studies in History, Economics and Public Law, No. 573 (New York: Columbia University Press, 1951) [reprint; New York: Octagon, 1966], p. 157; Nye, *Crime, Madness, and Politics,* pp. 187–88.

54. Sicard de Plauzoles, *La maternité et la défense nationale contre la dépopulation* (Paris: V. Giard et E. Brière, 1909), p. 249; Boxer, "French Socialism, Feminism, and the Family," pp. 138–41.

murderer."[55] Pregnancy, childbirth, and child care were so hard and painful for poor women that their fear of conception was natural. Ultimately, the solution was a just social and economic system that ensured healthy living and working conditions, adequate food, housing, and clothing, and equal education for all. In the meantime, socialists supported the proposed protection of working-class maternity as a palliative measure.

Radical Republicans made essentially the same argument about maternity, but their ultimate goal was to save the Republic. When in 1913 the parliament finally passed legislation requiring women to take maternity leaves and providing partial compensation for lost wages, the minister of the interior reminded the prefects that the legislature had been motivated by the population crisis. Thanks to the legislation, the minister predicted, mothers would be able to breast-feed their children and provide them with the necessary care. In addition, women would be spared the complications of childbirth which so often harmed their health and led them to fear the coming of another pregnancy if they did not destroy fertility altogether.[56] The minister concluded that because the legislation addressed the problem of women's wage labor it would not only prevent infant mortality but would affect the birthrate as well. Radical Republicans criticized the exploitation of women in industry but they saw the social implications of maternal and child protection as conservative. A group of deputies summed up this position: "The protection of the woman, at the time she becomes a mother, is the surest safeguard of the child's life; fertility is the very condition of existence of the nation; by protecting maternity, the nation protects itself and guarantees its power and its existence."[57] Thus Radical Republicans argued that the economic insecurity of the working class was bad for the Republic—not only because it bred radicalism and militant strike activity but because a miserable working class would fail to reproduce itself.[58]

Despite its concern for the preservation of morality and its focus

55. Chambre des Députés, Annexe au procès-verbal de la 1ère séance du 8 novembre 1912, *Proposition de loi tendant à établir l'assistance maternelle obligatoire et à fixer les indemnitées et les primes de natalité et d'allaitement aux mères qui élèvent elles-mêmes leurs enfants,* p. 15.

56. Ministre de l'intérieur et des cultes, Circulaire aux préfets, *Journal officiel,* August 11, 1913: 7244.

57. Chambre des Députés, Annexe au procès-verbal de la séance du 23 juin 1910, *Proposition de loi relative à la protection de la maternité.*

58. See Stone, *Search for Social Peace,* p. 4.

on the family as the preserver of social order, the French government was willing to sacrifice certain moral imperatives to the "power and existence" of the nation. Perhaps one of the most striking aspects of French maternal and child welfare policy was the consideration it gave to single mothers. In the late nineteenth century about one-quarter of the children born in Paris were illegitimate. Illegitimate children constituted about 30 percent of those placed out to nurse and made up most of the thousands of children abandoned each year.[59] Whether their mothers kept them or not, they died at a much higher rate than legitimate children.[60] Catholic charitable institutions frequently either refused aid to single mothers or specialized in assisting single women guilty of only one offense; the Republican state, on the other hand, defined all children as equally valuable and considered all poor mothers worthy of assistance.

In 1904, despite the opposition of conservative Catholics, the parliament even passed legislation providing assistance to poor parents to prevent abandonment, specifically with single mothers in mind. This legislation was designed to save both children and state funds, since abandoned children automatically became wards of the state. When the Conseil supérieur de l'assistance publique, a government body that formulated and monitored public welfare legislation, drew up a bill that would require all departments to provide maternity care for poor women, protecting single mothers from social ostracism was a primary concern of the council members. Although one or two argued that endowing single mothers with the right to public assistance would promote immorality and dependence, most insisted that the welfare of the child demanded protection of the mother, even if this meant respecting her request for secrecy to the point of allowing her to give a false name. As one member pointed out, "They are numerous, the children who are gotten rid of, the children killed while living with a nurse, the children lost through abortions; they are a veritable army that never comes to light and that would, how-

59. See Fuchs, *Abandoned Children*, pp. 67–69, and Rachel Fuchs, "Morality and Poverty: Public Welfare for Mothers in Paris, 1870–1900," *French History* 2 (1988): 288–311; George D. Sussman, *Selling Mothers' Milk: The Wet-Nursing Business in France, 1714–1914* (Urbana: University of Illinois Press, 1982), p. 182.

60. In his report to the Commission de dépopulation, Pierre Budin reported an infant mortality rate of 326.5/1000 for illegitimate children and 167.5/1000 for legitimate children in the years 1856–1865. Commission de dépopulation, Sous-commission de la mortalité, *Séances, 1902–3*, Séance du 12 novembre 1902, p. 28.

ever, render great services if it [the army] was under the flags of France."[61]

French reformers inevitably saw infant mortality in terms of the problem of depopulation, which was itself at the center of the discourse on the physical and moral degeneration that threatened both France's international position and its internal stability. Radical Republican maternal and infant health policy thus grew out of a larger program of social reform which sought to save the Republic by increasing the strength and numbers of the population and fostering social harmony.

Eugenics and the Infant Health Movement in the United States

Like their French counterparts, social reformers in the United States argued that the nation had an interest in child health. Historians have often identified children as a central concern of Progressive reform. It was common for Progressives to argue that children constituted a valuable national resource and that the state ought to make an investment in the production of healthy and useful citizens. Advocates of mothers' pensions, for example, insisted that benefits granted to mothers were not charity but payment for services rendered to society. Theodore Roosevelt too linked the nation's military and economic vigor with the strength of the family and likened motherhood to military service.[62] In the United States, however, a belief that the nation's survival depended on saving the lives of infants did not guide

61. Conseil supérieur de l'assistance publique, *Comptes-rendus*, Fascicule No. 37, Session de janvier 1892, p 91. See also Chambre des Députés, Annexe au procès-verbal de la séance du 7 mars 1899, *Proposition de loi sur la protection de la mère et de l'enfant nouveau-né;* Fuchs, "Morality and Poverty," p. 289.

62. Robert Wiebe, *The Search for Order, 1877–1920* (New York: Hill and Wang, 1967), p. 67; Meckel, *Save the Babies,* p. 103; Harold Underwood Faulkner, *Quest for Social Justice, 1898–1914* (New York: Macmillan, 1931), p. 177; Robert H. Bremner, *From the Depths: The Discovery of Poverty in the U.S.* (New York: New York University Press, 1956), p. 213; Theodore Roosevelt, Opening Address, in National Congress of Mothers, *First International Congress on the Protection of Children,* 1908, p. 15; Mary Madeleine Ladd-Taylor, "Mother-work: Ideology, Public Policy, and the Mothers' Movement, 1890–1930," Ph.D. diss., Yale University, 1986, pp. 248–49; Irving Fisher, "National Vitality, Its Wastes and Conservation," in U.S. Cong., Senate, 60th Cong., 2d Sess., Document No. 676, *Report of the National Conservation Commission,* 1909, vol. 3, p. 673.

maternal and infant health care reform. Instead, ideas about the value of child life to the nation focused on the ethnic composition of the population and the perfection of its physical, mental, and moral health.

The Progressive conservation movement encompassed human as well as mineral and vegetable resources. As Samuel P. Hays has shown, concern for the elimination of the waste of natural resources was part of a wider gospel of efficiency.[63] Theodore Roosevelt wrote to Irving Fisher, a professor of political economy at Yale University and author of a report on national vitality for the National Conservation Commission: "Our national health is physically our greatest national asset. To prevent any possible deterioration of the American stock should be a national ambition. We can not too strongly insist on the necessity of proper ideals for the family, for simple living and for those habits and tastes which produce vigor and make men capable of strenuous service to their country."[64] Roosevelt did not see sheer numbers as an urgent consideration, and while he clearly had an interest in military service, national "vitality" more often implied economic efficiency and prosperity than military might. In the Progressives' vision insurance for future national prosperity and efficiency would depend on three factors: preventing reproduction of the least fit members of the population; increasing the number of children born to the genetically superior; and measures, both personal and public, to improve the health of those who were born.

Mainstream social thought in the United States did not exhibit the antipathy to birth control seen in French literature, and birth control for the unfit almost always constituted an important element of the social program of Progressive reformers. In the first decades of the twentieth century, radical birth control advocates in the United States, like French Neo-Malthusians, agitated for the legalization of the dissemination of birth control devices and information as part of a larger revolutionary program.[65] Members of this group frequently couched their arguments in terms of child welfare.

    63. Samuel P. Hays, *Conservation and the Gospel of Efficiency: The Progressive Conservation Movement, 1890–1920* (Cambridge, Mass.: Harvard University Press, 1959), p. 124; Ladd-Taylor, "Mother-work," pp. 302–4.
    64. Quoted in Manfred J. Waserman, "The Emergence of Modern Health Care: Pediatrics, Public Health, and the Federal Government," Ph.d. diss., Catholic University, 1982, p. 63.
    65. See Gordon, *Woman's Body, Woman's Right,* chap. 9.

The Voluntary Parenthood League published a series of pamphlets around 1916 which pointed out a connection between a high birthrate and infant mortality and urged the dissemination of contraceptive information in the interests of child welfare. It was a crime, the authors of one pamphlet argued, that the U.S. Children's Bureau was prohibited from providing information about birth control. It could give endless information to poor mothers on baby care but it could not tell her "how not to have a rapid successsion of feeble babies, each one further draining the mother's vitality, and competing vainly with its brothers and sisters for a cruelly scant food supply."[66] Margaret Sanger wrote: "Three hundred thousand babies die in the United States each year before they are one year old, and three hundred thousand mothers remain in ignorance of how to prevent three hundred thousand more babies from coming into the world the next year to die of misery, poverty and neglect."[67] Leaders of the Voluntary Parenthood League considered the bureau an important potential ally; in particular they sought the endorsement of its director, Julia Lathrop, who privately supported the league's position but steadfastly refused to take a public stand for fear it would threaten the bureau's public and legislative support.[68]

It was risky for a public figure openly to advocate the dissemination of contraceptive information and devices, since such advocacy implied support for free sexual expression. The argument that birth control would help solve the social problems of the poor and protect their children, however, was attractive to a wide variety of social and political activists, from such socialists as Margaret Sanger to members of charity organization societies. Just as pronatalism appeared in French discourse across the political spectrum, articles supporting birth control appeared in publications ranging from the *Progressive Woman* to the *Boston Medical and Surgical Journal.*[69] The editors of the *New Republic,* for example, advocated birth control as a humanitarian

66. Quote in "Can the Baby Crop Be Guaranteed?" See also "That Grasshopper" (Voluntary Parenthood League, n.d.) (U.S. Children's Bureau, 4-0-2).
67. Margaret Sanger, "To My Friends," 3/3/16 (ibid., 4-0-2).
68. Mary Ware Dennett to Julia Lathrop, 1/21/16 (ibid., 4-0-2).
69. Clyde Wright, "The Economic Side of the Mother Question," *Progressive Woman* 6 (January 1913): 6; Arthur E. Howard, "The Importance of Milk Stations in Reducing City Infant Mortality," *Boston Medical and Surgical Journal,* May 23, 1912: 773–75; Helen Richards Watkins to Julia Lathrop, 4/29/13 (U.S. Children's Bureau, 4-0-2); Annette Fiske, "Where Race Suicide Does not Prevail," *The Survey* 29 (1912): 246.

measure. In all decency, they wrote, no child should be born unless there was a home anxious to receive it: "[A nation] cannot waste [children] in peace or war with that insane prodigality which is characteristic of the great spawning and dying nations where the birthrate and the death rate are both exorbitant, where men breed to perish."[70]

The corollary of the argument that large families were the cause of infant mortality and poverty, however, was that native-born middle-class women were having too few children and neglecting the ones they had, thus reneging on their civic responsibiities. "Race suicide" provided the fuel for antifeminist writers who emphasized the failure of well-off mothers to breast-feed or take responsibility for their children's care, just as French physicians condemned their female compatriots for valuing their appearance and their social status above their children's lives.

In an article titled "Why American Mothers Fail," published in the *Atlantic Monthly* in 1903, one female writer berated a generation of irresponsible women; she cited the high divorce rate and accused wealthy mothers of leaving their children's education to schools and feeding them unwholesome food but at the same time neglecting their husbands in favor of their children. "Any system of education," she wrote, "that fails to impress upon our girls the immense civic value of motherhood, its imposing dignity, its grave responsibilities to the state itself, fails of its purpose."[71] Another female observer criticized women in the "so-called educated class" for refusing to breast-feed, for entering the labor force, and for submitting to an "inordinate love of ease and pleasure . . . and certain diseases of over-civilization."[72]

As Theodore Roosevelt argued in an address before the National Congress of Mothers in 1908, the United States could not get along as a nation without the right kind of home life; the woman who shirked her duty as mother should be condemned as heartily as a soldier who fled from battle.[73] Pronatalism, however, never constituted a rationale for public measures to prevent infant mortality in

70. "The Control of Births" (reprinted from *New Republic* [n.d.] for the National Birth Control League), (U.S. Children's Bureau, 4–0–2).

71. Anna Rogers, "Why American Mothers Fail," *Atlantic Monthly,* March 1903: 289. On race suicide generally, see Gordon, *Woman's Body, Woman's Right,* chap. 7.

72. Elaine G. Eastman, "The Waste of Life," *Popular Science Monthly* 87 (August 1915): 189.

73. Theodore Roosevelt, Opening Address, National Congress of Mothers, *First International Congress on the Protection of Children,* p. 15.

the United States because the babies of wealthy women did not die in large numbers; all researchers confirmed that infant mortality rates rose in inverse relation to the wealth of a community. Given the obvious concern with the composition of the population and the influence of Social Darwinism on social thought in the United States, it would not be surprising to find writers who maintained that infant mortality was nature's way of weeding out the unfit. Few if any observers actually espoused such a position publicly but it is suggestive that many found it necessary to refute this argument.[74] Those in favor of measures to prevent infant mortality argued that allowing children to die was not only cruel but had a harmful effect on the strength of the population as a whole because diseases that killed infants left many survivors permanently disabled or weak.

A few eugenists did go so far as to oppose humanitarian reforms on eugenic grounds. Though Paul Popenoe and Roswell Hill Johnson favored the abolition of child labor and compulsory education legislation because these measures would cause the poor to restrict their fertility, they opposed such supplements as free lunches and textbooks for schoolchildren on the grounds that these would undermine the effectiveness of efforts to reduce the working-class birthrate.[75] In the South, outside of the organized eugenics movement, similar ideas held sway when whites discussed public health measures for blacks.

In the 1910s, southern white physicians and public health officials were engaged in a debate over whether or not the particular health problems of blacks were the result of genetic inferiority—or at least the inability to adapt to a cold climate or to urban life—or the result of social and environmental handicaps. In 1914, when the American Public Health Association held its annual meeting in Jacksonville, Florida, and made African-Americans the focus of their discussion, some health officials maintained that because African-Americans were unable to adapt to urban life they were becoming extinct; some argued outright that spending money in the African-American community was therefore a waste.[76] Though the tendency was increasingly toward

74. A few British writers did argue that preventing infant mortality was dysgenic; see J. H. Kellogg in *Proceedings of the First National Conference on Race Betterment*, pp. 437–39.
75. See Hofstadter, *Social Darwinism in American Thought*, p. 142.
76. See Edward H. Beardsley, *A History of Neglect: Health Care for Blacks and Mill*

a social and environmental explanation for high mortality rates from
tuberculosis and syphilis, even those southern health officers who
vocally supported public health work among African-Americans
often simultaneously expressed contempt and racial hostility. Their
standard arguments were that African-Americans would always be
dependent on whites and that therefore taking care of them was a
moral responsibility of the white community and that disease, immorality, and ignorance in the African-American community were a
threat to all.[77]

Such attitudes without a doubt retarded the development of public
health work in the South. Efforts to improve maternal and infant
health, however, were conceived in the context of a eugenic social
reform movement strongly influenced, as in France, by Neo-
Lamarckian evolutionary thought. Thus, although by 1905 scientists
had rejected the theory that acquired characteristics could be inherited,
most reformers believed that improving the health of the existing
population was a form of eugenics and would lead to the birth of
more vigorous children in the future.[78] Though they assumed that
the offspring of alcoholics, delinquents, and people with tuberculosis
had congenital moral or physical defects, they believed that providing
a wholesome environment for children would prevent them from
becoming criminals or alcoholics. In general, they reserved "negative" eugenic solutions for the more extreme cases of mental, physical,
or social deviance. As one historian has written, "The concept of
'defective classes' enabled the reformer to place a portion of mankind
outside the pale of normal human sympathy," while retaining their
self-image as humanitarians.[79] Even active eugenists believed that
child health measures would improve the health of the population in
the long run. Irving Fisher, for example, supported measures to seg-

Workers in the Twentieth-Century South (Knoxville: University of Tennessee Press,
1987), p. 130.

77. William F. Brunner, "The Negro Health Problem in Southern Cities," *Amer-
ican Journal of Public Health* 5 (1915): 183–90; L. C. Allen, "The Negro Health
Problem," ibid.: 194–203; Lawrence Lee, "The Negro as a Problem in Public Health
Charity," ibid.: pp. 207–11.

78. Pickens, *Eugenics and the Progressives,* pp. 42–43; Elmer Gates, "The Art of
Rearing Children," in National Congress of Mothers, *The Work and Words of the
National Congress of Mothers (First Annual Session)* (New York: D. Appleton, 1897).

79. Rudolph J. Vecoli, "Sterilization: A Progressive Measure?" *Wisconsin Magazine
of History* 43 (1960): 192.

regate and sterilized the "unfit" but he also saw hygiene as an essential aspect of eugenics.[80] He admitted that child hygiene prolonged the lives of the weak, but it also prolonged the lives of the strong. In Russia, for example, a high rate of infant mortality was not associated with longer life for those who reached adulthood; instead, childhood diseases stunted all life and the whole nation suffered. The cost of keeping people healthy in the first place, Fisher concluded, was trivial in comparison with the economic losses to society resulting from needless fatigue, sickness, and death: "the rate of this return is quite beyond the dreams of avarice."[81] The longer-lived and more vigorous a people, the better it could make use of its other natural resources.

Other eugenists agreed with Fisher that protecting the lives of working-class and immigrant babies would help to counteract the harmful effects of race suicide. In 1913, for example, Meyer Solomon warned that national deterioration and degeneration were the results of the high birthrate among the lower social classes—people who had a "constitutional inferiority, physical or mental, which makes an individual of less civic worth." The "sensible eugenist," however, did not oppose measures to prevent infant mortality, a scourge that destroyed the fit as well as the unfit. Besides, Solomon added, nine out of ten children were really born fit if only given the chance.[82]

Solomon thus rejected as "permanently defective" as many as 10 percent of the population, including paupers and "feeble-minded," insane, epileptic, and criminally inclined people. All of these, Solomon wrote, were "positive drains on the vital functions of society, who sap the very life's blood and weaken the constitution of the social organism."[83] He believed, however, that other hereditary defects could be prevented. Syphilis and other infections, malnutrition, and exhaustion in the parents affected offspring not through true heredity but rather through the action of some toxin on the germ cells. Ultimately, social and economic conditions were responsible for such defects. Fisher agreed that inheritance probably depended largely on the physical condition of the parents at the time of conception and

80. Fisher, "National Vitality, Its Wastes and Conservation," p. 673.
81. Ibid., p. 746.
82. Meyer Solomon, "Infant Mortality and Eugenics," *Illinois Medical Journal* 23 (1913): 266.
83. Ibid., 259.

not, therefore, on the parents' own genetic background.[84] Thus even these eugenists believed that social and economic conditions and education affected physical degeneration as much as genetic or "racial" characteristics.

This conception of eugenics, with its emphasis on education and public health measures, had a significant influence on the infant health movement. The baby health contests popular among women's organizations provide the most obvious example, but a concern for improving the "race" also prevailed among physicians and other social reformers active in the movement to prevent infant mortality. As S. W. Newmayer, head of the Philadelphia Division of Child Hygiene, put it, "The gardener destroys the undesirable blooms to give a hardier plant, but he studies how to obtain from the seed only the best and strongest plants."[85] S. Josephine Baker agreed. She wrote in the *Woman's Home Companion:* "We are awakening to the fact that the conservation of child life and health is the key of our whole health problem and is our most vital national need. The world does not need more babies, but it does need better babies; for the physical vigor and mental and moral well-being of any race of people determines not only their power to live out their lives to their fullest development but, indeed, their ability to perpetuate themselves and to endure as a race."[86] Both Newmayer and Baker, engaged in the every-day work of urban public health departments, thus viewed their work as contributing to the larger goals of racial improvement.

In 1909 the American Academy of Medicine sponsored a national conference on infant mortality. The physicians, social workers, nurses, and public health officials who attended represented a wide variety of public and private organizations. Out of this meeting was born the American Association for the Study and Prevention of Infant Mortality. The prominent place given to eugenics in the proceedings of this organization suggests that many of its members were at least as interested in improving the "race" as in saving lives.

From its inception, the organization included a section on eugenics. Among the speakers at early meetings were prominent eugenists,

84. Fisher, "National Vitality, Its Wastes and Conservation," p. 723.
85. S. W. Newmayer, "The Warfare against Infant Mortality," *Annals of the American Academy of Political and Social Sciences* 37 (1911): 533.
86. S. Josephine Baker, "The Importance of Good Health," *Woman's Home Companion,* January 1914: 44.

including Henry H. Goddard, pioneer in intelligence testing and an important figure in the development of hereditarian ideas about intelligence, and Roswell Johnson, author, with Paul Popenoe, of a standard textbook on applied eugenics.[87] Participants in the section on eugenics addressed such questions as the importance of heredity as a cause of infant mortality, the hereditary effects of alcoholism, syphilis, and tuberculosis on infant health, and the need for measures to compensate for the dysgenic effects of "indiscriminate" infant conservation. In 1911 the organization as a whole adopted resolutions calling for efforts to "produce the highest type of physical, intellectual and social man." Thus the association advocated a campaign of public education and moral suasion, especially by churches, to encourage greater productivity among the "best elements of our stock," as well as segregation and in extreme cases surgical sterilization of the "racially unfit."[88] As Charles Richmond Henderson, president of the association for 1911, argued in his official address, "The end is not merely to increase the number of our population, already vast, but especially to improve its quality, energy, efficiency, by giving to every infant born the chance to have a right start."[89]

Henderson did not refer simply to improving the physical health of the population. He was just as concerned with preventing crime, prostitution, and economic dependency and saw these as appropriate subjects of discussion for an infant health organization. Henderson and his some of colleagues believed that mental retardation, immorality, and antisocial behavior were all inherited and that they were manifestations of defects of the nervous system. If the public took on the humanitarian task of caring for the sick and defective, including saving the lives of all children born, it had every right to take steps to prevent the propagation of those predisposed to illness and deviance. Abraham Jacobi, a leading pediatrician, and Joseph Neff, head of the Philadelphia Department of Health, both argued that the pro-

87. Henry H. Goddard, "Infant Mortality in Relation to the Hereditary Effects of Mental Deficiency," *Transactions of the American Association for the Study and Prevention of Infant Mortality* 3 (1912): 167–71; Roswell H. Johnson, "Eugenics and Mental Variations," ibid., pp. 164–66.

88. *Transactions of the American Association for the Study and Prevention of Infant Mortality* 2 (1911): 114, 116.

89. Charles Richmond Henderson, "Greetings by the President for 1911," *Transactions of the American Association for the Study and Prevention of Infant Mortality* 1 (1910): 20.

hibition of marriage among the unfit and even forced sterilization
were justified not only to prevent infant deaths from syphilis and
tuberculosis but also as measures that would save taxpayers money
for prisons, reformatories, hospitals, and asylums.[90]

The American Association for the Study and Prevention of Infant
Mortality, and the infant health movement more generally, reflected
a wide range of positions on eugenics. Julia Lathrop and other leaders
of the U.S. Children's Bureau, for example, departed significantly
from the eugenic position, defining the bureau's work in terms of
the rights of children and mothers rather than in terms of their utilitarian value. This view was not characteristic of the women's infant
health movement as a whole, however; several of the female leaders
of the baby health contest movement saw their work primarily as
scientific eugenics, while leaders of the National Congress of Mothers
had a religious and moral vision of racial improvement. A concern
with race betterment could also coincide with belief in women's right
to maternity care, as they did in the case of Florence Sherbon, who
was an active proponent of the baby health contest and later conducted
surveys of rural child welfare for the Children's Bureau. Thus there
were tensions within the infant health movement, and within the
women's movement, that would be manifested in the controversy
surrounding the baby health contests in 1913 and 1914 and in the
Children's Year campaigns of the World War I period.[91]

Public health programs for preventing infant mortality reflected a
hybrid of hereditarian and environmentalist understandings of eugenics. In 1916, when the *New York American* launched a campaign
to "teach the women of America to produce better babies," the topics
it covered included eugenics, the care of pregnant women, and the
care of babies. In this context, eugenics referred to temperance, moderation in food consumption, and sexual morality as much as to
segregation or sterilization of the unfit. The *New York American*'s
program emphasized the importance of health in choosing a spouse
and of avoiding diseases that parents would pass on to their offspring:
alcoholism, syphilis, tuberculosis, epilepsy, and insanity. Such eu-

90. Joseph Neff, "A City's Duty in the Prevention of Infant Mortality," ibid., 1 (1910): 154; A. Jacobi, "Address," ibid: 44–45.

91. Julia C. Lathrop, "The Children's Bureau," *Thirty-ninth National Conference of Charities and Corrections,* 1912, pp. 29, 33. On the National Congress of Mothers see Ladd-Taylor, "Mother-work," pp. 79–80.

genic education was within the tradition of American moral reform, because the laws of hygiene were consistent with conservative evangelical morality; both prescribed cleanliness, abstinence from alcohol, and sexual self-control.[92]

The *New York American*'s program would have fitted well into Adolphe Pinard's course on *puériculture*. Eugenics, Neo-Malthusianism, and pronatalism all coexisted within Progressive social reform, just as they all contributed to French family policy. In both countries, the discourse on infant mortality was embedded in hereditarian thought. Because early-twentieth-century eugenic reformers accepted the notion that certain types of acquired characteristics could be inherited, public health and social welfare programs played an important role in the quest for racial improvement. Infant health campaigns in both countries can thus be described as part of the larger movement toward state regulation of reproduction, in both cases a reaction to a perceived national decline.

In each country the discourse on infant mortality reflected a faith in the capacity of science and social science to guide the management of human resources so as to maximize national power. Political culture, however, as well as contemporary political and social developments, shaped the implementation of this vision. American reformers viewed national integrity primarily in terms of the preservation of ethnic purity and a particular set of moral and political values, while French Republicans perceived the nation to be threatened both by its declining international position and by class conflict. In France, therefore, the birthrate clearly constituted the overriding concern of population policy, while creating better citizens was the ultimate goal of Progressive maternal and child welfare policy in the United States. It is consistent that "negative" eugenic measures such as segregation and sterilization of the "unfit" were more prominent in the United States than in France.

In 1910, Jules Jusserand, a French diplomat, drew attention to this difference as he tried to explain to members of the American Association for the Study and Prevention of Infant Mortality why depopulation was the cause of grave concern in France. "What do you think

92. Helen Lowry to Julia Lathrop, n.d. (U.S. Children's Bureau, 14–1–9–2); Pickens, *Eugenics and the Progressives,* pp. 15–16; E. Mather Sill, "How May at Least 100,000 Babies Be Saved from an Untimely Death Each Year and So Lessen the Present Fearful Mortality in this Country?" *Virginia Medical Semi-Monthly* 17 (1912): 135.

of your ancestors?" he asked. "Have you any fondness, any respect for them; any admiration for the principles they handed down to you? If you have, then hand those principles, with your blood, down to your children, and having children, keep them healthy. Do not allow the whole earth to go to the children of others." No wonder, he added, infant mortality drew the attention of "some of our best men."[93] Those in the audience who suspected that a superior variety of political and moral principles was indeed inherited with Anglo-Saxon blood must have understood Jusserand's point. Irving Fisher, however, suggested an analogy that better explained population politics in the United States. Both the United States and France were in the midst of an evolutionary process toward "vital economy," Fisher argued; decreasing the infant mortality rate was simply part of this process of conserving all human life. He cited Aesop's fable of the fox and the lion to illustrate his point: when the fox taunted the lion about having so few children, the lion replied, "Yes, but every child is a lion."[94]

93. Jules Jusserand, "Some Checks to Infantile Mortality," *Transactions of the American Association for the Study and Prevention of Infant Mortality* 1 (1910): 33.
94. Irving Fisher, "Address," ibid., 1 (1910): 41.

2

Puériculteurs and Pediatricians: The Medical Supervision of Infant Health

In 1865 members of the Académie impériale de médecine, France's most prestigious medical organization, heard a report by Gustave Lagneau on the decline of the French birthrate. Thirty years later one member recalled the "feeling of patriotic distress with which we heard this information, and how we all joined in the sorrow expressed by our colleague. . . . Today the peril is no less. . . . We must react at all cost."[1] This patriotism, French and American writers agreed, stimulated a zeal for saving infant lives among French physicians. It was no coincidence that by the early twentieth century French men could claim the credit for the invention of the two most widely known infant health institutions, the clean milk station and the infant health consultation.

Designed primarily to prevent infant deaths from diarrhea—the single most important killer of infants—milk stations and infant health consultations encouraged breast-feeding, distributed clean or sterilized milk for infants fed artificially, provided medical supervision of infants, and instructed their mothers in "scientific" hygiene. When American physicians and public health officials began to consider systematic measures to prevent infant mortality they drew heavily on the French models, for they too believed that instructing mothers

1. Académie de médecine, *Rapport annuel de la Commission permanente de l'hygiène de l'enfance*, 1897, p. 5.

and making pure milk available would save most of the thousands of children who died each year from gastrointestinal diseases.

French *gouttes de lait* and American clean milk stations, French *consultations de nourrissons* and American infant welfare centers had goals in common: the elimination of maternal ignorance, the dissemination of modern hygiene, and the distribution of pure milk. In addition, both French and American physicians sought recognition as legitimate experts in the care of infants and thus as necessary advisers to mothers of all social classes. In the nineteenth century, physicians began to reach middle- and upper-class women through private practice and advice books; in the late nineteenth and early twentieth centuries, campaigns to prevent infant mortality brought them into contact with children of the working class.[2] Establishing the habit of regular and frequent medical examinations for infants and instruction of mothers in the principles of scientific hygiene enunciated by physicians were central goals of milk stations and infant health consultations on both sides of the Atlantic. By increasing women's dependence on the medical profession, campaigns to prevent infant mortality contributed to the ongoing process by which professional intervention in the family was established and physicians claimed authority in all aspects of child care.

Jacques Donzelot describes public intervention in the family as a deliberate policy, designed to "make everything that composes the state serve to increase its power, and likewise, serve the public welfare."[3] In Donzelot's model such institutions as general hospitals, convents, and foundling homes served as "a strategical base for a whole series of corrective interventions in family life."[4] They simultaneously served as a laboratory for the observation of working-class behaviors, a means of launching measures to counteract these behaviors, and a tool for reorganizing working-class family life in terms of socioeconomic imperatives. An important element of the process was the medicalization of definitions of deviance.

2. See Jacques Donzelot, *The Policing of Families* (New York: Pantheon, 1979), p. 45; Sylvia Hoffert, *Private Matters: American Attitudes toward Childbearing and Infant Nurture in the Urban North, 1800–1860* (Urbana: University of Illinois Press, 1989); Richard Meckel, *Save the Babies: American Public Health Reform and the Prevention of Infant Mortality, 1850–1920* (Baltimore: Johns Hopkins University Press, 1990), pp. 45–61.

3. Donzelot, *Policing of Families*, p. 7.

4. Ibid., p. 26.

Robert Nye has also described the pervasiveness in nineteenth-century French politics and social reform rhetoric of a medical model of degeneration, which was essentially a vehicle for expressing class and national anxieties about exhaustion and decline.[5] Historians of the medical profession in France have emphasized the extent to which the French medical profession claimed expertise not only in individual health but in public hygiene. To a much greater extent than in the United States, as early as the late eighteenth century French governments called on the medical profession to serve as police in their concerted, often centralized, efforts to prevent disease. Thus the "autonomy" of the French medical profession went hand in hand with dependence on the state and bureaucracy.[6] Jacques Léonard also argues that the Third Republic in particular integrated medicine increasingly into its "grand demographic maneuvers," transforming the physician into expert, inspector, and agent of protective laws. The state contributed fundamentally to the restructuring of the health care system; medical assistance to the poor, and, in the twentieth century, social security, greatly increased the demand for medical services.[7] In seeking to protect child life as part of its efforts to counter the nation's population and social crises, the French government called heavily upon the medical profession. In turn, physicians had a significant voice in the framing of maternal and infant health policy.

The French model of medicalization cannot be applied easily to the American context, however. The United States lacked the bureaucratic administrative structures necessary to carry out the policies of an interventionist state, especially on the federal level. Furthermore, American political culture did not permit overt public efforts to influence social behavior. As the previous chapter showed, social re-

5. Robert A. Nye, *Crime, Madness, and Politics in Modern France: The Medical Concept of National Decline* (Princeton, N.J.: Princeton University Press, 1984), p. 338.
6. See ibid., p. 45; *Professions and the French State, 1700–1900*, ed. Gerald L. Geison (Philadelphia: University of Pennsylvania Press, 1984), p. 3; Jan Goldstein, " 'Moral Contagion': A Professional Ideology of Medicine and Psychiatry in Eighteenth- and Nineteenth-Century France," in ibid., p. 197; George D. Sussman, "Enlightened Health Reform, Professional Medicine and Traditional Society: The Cantonal Physicians of the Bas-Rhin, 1810–1870," *Bulletin of the History of Medicine* 51 (1977): 3.
7. Jacques Léonard, *La médecine entre les savoirs et les pouvoirs: Histoire intellectuelle et politique de la médecine française au XIXe siècle* (Paris: Aubier Montaigne, 1981), p. 302; Matthew Ramsey, "Review Essay: History of a Profession, *Annales* Style: The Work of Jacques Léonard," *Journal of Social History* 17 (1983): 327–28.

formers, public health officials, and politicians in the United States
were interested in controlling sexual morality, regulating reproduction, and improving economic efficiency; the institutions they created,
however, had to conform to an ideology that emphasized voluntarism, informed good citizenship, and the appearance of social harmony
and political consensus.

This political culture shaped the ideology of the medical profession
as well. The ideology of free enterprise and the absence of centralized
educational and licensing structures hampered the medical profession
in its struggle for legal monopoly. While French physicians did not
face a serious challenge to their control over medical practice, "regular" physicians in the United States faced extensive competition from
other practitioners until the late ninteenth century. Nonetheless, by
the end of the Progressive Era, organized medicine in the United
States would see its fate as linked with preservation of a free market
in health care, not with public health or a welfare state.[8]

In the late nineteenth and early twentieth centuries, many leaders
of the medical profession actively supported public health programs,
including limited centralization of public health policy in a federal
department of public health. The profession was split over support
for public health, however, and over the extent to which medical
organizations should become involved in social issues. Many, especially those outside of the elite leadership, feared that any kind of
public medicine would deprive them of patients and income. Pediatricians and obstetricians concerned to develop clinical and research
opportunities in their specialties, however, played a major role in
campaigns to prevent infant mortality among the urban poor, and
by the late 1920s public health programs such as those created by the
Sheppard-Towner Act and school health work had taught mothers
to bring their children to pediatricians for routine examinations. Female physicians occupied a particular niche in the medical profession.
The free enterprise system of medical education and health care made
the profession less exclusive and allowed women to obtain training
and to practice with relative ease, especially in maternal and infant
care.[9]

8. See Matthew Ramsey, "The Politics of Professional Monopoly in Nineteenth-
Century Medicine: The French Model and Its Rivals," in *Professions and the French
State,* pp. 250–53, 276–77.
9. See Regina Markell Morantz-Sanchez, *Sympathy and Science: Women Physicians*

Public health was a field of low prestige in the United States, however; public policy failed to provide doctors with the kind of authority derived by French physicians from centralized, interventionist social policy.[10] Thus, while French physicians had at their disposal a range of bribes and threats—including, in certain programs, the withholding of essential material benefits—with which to coax women into obeying the laws of scientific hygiene, American pediatricians and obstetricians relied more on persuasion and on private institutions in their efforts to foster dependence on their professional expertise.

Physicians and the Causes of Infant Mortality

The primary target of infant health campaigns around the turn of the century was infant diarrhea, the cause of more than one-third of infant deaths in both countries. The problem was greatest during the yearly epidemics of "summer diarrhea" among urban babies, especially those who were not breast-fed. Thus, for example, in France in 1901–5, the infant mortality rate for August was nearly double that for November.[11] Physicians attributed another 17 to 20 percent of

in American Medicine (New York: Oxford University Press, 1985), esp. chap. 4 and 10.

10. See Paul Starr, *The Social Transformation of American Medicine* (New York: Basic Books, 1982), pp. 186–87; James B. Burrow, *Organized Medicine in the Progressive Era: The Move toward Monopoly* (Baltimore: Johns Hopkins University Press, 1977), pp. 85–95, 100–101; Naomi Aronson, "Fuel for the Human Machine: The Industrialization of Eating in America," Ph.D. diss., Brandeis University, 1978, pp. 94–95; Manfred J. Waserman, "The Emergence of Modern Health Care: Pediatrics, Public Health, and the Federal Government," Ph.D. diss., Catholic University, 1982, p. 53.

11. Françoise Thébaud, "Donner la vie: Histoire de la maternité en France entre les deux guerres," thèse du 3ème cycle, Université de Paris-VII, 1982, p. 382; E. Van Goidtshoven, "Infant Mortality, Its Prime Cause and Prevention," *Atlanta Medical and Surgical Journal* 14 (1897): 302; E. Ausset, "La mortalité infantile dans le département du Nord," *Revue d'hygiène et de médecine infantiles* 4 (1905): 446; Pierre Budin, "Les consultations de nourrissons," *Revue d'hygiène et de médecine infantiles* 4 (1905): 123; Michel Huber, *La population de la France pendant la guerre* (Paris: Presses universitaires de France, 1931), p. 303; Rose A. Cheney, "Seasonal Aspects of Infant and Childhood Mortality: Philadelphia, 1865–1920," *Journal of Interdisciplinary History* 14 (1984): 563; A. Balestre and A. Giletta de Saint-Joseph, *Etude sur la mortalité de la première enfance dans la population urbaine de la France de 1892 à 1897* (Paris: O. Doin, 1901), p. 31. Where the death rate from gastrointestinal diseases was low, "congenital debility" could be the most common cause of death. This was true, for example, in Saginaw, Michigan, where only 9.6 percent of infant deaths were due to gastroin-

infant deaths, including most of those that took place in the first two weeks of life, to "congenital debility" due to prematurity, low birth-weight, malformations, injuries at birth, and "lack of vitality." Deaths from respiratory diseases, particularly common in cold weather, made up the third large category of infant deaths.

Physicians were confident that they could easily eliminate almost all infant deaths from gastrointestinal diseases. For one thing, breast-fed babies were largely immune to such disturbances: studies showed that these children had a death rate five to seven times lower than that of artificially fed babies.[12] Before 1920 those active in infant health campaigns unanimously agreed on the superiority of breast-feeding. Some even proposed that the failure to breast-feed be considered a crime, with exemptions for women who had medical certification of their physical incapacity to nurse.[13] Physicians agreed, however, that given proper nutrition and expert guidance the vast majority of women were physically able to breast-feed.

The rhetoric surrounding breast-feeding provides an excellent example of the way in which medical prescriptions supported social and political objectives. The significance physicians attached to breast-feeding far transcended its physiological importance. Breast-feeding, they argued, was a mother's most fundamental responsibility; it was a woman's sacred duty as well as her most tender, beautiful, and emotionally fulfilling moment. French Catholics and anticlerical Republicans alike believed that it even had the potential to redeem women who gave birth to illegitimate children. French writers romanticized breast-feeding to a high degree. One French author wrote,

testinal ailments; 49.4 percent from congenital debility. Nila F. Allen, *Infant Mortality: Results of a Field Study in Saginaw Michigan,* U.S. Children's Bureau, Infant Mortality Series No. 9 (Bureau Publication No. 52) (Washington, D.C.: Government Printing Office, 1919), p. 3; U.S. Cong., Senate, *Report on Condition of Woman and Child Wage-Earners in the United States,* 61st Cong., 2d Sess., Document No. 645, vol. 13, "Infant Mortality and Its Relation to the Employment of Mothers," 1912, p. 85.

12. Jacques Bertillon, "De l'influence de l'alimentation des jeunes enfants sur leur mortalité à Berlin," *Bulletin de la Société de médecine publique et d'hygiène professionnelle* 12 (1889): 126; Deborah Bernson, *Nécessité d'une loi protectrice pour la femme ouvrière avant et après ses couches* (Paris: Société d'éditions scientifiques, 1899), pp. 72, 85; Mark Reuben, "Infant Mortality," *Medical Record* 84 (1913): 238; Auguste Luling, *De la mortalité des nourrissons en rapport avec la modalité de leur alimentation* (Versailles: Imprimerie Aubert, 1901), p. 2.

13. Sicard de Plauzoles, *La maternité et la défense nationale contre la dépopulation* (Paris: V. Giard et E. Brière, 1909), p. 260; comments by Hastings Hart in the *Transactions of the Conference on the Prevention of Infant Mortality,* 1909, p. 53.

"Poets have made of it a divine vision descended from heaven to earth. In that stardust, that white, luminous trail which is called the *milky way,* the Vedas saw the milky trail of a cow with a swollen udder grazing in the field of stars."[14]

At a time when the birthrate was decreasing, observers in both France and the United States described the decline in breast-feeding as the most powerful evidence of women's refusal to fulfill their natural role. In France especially, "natural role" had a political definition as well as a biological one. Physicians were particularly critical of wealthy women who chose not to breast-feed out of vanity or of fear that their social life would be interrupted. This denial of their most fundamental maternal duty symbolized the decadence of the French bourgeoisie and their denial of social responsibility, often cited as a prime cause of depopulation.

Clearly seeking to frighten women into returning to their traditional role, physicians described the decision not to breast-feed as a denial of one's femininity. One French physician warned that in certain families and nations—England was a good example—so few mothers nursed their children that women no longer had breasts.[15] On the other hand, French physicians noticed that most working-class women gave up breast-feeding because they had to work outside their homes. These observers lamented the economic system that deprived infants of their mothers' breasts and made heroines of those mothers who worked to earn a wage and yet struggled to care for their families. Making it possible for working women to nurse their infants was thus a goal of much French legislative activity.[16]

While breast-feeding was not associated with national survival in the United States, some American physicians attacked women who failed to fulfill this essential maternal function. The writings of these men are reminiscent of threats made to childless or educated women

---

14. "L'allaitement dans l'art," *Le Puériculteur* 3 (1908): 138.

15. G. Eustache, *La puériculture, hygiène, et assistance* (Paris: J.-B. Baillière, 1903), p. 179; Fernand Pestre, *Les oeuvres d'assistance et de protection à la mère, au nouveau-né et aux enfants du premier âge, ce qu'elles sont à Avignon* (Montpellier: Gustave Firmin, Montane et Sciardi, 1907), p. 11.

16. Maurice Melin, *L'assurance maternelle* (Paris: Librairie de la Société du Recueil Sirey, 1911), p. 43; George D. Sussman, *Selling Mothers' Milk: The Wet-Nursing Business in France, 1715–1914* (Urbana, Ill.: University of Illinois Press, 1982), pp. 121–29; Mary Lynn Stewart, *Women, Work, and the French State: Labour Protection and Social Patriarchy, 1879–1919* (Kingston, Ont.: McGill-Queen's University Press, 1989).

by antifeminist men who asserted that too much education drained
away energy needed to develop female reproductive organs. J. W.
Dupree warned, for example, that women who fed their children
artificially would be punished with physical suffering and pain, pos-
sibly even with some "loathsome disease": "Nature's laws," he
wrote, "are immutable and irrevocable, and their infractions are as
surely followed by penalties as the day by night."[17]

If physicians saw encouraging breast-feeding as their first task, all
agreed that more complex social factors contributed to infant mortality. Even when breast-fed, the children of poor mothers had a
higher death rate than the breast-fed children of the bourgeoisie.[18]
Well-to-do women were also able to feed their children cows' milk
much more successfully than working-class women. The quality of
milk available in cities was often appalling: it was skimmed, diluted,
adulterated, and a perfect home for flourishing colonies of bacteria.
Researchers could associate no definite microorganism with the annual epidemics, but they consistently found that children fed sterilized
or pasteurized milk had a good chance of flourishing, though still not
as good as that of breast-fed babies. Physicians were certain, however,
that overfeeding or feeding solid foods too early was also an important
factor in infant ill health; some thought that overfeeding could cause
diarrhea even in the absence of pathological organisms. Others argued
that heat in itself might be responsible for the high summer rate of
infant mortality among children living in slums.[19]

Although by the early twentieth century there was a general consensus that infant diarrhea was caused by contaminated milk, physicians also blamed insanitary domestic conditions of all kinds. They
believed, for example, that lack of sunlight impeded development,
that cracked and dirty walls harbored dangerous microbes, and that

17. J.W. Dupree, "Infant Mortality in My Own Field of Observation, with Some
Suggestions for Its Diminution," *Transactions of the Louisiana State Medical Society,*
1892, pp. 101–2; Carroll Smith-Rosenberg, *Disorderly Conduct: Visions of Gender in
Victorian America* (New York: Knopf, 1985), p. 187.

18. Bernson, *Nécessité d'une loi protectrice pour la femme ouvrière,* p. 72; H. Vildermann, *Moyen pratique de diminuer dans de notables proportions la mortalité des nourrissons
dans les classes pauvres de Paris* (Mâcon: X. Perroux, 1895), p. 6.

19. Commission de la dépopulation, Sous-commission de la mortalité, *Séances,
1902–3,* Séance du 12 novembre 1902, p. 15; E. Maurel, *Etude sur la mortalité qui suit
la naissance; ses principales causes* (Toulouse: Imprimerie C. Marquèz, 1902), p. 20; J.
W. Schereschewsky, "Heat and Infant Mortality," *Transactions of the American Association for the Study and Prevention of Infant Mortality* 4 (1913): 99–128.

air in confined places lacked sufficient oxygen and was poisoned with the volatile products of decayed matter or body excretions. Inadequate ventilation and cold temperatures seemed to be the primary causes of fatal respiratory diseases. Thus the common practice of drying wet soiled diapers in front of the family fire could be fatal; so could leaving milk in uncovered containers, keeping food in bedrooms (where it was exposed to bodily exhalations), and keeping windows closed at night.[20] Some of these conditions were beyond the mothers' control. Poverty, for example, often made it impossible for them to afford good-quality milk even if it was available and forced families to live in crowded and insanitary housing. Still, physicians on both sides of the Atlantic were convinced that if women applied the basic principles of scientific hygiene their babies would live. This conviction formed the basis for the infant health consultation and the milk station.

Neither French nor American physicians had faith in the natural maternal ability or common sense of the average woman; they also denigrated the precepts passed by women from generation to generation. The most important factor in infant mortality, wrote Julius Levy, head of the Division of Child Hygiene of Newark, New Jersey, was "ignorance made hidebound by prejudice."[21] Unlike other medical specialists, who focused on diseases of specific organs, pediatricians built their specialty largely as experts in the prevention of disease. Thus, as part of their quest for professional authority, both French and American pediatricians deliberately tried to undermine women's traditional wisdom and to replace the older neighbor or relative, the midwife, or the local herbalist as the authority on child care.[22]

American physicians found the child care and health care practices of eastern and southern European immigrants and African Americans

20. B. Roussy, *Education domestique de la femme et rénovation sociale* (Paris: Delagrave, 1914), pp. 53–55; R. Felhoen, *Etude statistique sur la mortalité infantile à Roubaix et dans ses cantons comparée avec celle de Lille et Tourcoing, 1871–1905* (Paris: Vigot Frères, 1906), p. 15; Meckel, *Save the Babies*, pp. 41–46, 72–74, 95–98.

21. *Baby-Saving Campaigns: A Preliminary Report on What American Cities Are Doing to Prevent Infant Mortality*, U.S. Children's Bureau, Infant Mortality Series No. 1 (Bureau Publication No. 3) (Washington, D.C.: Government Printing Office, 1913), p. 33.

22. Henri Bouquet, *La puériculture sociale* (Paris: Blond, 1911), p. 283; Luc Boltanski, *Prime éducation et morale de classe* (Paris: Mouton, 1969), pp. 22, 34; Meckel, *Save the Babies*, p. 51; Sydney A. Halpern, *American Pediatrics: The Social Dynamics of Professionalization, 1880–1980* (Berkeley: University of California Press, 1988), p. 51.

especially foreign and therefore especially irrational. Abraham Jacobi, one of the pioneers of American pediatrics in the second half of the nineteenth century, argued that his specialty was essential for the preservation of American institutions and social values. "Unless the education and training of the young," he wrote, "is carried on according to the principles of sound and scientific physical and mental hygiene, neither the aim of our political institutions will ever be reached nor the United States fulfill its true manifest destiny."[23]

The Regulation of the Nursing Industry in France

The first target of French infant health campaigns was the peasant nurse. Children placed out to nurse, whether breast-fed or not, had a much higher mortality rate than children living with their parents, but other characteristics also made wet-nurses and other caretakers obvious subjects of infant health reforms. Though French physicians and legislators considered the nuclear family sacred and inviolable, they had few qualms about interfering in the care of children living outside of their parents' homes, especially if the caretakers were poor peasant women. Eugen Weber has traced the efforts of the French urban bourgeoisie and the Republican government to "civilize" the peasantry in the nineteenth century in an attempt to destroy rural irrationality, ignorance and superstition, and provincial languages, and to teach, in their place, reading, cleanliness, patriotism, and an industrial work ethic.[24] Just as the government saw peasant traditions as an obstacle to political unity and social homogeneity, physicians saw them as the most obstinate source of resistance to the propagation of scientific hygiene.

One physician, trying to explain why the rate of infant mortality among children placed out to nurse was so high even in regions where breast-feeding prevailed, eloquently expressed the contempt for the peasant nurse typical of French physicians: "What misappreciation of the precepts of hygiene, what customs, what habits, what prejudices, what stupidity could so be packed into the age-old filth of the coun-

23. Quoted in Halpern, American Pediatrics, p. 52.
24. Eugen Weber, Peasants into Frenchmen: The Modernization of Rural France, 1870–1914 (Stanford, Calif.: Stanford University Press, 1976), pp. 5, 19–20.

tryside to mask or rather, alas! to extinguish the fortunate effect of the most certain law of child nutrition; the minimal mortality among breast-fed children?"[25] Peasants often lived in abject poverty and in primitive structures, and their traditions of child care seemed antithetical to the ideas of physicians trained in the germ theory. Physicians described the middle-aged and older women, many of them widows, who often took in infants as superstitious old wives. This portrait resembled in some respects that of the immigrant midwife in the United States as sketched by obstetricians seeking to destroy the profession of midwifery.[26] Both were the bearers and teachers of traditional female lore, and both threatened physicians' crusade to bring modern medicine into the homes of the working class.

The "ignorance" of peasant nurses was not the only reason that they attracted the attention of legislators and physicians. The practice of placing children out to nurse also seemed to epitomize the disintegration of French family values, particularly the tendency of women to abandon their maternal responsibilities. French writers thus viewed the nursing industry as an important aspect of the problem of depopulation.[27]

By the late nineteenth century, placing children out to nurse in the countryside was a working-class practice in France. Most wealthy women kept their children at home, following nineteenth-century domestic ideology, though many hired live-in wet-nurses. Married working-class women, however, made essential economic contributions to their families as well as to the French economy; they simply could not afford to stay at home and devote themselves to their infants. Women in textile towns tended to leave their children with neighbors or relatives during the day, but in Paris and other com-

25. J. Jarricot, *Rôle social et pratique du fonctionnement des consultations de nourrissons et des gouttes de lait* (Trévoux: Jeannin, 1909), p. 74.

26. On the campaign to eliminate midwives see Judy Barrett Litoff, *American Midwives 1860 to the Present* (Westport, Conn.: Greenwood Press, 1978); Frances E. Kobrin, "The American Midwife Controversy: A Crisis in Professionalization," *Bulletin of the History of Medicine* 40 (1966): 350–63.

27. See Anne-Martin Fugier, "La fin de nourrice," *Le Mouvement social*, no. 105 (October–December 1978): 27. Fugier argues that legislators also saw a correlation between the decadence of rural civilization and the deteriorating quantity and quality of nurses' milk. See also Sussman, *Selling Mothers' Milk*, pp. 7, 28–29; Karen Offen, "Depopulation, Nationalism, and Feminism in Fin-de-Siècle France," *American Historical Review* 89 (1984): 652.

mercial and artisan cities 20 to 30 percent of infants were sent out to
nurse. In those sections of Paris where retail trade, artisinal crafts,
office work, and domestic service predominated, as many as 45 to
60–70 percent of parents sent their children away.[28] While physicians
proposed comprehensive regulation of the wet-nursing industry, they
hoped eventually to make it possible for working women to keep
their children at home by making them, in a sense, the paid nurses
of their own children.

The campaign launched by physicians in the 1860s and 1870s to
create a national system to regulate nursing was part of an international movement to protect children from physical abuse. The debate
over nursing in France paralleled the British "baby farming" scandals
of the same period which also focused on the shockingly high death
rate of infants living with paid caretakers; the same years saw the
founding of societies for the prevention of cruelty to children in cities
in the United States as well.[29] The French campaign was distinctive,
however, in making the connection between infant mortality and
depopulation.

The Académie de médecine took up the issue of infant mortality
in 1866, when the government asked this prestigious medical association to consider the implications of a report by one of its members
on the appalling mortality rate of children placed out to nurse in the
Morvan, a traditional region for the placement of Parisian children.
Another member presented statistics suggesting that the pattern in
the Morvan was replicated throughout the nation; in all departments,
the mortality rate of children placed out to nurse was 55 to 70 percent.
These deaths, the reporter concluded, must have a significant effect

28. In 1907 only 2 percent of the fathers of children from the Seine placed out to
nurse were professionals; 11 percent were shopkeepers or merchants, 24 percent
worked in commerce, 40 percent were laborers, and 19 percent were domestic or day
laborers. Fugier, "La fin de nourrice," p. 14; Sussman, *Selling Mothers' Milk,* p. 168;
Catherine Rollet, "Allaitement, mise en nourrice et mortalité infantile en France à la
fin du XIXe siècle," *Population* 33 (1978): 1197.

29. See Linda Gordon, *Heroes of Their Own Lives: The Politics and History of Family
Violence, Boston, 1880–1960* (New York: Penguin, 1988), pp. 27–30; Meckel, *Save the
Babies,* pp. 30–31; George K. Behlmer, *Child Abuse and Moral Reform in England 1870–
1908* (Stanford, Calif.: Stanford University Press, 1982); Le Vicomte de Bernis, *Protection de la première enfance* (Paris: V. Giard et E. Briére, 1898), p. 312. On baby
farming and its critics in the United States see Sherri Broder, "Child Care or Neglect?
Baby Farming in Late Nineteenth-Century Philadelphia," *Gender and Society* 2 (1988):
128–48.

on the declining rate of population growth. In 1867 the academy appointed a commission on the mortality of nurslings, the Commission de la mortalité des nourrissons, to study the wet-nursing business and propose a system of regulation; by 1870 the academy had devoted thirty-four sessions to this issue.[30]

The commission's report drew heavily on existing or former statutes regulating the Parisian wet-nursing business, dating back to 1715, which included provisions for the registration of nurses.[31] The commission introduced a medical element into the system, however. The report suggested that each nurse undergo a medical examination to determine her health and ability to nurse and that the children be certified free of venereal disease. It also proposed that a medical inspector make regular visits to ensure that the nurses followed the basic rules of infant hygiene.[32] In proposing this system of inspection the commission was inspired by the work of a private organization of physicians, the Société protectrice de l'enfance. This society had been organized in 1865 to combat infant mortality; its first effort was to advertise to parents in Paris, offering to have a physician visit each child every month and report on its health and care.[33] Physicians in several other cities soon followed the Parisian example.

Among the many criticisms of the report by members of the academy, the most cogent was that the commission had ignored the underlying causes of infant mortality. Poverty and the negligence of wealthy women, the critics argued, lay at the root of the problem.[34] In its final report, presented in 1870, the commission incorporated this argument; though devoted mostly to the regulation of the nursing business, the report also proposed financial assistance to encourage poor mothers to breast-feed and educational campaigns to reawaken the maternal sentiment of bourgeois women. These measures, members of the academy agreed, would ultimately lead to the elimination

30. *Bulletin de l'Académie de médecine* 31 (1866–67): 96–355; Jules Renault and G. Labeaume, "L'évolution de la protection de l'enfance," *Bulletin de l'Académie de médecine*, 3d ser. 117 (1937): 771. For the history of the Académie de médecine see Erwin H. Ackerknecht, *Medicine at the Paris Hospital, 1794–1848* (Baltimore: Johns Hopkins University Press, 1967), p. 115. See also Sussman, *Selling Mothers' Milk*, pp. 122–28.
31. See Sussman, *Selling Mothers' Milk*, pp. 31, 102–3, 128.
32. *Bulletin de l'Académie de médecine* 34 (1869): 257.
33. Archives de la Ville de Paris, VD⁶ 1575, No. 3; *Bulletin de l'Académie de médecine* 34 (1869): 966; Sussman, *Selling Mothers' Milk*, p. 123.
34. *Bulletin de l'Académie de médecine* 34 (1869): 1014, 1256–80.

of the nursing business.[35] These larger issues addressed by the commission lay at the heart of later legislative debates.

In March 1869, in response to the academy's work, the minister
of the interior appointed a commission of legislators, administrators,
and physicians, including four members of the academy's commission, to study the relationship between the nursing business and infant
mortality. War interrupted the work of the official commission but
the project survived the change in government. In 1873, when Théophile Roussel, Republican deputy from Lozère and a member of the
Académie de médecine, proposed legislation based largely on the
academy's report, the new administration lent its support.[36]

Like the academy's proposals, Roussel's bill borrowed heavily from
Parisian regulations dating back to the eighteenth century, but it
created a national administrative structure to make possible their application to the entire country. The legislation required each nurse to
obtain a health certificate from a physician and a certificate of morality
from the mayor of the commune she lived in. All children under two
years old who were placed out to nurse would be registered with the
local authorities and were placed under the official protection of the
state. Medical inspectors would visit each child placed out to nurse
once a month to examine the child and assess the general sanitary
conditions and cleanliness of the house. The inspectors would have
the authority to recommend the removal of children from incompetent nurses.

The bill also provided for systematic community supervision of
nurses through local commissions composed of clergymen, representatives of local charitable societies, and respectable married
women. The law itself and the officials who first developed the regulations governing its execution foresaw these local commissions as
principal agents of the protective service. The commission members
were to live near the protected children and make frequent unannounced visits, thus supplementing the monthly visits of the medical
inspector. Their job was to investigate the "way of life" of the nurse
and her family and the hygiene and safety of the home, and to assess
the quality of her care of the nursling. They were to ensure that the
nurse followed the instructions of the medical inspector and called a

35. Bulletin de l'Académie de médecine 35 (1870): 259.
36. Ibid.; Bulletin de l'Académie de médecine 40 (1874): 292. Léonard discusses Roussel's life in La médecine entre les savoirs et les pouvoirs, p. 299.

physician in case of illness. The commission had the power to remove a child from a refractory nurse and to commend and reward those who performed well.[37] This assignment of the role of voluntary home visitor to bourgeois women foreshadowed their place in maternal and infant health policy after the turn of the century.

Roussel feared opposition to his proposal in the parliament, because the law would be an expensive one and interference with parental prerogatives was a delicate issue. Nonetheless the legislature passed the law unanimously and without debate. As some observers noted, such legislative successes were rare in the stormy course of French parliamentary politics.[38] In a sense the Roussel Law, passed in the wake of France's military defeat in 1871, stood as the first legislative effort to counteract the population crisis. The legislators agreed, almost to a man, that the nation faced an urgent crisis, and they could concur on few pronatalist measures. Because the Roussel Law did not address the volatile economic and religious issues that defined the depopulation debate, however, it proved relatively uncontroversial.

The departments began to execute the law only gradually. Several departmental assemblies failed to vote funds for the service, either on the grounds that the nursing business did not exist in their department or that the law violated parental authority.[39] Where the law was in effect those involved in its execution criticized the functioning of the unwieldy bureaucracy the system required and pointed out major gaps in the law. Medical inspectors and mayors repeatedly complained in their annual reports that the administration required too much paperwork or that the necessary paperwork did not get done. Phy-

37. Jarricot, *Rôle social et pratique*, pp. 75, 84–87; Préfecture de Police, 1re Division, 5e Bureau, *Protection des enfants du premier âge: Historique de la réglementation du service dans le Départment de la Seine* (Paris: Imprimerie administrative, 1910), p. 3; Préfet de Police to Maire du 7e arrondissement, January 9, 1878, Archives de la Ville de Paris, V.D.⁶ 1575, No. 4; Préfecture de Police, "Instruction générale du 15 juin, 1877," in *Protection des enfants du premier âge* (Paris: 1909), p. 28.

38. *Bulletin de l'Académie de médecine* 40 (1874): 1149.

39. Académie de médecine, *Rapport annuel de la Commission permanente de l'hygiène de l'enfance*, 1903, p. 15; Hélène Moniez, *Les commissions locales du protection du premier âge: Rapport présenté au nom de la deuxième section à la Société internationale pour l'étude des questions d'assistance* (Paris: Masson, 1904), pp. 11–13; Conseil supérieur de l'assistance publique, *Comptes-rendus*, Fascicule No. 76, Statistique des dépenses publiques d'assistance en 1896; Comité supérieur de protection des enfants du premier âge, *Rapport concernant l'application de la Loi du 23 décembre 1874 présenté à M. le Ministre de l'Intérieur*, 1886.

sicians protested that local authorities failed to notify them when
infants arrived in their districts, that nurses refused to call a physician
in case of illness because they had no way to pay the fees, that children
only a few days old were transported in cold, insanitary railroad cars,
that the local commissions did not exist; and that many nurses were
never paid.[40]

Nonetheless, by 1898 11 percent of all children born in France,
including 30 percent of those born in Paris, came under the supervision of the protective services. By 1900 even most of those who
expressed significant criticisms of the law considered its efficacy to
be beyond doubt and none proposed its abolition. In 1884 the minister
of the interior wrote: "It would be superfluous to enter here into long
expositions to demonstrate once more that medical inspection constitutes the essential and direct work of the protection of infancy; that
is a truth recalled in all circulars calling for the cooperation of departmental assemblies, a truth that experience makes clearer each
year."[41] Statistics certainly indicated that the mortality of children
placed out to nurse was declining rapidly. In 1857–66 the mortality
rate had averaged 204.2 per thousand; by the 1890s, it had been
reduced to 161.7 per thousand By the end of the century some observers began to point out that, at least in certain communes and
regions, nurses were apparently doing a better job of caring for children than mothers were.[42]

The majority of those involved in the administration of the law

40. Département des Basses-Pyrénées, Assistance publique, *Rapports présentés à M. le Préfet des Basses-Pyrénées par M. Adolphe Augé, Inspecteur départemental de l'assistance publique,* 1908; E. Vidal, "Résultats de la Loi Roussel dans le dèpartement du Var," *Progrès médical,* 2d ser. 20 (1894): 73–76; Département de Meurthe-et-Moselle, Assis-tance publique, *Rapport de M. G. Chevillet, Inspecteur départemental, sur l'ensemble des diverses branches des services de l'enfance, année 1907* (Nancy: Berger-Levrault, 1908); Département de la Haute-Vienne, Inspection de l'assistance et de l'hygiène publique, services de l'enfance, *Rapports de M. A. Gourivand, année 1912* (Limoges: Henri-Charles LaVauzelle, 1913). See also the annual reports of the Comission permanente de l'hy-giène de l'enfance of the Académie de médecine.

41. *Bulletin de l'Académie de médecine* 51 (1885): 355.

42. Conseil superiéur de l'assistance publique, *Comptes-rendus,* Fascicule No. 76, p. 23; Département des Basses-Pyrénées, Assistance publique, *Rapports présentés à M. Le Préfet des Basses-Pyrénées,* p. 67; *Congrès national d'assistance publique* (Lyons: An-cienne imprimerie A. Waltener, 1894), vol. 2, pp. 169–70; Vidal, "Résultats de la Loi Roussel dans le département du Var," p. 74; A. Chaudet, *Un exemple d'initiative privée: La commission d'inspection des nourrissons de Sainte-Jamme-sur-Sarthe* (Le Mans: Impri-merie Ch. Blanchet, 1902), p. 17.

believed that the medical inspectors had made significant progress in the dissemination of modern hygiene into the countryside. By the 1890s some medical inspectors still complained about the care nurses provided, but they generally reported that most of the nurses were conscientious and clean and that they obediently followed the new rules. They observed that the practice of swaddling children tightly from neck to foot had disappeared, that nurses no longer fed young infants on thick soups or bread and water, and that the number of diarrheal deaths had declined sharply.[43]

The Roussel Law provided an important public role for physicians, one consistent with the ethos of the organized medical profession. Members of the Académie de médecine were beginning to see their organization as a semiofficial agency and insisted that the government consult them on issues they felt required medical expertise, including infant health programs. Physicians sat on the Comité supérieur de protection de l'enfance du premier âge, the agency created by the Roussel Law to administer the infant protective services, and the academy's permanent commission on child hygiene took on the task of putting together an annual report on the functioning of the law and collecting the reports of medical inspectors, mayors, and local commissions in all the departments. The institution of a national system of medical inspection, the first in France, brought several hundred local physicians all over the country into government service.[44] The official role of these physicians and the influence of the Académie de médecine on national policy gave an important section of the medical profession a stake in social control and provided legitimacy and prestige for the practice of pediatrics and obstetrics.

The medical inspectors demanded still more authority and better pay. Some argued that they should be able to take coercive action

43. Delobel, "Dix années de protection des enfants du premier âge," *Archives de médecine des enfants* 2 (1899): 27; Département de la Seine, Protection des enfants du premier âge, *Rapport annuel*, 1891, p. 99; Département de Meurthe-et-Moselle, Assistance publique, *Rapport de M. G. Chevillet, Inspecteur départemental*; Département de la Haute-Vienne, Inspection de l'assistance et de l'hygiène publique, services de l'enfance, *Rapports de M. A. Gourivand*; Département des Basses-Pyrénées, Assistance publique, *Rapports présentés à M. le Préfet des Basses-Pyrénées; Bulletin trimestriel de la Ligue contre la mortalité infantile* 12 (1913): 35–39.

44. The number of inspectors varied from department to department, from about twenty to seventy; an inspector might have only one child to supervise. See, for example, Département des Basses-Pyrénées, Assistance publique, *Rapports présentés à M. le Préfet des Basses-Pyrénées*, p. 72.

against the nurses; as it was, they had only a consultative voice in the local commissions, which had the authority to remove a child from an incompetent or unscrupulous nurse.[45] More important, the medical inspectors argued that the benefits of their supervision should be extended to other groups of children. As the mortality rate of nurslings approached that of children living with their parents, the emphasis of the law shifted from inspection to instruction and the attention of physicians and legislators turned from paid nurses to mothers themselves.

A few even proposed the extension of official medical supervision to all infants, with the provision that parents could choose to have their family physician make monthly official reports.[46] This suggestion ran into opposition from those who hesitated to infringe on the sanctity of the home or to threaten paternal authority. It was possible, however, to extend the protection of the law to a large number of children without violating these principles. Most supporters of the Roussel Law agreed, for example, that the law should cover all children living apart from their parents whether with paid nurses or not. In particular, the government could subject illegitimate children who lived with grandmothers or aunts to supervision without encountering the accusation that it was violating parental authority. Physicians were especially eager to protect children from their grandmothers, who had little exposure to modern hygiene and clung to their traditional "prejudices" and superstitions.[47]

45. Charles Mercier, *Les Petits-Paris: Etude critique et conseils pratiques sur l'hygiène infantile* (Paris: G. Steinheil, 1898), p. 165; Académie de médecine, *Rapport annuel de la Commission permanente de l'hygiène de l'enfance*, 1900, p. 39; E. Ravon, *Guide du médecin examinateur de l'assistance aux vieillards, infirmes et incurables et du médecin inspecteur des enfants protégés et assistés et des écoles* (Paris: Berger-Levrault, 1911), p. 26; Eustache, *La puériculture*, p. 304; Pestre, *Oeuvres d'assistance et de protection*, p. 26; "La protection de l'enfance," *Le Matin*, August 21, 1901.
46. Julien Guillemin, *De la protection des enfants du premier âge* (Paris: V. Giard et E. Brière, 1901), pp. 175–77; Hélène Bérot-Berger proposed the appointment of *inspectrices d'enfants malades* in each department to visit all children under the age of three years. Bérot-Berger, "Nominations d'inspectrices permanentes d'enfants malades," *Bericht über den III. Internationalen Köngress für Sauglingsschutz (Gouttes de Lait)* (Berlin: Georg Stilke, 1912), p. 753; Urbain Gohier, "La Loi Roussel pour la protection de l'enfance," *Le Matin*, July 12, 1907; Académie de médecine, *Rapport annuel de la Commission permanente de l'hygiène de l'enfance*, 1896, p. 9.
47. *Bulletin trimestriel de la Ligue contre la mortalité infantile*, October 1913: 38; E. Barthès, "Modifications à apporter à la loi du 23 décembre 1874," *Congès international de la protection de l'enfance (Bordeaux 1895)* (Bordeaux: Bourlange, 1896), p. 295; F. Lédé, "Rapport sur l'application de la loi du 23 décembre 1874," in ibid., p. 218;

Many physicians and public welfare authorities also believed that women who received public assistance or private charity had forfeited their right to privacy. The Académie de médecine, the Congrès national d'assistance, and the Congrès des sociétés protectrices de l'enfance all passed resolutions urging that all children whose parents were recipients of public assistance should be covered by the protective services. In effect, argued Charles Delplanque, who ran infant health programs in Lille, by providing aid to prevent abandonment the state was buying the lives of the children it saved and therefore had the right to verify that the assistance was being used for its intended purpose and that the mother was caring for her baby properly. By 1901 the departments of the Loiret and the Eure-et-Loire put these ideas into practice and hired medical inspectors to visit children receiving certain forms of public assistance.[48] Legislators did not extend the Roussel Law to cover children living with their parents, although the law served as a model for private and public programs aimed at mothers rather than at nurses.

Physicians reporting on the functioning of the law attributed its success to a combination of factors. Some argued that nurses genuinely understood and accepted the laws of hygiene. Others thought that the nurses followed the medical inspector's instructions only when they feared his visit. Rewards, reprimands, and the threat of punishment worked together to foster a beneficial spirit of competition among the nurses, argued the reporter for the permanent commission on child hygiene of the Académie de médecine in 1900.[49]

Though physicians came increasingly to see the medical inspection of nurslings as an educational enterprise, it remained essentially a

---

Académie de medicine, *Rapport annuel de la Commission permanente de l'hygiène de l'enfance,* 1891, pp. 37–39; 1893, p. 93.

48. Moniez, *Les commissions locales du protection du premier âge,* p. 5; Charles Delplanque, *Assistance aux enfants du premier âges privés de ressources (avant et après la naissance); fonctionnement des consultations du Bureau de bienfaisance de Lille* (Lille: Wilmot-Courtecuisse, 1910), p. 14; Commission de la dépopulation, Sous-commission de la mortalité, *Rapport général sur les causes de la mortalité, présenté par M. Paul Strauss* (Melun: Imprimerie administrative, 1911), p. 25; Académie de médecine, *Rapport annuel de la Commission permanente de l'hygiène de l'enfance,* 1901, p. 56; E. Barthès, "Des causes de la mortalité des enfants dans leur première année d'existence et des moyens d'y remédier," *Revue d'hygiène* 20 (1898): 645.

49. Académie de médecine, *Rapport annuel de la Commission permanente de l'hygiène de l'enfance,* 1900, p. 41; 1903, p. 16; Marie Roget, "Des nourrices: Nourrices à la campagne," *Le Puériculteur* 1 (1906): 181; Ravon, *Guide du médecin examinateur,* p. 76.

system of surveillance backed up by the threat of removing the nurse's livelihood. In principle, the sanctions were necessary because nurses had no natural affection for the children they cared for; as one author put it, Roussel "understood that it would be more effective to frighten nurses than to teach mothers their duty [to breast-feed]."[50] Nonetheless, this approach, one that combined instruction with rewards and punishments, served as the model when physicians began to try to instruct mothers. Following certain rules of hygiene or attending infant health consultations later became a condition for a variety of material assistance and services: free meals, crèches, clean milk, and maternity benefits.

Consultations de Nourrissons

The most important institution for the medical supervision of infants and the instruction of their mothers was the *consultation de nourrissons,* or infant health consultation. The man credited with the invention of the infant health consultation was Pierre Budin, who had links with solidarist Radicals and was chief of the obstetrical service of the Hôpital de la Charité in Paris. Budin had noticed that infants who left the hospital in good health often sickened and died at home; because no medical service admitted children so young, he later wrote, their mothers were left to flounder without any medical instruction. In 1892, Budin obtained permission from the general director of the Assistance publique of Paris, the city's public welfare department, to have the children born in his service brought back once a week for examination and weighing. Budin's primary goal was to encourage breast-feeding, but the consultation supplied sterilized cows' milk if the mother did not have enough milk. Within a few years physicians had established infant health consultations in three other Parisian hospitals and in several charitable and municipal dispensaries.[51]

The *goutte de lait,* or milk station, was similar to the infant health consultation but was designed primarily to combat infant mortality

50. Bernis, *Protection de la première enfance,* p. 310.
51. Pierre Budin, "Les consultations de nourrissons," *Revue d'hygiène et de médecine infantiles* 4 (1905): 118, 121; Commission de dépopulation, Sous-commission de la mortalité, *Séances, 1902–3,* Séance du 12 novembre 1902, pp. 30–31.

among artificially fed infants. A Dr. Dufour, who organized a milk station in Fécamp in 1894, coined the term *goutte de lait,* literally, "drop of milk." He distributed milk free or for a fee depending on the parents' ability to pay and required the mothers to attend a weekly medical consultation. Dufour considered this instruction of individual mothers an important aspect of the work of the milk station; he conducted the consultations like a class, insisting that all the mothers remain quiet so as to profit from the instructions given to each one.[52] In 1892 Gaston Variot had organized a similar service in his dispensary in the Belleville section of Paris, though in this case most of the children were already sick.[53]

Though the consultation and the milk station had quite similar goals, their respective advocates hotly debated the relative merits of the two institutions. Supporters of the consultation argued that milk stations encouraged women to give up breast-feeding; supporters of the milk station countered that social and economic conditions made artificial feeding a necessary evil that could not be ignored.[54] In fact, there were few consultations that did not supply sterilized or pasteurized milk to mothers who could not breast-feed and most milk stations distributed milk to mothers only after a physician had certified their inability to breast-feed. Institutional differences determined to some extent the different emphases of the consultations and the milk stations. Consultations, which were often attached to maternity hospitals, could encourage women to breast-feed when they were still in the hospital, while milk stations, which tended to be independent of hospitals, more often saw children only after their mothers had already given up nursing.[55]

Infant health consultations and milk stations proliferated in both urban areas and small towns under the sponsorship of a variety of public and private maternal and child welfare agencies. Many medical inspectors welcomed the consultation as an addition to the work of

52. Léon Dufour, *Comment on crée une goutte de lait* (n.p.: Oeuvre Fécampoise de la Goutte de Lait, 1902).

53. *Organisation et fonctionnement de la Goutte de lait de Belleville, 1892–1911* (Paris: A. Davy, 1911), p. 9.

54. E. Ausset, "La vulgarisation de la puériculture et de l'hygiène alimentaire des nourrissons dans le grand public," *Bericht über de III. Internationalen Kongress für Sauglingsschutz,* p. 324; George F. McCleary, *The Early History of the Infant Welfare Movement* (London: H. K. Lewis, 1933), p. 50.

55. Budin, "Les consultations de nourrissons," p. 122.

the Roussel Law. In the country, or wherever nurses were widely scattered, visiting all the children in a district could be very time-consuming; the inspectors often complained that their fee was ridiculously low in relation to the time they spent. Budin cited the example of a former student of his who spent ten full days each month visiting the three hundred children in his district (an unusually large number). In communes where the children were concentrated enough, Budin suggested, gathering the nurses in a single place for consultations could replace at least some of the home visits.[56]

In 1903 the Senate passed a resolution urging that the infant protective services establish infant health consultations and milk stations to supervise children protected under the Roussel Law and those whose mothers received certain forms of public assistance, and to offer their services to other mothers. The minister of the interior called upon the prefects to encourage the creation of consultations as an important weapon in the nation's battle against depopulation, particularly in conjunction with the administration of the Roussel Law. Authorities in some departments followed these instructions. In 1902, for example, following a lecture by Budin in Arras, the prefect of the Pas-de-Calais asked all mayors in the department and the directors of large coal companies to establish consultations. By 1904 there were 116 in the department, including several run by mining corporations.[57]

Over the next ten years consultations became an integral part of the system created by the Roussel Law in many areas. Perhaps the most complete system of consultations in connection with the Roussel Law was in the Yonne; in 1911 this department boasted 133 consultations.[58] Medical inspectors and mayors praised the innovation and reported that nurses and mothers alike attended willingly. The consultation, they argued, fostered a healthy spirit of competition among the nurses as they vied for praise from the physician. The consultation also enabled medical inspectors to extend their supervision to legitimate children living in their parents' homes, though some medical

56. Pierre Budin, "La Ville de Paris et la mortalité infantile," *Revue philanthropique* 14 (1904): 412.

57. Ravon, *Guide du médecin examinateur*, p. 78.

58. Elie Decherf, "Etude critique des oeuvres françaises de protection de l'enfance," *Bericht über den III. Internationalen Kongress für Sauglingsschutz*, p. 409; Commission de la dépopulation, Sous-commission de la mortalité, *Séances, 1902–3*, Seance du 3 décembre 1902, p. 8.

inspectors complained that the consultations unfairly forced them to give free care to those who were not entitled to it.[59]

In the early 1900s, as consultations and milk stations became more popular, public assistance agencies and charities that aided mothers with children began to make medical supervision a condition of receiving material aid. Several writers proposed that the law of 1904 which provided assistance to indigent mothers as a way of preventing child abandonment be modified to require the mothers to attend a consultation, but the parliament never seriously considered this suggestion.[60] Some muncipalities, however—Roubaix and Lille, for example—required that women receiving assistance from the local welfare bureau attend a consultation; those who attended regularly also received supplemental aid. For women who were not breast-feeding, receiving milk free or at minimal cost was considered incentive enough. The welfare bureau in Lille lured women with gifts of meat and distributed bonuses of ten francs to those who continued to nurse for an entire year. In Roubaix mothers who attended regularly for a full year received a set of clothes and linens as a reward.[61]

Most municipalities, however, did not make attendance a condition of receiving public assistance. In 1910 the authors of a survey of 150 of France's largest cities concluded that only eight supervised the health of infants with any care. Several cities, including Paris, had consultations that poor women were encouraged to attend; others arranged for private milk stations to provide milk for their clients; still others insisted on supervision only for artifically fed children. Welfare officials in the Vendée required that wards of the state, children placed out to nurse, and those whose mothers received aid to prevent abandonment attend consultations. In 1911, however, there were only eight consultations in the entire department—probably not nearly enough to serve all the children in these groups.[62]

59. Jarricot, *Rôle social et pratique*, p. 96; Ravon, *Guide du médecin examinateur*, pp. 80–81; R. Marois, *Les consultations de nourrissons dans l'Yonne en 1910* (Auxerre: A. Jacques, 1911), pp. 42–46, 51–53, 59–66.

60. Eustache, *La puériculture, hygiène, et assistance*, p. 269; Delplanque, *Assistance aux enfants du premier âge*, p. 53.

61. Felhoen, *Etude statistique sur la mortalité infantile*, p. 212; Bureau de bienfaisance de Lille, *Rapports sur les consultations obstétricales*, 1910, p. 21; Delplanque, *Assistance aux enfants du premier âge*, pp. 43–45.

62. *L'enfant* 20 (1911): 111–12; Delplanque, *Assistance aux enfants du premier âge*, pp. 39–43.

By the 1910s most private charities also provided medical super-vision. Many maternal charity societies, which had traditionally aided poor married women, opened consultations. When the Roussel Law took over the medical supervision of children placed out to nurse, the *sociétés protectrices de l'enfance* turned their attention to providing material assistance to enable mothers to keep their children at home and to make breast-feeding possible. After 1900 these organizations added infant health consultations to their programs. Crèches em-ployed physicians to examine the children regularly and often insti-tuted some form of instructive consultation for the mothers, and maternal mutual aid societies usually required their members to attend consultations. Free restaurants for nursing mothers, which did not even require beneficiaries to give their names, began to insist that they bring their children to be examined by a physician.[63]

Independent milk stations or consultations also became agencies of maternal and child assistance. Their organizers recognized that many working-class women could afford neither good quality milk for their children nor the nutritious food necessary to maintain an adequate supply of breast milk. If the consultations were going to encourage breast-feeding, they had to make it materially possible. Rarely was the aid sufficient to enable a woman to forego her wages and devote herself to her child, however. The consultations frequently resorted to cash and in-kind gifts simply in order to attract clientele.[64]

Physicians frequently asserted that mothers attended consultations only to receive the inexpensive milk or other material assistance, though others thought that the spirit of competition among the moth-ers or even maternal instinct provided sufficient motivation.[65] They

63. A. Vallin, *La femme salariée et la maternité* (Paris: Arthur Rousseau, 1911), p. 140; A. Balestre and M. d'Oelsnitz, "Création d'une goutte de lait par la Société protectrice de l'enfance de Nice," *Bericht über den III. Internationalen Kongress für Sauglingsschutz,* p. 790; Société protectrice de l'enfance de la Gironde, *Exercises 1928 et 1929* (Bordeaux: Imprimeries Gounouilheu, 1930), p. 15.

64. Decherf, "Etude critique des oeuvres françaises de protection de l'enfance," p. 6; Jarricot, *Rôle social et pratique,* p. 167.

65. For example, see Fernand Merlin, "Un moyen efficace de protection générale de l'enfance—la mutualité maternelle élargie," *Bericht über den III. Internationalen Kon-gress für Sauglingsschutz,* p. 905; Jarricot, *Rôle social et pratique,* p. 133; Louis Ciando, *La culture des nourrissons: De l'organization des nourrissons* (Nice: Imprimerie des Alpes-Maritimes, 1908), pp. 22, 30; Budin, "La Ville de Paris et la mortalité infantile," p. 397; Vildermann, *Moyen pratique,* p. 31.

usually considered free milk a sufficient incentive for mothers who bottle-fed their infants. It was difficult to demonstrate, however, that gifts of milk did not encourage women to give up breast-feeding, so most private consultations offered some kind of material aid to breast-feeding women as well. The consultations in Le Havre, for example, distributed cash and in-kind prizes at a public ceremony every three months, and all women who attended regularly got meat each week.

The patrons of the Le Havre consultations frankly admitted that they offered these gifts simply as an incentive to stimulate breast-feeding. They also offered a more exalted explanation, however: the rewards, they argued, made mothers feel the price attached to their devotion to their children and fortified them to persevere in their noble mission of raising French citizens.[66] It was perfectly natural, they concluded, to pay mothers for the work they did for the state.

The notion that poor mothers could legitimately be made the paid nurses of their own children because motherhood was a service to the state was a common French rationale for the financial assistance of poor mothers, whether through infant health consultations, through the temporary aid provided by the law of 1904, or through the maternity benefits later allocated under the Strauss Law of 1913. French physicians advocated supervision of infants and instruction of their mothers as a critical element of programs to prevent infant mortality. They did not, however, believe that instruction alone would suffice; they recognized that poverty and employment prevented working-class mothers from carrying out their maternal duties. A system of maternal and infant health care which combined education with material assistance thus gradually emerged in France. The Strauss Law, for example, provided maternity benefits only to women who actually rested and provided proper "hygienic" care for their infants.[67] The population crisis and an increasingly comprehensive system of public welfare facilitated the efforts of French pediatricians to become the recognized authorities on child care, for both mothers and policy makers.

66. La consultations de nourrissons au sein, *Statuts: Compte rendu de l'Assemblée générale*, 1907, p. 16.

67. See Stewart, *Women, Work, and the French State*, p. 189, for general provisions of the law.

Milk Stations in the United States

The child health movement also provided physicians in the United States, particularly the members of the emerging pediatric and obstetric specialties, with opportunities to develop their professional legitimacy. Around the turn of the century these specialists were working to create institutions that would provide them with clinical, research, and training facilities. Because of the decentralized nature of social welfare in the United States, these institutions were developed primarily in the context of philanthropy and of municipal public health and social reform, rather than in the context of national policies or structures, as in France.

In the northeastern and midwestern cities where these physicians were concentrated, Progressive reform efforts focused on the integration of the "new" southern and eastern European immigrants into American society. Pediatricians and obstetricians were not the only group bent on shaping the health and child care habits of these immigrants; the women devoted to the development of the new, independent profession of public health nursing played a vital role in urban public health programs. In addition, the ideology of settlement leaders and social workers who sought to mold the new urban immigrants into independent, responsible, intelligent citizens seemed at times to conflict with the medical specialists' goal of increasing women's dependence on professional expertise. What all of these groups shared was a belief that the best way to prevent infant mortality was to educate mothers in infant care and feeding. Milk stations in the United States frequently included some charitable component, and American reformers recognized the consistent association between high infant mortality rates and poverty. Nonetheless, they never saw the relief of poverty as essential to their efforts. Thus, while the founders of milk stations and child welfare centers in the United States consciously imitated the French *consultations de nourrissons* and *gouttes de lait,* the American institutions differed in important respects from their French models.

The milk station—the American *goutte de lait*—provided the basis for urban infant health programs in the United States. The first milk stations, an outgrowth of campaigns to improve the urban milk supply through pasteurization, inspection, and certification, aimed simply to provide milk that was free of chemical and microbial contamination. Convinced that infant mortality from diarrhea was caused by such contamination, scientists and physicians in the 1890s and early 1900s disagreed over the relative merits of pasteurization and certification (a system of close medical supervision of milk production for infants and sick people proposed by Henry Coit, a physician from Newark, New Jersey). Futhermore, because physicians had not come to any definitive conclusion as to the mechanism by which milk became toxic, they did not agree on the proper methods of testing and regulating a city's milk supply.[68] In the meantime, a few individuals took the initiative to make pure milk available to the most vulnerable groups.

Henry Koplik, a New York physician, established the first milk station in the United States, supplying clean milk to sick children on the Lower East Side beginning in 1889. The most influential figure in the milk station movement in the 1890s, however, was Nathan Straus, a wealthy New York philanthropist and ardent advocate of pasteurization. Beginning in 1893 he began to supply pasteurized milk to poor infants. By 1896 he supplied over 600,000 bottles a year and had donated pasteurization plants to Philadelphia and Chicago.[69] In 1908, when Wilbur Phillips was hired by the New York Association for Improving the Condition of the Poor to open milk stations under the auspices of the New York Milk Committee, there were already seven operating year-round in the city: six owned by Straus and feeding about two thousand babies a day, and one run by the Good Samaritan Dispensary providing milk to two hundred.

The seven stations opened in 1908 by the New York Milk Committee differed from these older stations: from the outset Phillips conceived their primary task as one of education. At the new stations volunteer physicians held weekly classes for mothers where they ex-

68. For discussions of the pure milk movement see Meckel, *Save the Babies,* pp. 63, 80–89; Judith Walzer Leavitt, *The Healthiest City: Milwaukee and the Politics of Health Reform* (Princeton, N.J.: Princeton University Press, 1982), pp. 159–85; McCleary, *Early History of the Infant Welfare Movement,* pp. 61–67.

69. See McCleary, *Early History of the Infant Welfare Movement,* pp. 55–56; Rima Apple, *Mothers and Medicine: A Social History of Infant Feeding, 1890–1950* (Madison: University of Wisconsin Press, 1987), p. 144; Nathan Straus, "A Report on the Progress Made in America in the Protection of Childlife," *Bericht über den III. Internationalen Kongress für Sauglingsschutz,* pp. 412–19; Nathan Straus, "Twenty Years' Practical Experience in Modifying and Pasteurizing Milk for Infant Feeding," in ibid., pp. 646–49.

amined and weighed children, prescribed a formula for each child's feedings, and lectured the mothers on infant feeding and hygiene. Trained nurses supervised the distribution of milk modified in the committee's laboratory, assisted the physicians in the classes, and visited the children's homes to see that the mothers carried out their directions. The committee claimed to encourage breast-feeding through education and provided milk only to mothers who could not nurse.[70]

As he later wrote, Phillips, a Harvard-educated newspaper reporter, knew nothing about babies, milk, or mortality when he was hired. The membership of the Milk Committee included an impressive array of eminent bacteriologists and public health authorities—basically, Phillips quipped, the makings of an imposing letterhead. Phillips was influenced by Budin's work in Paris, but his educational approach was also shaped by his own and his employers' commitment to social work with the poor and by the work of visiting nurses.[71] The new emphasis on instruction of mothers reflected the reorientation of American public health toward the reform of personal and household hygiene through public education. Public health officials in the late nineteenth century had focused their efforts on public sanitation and the isolation and prevention of communicable diseases. By the early twentieth century, largely successful in their campaigns to clean up the streets and to protect water and milk supplies, they began to see domestic and individual cleanliness as important factors in the spread of contagious diseases, including infant diarrhea.[72]

In the new public health movement, one segment of the nursing profession found an opportunity to carve out a professional niche that allowed significant independence and an influential role in social reform. The first American visiting nurse associations were organized by wealthy women in the 1880s to provide nursing care for the sick poor. By 1900 there were 115 visiting nurse associations

70. Wilbur C. Phillips, "The Mother and the Baby," *The Survey* 22 (1909): 626; Frederic J. Haskin, "Better Care for Babies," May 13, 1916 (Records of the U.S. Children's Bureau, National Archives, Washington, D.C., 4–15–4–3).

71. Wilbur C. Phillips, *Adventuring for Democracy* (New York: Social Unit Press, 1940), pp. 5, 18, 23.

72. Leavitt, *Healthiest City*, pp. 70, 243–44; Meckel, *Save the Babies*, pp. 93–97, 120; Waserman, "Emergence of Modern Health Care."

in the United States; these agencies copied the English system of dividing the city into districts, assigning a nurse to each. The primary responsibility of public health nurses, however, like that of English "health visitors," was not bedside nursing. Instead, these women were trained to teach the prevention of disease through proper nutrition, cleanliness, sleep and exercise habits, clothing, and ventilation.[73]

In the work of these nurses, the "new" public health merged with Progressive social reform and settlement work; many public health nurses found that without housing reform and measures to protect children and workers, for example, instruction in hygiene was an incomplete solution to the health problems of the poor. Phillips shared this perspective; he was determined to mold the milk stations into social as well as medical institutions. Not only did he enlist the aid of charitable organizations such as the St. Vincent De Paul Society, the Charity Organization Society, and the United Hebrew Charities, but he also called on leading female social reformers, including Lillian Wald, Alice Lakey, who was active in the General Federation of Women's Clubs and the National Consumers' League, and Elizabeth Williams and Grace White, both head workers in settlements.[74]

A year later, in 1909, when the American Association for the Study and Prevention of Infant Mortality was founded, the new organization included social workers, educators, and public health nurses, many of them women, as well as physicians, bacteriologists, and public health officials. This organization incorporated the perspectives of these diverse professionals and treated infant mortality as a social problem that required a multipronged attack. In practice, instruction of mothers was the basis of all their work.

The New York Milk Committee's work served as the model for virtually all the milk stations opened in the United States over the

---

73. See Karen Buhler-Wilkerson, *False Dawn: The Rise and Fall of Public Health Nursing, 1900–1989* (New York: Garland, 1989), pp. 12–13, 47–48, 90–92; Deborah Dwork, *War Is Good for Babies and Other Young Children: A History of the Infant and Child Welfare Movement in England, 1898–1918* (London: Tavistock, 1987), pp. 125–27, 132–45, 158–60; *Transactions of the American Association for the Study and Prevention of Infant Mortality* 2 (1911): 392–93, 385–86.

74. Wilbur C. Phillips, "A Plan for Reducing Infant Mortality in New York City," *Medical Record* 73 (1908): 890–91; Phillips, *Adventuring for Democracy*, pp. 24–25, 48–50; Buhler-Wilkerson, *False Dawn*, pp. 94–97.

next ten years. In 1910 the New York City Council appropriated funds for fifteen year-round milk depots in addition to the privately funded stations, based on this model, and by 1912 there were a total of fifty-five milk stations in the city. By 1911 only two other cities— Pittsburgh and Rochester—had municipal milk stations; in most cities, private organizations provided the funds for infant health campaigns. Children's aid societies, charitable dispensaries, Red Cross chapters, Associated Charities, civic organizations, and visiting nurse associations organized "Babies Milk Fund" associations and "Milk and Baby Hygiene" associations to create milk stations, hire visiting nurses and recruit volunteer physicians. Public health officials cooperated, lent the services of school nurses, and solicited public funds.[75]

A few large cities had quite extensive systems in operation by 1911 or 1912. Cleveland, for example, had a centralized network of thirty-one privately operated "prophylactic" dispensaries and twenty-two visiting nurses. In 1902, a philanthropist had donated funds to establish a dispensary that would provide free modified milk to infants in addition to the usual medical care. This proved so expensive that the station could only serve a few children, so the administrators decided instead to supply good raw milk at a low price.

In 1906 H. J. Gerstenberger, a German-born and trained physician suggested that this Milk Fund Association cooperate with the Visiting Nurse Association to form an institution on a German model, combining medical consultations, home nursing care, and a milk station. In July 1906 the new Infants' Clinic was opened in the poorest part of the city, offering its services to mothers who could not afford a private physician. In December the Clinic was incorporated as the Babies' Dispensary and Hospital. This dispensary served both sick and well infants. It housed a milk laboratory and was the center of a network of branch dispensaries for healthy

75. On New York, see Edward Bunnell Phelps, "The World-Wide Effort to Diminish Infant Mortality—Its Present Status and Opportunities," *Transactions of the Fifteenth International Congress on Hygiene and Demography* (1912), vol. 6, p. 166. On other cities, see reports of affiliated societies in the annual *Transactions of the American Association for the Study and Prevention of Infant Mortality;* U.S. Children's Bureau, *Baby-Saving Campaigns: A Preliminary Report on What American Cities Are Doing to Prevent Infant Mortality,* Infant Mortality Series No. 1 (Bureau Publication No. 3) (Washington, D.C.: Government Printing Office, 1913).

babies. The nurses from the branch dispensaries sent their sick patients to the central dispensary and reported there daily. These children served as teaching material for medical students at Western Reserve University. In 1911 the City Council appropriated funds for five new branch dispensaries and in 1912 took over all the branch dispensaries and opened two more, leaving the Central dispensary free to deal with sick children only.[76]

Infant health work in Chicago, less extensive and less centralized, was more typical of American cities. Chicago's United Charities initiated an infant health campaign in 1910; several charitable and municipal agencies contributed names of babies for a central register, and the Visiting Nurse Association and the Health Department supplied nurses to visit these children's homes. Members of the Pediatric Society donated their services, and the Elizabeth McCormick Memorial Fund operated ten open-air hospital tents for sick babies. Other charitable organizations provided clean milk and ice to poor infants. The Infant Welfare Society formed in 1911 to coordinate the work of milk stations run by various agencies; each held consultations twice a week and distributed certified milk at low prices.[77]

The development of infant health work followed a similar patchwork pattern in smaller cities. In Louisville, Kentucky, for example, the Babies' Milk Fund Association opened seven stations in 1910 with the aid of municipal funds.[78] In 1910 the Children's Aid Association of Indianapolis reported five stations that treated children requiring special care or feeding; the city contributed half of the necessary funds.[79] In Utica, New York, members of the Municipal League raised funds for a milk station, which they opened in the summer of

---

76. H. J. Gerstenberger, "The Organization of Infant Mortality Work in Cleveland," *Pediatrics* 26 (1914): 129–40.

77. George B. Young, "Municipal Measures against Infant Mortality in Chicago," *Transactions of the American Association for the Study and Prevention of Infant Mortality* 2 (1911): 29–30; Sherman C. Kingsley, "The Relation of Infant Welfare Work to the General Social Movement," ibid., 1 (1910): 70–71.

78. Reports of Affiliated Societies, *Transactions of the American Association for the Study and Prevention of Infant Mortality* 1 (1910): 306–7; 2 (1911):334–35, and 4 (1913): 377.

79. Ibid., 3 (1912): 383; U.S. Children's Bureau, *Baby-Saving Campaigns*, pp. 26–27.

1912. The Waterbury, Connecticut, Visiting Nurses' Association established a milk station at a settlement house in the summer of 1908 and beginning in 1909 had one nurse who specialized in caring for infants and instructing mothers in their homes.[80]

Visiting Nurses in the United States

While French writers maintained that the only requirements for a *consultation de nourrissons* were a willing physician, a pair of scales, and a room, Americans argued that a visiting nurse was the one essential factor in all infant health work. The founders of French milk stations and consultations frequently recruited female patrons to distribute material aid and police its use through home visits, but in American cities the nurses' home visits were the heart of the program. In 1912 a survey of all cities in the United States with populations over fifteen thousand revealed that education of mothers, as opposed to any form of material assistance, was the primary goal of all infant health work in the United States. Thirty-two of the cities surveyed had infant welfare stations that did not distribute milk at all; 38 had milk stations; and 43 had visiting nurses.[81]

Another survey showed that 42 of the 43 milk stations operating in the United States in 1911 had some educational component; all but two employed nurses to instruct mothers in their homes. In fourteen cities nurses visited all children born in certain districts, all those whose births had been attended by midwives, or those discharged from the free wards of local hospitals.[82] New York's first systematic municipal infant health campaign, in the summer of 1908, involved the city's thirty-odd school nurses. Supplied each day with a list of the babies whose births had been reported the previous day, the nurses visited the home of each to meet the mother and give her detailed

80. "Reports of Affiliated Societies," *Transactions of the American Association for the Study and Prevention of Infant Mortality* 3 (1912): 353; 2 (1911): 396.

81. "Report of the Executive Secretary," *Transactions of the American Association for the Study and Prevention of Infant Mortality* 3 (1912): 18.

82. J. W. Schereschewsky, "The Present Status of Infant Welfare Work in the United States," *Transactions of the American Association for the Study and Prevention of Infant Mortality* 2 (1911): 40–43.

instructions on breast-feeding, how to bathe and clothe her child, and general household hygiene.[83]

Similarly, in Boston the work of the Milk and Baby Hygiene Association emphasized education over the provision of milk; modified milk was prescribed only as a last resort.[84] When the division of Child Hygiene of the Philadelphia Bureau of Health began doing infant health work, its staff provided instruction only in the mothers' homes. In most cases a nurse directed the work of the milk stations while physicians volunteered their time on a rotational basis. The nurse, wrote Wilbur Phillips of the New York Milk Committee, was the "soul of the depot"; her tact and sympathy were essential to the milk station's success. Phillips even suggested that the nurses, in consultation with local social workers, should select the station's physicians.[85]

The visiting nurse brought a distinctive tone to the American milk station. In theory she offered friendship and sympathy to the mothers she visited and information they were sure to accept gratefully once made aware of its intent. American public health nurses and public health officials maintained that most mothers eagerly attended consultations and followed instructions once they observed their children thriving. Further, the health-care workers believed that it was essential that women attend voluntarily and that they understand the principles behind the instructions they received.

In the tradition of "friendly visiting," the public health nurse tried to create a personal bond with the mothers she visited.[86] American milk stations and infant health centers relied on this personal contact for attendance at the consultation, but the home visit was more than

83. S. Josephine Baker, *Fighting for Life* (New York: Macmillan, 1939), p. 86.

84. *Transactions of the American Association for the Study and Prevention of Infant Mortality* 1 (1910): 316. On infant welfare work in Boston more generally, see Sonya Michel and Robyn Rosen, "The Paradox of Maternalism: Elizabeth Lowell Putnam and the American Welfare State," *Gender and History* (forthcoming).

85. Wilbur C. Phillips, "Infants' Milk Depots and Infant Mortality," *Transactions of the American Association for the Study and Prevention of Infant Mortality* 1 (1910): 78–80; Comments of Harriet Hartley, Round Table Conference on Divisions of Child Hygiene, *Transactions of the American Child Health Association* 11 (1920): 253.

86. Buhler-Wilkerson, *False Dawn*, p. 21; Minnie H. Ahrens, "Infant Welfare or Milk Stations," *Transactions of the American Association for the Study and Prevention of Infant Mortality* 2 (1911): 291–92; Harriet L. Hartley, "The City Nurse as an Agent for the Prevention of Infant Mortality," ibid. 9 (1918): 123.

just a way to recruit mothers. Though the visiting nurse had the task of improving the infant's physical environment, she was trained in social work as well as nursing. She personified the Progressives' faith in the power of the physical environment to shape character and social relationships. The milk station, Phillips wrote, for example, should contain pictures, curtains, flowers, comfortable chairs, and a coat of white enamel, so that it could serve as a haven of rest for overworked mothers and a model of clean living.[87]

An exhibit at the Philadelphia Baby-Saving Show in 1913 featured "before" and "after" models illustrating how a visiting nurse had helped to transform a tenement to conform to her social ideals. Following the nurse's advice, the family had cleaned and painted its rooms, obtained an icebox to keep milk cold, and put screens in the windows—an important health measure at a time when flies were a major source of disease transmission. The family also added a geranium, a rocking chair, a calendar, and an alarm clock.[88] While these changes might be interpreted to suggest that an underlying motivation of the work was the desire to inculcate an industrial work discipline into immigrants, public health nurses were not necessarily intent on molding efficient factory workers. A kind of time discipline was basic to the rules of "scientific" infant hygiene; infant care manuals, such as that published by the U.S. Children's Bureau, placed a great deal of emphasis, for example, on establishing a regular feeding schedule. While domestic conditions undoubtedly did contribute to the transmission of contagious diseases such as tuberculosis and diarrhea, "scientific" hygiene and social health were inseparable in the reformers' minds.[89]

87. Phillips, "Infants' Milk Depots and Infant Mortality," p. 78.
88. *Report of the Philadelphia Baby Saving Show* (Philadelphia: Executive Committee, 1913), pp. 68–69.
89. See Cheney, "Seasonal Aspects of Infant and Childhood Mortality," p. 574. Nancy Pottishman Weiss, "Mother the Invention of Necessity: Dr. Benjamin Spock's 'Baby and Child Care,' " *American Quarterly* 24 (1977): 519–46. Weiss argues that the Children's Bureau manual was relatively harsh to children in imposing a strict schedule on them but that this approach also reflected a sympathy for mothers' needs. Spock's system, on the other hand, required constant attention and infinite flexibility on the mother's part. For an analysis of the ways in which early-twentieth-century child-rearing experts sought to shape children to fit the industrial world see Barbara Ehrenreich and Deirdre English, *For Her Own Good: 150 Years of the Experts' Advice to Women* (Garden City, N.Y.: Anchor Books, 1978), pp. 201–5. In her study of the infant welfare movement in England, Deborah Dwork takes issue with several historians who criticize the British movement for focusing on personal behavior rather

The campaign to educate schoolgirls in infant hygiene, through "Little Mothers' leagues," was consistent with reformers' political and social goals. The leagues taught hygiene to schoolgirls and through them disseminated the principles of infant hygiene to immigrant mothers. They also trained the girls in voluntarism, thus reflecting the activist role women played in Progressive reform.

"Little mothers," the young girls who took care of their younger siblings while their mothers worked, were objects of the pity and horror of middle-class and upper-class reformers.[90] It was Josephine Baker's idea to recruit these girls as allies of the New York City Division of Child Hygiene by organizing after-school classes in infant care. Not only would they care better for their little brothers and sisters, Baker argued, but they would exert an educational influence in their families and be better prepared for their own future maternal duties. By 1911 there were 239 Little Mothers' leagues in New York City with a total of twenty thousand members, and the idea had spread to several other large cities.[91]

Members of the leagues met weekly with a public health nurse for lessons in hygiene, but they were also schooled in civics. Each member pledged to "act as a voluntary aid of the Department of Health of the City of New York in its efforts to reduce infant mortality."[92] The girls followed parliamentary procedure, elected officers, and appointed committees. Their activities extended beyond the schoolyards where they met into the community, where they acted as missionaries for the public health department. The girls

---

than on poverty and for describing such work as social control and as rooted in class bias. English physicians, Dwork argues, did not deny the association between poverty and infant mortality, but they addressed the problem conscientiously, given the limits of their knowledge and resources; the relevant bacteriological research suggested that their approach made sense. Dwork seems to see social control as necessarily conscious and insincere. This chapter assumes that class bias is by nature unconscious and that scientific ideas, even those that are "proven" through honest experimentation, are always influenced by their social context. Dwork, *War Is Good for Babies*, pp. 226–27. See also Anna Davin, "Imperialism and Motherhood," *History Workshop Journal* 5 (Spring 1978): 9–66; Carol Dyhouse, "Working-class Mothers and Infant Mortality in England, 1895–1914," *Journal of Social History* 12 (1978): 248–67; Jane Lewis, *The Politics of Motherhood: Child and Maternal Welfare in England, 1900–1939* (London: Croom Helm, 1980).

90. The term was popularized by John Spargo in *The Bitter Cry of the Children* (1906; reprint, Chicago: Quadrangle Books, 1968).

91. U.S. Children's Bureau, *Baby-Saving Campaigns*, p. 31; Baker, *Fighting for Life*, p. 134.

92. "Instructions to Medical Inspectors and Nurses Regarding the Preliminary and Subsequent Lectures to Members of the Little Mothers' Leagues"; Kansas State Board of Health, Division of Child Hygiene, "Little Mothers' Leagues" (U.S. Children's Bureau, 14–1–9–2–1); Baker, *Fighting for Life*, p. 133.

learned the rewards of voluntarism as they canvassed tenements for
sick babies, persuaded women they knew to try the baby health
stations, checked up on mothers whose attendance had fallen off,
and passed on their new knowledge to mothers they met on the
street.[93]

The explicit strategy of the Little Mothers' leagues was to intervene
in the immigrant family at a vulnerable point. As Baker told members
of the American Association for the Study and Prevention of Infant
Mortality, children acted as interpreters of both language and custom
for their immigrant parents; their word had the weight of authority
when it concerned the manners and methods of the new world.[94] A
favorite project was to write and enact plays for groups of mothers.
In the typical scenario an ignorant mother, at her wit's end with a
fussy baby, is enlightened by a competent Little Mother who tells
her to feed the child regularly, keep it clean, give it fresh air, and
abandon tight swaddling clothes. "The Little Mothers in the cast,"
Baker wrote, "[burst] with pride in their own superior knowledge."[95]
The public health nurse, a female professional figure in an impressive
uniform, won over the leagues' members by offering them the opportunity to earn respect in their community; the nurse entered the
home through the daughter as a figure of authority in competition
with the mother. Little Mothers' leagues served the particular goals
of American urban social reformers; their ultimate target was the
working-class immigrant home, their message political and social as
well as scientific.

Physicians and Mothers in the Unitd States and France

Little Mothers' leagues had their French counterpart in the teaching
of *puériculture,* or the science of child rearing, in schools. While bourgeois French schoolgirls learned that their feminine duties included
charity as well as motherhood, *puériculture* did not imply an activist

93. Anna W. Kerr, "The School Nurse as an Organizer," *Public Health Nurse
Quarterly* 7 (1915): 55–56.
94. S. Josephine Baker, "Little Mothers' Leagues," *Transactions of the American
Association for the Study and Prevention of Infant Mortality* 2 (1911): 307.
95. Baker, *Fighting for Life,* p. 135.

role for women, as Little Mothers' leagues did. *Puériculture* had an unambiguous political goal: the indoctrination of girls with the idea that bearing children was simultaneously their patriotic duty and their biological destiny. French Republican leaders treated the schools as a valuable political tool, one that had the capacity to mold citizens imbued with patriotism, a sense of social responsibility, and moral fortitude. In wresting control over the nation's schools from the clergy, the government explicitly sought control over the hearts and minds of future French citizens. Posted in every commune in the country, schoolteachers were missionaries of the Republic.[96] To pronatalist activists, the schools seemed an obvious means of influencing the next generation of parents.

Adolphe Pinard, who personally taught a model course in *puériculture* to schoolgirls, wrote: "We must imbue the young girl with this idea, namely: that if she has breasts, it is for feeding. We must ceaselessly prepare her for that function which is so natural, so great and so beautiful, *motherhood of the breast*."[97] Pinard considered the instruction of future teachers to be an urgent priority; familiarity with motherhood, he argued, was as important a qualification as intellectual attainment for those who taught young girls. Pinard advocated the creation of a little "institute of *puériculture*" attached to each normal school. Another proposal popular among physicians was to arrange for students or future teachers to assist at infant health consultations. Teachers, Pinard found, almost all single and middle-aged, too often had no interest in teaching *puériculture*.[98] The

96. See Mona Ozouf, *L'école, l'eglise, et la Republique, 1871–1914* (Paris: Armand Colin, 1963), p. 213; Barry Bergen, "Molding Citizens: Ideology, Class, and Primary Education in Nineteenth-Century France," Ph.D. diss., University of Pennsylvania, 1987, chap. 4; Linda L. Clark, *Schooling the Daughters of Marianne: Textbooks and the Socialization of Girls in Modern French Primary Schools* (Albany: State University of New York Press, 1984), p. 13.

97. Quoted in A. Dufour, "De la puériculture," *Le puériculteur*, 1 (1906): 3; Clark, *Schooling the Daughters of Marianne*, p. 39; Ausset, "La vulgarisation de la puériculture," pp. 321–22.

98. A. Pinard and Méry, *L'enseignement de la puériculture*, Publications du Musée pédagogique, new ser. no. 20 (Paris: Imprimerie nationale, 1912), p. 2; G. Variot, *L'hygiène infantile: Allaitement maternel et artificiel* (Paris: Librairie Hachette, 1908), pp. 8–9; Oeuvre des nourrissons de Marseille, *Fonctionnement et résultats: Rapport présenté à l'Assemblée générale du 25 mai 1908* (Marseilles: Imprimerie Marseillaise, 1908), p. 15.

contact with real children would, in theory, reawaken the maternal feelings of these overeducated girl students, to whom "the essential role of woman easily seems . . . as a social accident and not as a natural phenomenon."[99]

Strictly defined, *puériculture* meant simply the techniques of infant care based on scientific principles; more broadly, it also could encompass the whole of woman's social mission. B. Roussy, for example, defined *puériculture* as the knowledge and practices necessary to foster the development of those qualities of the body, heart, intelligence, character, and will of children needed to ensure the extension and perfection of their families and their nation. Like other French Republicans trying to define the nature of the commitment they sought, Roussy ironically turned to a religious analogy. The Catholic church had carefully cultivated the hearts and minds of women, he wrote, making of them its most valuable allies; the Republic must teach its own "great moral and social ideal" to young children.[100] The education of women in *puériculture*, he argued, would make possible the repopulation and regeneration of France. Just as depopulation was only one aspect of the larger problem of social degeneration, the nation needed more than bodies alone; it needed citizens imbued with patriotic fervor and a sense of social responsibility.

The form and tone of French physicians' efforts to instruct mothers reflected a deep-seated mistrust of the maternal instincts of French women. Physicians in both France and the United States maintained that the education of mothers was the key to the prevention of infant mortality. Both saw their task as one of rooting out superstition, combating the influence of older female relatives and neighbors, and increasing the authority of the medical profession. American leaflets on infant care invariably warned mothers not to follow the advice of other women, while French physicians waged a war against "herboristes" and "bonnes femmes."[101]

French physicians in particular exhibited an authoritarian attitude toward the mothers they instructed. A French writer would occa-

99. Jarricot, *Rôle social et pratique*, p. 281.
100. Roussy, *Education domestique de la femme et rénovation sociale*, pp. 234–36; Bergen, *Molding Citizens*, p. 160; Boltanski, *Prime éducation et morale de classe*, p. 25.
101. Boltanski, *Prime éducation et morale de class*, p. 34.

sionally suggest the importance of gaining the mothers' confidence, but French physicians more often advised one another to be strict with mothers. Henri de Rothschild, a student of Budin's, argued, for example, that the success of a consultation depended almost exclusively on the firmness of the physician and the director. They must watch that infractions of the regulations were punished: "a first disobedience, a first offense, deserves a severe reprimand, the second must bring about definitive expulsion." "Making a mother cry, often means saving her child," wrote another physician.[102]

The same authors emphasized the value of lavish praise and material rewards for those who successfully followed medical instructions. Both approaches reflected the contempt on the part of the physicians for the mothers' intelligence and good will. Thus, through a system of rewards and punishments, French physicians attempted to exact obedience. They assumed, like the advocates of school courses in *puériculture,* that women's attitude toward maternity was the source of many of France's problems.

Pinard, Roussy, and their fellow *puériculteurs* argued that adherence to the laws of scientific hygiene was fundamental to patriotic allegiance.[103] Pediatricians and obstetricians attempted to exploit this argument in their efforts to gain recognition of the legitimacy of their specialities. For several reasons, French obstetricians and pediatricians were in a more favorable position than their colleagues in the United States. French physicians were the first in Europe to obtain a legal monopoly over the practice of medicine; beginning in 1803 the state had the sole right to confer medical degrees.[104] Though they did not face a serious challenge to their monopoly from alternative practitioners, there was a glut of physicians throughout most of the nineteenth century, exacerbated by the existence of a class of semi-

102. Henri de Rothschild, *Les gouttes de lait: Organisation d'une "goutte de lait" et d'une "consultation de nourrissons"* (Paris: O. Doin, 1902), p. 6; Pestre, *Les oeuvres d'assistance et de protection,* p. 55; Luc Boltanski describes the tone of books by French physicians on child care as increasingly authoritarian after 1870. *Prime éducation et morale de classe,* p. 45.

103. On the symbolic political role of the germ theory in France, see Dominique Maingueneau, *Les livres d'école de la République, 1870–1914* (Paris: Le Sycomore, 1979), pp. 310–21, 328–29.

104. See Ackerknecht, *Medicine at the Paris Hospital,* p. 38; Ramsey, "The Politics of Professional Monopoly," pp. 228, 237–40.

professional practitioners called *officiers de santé*, who were supposed to provide health care in rural areas. Jan Goldstein argues that the response of the medical profession to the deep sense of insecurity created by these conditions was to turn to the state as a source of salaried positions. Other historians of French medicine agree that by the end of the nineteenth century physicians had acquired institutional and political positions that provided them with significant opportunities to influence public policy.[105]

Also important for the development of the French medical profession was the hospital. By the beginning of the nineteenth century, large state-owned hospitals constituted a fundamental part of the nation's poor-relief system. These hospitals provided much greater opportunities for clinical instruction and research than had existed before and also led to the emergence of a new type of doctor-patient relationship: because the hospital patients were poor, physicians naturally dealt with them in an authoritative manner and readily used them as clinical subjects. Hospital consultants now became the elite among medical practitioners; internships had to be won through competitive examinations and constituted the essential basis for lucrative and prestigious careers.[106]

Luc Boltanski points out that the physicians most prominent in the maternal and infant welfare movement in France—Variot, Budin, Pinard, and de Rothschild, for example—were among the "princes of medicine," the *grands bourgeois* who held the prestigious teaching positions in charitable hospitals which paved the way to lucrative private practice among the wealthy.[107] These physicians were prominent among the members of the government's commission on the mortality of nurslings, the Commission de dépopulation, and permanent public health and welfare committees; some were elected to

105. Goldstein, " 'Moral Contagion,' " p. 200; Ramsey, "The Politics of Professional Monopoly," p. 237; Ramsey, "Review Essay," pp. 324–25; Léonard, *La médecine entre les savoirs et les pouvoirs*, pp. 279–82; Nye, *Madness, Crime, and Politics*, pp. 44–45.

106. See Ackerknecht, *Medicine at the Paris Hospital*, pp. 17, 302; Ivan Waddington, "The Role of the Hospital in the Development of Modern Medicine: A Sociological Analysis," *Sociology* 7 (1973): 212–21; Toby Gelfand, " 'A Monarchical Profession' in the Old Regime: Surgeons, Ordinary Practitioners, and Medical Professionalization in Eighteenth-Century France," in *Professions and the French State*, p. 172; Colin Jones, *The Charitable Imperative: Hospitals and Nursing in Ancien Regime and Revolutionary France* (London: Routledge, 1989), pp. 7, 16.

107. Boltanski, *Prime éducation et morale de classe*, p. 35.

the Senate or the Chamber of Deputies, where they participated in framing social welfare and health care legislation that provided an authoritative role for the medical profession.

"Regular" doctors in the United States did not achieve a legal monopoly until the mid- to late nineteenth century; not until 1888 did the Supreme Court rule that a state could make licensing mandatory. For most of the nineteenth century, qualifications for medical practice were not standardized, and the dissident sects thrived.[108] Physicians in the United States lamented the scarcity of hospital and other clinical facilities, so plentiful in Europe, which would help to establish a scientific basis for their specialties and the possibility of pursuing a career based on clinical teaching and research. Only in the late nineteenth and early twentieth centuries did they begin to achieve this objective.[109] For pediatricians and obstetricians, the infant health campaigns were a critical junction.

In the large cities where these physicians were concentrated, infant health programs often offered services that lured poor women and children to depend on hospitals and clinics, where they served as valuable teaching and research material.[110] The movement to prevent infant mortality made possible the founding of hospitals for infants and children which later became prestigious teaching and research institutions. Babies and Children's Hospital in Cleveland is but one example. In that city the prophylactic dispensaries directed sick babies to the new hospital, where medical students at Western Reserve University received pediatric clinical training. The milk laboratory that sterilized and modified the milk prescribed by physicians at the branch dispensaries served as a center for research; H. J. Gerstenberger and his colleagues later developed an infant formula that was marketed commercially.[111]

108. See Ramsey, "The Politics of Professional Monopoly," pp. 253, 276.

109. See Charles Rosenberg, *The Care of Strangers: The Rise of America's Hospital System* (New York: Basic Books, 1987), pp. 178–79; 184–85, 199–201.

110. Virginia G. Drachman describes the effort of physicians to recruit poor women as subjects for teaching and research in the mid-nineteenth century in "The Loomis Trial: Social Mores and Obstetrics in the Mid-Nineteenth Century," in *Health Care in America,* ed. Susan Reverby and David Rosner (Philadelphia: Temple University Press, 1979), p. 80. See also Nancy Schrom Dye, "Modern Obstetrics and Working-class Women: The New York Midwifery Dispensary, 1870–1920," *Journal of Social History* 20 (1987): 550; Halpern, *American Pediatrics,* pp. 42–43, 58, 62–63.

111. H. J. Gerstenberger, "The Organization of Infant Mortality Work in Cleveland, Showing the Relationship between a Municipality, a Babies' Dispensary, and a

Pediatricians and obstetricians who wanted to achieve professional status and legitimacy, however, required more than institutions: they had to persuade women that their expertise was essential. Obstetricians campaigned to convince the general public that childbirth was a dangerous pathological event requiring the attendance of a highly trained medical specialist. In addition, they lobbied for legal obstacles to the practice of midwifery by midwives and created institutions designed to siphon off midwives' clientele.[112] Pediatricians sought to persuade women that infant care, especially artificial feeding, was a delicate undertaking requiring supervision by a physician with expertise in child hygiene.

Physicians, Milk, and Public Health

Milk stations were central to the establishment of pediatrics as a medical specialty in the United States, because early pediatricians based their claim to expertise largely on the difficulties of infant feeding. Historians of pediatrics have emphasized that the "scientific" method of infant feeding was central to pediatricians' efforts to strengthen their own authority and to increase women's dependence on their expertise.[113] Each child, the experts argued, was a new feeding problem; each required specific proportions of fat, protein, and sugar. It is interesting that French physicians did not for the most part engage in such a debate. A French physician surveying several of his colleagues who directed milk stations and infant health consultations reported that all but one agreed that pure sterilized milk was suitable for all infants, though some suggested diluting it slightly with water for newborns. The only dissenter advocated a simple dilution of one part sugared water to two parts whole milk.[114] French physicians still

University," paper read at the Conference on Infant Mortality, London, August 5, 1913 (U.S. Children's Bureau, 4–15–2–3).

112. For example, George W. Kosmack, "Does the Average Midwife Meet the Requirements of a Patient in Confinement?" *Transactions of the American Association for the Study and Prevention of Infant Mortality* 3 (1912): 23; J. Whitridge Williams, "The Midwife Problem and Medical Education in the United States," ibid., 2 (1911): 1183; C. E. Ziegler, "The Elimination of the Midwife," ibid, 3 (1912): 233; Kobrin, "The American Midwife Controversy"; Litoff, *American Midwives*, chaps 5–8.

113. Apple, *Mothers and Medicine*, p. 17; Meckel, *Save the Babies*, pp. 47–57; Halpern, *American Pediatrics*, pp. 64–65; Harvey Levenstein, " 'Best for Babies' or 'Preventable Infanticide'? The Controversy over Artificial Feeding of Infants in America, 1880–1920," *Journal of American History* 70 (1983): 82.

114. Ciando, *La culture des nourrissons*, pp. 17–19; G. Variot, *La puériculture et la*

insisted that raising children, especially on cows' milk, was a very delicate operation, and that even breast-feeding mothers required careful instruction and supervision. Perhaps with other sources of prestige and legitimacy, however, they did not depend on the mystification of milk modification to the same extent as did pediatricians in the United States.[115]

S. Josephine Baker criticized the school of milk modification developed by the physician Thomas Rotch, a complicated system for prescribing various mixtures of milk, cream, milk-sugar, and lime water to meet the idiosyncratic needs of each infant for specific percentages of fat, sugar, and protein. This method, Baker quipped, was "based on consideration of the baby's age, health, complexion and astrological data—or at least so it seemed when you started working with it." Baker risked her professional reputation, she wrote in her autobiography, and all her hopes of cooperation from the medical profession, when she started modifying milk according to the baby's weight alone. Three well-known pediatricians who contributed to her formula made her promise not to let their names be associated with it.[116]

Such systems of modifying milk could interfere with the goals of milk stations. While pediatricians often sought obedience from mothers, their efforts to foster mothers' dependence on their professional authority were challenged by reformers such as Baker and Wilbur Phillips. In her work on the history of infant feeding in the United States, Rima Apple suggests that the new educational focus of milk stations created a dilemma for pediatricians; by the 1920s they found that women had become too independent. Physicians wanted women

---

guerre: Conférences faites à l'Institut de puériculture de l'Hospice des enfants assistés en 1915, 1916, et 1917 (Paris: O. Doin, 1918), pp. 112–13. Meckel observes that European pediatricians generally were never as enamored as Americans with complicated feeding methods. *Save the Babies*, p. 59. French physicians did debate the question of whether paid nurses could be taught to sterilize and prepare milk in their homes. See Département de la Seine, Protection des enfants du premier âge, *Rapport annuel*, 1896, pp. 76–93.

115. In his history of American medicine, Paul Starr quotes Arpad Geister, a young Hungarian physician who, after visiting the United States in the 1870s, observed that American physicians were more concerned than European practitioners with winning the trust and confidence of their patients. He concluded that the chief reason for this difference was that in Europe "the medical degree itself invested the physician with a social standing and authority unknown in America," while the majority of American physicians ranked, in terms of education, little above the level of their patients." *Social Transformation of American Medicine*, pp. 80–81.

116. Baker, *Fighting for Life*, p. 129.

to be aware enough of scientific principles that they would follow medical advice, but not so educated that they felt they knew better than the doctor. Apple also points out that scientific infant feeding brought out some of the contradictions inherent in the ideology of scientific motherhood: on the one hand, it gave women status because it implied a professional role, but on the other hand it denied women control over their work because they now needed professional supervision.[117]

This contradiction led to disagreements among physicians and other infant health workers over the issue of whether women could be taught to prepare infant formulas in their homes. Most early milk stations dispensed milk in individual feedings already modified according to a physician's prescription to save mothers the difficult tasks of keeping the milk clean, sterilizing utensils, and mixing a complex formula. Responding to a survey by the *Delineator* magazine in 1909, however, Nathan Straus said that he thought there should be a pasteurization device in every home. Other experts, including Charles Chapin, who directed municipal infant welfare work in Providence, Rhode Island, and J. W. Kerr, assistant surgeon-general, also supported home modification.[118] On the other hand, in the same year, when the New York Milk Committee decided to close its laboratory and teach mothers how to prepare milk in their homes, some of the physicians on the committee resigned in protest.[119] J. H. Mason Knox of Baltimore feared that the milk would be contaminated in poor mothers' unsanitary homes. In Washington, D.C., when the Diet Kitchen, which distributed food and milk to the poor, announced that it would teach home modification, many white observers were skeptical that the city's African-American mothers could learn.[120]

For Phillips, the question of milk modification was not just a practical issue. Not only did home modification save money, he argued, but dispensing prepared feedings deprived mothers of the opportunity to exercise their intelligence and made them unnecessarily dependent

117. Apple, *Mothers and Medicine,* pp. 216–18, 289.
118. "How Shall We Get Safe Milk for Babies," *Delineator,* July 1909: 52.
119. See Phillips, *Adventuring for Democracy,* p. 28; Levenstein, " 'Best for Babies' or 'Preventable Infanticide'?" p. 89.
120. Phillips, "Infants' Milk Depots and Infant Mortality," p. 87; report by Mary Gwynn, *Transactions of the American Association for the Study and Prevention of Infant Mortality* 4 (1913); 337–38. Gwynn reported that the critics were proven wrong; the station workers found the black mothers to be "natural cooks."

on charity. Gifts of knowlege, not of milk, Phillips wrote, would develop women with initiative and self-reliance rather than "helpless women dependent upon four-legged cows and bottling machines."[121] L. T. Royster, of Norfolk, Virginia, agreed that teaching women to modify their own infants' milk would make them feel an additional sense of responsibility in the rearing of their children.[122]

Lillian Wald and Josephine Baker shared a conviction that mothers were intelligent enough to prepare their infants' food. Wald argued, "In the last analysis babies of the poor are kept alive through the intelligence of the mothers." Rarely did her nurses report a woman incapable of learning. Phillips agreed: "Tenement mothers," he found, "did possess common sense. Given sound instruction, they could, would and did learn to care for their babies intelligently."[123]

These reformers' attitudes grew out of their larger political and social philosophies. Phillips was a socialist who hoped that infant welfare stations would grow into neighborhood health centers that would provide preventive health care to people of all ages. He was also committed to a form of participatory democracy in the governing of the centers. After he left New York he was employed by the socialist municipal government of Milwaukee. There he consulted with local midwives and enlisted physicians from the community rather than outside specialists. With the aid of the local priest he selected respected neighborhood women to recruit clientele for the infant welfare stations he started.[124] Wald shared with other female settlement leaders a sympathy with the plight of poor women, a belief in democracy, and a faith that education and environmental reform would enable all to participate as equals in American politics and society. These convictions mingled uneasily in the American infant health movement with the professional and scientific goals of pediatricians and obstetricians.

While much of the medical elite supported municipal infant health

121. Phillips, "Infants' Milk Depots and Infant Mortality," p. 80.
122. Ibid., p. 85.
123. Lillian Wald, *The House on Henry Street* (New York: Henry Holt, 1915), p. 55–56; Phillips, *Adventuring for Democracy*, p. 28; Baker, *Fighting for Life*, p. 129.
124. See Phillips, *Adventuring for Democracy*, pp. 77–78, 90–91; Leavitt, *Healthiest City*, pp. 217–27, 261; Patricia Mooney Melvin, "Make Milwaukee Safe for Babies: The Child Welfare Commission and the Development of Urban Health Centers 1911–1912," *Journal of the West* 17 (1978): 83–93; George Rosen, "The First Neighborhood Health Center Movement—Its Rise and Fall," *American Journal of Public Health* 61 (1971): 1625.

work, partly because it provided valuable clinical experience for young doctors, other practitioners were often hostile to such reforms, as they were to any form of free care.[125] Josephine Baker recalled that in the early days of New York City's infant health campaigns thirty-odd Brooklyn physicians sent her a petition demanding the closing of a baby welfare station in Brownsville. They claimed that the station, by keeping babies well, was ruining their medical practices.[126] Some medical specialists feared that this negative attitude toward public health work was a dangerous one for the profession. In 1912 the president of the American Pediatric Society warned the members that if they failed to give their expert advice they inevitably "relegated many topics to semi-medical organizations, over which we exert only indirect control."[127] "The ignorant though humane" laity, Thomas Rotch asserted, should not be allowed to impinge on areas in which physicians were the rightful authorities. By their indifference, Henry Shaw told members of the Vermont State Medical Society in 1913, physicians were opening the "portals of this important field of preventive medicine to social workers and philanthropists."[128]

Perhaps Shaw had in mind the U.S. Children's Bureau, then just one year old. Though it lacked a medical staff, the bureau had begun a series of investigations into the social causes of infant mortality; from the beginning this federal agency reflected the views of its director, Julia Lathrop, a former Hull House resident, more than those of pediatric and obstetric specialists. The bureau challenged the priorities of the pediatric and obstetric specialties by defining maternal and infant health as an issue with broad social ramifications and not as a purely medical problem.

Pediatricians and obstetricians in both the United States and France

125. See Meckel, Save the Babies, pp. 128–29; Burrow, Organized Medicine in the Progressive Era, pp. 111–13; Starr, Social Transformation of American Medicine, pp. 186–87. Judith Leavitt writes that physicians in Milwaukee rarely opposed public health efforts except when they threatened to intrude on private practice—for example, school health-advice stations. Healthiest City, pp. 200–201.

126. Baker, Fighting for Life, p. 139.

127. Walter Lester Carr, "The Relation of the American Pediatric Society to the Reduction of Mortality in Infancy and Childhood," Archives of Pediatrics 24 (1912): 406.

128. Thomas M. Rotch, "The Position and Work of the American Pediatric Society toward the Public Question," Transactions of the American Pediatric Society 21 (1909): 8; Henry K. Shaw, "Infant Mortality," Albany Medical Annals 34 (1913): 719.

ultimately won their struggle for the medical definition and control of maternity and infant care. In France the authority of male physicians was enhanced by pronatalism; their professional identity and legitimacy were defined within an increasingly comprehensive social welfare system. Most American physicians, however, believed that their interests would be best served within a private system of medical care, and by the late 1920s they could claim victory in their struggle against public health care. Lay reformers, however, especially the members of women's organizations, exerted a significant influence on infant health policy in the 1910s and 1920s.

3

French and American Women and Infant Health

In 1939, reviewing her long career in child health, S. Josephine Baker recalled that in 1924, three years after the passage of the Sheppard-Towner Act, only three of the forty-five state directors of federal child welfare work were men. Fifteen years later, four years after the passage of the Social Security Act of 1935, only one-quarter were women. "I am not impugning the capacity of any of these men as individuals," Baker wrote, "when I say that that looks very strange in a line of activity which was invented and developed by women."[1]

So extensive and widespread was the activity of women's organizations in the area of child welfare that in 1926 the participants of an international congress on the child voted to recognize "that a large number of the best works are due almost exclusively to the devotion of women and to their intelligent work."[2] Women's work in maternal and child welfare reform was a natural outgrowth of the dedication

1. S. Josephine Baker, *Fighting for Life* (New York: Macmillan, 1939), p. 201.
2. Denise Moran, "Le premier Congrès générale de l'enfant," *Le Quotidien,* January 26, 1926 (clipping in Bibliothèque Marguerite Durand, Dos. CON/ENF). On women's preeminence in child welfare policy in the United States see Robyn Muncy, *Creating a Female Dominion in American Reform, 1890–1935* (New York: Oxford University Press, 1991). Some of the ideas in this chapter and the next are summarized in Alisa Klaus, "Women's Organizations and the Infant Health Movement in France and the United States, 1890–1920," in *Lady Bountiful Revisited: Women, Philanthropy, and Power,* ed. Kathleen D. McCarthy (New Brunswick, N.J.: Rutgers University Press, 1990), pp. 157–73.

to improving motherhood, the care and education of children, and the home which characterized women's interest in moral reform and charitable work in both France and the United State in the nineteenth century. Women played strikingly different roles in social policy in the two countries, however. This chapter examines the social and political factors that determined the influence of women in maternal and child welfare policy in both countries and traces the development of the distinctive role women played as volunteers in French infant health institutions before World War I. Chapter 4 focuses on the popular "Better Baby" movement in the United States and compares it with the charitable activity of French feminists.

Women in the United States actively influenced policy at all levels as professionals and often as public officials. They had a significant voice in the American Association for the Study and Prevention of Infant Mortality, chaired sessions at the annual meetings, and were among its officers. For a few years they ran a committee of the American Medical Association devoted to the welfare of women and children. Women headed many municipal and state divisions of child hygiene and, perhaps most important, organized, administered, and staffed the U.S. Children's Bureau. These professional women saw themselves as the leaders of a massive popular movement whose rank-and-file were the members of women's clubs and mothers' congresses. As a result, state and federal maternal and infant health policy responded to the needs and visions of these mostly white, middle-class women. The Sheppard-Towner Act, creating the nation's first federal social welfare program, was largely the fruit of a decade of female political activity.

French women, too, campaigned for legislation they hoped would improve women's status as mothers and supported measures they believed would provide moral and economic protection for the family and children. Their influence in pediatric institutions and on maternal and child welfare policy did not reflect the extent of their voluntary activity; they lacked the institutional and political power to shape policy. They virtually never sat on official commissions to investigate maternal and infant health, and, if any were present, they never spoke up in debates on infant mortality in the Académie de médecine. Very few positions in public or private welfare agencies of any kind were open to women, and as late as 1919 a feminist journalist complained that even women who had founded and administered private insti-

tutions and served as the leaders of national organizations were unable
to find paid employment.[3]

To a certain extent the visibility of women in maternal and child
welfare policy in the United States can be explained by the comparative indifference of politicians and male physicians. As Alice Hamilton, pioneer in industrial medicine, observed, "The American man
gives over to the woman all the things he is profoundly disinterested
in, and keeps business and politics to himself."[4] In France, where the
birthrate was an issue of national political significance, male politicians
thought maternal and child welfare too important to be delegated to
women. Other factors influencing the participation of women in public policy were equally important, however. Historians studying the
role of gender in the formation of the welfare state in comparative
perspective have suggested that in all countries in western Europe,
as in the United States, emerging welfare policies were nurtured by
women's charitable and reform organizations. At the same time, however, the nature of state structures in each country determined the
degree to which women were able to translate their voluntary role
into professional and political power. In the United States and Britain,
relatively weak state institutions allowed women to make significant
inroads into new public welfare bureaucracies. In contrast, in Germany, a strong welfare state developed early; in the late nineteenth
and early twentieth centuries women were unable to break into the
male-dominated system.[5]

Centralized state structures and a tradition of social intervention
effectively excluded French women from policy making; the centralized, state-controlled system of medical education and licensing
also hindered their professional advancement. The specific political
conditions under which women organized for "maternalist" goals in
France prevented them from becoming a distinctive female political
force. Not only did the ongoing struggles between anticlerical Republicans and the Catholic church and other conservative forces en-

3. Mme Remember, "Le vote familial et la repopulation," *Féminisme intégral,* July
1919.
4. Quoted in Barbara Sicherman, *Alice Hamilton: A Life in Letters* (Cambridge,
Mass.: Harvard University Press, 1984), p. 3.
5. See Seth Koven and Sonya Michel, "Womanly Duties: Maternalist Politics and
the Origins of Welfare States in France, Germany, Great Britain, and the United
States, 1880–1920," *American Historical Review* 95 (1990): 1079–80.

gage women on both sides, but the depopulation crisis provided fuel for antifeminist rhetoric and policies. Certain French female activists sometimes articulated an approach to maternal and infant welfare which was consistent with their demands for civil and political equality, but they did not challenge the ideological basis of patriotic pronatalism.

The French government did not, however, completely take over the work of the private charities that had traditionally provided assistance to mothers and infants. Instead, it sought to utilize the material and human resources of these organizations while limiting their autonomy through regulation or through subsidies contingent on conformity to a particular social orientation. Republican political leaders hoped that they could call on the female virtues of bourgeois French women to fight depopulation and class conflict. This policy encouraged the growth of women's charitable organizations, but it also placed constraints on their ability to develop and implement their own vision of maternal and child welfare. In general, women's organizations served goals defined by male politicians and physicians, often working under the direction and influence of men.

Women in the Medical Professions in the United States and France

Much of the leadership of the women's infant health movement in the United States was provided by women in the medical and public health nursing professions. In the United States, women who aspired to careers in medicine benefited from the free market in medical education and the relatively late development of a legal monopoly by the "regular" physicians. As medical colleges proliferated, homeopathic institutions and state universities found it hard to attract competent students and turned to women as a source of qualified candidates. Nonetheless, women continued to face hostility from male professors, students, and practitioners. The jobs open to these women were extremely limited. In the 1890s only seven American hospitals regularly accepted women interns; all of these specialized in the treatment of women and children. Women were largely excluded from teaching positions in coeducational or all-male schools and from clinical positions in hospitals.[6] The women's medical colleges and hospitals founded between 1850 and 1900 played a central role in facilitating women's entrance into the profession. Over one-half of female physicians graduated from the women's medical colleges.

The women's medical colleges—funded, promoted, administered, and patronized by women—provided clinical training often not available to women anywhere else. They also provided role models, an atmosphere that was emotionally supportive, professional connections, and an opportunity for white women to hold teaching and administrative positions.[7] Although the women's medical colleges did accept a few African-American students, however, most African-American women physicians were trained at Meharry and Howard, the two leading institutions among the eleven black medical schools founded between 1869 and 1900.[8]

The women's institutions focused their attention on the health of women and children. They excelled in obstetrics and gynecological surgery, but they were also pioneers in preventive medicine. The Medical College of the New York Infirmary for Women and Children, for example, was the first to establish a chair for the teaching of hygiene and in 1859 appointed a "sanitary visitor" to instruct poor mothers in infant care and family health. When S. Josephine Baker was a student at the college in the 1890s Annie Sturgis Daniel taught a course required of all students called "The Normal Child." At the time, Baker later recalled, no other medical college offered a course on the "normal" anything.[9] The Woman's Medical College of Pennsylvania was well known for its obstetrical teaching and the instruction of women in prenatal care. In 1880, Anna Broomall, one of the faculty members, opened a dispensary at her own expense which

6. See Regina Markell Morantz-Sanchez, *Sympathy and Science: Women Physicians in American Medicine* (New York: Oxford University Press, 1985), pp. 160, 164–65; Mary Roth Walsh, *"Doctors Wanted: No Women Need Apply": Sexual Barriers in the Medical Profession, 1835–1975* (New Haven: Yale University Press, 1977), p. 221; Thomas Neville Bonner, "Medical Women Abroad: A New Dimension of Women's Push for Opportunities in Medicine, 1850–1914," *Bulletin of the History of Medicine* 62 (1988): 58–73.

7. See Morantz-Sanchez, *Sympathy and Science*, pp. 109–12, 245.

8. See Bettina Aptheker, *Woman's Legacy: Essays on Race, Sex, and Class in American History* (Amherst: University of Massachusetts Press, 1982), p. 100; Darlene Clark Hine, "Opportunity and Fulfillment: Sex, Race, and Class in Health Care Education," *Sage* 2 (Fall 1985): 15.

9. Baker, *Fighting for Life*, pp. 34, 41.

made it possible for students to care for obstetrical patients in their homes.[10] The New England Hospital for Women and Children was the only Boston institution to provide both obstetrical and gynecological services; it also opened the first hospital social service department in the country.[11]

Despite women's interest in the care of women and children, the pediatric and obstetric specialties were dominated by men; the American Pediatric Society did not admit its first female member until 1928, forty years after its founding.[12] It was in public maternal and child health, far less prestigious than the clinical and research specialties, that female physicians were able to have their greatest impact. The tendency of female physicians to work in public health or preventive medicine was not simply a result of their exclusion from other areas, however. Many women physicians in the late nineteenth and twentieth centuries shared with other women activists a belief that women had a unique role to play in the public realm, one that focused on the improvement of the family and the protection of women and children. It was their special sense of public responsiblity which frequently led female physicians to careers in public service.[13]

Women physicians carried their commitment to public health into the American Medical Association in 1909, when they formed a Public Health Education Committee. Rosalie Slaughter Morton, a New York surgeon, proposed to the organization that the female members act through women's clubs and mothers' organizations in their own communities to disseminate information on prenatal and child care and other health issues. As she recalled in her autobiography, "I considered it odd that men physicians were just waking up to preventive medicine, while women doctors had for fifty years been

---

10. Lida Stewart-Cogill, "The Importance of Prenatal Care as Demonstrated at the Woman's Medical College, Its Hospital, the Woman's Hospital of Philadelphia, and the West Philadelphia Hospital for Women," *Transactions of the American Association for the Study and Prevention of Infant Mortality* 9 (1918): 140.

11. Walsh, *"Doctors Wanted,"* pp. 92, 96. See also Virginia G. Drachman, *Hospital with a Heart: Women Doctors and the Paradox of Separatism at the New England Hospital, 1862–1969* (Ithaca: Cornell University Press, 1984).

12. See Sydney A. Halpern, *American Pediatrics: The Social Dynamics of Professionalism, 1880–1980* (Berkeley: University of California Press, 1988), pp. 44, 180–81, n.35.

13. See Morantz-Sanchez, *Sympathy and Science,* pp. 60, 270–72, 283, 303, 308. On the female professional ethos see Muncy, *Creating a Female Dominion,* pp. 20–22.

stressing the importance of educating mothers in the care of children's health, in prenatal care of mothers, etc."[14]

Morton's resolution passed, over the laughter of many of the men present, and she was appointed to organize the committee of six women and four men who recruited over three hundred female physicians to carry out the program. The committee survived in its original form for just four years before being taken over by the new Council on Public Health Instruction in 1913. The work it accomplished testified not only to the belief of women physicians that they had a special role to play but to the strength of the links between female members of the medical profession and women's voluntary organizations.[15]

The few black women trained as physicians played a special role in their communities. They worked primarily within the institutions created by black philanthropists, women's organizations, and physicians to provide health care to blacks, rather than in all-female clinics or hospitals. Matilda Evans, for example, educated at Oberlin and the Woman's Medical College of Pennsylvania, was the first black woman to practice medicine in Columbia, South Carolina. She opened the first black hospital in that city, with three clinics and a training school for nurses. In 1916 she organized the Negro Health Association of South Carolina, with the goal of putting a black nurse in every county in the state. The effort was a failure because the association received no encouragement from the state's white health establishment.[16] Thus the same system that left room for the women's medical colleges also enabled black men and women to enter the profession, because it allowed the existence of separate schools and hospitals. Racism, however, hampered the political struggles of black female physicians.

Given the expansion of public health work in the Progressive period, white women doctors who started out in low-status jobs in public health could soon find themselves in responsible positions.

14. Rosalie Slaughter Morton, *A Woman Surgeon* (New York: Frederick A. Stokes, 1937), p. 165.

15. Ibid., pp. 165–74; Morantz-Sanchez, *Sympathy and Science,* pp. 284–88; Morris Fishbein, *A History of the American Medical Association, 1847 to 1947* (Philadelphia: W. B. Saunders, 1947), pp. 263, 273, 287, 997–98.

16. See Edward H. Beardsley, *A History of Neglect: Health Care for Blacks and Mill Workers in the Twentieth-Century South* (Knoxville: University of Tennessee Press, 1987), p. 83.

Baker, for example, began her medical career as a tenement inspector in New York City and was one of the physicians assigned to seek out sick infants as part of the city's first campaign to prevent infant mortality, in the summer of 1902. When the Division of Child Hygiene was created in 1908 she became its first director. She served in that position for more than twenty years with increasingly large funds at her disposal, and several generations of male and female physicians worked under her direction. She became one of the nation's foremost authorities on child welfare.[17]

Other female physicians achieved national prominence as activists in private organizations and later became public health officials. As director of the Children's Department of the *Woman's Home Companion,* Lydia Allen DeVilbiss helped launch the baby health contest movement in 1913. When the Kansas State Board of Health created a Division of Child Hygiene, DeVilbiss moved west to serve as its director. Florence Sherbon, secretary of the American Baby Health Contest Association in 1913, later conducted surveys for the U.S. Children's Bureau for several years, and she succeeded DeVilbiss in Kansas in 1920. Frances Hollingshead and Dorothy Reed Mendenhall directed the State Child Hygiene divisions of Ohio and Wisconsin, respectively.

Perhaps the most significant public health positions held by women were in the U.S. Children's Bureau, headed by Julia Lathrop, a former Hull House resident and a close friend of Jane Addams'. A few of the statistical staff of the bureau were male, but the physicians hired to do fieldwork, their assistants, and the division heads were women. Several were personal friends of women in the social settlement movement and some were members of the General Federation of Women's Clubs. The bureau staff viewed themselves as leaders of the larger women's infant health movement, and women throughout the nation saw the staff as their allies and often wrote for advice on child care or on organizing child welfare programs.[18] The bureau responded with friendly guidance and inspiration and appealed to local women's organizations for assistance in carrying out their programs.

17. Baker tells the story of her career in her autobiography, *Fighting for Life.*
18. For examples, see *Raising a Baby the Government Way: Mothers' Letters to the Children's Bureau, 1915–1932,* ed. Molly Ladd-Taylor (New Brunswick, N.J.: Rutgers University Press, 1986). On the Children's Bureau more generally, see Muncy, *Creating a Female Dominion,* chap. 2.

Thus, as professionals, white female physicians were the beneficiaries of the new public health and welfare institutions they helped
to build. In other ways as well, the Progressive Era was a high point
for women in the medical profession in the United States; in 1910,
6 percent of all physicians in the country were women, a number
that would not be reached again until 1950. They made up an even
greater percentage in major cities: from 9.1 percent in Philadelphia
and 11.6 percent in Chicago to 13.5 percent in San Francisco and
Boston and 17.9 percent in Los Angeles.[19]

French women who met American women professionals were impressed with the respect they commanded. Jeanne Forpomès, a Parisian woman who wrote about the work of the American Red Cross in
France during World War I, was struck by the importance of female
physicians in that organization. She felt a shock of surprise on meeting
a woman who was chief physician in a hospital for soldiers with tuberculosis. That a woman should be invested with such a high and serious
position in a hospital devoted only to men, she exclaimed, was "so
contrary to our customs!" Were French women, wondered Forpomès,
intellectually and morally so inferior to American women?[20]

The first woman was admitted to the Faculté de Médecine in Paris
in 1865, and by 1900 the schools of Law and Pharmacy and the Faculty
of Arts and Sciences were all open to women. According to Regina
Morantz-Sanchez, women from the United States found the medical
schools and hospitals in Paris, as in other western European countries,
"quite cordial to women in the late nineteenth century."[21] As French
feminists observed, however, few French women chose to pursue the
liberal professions, partly because it was very difficult for girls to
obtain the preparatory education necessary for the baccalauréat unless
their parents provided private tutors.[22] The highly structured and
exclusive system of exams and competitions for places in French

19. See Morantz-Sanchez, *Sympathy and Science,* p. 234; Walsh, *"Doctors Wanted,"*
pp. 185–86.
20. [Jeanne Forpomès], *Notre oncle d'Amérique: Souvenirs et impressions d'une parisienne sur les travaux de la Croix-rouge Américaine* (Paris: Perrin, 1919), pp. 167–68.
21. Morantz-Sanchez, *Sympathy and Science,* p. 167.
22. The lycées created under the educational reforms of 1879 did not train girls
for the *baccalauréat.* Deuxième Congrès international des oeuvres et institutions féminines (1900), *Compte rendu des travaux* (Paris: Charles Blot, 1902), vol. 4, p. 137; Claire
Goldberg Moses, *French Feminism in the Nineteenth Century* (Albany: State University
of New York Press, 1984), p. 233.

medical schools, for hospital appointments, and for teaching positions also constituted a major obstacle to French women seeking to enter the medical profession.

The opening of each new position to women required official government action. For example, in order to take the exam for the Paris hospital internship in 1887, Blanche Edwards-Pilliet had to convince the prefect of the Seine to sign a decree giving women the right to compete. Women who broke down barriers also encountered virulent hostility; like the first American women to enter medical schools they were excluded from some laboratories and classrooms, ostracized by their fellow students, and harassed by unsympathetic faculty. Protestors tried to force open the door of the building where Edwards-Pilliet was taking the exam for the internship, and some threatened to kidnap her, screaming, "Down with Blanche!" That evening students burned her in effigy in front of the Hôtel de Ville.[23] Unlike women in the United States, however, French women were not able to create separate institutions to ease their way.

By 1900 women had gained the right to compete for hospital internships and a few women held official appointments under various ministries—as physicians attached to local welfare bureaus and schools for girls, teachers in nursing schools, members of the Comité consultatif d'hygiène, and medical inspectors for the infant protective services. They were, however, not allowed to compete for medical teaching positions and they lacked the financial support and professional network needed to open clinics and dispensaries.[24] At least one group of women recognized that the reputations of many famous French physicians had been born in clinics, and they organized a clinic to provide female physicians and dentists with this kind of advantage. The Société des consultations gratuites pour femmes et enfants par femmes docteurs en médecine et les femmes chirurgien-dentistes, founded in 1897 and subsidized by the municipal council of Paris, offered free consultations daily. In an attempt to carve out a special niche for women doctors, the organizers hoped to attract working-class women who were afraid to go to clinics because they would be

23. See Hélène Bory, "Maternité finit par l'emporter," *Le Jour,* January 1935 (clipping, Bibliothèque Marguerite Durand, Dos. EDW.)

24. Women were not allowed to pass the *agrégation* or to become *chirurgiens* or *médecins d'hôpital.* Deuxième Congrès international des oeuvres et institutions féminines (1900), *Compte rendu des travaux,* vol. 4, p. 110.

used as teaching material for students, and children who were afraid of male doctors and dentists.

The Conseil national des femmes françaises also passed a resolution calling for the creation of a hospital staffed and administered by women.[25] The idea did not catch on, however, either because female physicians were simply too scarce or because French feminists could not or would not provide the same patronage that made the women's hospitals in the United States viable institutions.[26] Thus, though French women physicians were concentrated in maternal and child health, they did not achieve prominence in this area; the physicians who sat on official commissions and on the boards of private institutions were men.

While female physicians in the United States actively influenced the direction of maternal and child health policy in the United States, another group of women—public health nurses—forged their professional identity as they helped to build Progressive public health institutions. The first action of any private or public agency in the United States wishing to tackle the problem of infant mortality was almost invariably to hire a public health nurse. The work of the nurse—visiting mothers at home to teach child-care techniques—made up the heart of American infant health programs. In many cities the visiting nurse association, formed to provide home care for the sick poor, initiated the first infant health campaigns; sometimes their actions persuaded city governments to take over the work. In smaller towns and rural areas individual public health nurses employed by the Metropolitan Life Insurance Company, the Red Cross, county health commissions, and mining companies started infant welfare work on their own, often guided by U.S. Children's Bureau literature. Public health nursing, which reached the height of its influence

25. Deuxième Congrès international des oeuvres et institutions féminines (1900), *Compte rendu des travaux*, vol. 4, pp. 126, 145; Conseil national des femmes françaises, *Première assemblée générale publique*, 1903, pp. 73–74.

26. Denial of the right to own property may also have been a factor inhibiting the development of autonomous women's institutions in France. New York State granted married women the right to own property in 1860, and by 1890 all other states had followed. French married women were not allowed to open their own accounts in saving banks before 1881; they won the right to manage their own property in 1893, but not until 1907 were they entitled to complete control over their wages. Mary P. Ryan, *Womanhood in America from Colonial Times to the Present* (New York: New Viewpoint, 1979), pp. 102–3, 149; Patricia Branca, *Women in Europe since 1750* (London: Croom Helm, 1978), pp. 168–69.

in the 1910s and 1920s, potentially offered much greater autonomy and less subordination to the authority of physicians than bedside nursing offered.[27]

The history of the French nursing profession illustrates the way in which the politics of religion and the Republic influenced the formation of social welfare institutions and shaped women's opportunities. Since the seventeenth century nursing had been the domain of religious orders (most prominently the Daughters of Charity); its members were distinguished from nuns because they took only an annual vow. Though their original mission was bedside care, nursing sisters took on most of the administrative work in hospitals and supervised hospital pharmacies. Thus they wielded authority and influence independent of their relationship with physicians.[28] In the nineteenth century, ecclesiastical authorities and conservative political figures supported the establishment of new religious orders to dispense free health care in the countryside along with material assistance and a moral influence. Anticlerical politicians attacked this policy as a means of extending the arm of the clergy, and physicians charged that in selling drugs and practicing surgery the women overstepped the bounds of their authority.[29]

In hospitals, too, the religious and moral priorities of nursing sisters undermined physicians' authority and the utilitarian goals of Republican social policy. Even in the late nineteenth century, for example, nuns insisted on excluding single mothers, prostitutes, and women with venereal diseases from maternity hospitals in spite of the Republican policy that the lives of illegitimate and legitimate children were equally valuable to the state. Because nursing sisters provided an essential service, the Republican government was more tolerant of them than of the members of teaching orders. Physicians, however,

27. Mary Trugg Jackson and Eleanor Hopkins to U.S. Children's Bureau, 4/16/17 (records of the U.S. Children's Bureau, National Archives, Washington, D.C., 4–12–1); Marion M. Brown to Lathrop (received 12/15/15) (ibid., 4–15–4–3); interview by Grace Meigs with Miss Tracy, in charge of Public Health Nursing Association, Topeka, Kans., n.d. (ibid., 4–11–4–12); "A Trip to Lexington, Va., May 10 and 11, 1915" (ibid., 4–15–0); Karen Buhler-Wilkerson, False Dawn: The Rise and Fall of Public Health Nursing, 1900–1930 (New York: Garland, 1989), pp. 97–99, 107.

28. See Colin Jones, The Charitable Imperative: Hospitals and Nursing in Ancien Regime and Revolutionary France (London: Routledge, 1989), pp. 135–37, 196–98.

29. See Jacques Léonard, "Femmes, religion, et médecine: Les religieuses qui soignent, en France au XIXe siècle," Annales E.S.C. 32 (1977): 889, 898.

began to train nonreligious nurses, educated in orthodox scientific medicine and with a clear understanding of their place in the medical hierarchy.[30] Divisions between religious and nonreligious, and the suppression of the autonomy of nursing sisters by physicians and Republican politics, prevented French nurses from developing a clear sense of their profession before World War I. Though perhaps more scientifically sophisticated than the Daughters of Charity, the new nonreligious nurses probably had less power. When the profession of maternal and infant health visitor was recognized in France after World War I, its roots lay more in social work than in nursing.

Women's Activism in the United States and France

While women's access to the health care professions was an important factor in the determination of their roles in creating infant health policy, the larger history of the women's rights movement in each country is essential for an understanding of the influence of women's organizations in policy making. The comparative history of women's movements in the United States and France is rooted partly in the differences between Catholic and Protestant religious institutions. Historians have tended to see the Protestant Reformation as a mixed blessing for women. The new theology preached the spiritual equality of male and female souls and provided the justification for universal literacy. On the other hand, with the abolition of religious orders, Protestant women lost their only respectable alternative to marriage and the family and their only opportunities for intellectual and professional achievement.[31] In the United States and

30. See Yvonne Knibiehler, *Cornettes et blouses blanches: Les infirmières dans la société française, 1880–1920* (Paris: Hachette, 1984), chap. 1. I found one leaflet from before World War I advertising the Association des infirmières visiteuses de France; its *monitrices d'hygiène* were available to physicians and public and private welfare agencies to care for and supervise indigent poor patients at home and to act as intermediaries between the families and agencies. They were devoted particularly to combating infant mortality and tuberculosis (Bibliothèque documentaire internationale contemporaine, Dos. F Res. 221/1–1–16); Mme le Dr. Edwards-Pilliet, "Les femmes dans l'art de guérir depuis cinquante ans," in Deuxième Congrès international des oeuvres et institutions féminines (1900), *Compte rendu des travaux*, vol. 4, p. 109.

31. See Nancy Roelker, "The Appeal of Calvinism to French Noblewomen in the Sixteenth Century," *Journal of Interdisciplinary History* 2 (1972): 391–418; Natalie Zemon Davis, *Society and Culture in Early Modern France* (Stanford, Calif.: Stanford

Britain, however, evangelical Protestantism and women's isolation in the domestic sphere ultimately inspired and made possible the political organization of women and facilitated the creation of new autonomous female professional and educational institutions.

The nineteenth-century American women's rights movement traced its origins to the Second Great Awakening, when evangelical Protestantism provided the rationale for a great social reform movement. Evangelical theology was at the root of abolitionism, which gave such feminists as Elizabeth Cady Stanton, Lucretia Mott, and Sarah Grimke their first political experience and helped them to develop the theoretical basis for their feminism. Evangelicalism also inspired moral reform societies whose programs carried them into the public realm. Mothers' clubs, which originally had as their primary concern the moral training of children, increasingly took a broader interest in all aspects of education and in social reforms conducive to wholesome family life.[32] The National Congress of Mothers, founded in 1897, lay within this moral reform tradition. The program of the congress, which had hundreds of thousands of members by the early twentieth century, encompassed a wide variety of reforms including temperance, child labor legislation, abolition of the public drinking cup, regulation of drugs, repression of the white slave traffic, domestic and manual training in schools, mothers' pensions, medical inspection of schools, and laws prohibiting the marriage of "feeble-minded" and "degenerate" people.[33]

Like the program of the National Congress of Mothers, that of the General Federation of Women's Clubs was based on the ideology of separate spheres, though the federation was more secular and morally

University Press, 1975), pp. 65–95; Jane Rendall, *The Origins of Modern Feminism: Women in Britain, France, and the United States 1789–1860* (London: Macmillan, 1985), pp. 98–101; Nancy F. Cott, *The Bonds of Womanhood: "Woman's Sphere" in New England, 1780–1837* (New Haven: Yale University Press, 1977), p. 154.

32. See Ellen DuBois, *Feminism and Suffrage: The Emergence of an Independent Women's Movement in America, 1848–1869* (Ithaca: Cornell University Press, 1978), p. 32; Blanche Glassman Hersh, *The Slavery of Sex: Feminist-Abolitionists in America* (Urbana: University of Illinois Press, 1978), pp. 2–3; Gerda Lerner, *The Grimke Sisters from South Carolina: Rebels against Slavery* (Boston: Houghton-Mifflin, 1967).

33. "Resolutions Adopted by the Second International Congress on Child Welfare, National Congress of Mothers," *Child-Welfare Magazine* 5 (1911): 189–95. On the history of the National Congress of Mothers see Mary Madeleine Ladd-Taylor, "Mother-work: Ideology, Public Policy, and the Mothers' Movement, 1890–1930," Ph.D. diss., Yale University, 1986, chap. 2.

less conservative than the National Congress of Mothers and more committed to advocacy of women's rights as part of its maternalist agenda. Most of the member clubs had originated as cultural or literary societies but many became increasingly active in social reform toward the end of the nineteenth century. The federation was a leading advocate of Progressive social reforms, including mothers' pensions, public health measures, the protection of the custody rights of mothers and the property rights of married women, uniform marriage and divorce laws, strict enforcement of the White Slave Law, the appointment of female police officers and immigration inspectors, and the creation of the Bureau of National Parks. The federation also recommended that the Bible, as a literary classic, be part of the literary program of all federated clubs.[34] Along with the Women's Christian Temperance Union, the General Federation of Women's Clubs and the National Congress of Mothers reflected their members' convictions that women's moral superiority, their commitment to children and the family, and their detachment from party politics and business gave them the right to a voice not only in their own homes but in public debates.

Largely excluded from the National Congress of Mothers and the General Federation of Women's Clubs, African-American women formed separate organizations, also with a strong moral component, and with a sense of mission rooted in religious conviction. The activities of the local organizations that made up the National Association of Colored Women generally lay within the traditionally female sphere of child care, education, health, and moral rescue, but their struggle expanded into the political arena as well. These women believed that their maternal responsibilities extended beyond their families to the entire race. The services they provided often constituted the basic social welfare institutions in the African-American community. On occasion they waged political battles for municipal services, better schools, and funding for African-American health workers.[35]

34. General Federation of Women's Clubs, *Biennial Convention: Official Report,* 1912, pp. 596–602; Karen Blair, *The Clubwoman as Feminist: True Womanhood Redefined, 1868–1914* (New York: Holmes and Meier, 1980), p. 101; Ladd-Taylor, "Mother-work," p. 136.

35. Paula Giddings, *When and Where I Enter: The Impact of Black Women on Race and Sex in America* (New York: Bantam, 1984), p. 51; Cynthia Neverdon-Morton,

Although religious orders continued to provide professional opportunities for French women in education, nursing, and midwifery into the twentieth century, they were not a vehicle for independent women's political action or social reform. Like their American Protestant counterparts, French Catholic women who met to discuss their children began to take up social issues related to the economic and moral protection of women and children. In the context of Republican attacks on the church, however, Catholic women's organizations defended religious morality and the institutional power of the church. Consequently they did not develop a secular program that reflected distinctive female experience and interests. The Ligue patriotique des femmes françaises, founded in 1902 to defend religious liberty and freedom of education—in other words, to counter the state's attack on Catholicism—became the most powerful women's organization in the country, with 400,000 members in 1909.[36] Like the National Congress of Mothers and the General Federation of Women's Clubs, the Ligue patriotique developed a new rationale for women's political participation by linking public and private life and created an autonomous structure for female activism. The group's program, however, was that of the church; it attacked the "jacobin" regime, socialism, and usury (*"juiverie"*) and fought a prolonged battle against secular education. The Union nationaliste des femmes françaises supported such principles as women's right to work and equal pay for equal work, but it was also dedicated to the preservation of traditional family structures and its political loyalties, like those of the Ligue patriotique, lay clearly on the reactionary side.[37]

Other Catholic women activists mobilized within the camp of Social Catholicism. The Congrès Jeanne d'Arc concerned itself with such demands as votes for female heads of families, maternal custody

Afro-American Women of the South and the Advancement of the Race, 1895–1925 (Knoxville: University of Tennessee Press, 1989), pp. 191–93, 161; Jacqueline Anne Rouse, *Lugenia Burns Hope, Black Southern Reformer* (Athens: University of Georgia Press, 1989), pp. 6–8, 60, 90, 130; Eileen Boris, "The Power of Motherhood: Black and White Activist Women Reformers Redefine the 'Political,' " *Yale University Journal of Law and Feminism* 2 (1989): 25–89.

36. See Anne-Marie Sohn, "Les femmes catholiques et la vie publique en France, 1900–1930," in *Stratégies des femmes,* ed. Marie-Claire Pasquier et al. (Amsterdam: Editions Tierce, 1984), p. 105.

37. See Marie-Hélène Zylberberg-Hocquard, *Féminisme et syndicalisme en France* (Paris: Editions Anthropos, 1978), p. 101.

106   Every Child a Lion

rights, and women's right to work, thus associating the protection of children with increasing the autonomy of women. These women were inspired in part by the papal encyclical *Rerum novarum,* issued in 1891, which called for new efforts to aid the poor to prevent class warfare. In 1904, Pius X instructed women in particular to undertake works of true Christian *fraternité,* avoiding the superior attitude of traditional benefactors.[38] Thus, while supporting some social reforms, the Congrès, like the Action sociale de la femme, another women's Social Catholic organization, adhered strictly to Catholic church policy. The regulations of the Action sociale de la femme stipulated that all members had to be Catholic; the educational work of all its affiliates had to conform to Catholic doctrine; and the program of the congress had to be approved by ecclesiastical authority.[39]

While these "Christian feminists" defended Catholicism, the first loyalty of secular French women's rights activists lay with the Republic. Historians seeking to explain the relative weakness of the French women's rights movement in the late nineteenth and early twentieth centuries have argued that the movement suffered because its fate was linked with that of its leftist allies. Between 1848 and 1881, when Republican control over the government was secured, women's rights advocates were subjected to political repression and censorship. Not until the 1880s, then, did women's rights organizations and leaders have a chance to reach maturity. Under the Third Republic, however, the population crisis provided the grounds for antifeminist politics on the part of anticlerical Republican politicians as well as conservatives. Those men, such as Paul Strauss, who did not express outright hostility to calls for women's independence tended to paternalism and emphasized women's maternal duties rather than individual freedom. As a result, Karen Offen suggests, the most viable option for women seeking to expand their rights was "familial feminism," which sought to turn the population crisis and prevailing antifeminist attitudes to the advantage of women.[40]

38. See Yvonne Knibiehler, "Vocation sans voile, les métiers sociaux," in *Madame ou Mademoiselle? Itinéraires de la solitude féminine XVIIIe–XXe siècle,* ed. Arlette Farge and Christiane Klapisch-Zuber (n.p.: Montalba, 1984), p. 167.
39. Henri Rollet, *L'Action sociale des catholiques en France, 1871–1914* (n.p.: Desclée de Brouwer, 1958), p. 35.
40. See Moses, *French Feminism in the Nineteenth Century,* pp. 197–98; Karen Offen,

Rather than fight for political equality or the elimination of the sexual division of labor, familial feminists struggled to improve the position of women within the domestic sphere. They argued that women deserved respect for their social contribution and should receive the rights and resources to make material and moral choices about their children. Mostly bourgeois themselves, they also tried to improve the physical and material conditions of working-class women. In this context they sometimes argued that childbearing should be considered a social function and remunerated as such.[41] Society, they maintained, owed women adequate food and housing and the necessary rest to bear healthy children, so they need not look forward to childbirth as a burden or a shame.

Foremost among the secular women's rights organizations was the Conseil national des femmes françaises, founded in 1900. A moderate organization, the council's political philosophy generally coincided with that of the Radical Republicans. While committed to fighting for women's suffrage, its program also aimed at improving the education of girls and the professional opportunities of women, protecting women's working conditions, and promoting the welfare of children. These women did not, however, challenge the notion that motherhood was women's fundamental social and patriotic duty. The thirty-five original member organizations represented only twenty-one thousand women, far fewer than the Ligue patriotique repre-

"Depopulation, Nationalism, and Feminism in Fin-de-Siècle France," *American Historical Review* 89 (1984): 670–74.

41. See Offen, "Depopulation, Nationalism, and Feminism," pp. 660–70. The questions of whether these women are properly called "feminist" and whether "familial" or "relational" feminism has historically constituted a tendency distinct from "individualist" feminism have been the subjects of much recent debate. The issue is further complicated in this comparative study since, for example, certain French groups who would not have satisfied the American definition of feminism in the early twentieth century called themselves feminists. I have tried to avoid the labeling of groups of women activists as feminist or nonfeminist and have focused instead on describing their beliefs and goals. See Karen Offen, "Defining Feminism: A Comparative Historical Approach," *Signs* 14 (1988): 119–57 and replies by Ellen Carol Dubois and Nancy F. Cott, *Signs* 15 (1989): 195–209. The term "maternalism" has also been used to characterize those groups that Offen calls "familial feminists" i.e., those who made claims on the state based on women's distinctive needs and contributions to the state, particularly as mothers. See Koven and Michel, "Womanly Duties," p. 1079.

sented. The members were concentrated mostly in Paris and with a leadership that was disproportionately Protestant and Jewish.[42] Insofar as French women sought a voice in maternal and infant health policy to any significant extent they tended to come from the faction that made up the Conseil national des femmes françaises. Though their ideology had much in common with that of American organizations such as the General Federation of Women's Clubs, they had a structural relationship to medicine and family policy which was very different from that of American women reformers. In all areas of social welfare, French women were far more often relegated to political invisibility and professional inferiority than were their American counterparts.

Historians of female Progressive reformers in the United States have stressed the importance of autonomous women's institutions as a base for professional careers and activism. Perhaps foremost among these was the social settlement. In the settlement, American professional women could find a residential and social alternative to the family and an extensive network of women who shared their political goals and social status. Even those who did not live in settlement houses gained strength and emotional support from the network of settlement women. Hull House, in Chicago, in particular was the intellectual and social center of female activism; Lillian Wald's Henry Street Settlement in New York, which focused on health care, was another important center of women's activism.[43]

Following the example of reformers in the United States and Britain, several bourgeois and aristocratic Parisian women founded settlement houses (*résidences sociales* or *maisons sociales*) in the late nineteenth and early twentieth centuries, establishing residence in working-class neighborhoods, where they provided health and educational services. Though they shared with Anglo-American settlement workers a desire to effect class reconciliation, their work grew

42. Steven C. Hause with Anne R. Kenney, *Women's Suffrage and Social Politics in the French Third Republic* (Princeton, N.J.: Princeton University Press, 1984), pp. 36–39.

43. Estelle Freedman, "Separatism as Strategy: Female Institution Building and American Feminism, 1870–1930," *Feminist Studies* 5 (1979): 512–29; Kathryn Kish Sklar, "Hull House in the 1890s: A Community of Women Reformers," *Signs* 10 (1985): 658–77; Ellen Fitzpatrick, *Endless Crusade: Women Social Scientists and Progressive Reform* (Oxford: Oxford University Press, 1990), pp. 10, 16; Muncy, *Creating a Female Dominion*, chap. 1.

out of Social Catholic ideology. Yvonne Knibiehler notes that pious Catholic women who wanted to devote their lives to social work, and others disinclined to marry, were deprived in 1901 of their traditional refuge and careers by legislation severely limiting the activities and existence of religious orders, particularly in education. Many former nuns could thus be found in the first settlement houses. The settlement residents, however, did not take vows of obedience, and their new institutions provided them with a certain amount of independence. Ultimately, they built the foundations of professional social work, but this work would not develop until after World War I. Though through the settlement houses they found individual liberation from the bourgeois family and domesticity, their commitment was essentially a religious one. They respected an unspoken vow of chastity and sacrificed their personal fortunes to their mission.[44]

One of the most successful of the women's settlements in Paris was the Maison sociale founded in 1897 by the Marquise de Beauregard and organized by Marie Gahéry and later taken over by Mercédès La Fer de la Motte. Originally inspired by the Social Catholic ideals of rapprochement between upper-class and working-class women, the Maison became increasingly social in its orientation. Its program, not unlike that of American social settlements, included a workshop to enable mothers to work in their homes, a vacation colony, a residence for young workers, shelters for girls and boys, courses in home economics, day care for children, and evening classes for adults.

In 1909 scandal brought the institution's precarious financial situation to a head, however. The scandal was precipitated by a suit filed by the father of Jeanne Bassot, a woman who had decided to devote herself to social work and hoped to start her own settlement house where she planned to live alone with a friend. The General Bassot sued the institution in the civil courts for organizing an unauthorized religious order, and at the same time protested to Rome that the institution was heretical. He had his daughter certified as an imbecile and confined in an institution in Switzerland. She managed to escape, however, and filed charges of kidnaping. After a much-publicized trial she withdrew her complaint and was later able to found the Résidence sociale de Levallois in a Paris suburb, working closely with

44. Knibiehler, "Vocation sans voile," pp. 167–68.

parish clergy.[45] Another settlement that survived by maintaining good relations with religious authorities was the Résidence et le dispensaire de la Croix St.-Simon, which combined religious education and proselytizing with a dispensary and other health work, including an infant clinic.[46]

Probably more influential than these settlements was the work of Léonie Chaptal in a poor neighborhood on the outskirts of Paris. Great-granddaughter of a minister of Napoleon, daughter of a countess and sister of a bishop, Chaptal was a devout Catholic. At the age of twenty she adopted the faubourg of Plaisance, where her recently ordained brother, later to become a bishop, had been posted as assistant priest. After six years of social investigation, she decided to concentrate on the health problems of the poor, particularly tuberculosis and infant mortality. She opened a tuberculosis clinic in 1900, and in 1901 started a maternal and infant health program with *consultations de nourrissons,* home assistants for new mothers, and moral counseling for single mothers. The agency also distributed food coupons to nursing mothers and arranged for work that enabled them to stay at home and care for their children. In 1905, Chaptal opened a nursing school.

Chaptal was able to get recognition for her work, as well as official and scientific support; in 1909 she was one of two French delegates to the international antituberculosis congress in Washington. Her agency became a quasi-official one during the war, when its nurses took over the work of municipal visitors. Chaptal also played a principal role in the maternal and child welfare work funded by the American Red Cross during the war, through which public health nursing was first introduced into France on a large scale.[47] Thus to a limited extent French women were able to build female professions through social institutions not directly subject to religious authority. Because of the hierarchical, centralized nature of social welfare and charity,

45. Ibid.; Rollet, *L'Action sociale des catholiques,* pp. 116–30.
46. Ibid., pp. 126–130.
47. See Marguerite Peltier, *Mademoiselle Chaptal: Ses principales activités sociales* (Paris: Editions Spes, 1937); Rollet, *L'Action sociale des catholiques,* pp. 107–12; L. Chaptal, "La possibilité d'une éducation de la santé par l'assistance privé," *Alliance d'hygiène sociale* 14–15 (May 1913) (clipping, Bibliothèque Marguerite Durand, Dos. CHA).

however, these institutions depended heavily on official or clerical approval.

French Women's Voluntary Activity: The Société de charité maternelle

The lack of professional opportunities for French women became evident in 1892, when the city of Paris hired women to visit mothers and children receiving certain forms of public assistance. The Parisian local commission for administering the infant protective services established by the Roussel Law also included paid female inspectors as well as medical inspectors. The competition for these scarce jobs was fierce, however. In 1896 there were eighteen positions for female inspectors in the infant protective services and places for eleven volunteer substitutes. One hundred and twenty women were waiting for a chance for one of these jobs; there had not been an opening in three years and some of the applicants had been waiting for five or six years.[48]

The government encouraged private charity, however, and urged middle- and upper-class women to volunteer their services to aid in the protection of maternal and infant health. In the vision of the policy makers, not only would these volunteers save the government money, but their distinctive feminine qualities would help to counteract some of the harmful tendencies of public assistance. The French government, however, was not content to allow private charities free rein; its policy was to control their activities as much as possible while taking advantage of their resources and labor to aid in its efforts to quell class conflict and regenerate the population. Female charitable organizations thus found themselves under growing financial pressure and subject to close regulation in an increasingly bureaucratic social welfare system. The example of the Société de charité maternelle, France's oldest maternal charity society, illustrates this process. Although the society had aristocratic patrons and religious connections,

48. Madeleine, "Un nouvel emploi pour les femmes," *La Fronde*, October 14, 1899 (clipping, Bibliothèque Marguerite Durand, Dos. 614 MAT); memo, May 20, 1896 (Préfecture de Police, DB31); Rachel G. Fuchs, "Morality and Poverty: Public Welfare for Mothers in Paris, 1870–1900," *French History* 2 (1988): 296.

the Republican government encouraged and subsidized it, not only because it saved the state money but because Republican politicians believed that the traditional motives and goals of charity had a place in modern public welfare.

In 1784, Mme Fougeret and a group of her aristocratic friends in Paris had organized a society to prevent child abandonment by aiding poor married women at home at the time of childbirth and assisting them in caring for their newborn children. The founders also hoped that the assistance would help to preserve the children's families and to make sure that the babies were baptized. Thus the society aided only women who had been married in a religious ceremony and had three or more children, abandoned wives with two or more children, widows, and the wives of disabled men. Members of the society sought out poor women in their neighborhoods and delivered their gifts in person; they provided a layette, money at the time of birth, and an additional sum each month for a year on the condition that the mother care for and nurse her child. Within a few years aristocratic women in Arras, Rouen, and Lyons followed Fougeret's example.[49]

The society's founding was not due solely to the spontaneous charitable impulses of aristocratic women, however, or to a sense of female solidarity; the government and the church demonstrated an interest in the organization from its inception. Fougeret herself claimed to have been moved to action by a speech given by Jacques Necker, the controller-general, on abandoned children. Marie Antoinette adopted the Société de charité maternelle, declared herself its president, and favored it with a grant of 24,000 livres a year. In 1790 and 1791 the National Assembly voted to continue this grant permanently. In the Year II, when Mme Fougeret and her family went to prison and her husband to the scaffold, the society disappeared. It resurfaced, however, in 1801 with funding from the Bank of France and the bankers of the public treasury and under the patronage of several notable women. In 1810 Napoleon, unaware of the existence of this orga-

49. Albert de Mun, La Société de charité maternelle de Moulins (Paris: Imprimerie Crépin-Leblond, 1912), pp. 9–10; Paul Delauney, La Société de charité maternelle du Mans et ses origines (Le Mans: Imprimerie Monnoyer, 1911), p. 5; La France charitable et prévoyante (Paris: Librairie Plon, 1912); Victor Duval, La Charité à Rouen: Les oeuvres catholiques (Rouen: Ancienne imprimerie Lapierre, 1895); Bouchacourt, "Quelques vues et désiderata relatifs à l'assistance des femmes en couches à Lyon," Congrès national d'assistance (Lyons: Ancienne imprimerie A. Waltener, 1894), vol. 2, p. 267.

nization, decreed the formation of a Société maternelle in Paris with a branch in each of forty-four selected cities in the hopes that it would help to promote population growth. When informed that such an organization already existed, Napoleon appointed his wife to serve as its president and endowed the Société de charité maternelle with 500,000 francs in perpetual income.[50]

Under the instructions of Napoleon's minister of the interior each prefect initiated the effort to recruit women to patronize the local branches mandated by Napoleon. Some prefects were successful but others failed to drum up the necessary subscriptions even with the assistance of mayors and priests.[51] The society was never altogether independent of state regulation. Most of the new branches adopted the statutes and regulations of the original Paris society with few modifications. As the long struggle of the Dijon society to obtain approval of its regulation suggests, the leeway allowed by the authorities was slim, though this branch was able to function for twenty-two years without an approved set of regulations.[52]

Under the First Empire, the succeeding monarchies, and the Second Empire, the Société de charité maternelle resembled, in the words of one historian, an "official alms-purse."[53] As such, it was the beneficiary of royal patronage and generous government subsidies but it was also subject to official surveillance and vulnerable to political upheaval. After the Restoration, for example, Napoleon's decree was revoked and the provincial committees dissolved; only those branches for which the prefect proved the necessity continued to receive state funds.[54] Through the subsequent changes in regime only the official patron changed. Each branch had to submit the names of members

50. See De Mun, *La Société de charité maternelle de Moulins,* p. 12; Delauney, *La Société de charité maternelle du Mans,* p. 6.

51. The prefect of the Côte-d'Or successfully recruited the twenty-six subscriptions for the Dijon Société de charité maternelle, but the prefect of the Sarthe did not succeed until 1816. A historian of the Société de charité maternelle of Le Mans refers to evidence that official appeals were initially unsuccessful all over France. A. Cornereau, "Notice sur la Société de charité maternelle de Dijon," *Mémoires de l'Académie de sciences, arts et belles-lettres de Dijon,* 4th sér. 7 (1899–1900): 414–16; Delauney, *La Société de charité maternelle du Mans,* p. 10.

52. Cornereau, "Notice sur la Société de charité maternelle de Dijon," pp. 419–21.

53. Maurice Melin, *L'assurance maternelle* (Paris: Librairie de la Société du Recueil Sirey, 1911), p. 172.

54. Conseil supérieur de l'assistance publique, *Comptes-rendus,* Fascicule No. 76, Statistique des dépenses publiques d'assistance en 1896, pp. 26–28.

of the administrative council and its statutes and regulations for official approval to the duchesse d'Angoulême until 1830, to the queen under the July Monarchy, to the minister of the interior under the Second Republic, to the prefect in 1852–53, and finally to the empress.

Under the Third Republic the Société de charité maternelle faced a more serious challenge, as the government gradually denied the member organizations their favored status among maternal and child welfare agencies. Run by aristocratic women with moral and religious priorities and patronized by ecclesiastical notables, the society was not popular with Republican authorities. In 1883 the minister of the interior sent a circular to the prefects in which he announced continued support for the Société de charité maternelle but emphasized that only those branches that received departmental and communal support would henceforth be good candidates for government subsidies.[55] In 1888 the minister drew the attention of the prefects to the requirement that recipients present a certificate of religious marriage; because this rule conflicted with the principle of religious freedom, any society still adhering to this regulation had to change its practices in order to continue to receive government subsidies.[56]

According to information obtained from the prefects in 1894, sixteen branches still enforced the religious marriage requirement and twenty-two others had the rule on their books but no longer applied it.[57] Such practices, argued the reporter for the Conseil supérieur de l'assistance publique, accounted for the lack of local popularity and financial support. This was certainly true in Paris, where the municipal council withdrew its 10,000 francs in annual subsidy to the city's Société de charité maternelle on the grounds that it was of a denominational nature. Other branches lost their local funding for reasons that remain unclear, and state subsidies were also withdrawn in these cases. Thus while in 1886 77 branches had received a total of 79,000 francs in state subsidies, ten years later 68 received only 65,450 francs.[58]

<hr />

55. Ibid., Fascicule No. 6, Crèches, sociétés de charité maternelle, 1888, p. 3.

56. Cornereau, "Notice sur la Société de charité maternelle de Dijon," pp. 488–89.

57. Conseil supérieur de l'assistance publique, Compte-rendus, Fascicule No. 76, p. 30.

58. Ibid., pp. 25–28. The Société de charité maternelle of Dijon, which received one thousand francs from the state in 1886, lost its state funds in 1895 because the municipality and department both refused their support. Moulins withdrew its four-

As the number of maternal and child welfare institutions increased rapidly in the first years of the twentieth century, the national government began to use subsidies to private institutions as an important instrument of maternal and infant health policy. In 1908 the parliament increased the funds allocated for assistance to the Société de charité maternelle and to crèches, which provided day care for children, from 160,000 to 400,000 francs. It also changed the title of the relevant chapter in the budget to "assistance to works of maternal assistance and of infant protection," thus clearly removing any special claim to these funds on the part of the Société de charité maternelle.[59] The legislation stipulated that the distribution of the funds be administered by a special commission composed of legislators, public welfare administrators (including one female inspector), and the president of the Mutualité maternelle (maternal mutual aid society) of Paris. Like other organizations, maternal charity societies now had to send a dossier to the prefect of the department, who would forward the file to the minister of the interior with his recommendations after consulting with the Comité départemental de protection du premier âge, which oversaw the distribution of the funds in each department.[60]

To a certain extent the increased subsidies were a means of providing maternity benefits for which the state was not willing to pay directly. Legislators had been debating the question of mandatory maternity leaves for several years; one major objection was that requiring a woman to leave her job without providing any compensatory benefits was unjust and would harm rather than help her child's health. Encouraging private agencies that did provide material assistance was a possible way of getting around this problem.

The legislation increasing subsidies to private organizations also served to foster certain types of maternal and child welfare. Infant health consultations, for example, were favored because they were primarily educational, and all agencies were discouraged from dis-

---

hundred-franc subsidy of the local Société de charité maternelle in 1903 for unknown reasons. F. Gille, *La Société de charité maternelle de Paris* (Paris: Imprimerie V. Goupy et Jourdan, [1883]), p. 2; Mun, *La Société de charité maternelle de Moulins*, p. 3; Cornereau, "Notice sur la Société de charité maternelle de Dijon," p. 425. The Le Mans society also lost its public funding between 1870 and 1890. Delauney, *La Société de charité maternelle du Mans*, pp. 21–22.

59. Ministre de l'interieur, Circular, September 10, 1908 (Archives nationales, F[1a] 3157).

60. *Journal officiel: Bulletin des lois*, May 6, 1909: 737.

criminating against illegitimate children. Under the new regulations
no agency was eligible for funds if it distinguished among applicants
for aid by religious belief. Subsidies went by preference to those
institutions that encouraged breast-feeding, made an effort to instruct
as well as aid mothers, and did not limit their assistance to legitimate
children. Those agencies that provided mothers with material aid
sufficient to permit them to take a leave from work before and after
childbirth would receive additional funds.[61] The mutual aid society
was the favorite maternal welfare institution of Republican legislators
because it provided a possible vehicle for compensating women which
did not draw heavily on public funds. While in theory the *mutualité
maternelle* was a self-supporting institution designed to enable women
to provide for childbirth, in practice it was a charitable organization
supported largely by government subsidies and private donations
from "lady patrons" who distributed the aid and made sure the members rested and cared properly for their children. The self-help element
of the *mutualité maternelle* made it especially attractive to legislators.[62]

The government encouraged private agencies not only because they
provided social and medical services and material assistance the state
could not or would not afford; legislators also attempted to foster a
division of labor between public and private welfare agencies. Political
leaders believed that wealthy volunteers could exert the kind of moral
influence that fell by the wayside in public welfare, because they came
into personal contact with the poor and because their motives were
altruistic. Both conservative and Republican writers believed that
women had a special role in private charity, particularly in maternal
and child welfare. Despite its political drawbacks the sociétés de charité maternelle thus offered services the government considered valuable and not all of them lost out as a result of the change in policy.
As a group they did not benefit from the sharp increase in subsidies
in 1909—in 1913, for example, they received only 61,450 francs of

61. Décret, *Journal officiel: Bulletin des lois,* June 26, 1909: 1023–25; Conseil supérieur
de l'assistance publique, *Comptes-rendus,* Fascicule No. 110, Séance du 20 juin 1911,
pp. 7–8.
62. In 1911, 342 crèches received 121,000 francs; 281 *consultations de nourrissons* and
gouttes de lait received 192,291; 153 mutual aid societies received 11,836; 141 *sociétés
de charité maternelle* received 156,878; 107 *mutualités maternelles* received 104,200; and
67 communes received 13,795. Conseil supérieur de l'assistance publique, *Comptes-
rendus,* Fascicule No. 111, Séance du 10 décembre 1912.

the total of 536,750 francs distributed—but a few received larger grants than ever before. No organization in the country received more than the Parisian Société de charité maternelle and only one other received as much. Nineteen other branches received larger grants in 1913 than they had in 1886.[63] Those which adapted to suit the new requirements were rewarded. A government inspector heartily praised the Auxerre branch in 1910, for example, because it distributed its benefits without regard to marital status or religion but made aid contingent on vaccination and attendance at an infant health consultation. This society, the inspector concluded, was very useful and should receive the largest grant possible.[64]

Conservative supporters of the Société de charité maternelle considered the charitable nature of the work and the female gender of its members to be among the principal benefits of the institution. Count Albert de Mun wrote, "Charity, especially that which concerns mothers and cradles, is it not the glorious endowment of the Christian woman, as well as an effective apostolic instrument and the true way to show ourselves the disciples of He who said: 'Love each other as I have loved you.'"[65] F. Gille, a defender of the Société de charité maternelle of Paris, argued that only women possessed the true gift of charity. They knew how to be compassionate with the unfortunate and to find the words that could console and elevate.[66]

Because these men traced the decline in population growth to moral degeneration, they saw the religious orientation of the Société de charité maternelle as essential to its purpose and its defense of marriage as a patriotic task. Radical Republicans also developed a secular version of the charitable woman, herself a saint of sorts, whose altruistic sentiments were those of social solidarity and whose message was the gospel of scientific hygiene. Politicians hoped that as the bearers of material assistance, practical advice, and words of encouragement,

63. Conseil supérieur de l'assistance publique, *Comptes-rendus,* Fascicule No. 3, Rapport de M. Pichon sur le budget de 1889, pp. 39–40; Ministre de l'intérieur, "Rapport sur l'emploi du crédit ouvert au Ministre de l'Intérieur pour subventionner aux oeuvres d'assistance maternelle et de protection du premier âge," *Journal officiel,* January 16, 1913: 447–51.

64. R. Marois, *Les consultations de nourrissons dans l'Yonne en 1910* (Auxerre: A. Jacques, 1911), p. 15.

65. De Mun, *La Société de charité maternelle de Moulins,* p. 5.

66. Gille, *La Société de charité maternelle de Paris,* p. 25.

upper-class women would make motherhood more attractive to working-class women and also find their own maternal sentiments reawakened.

The "Lady Patron" in the Third Republic

Solidarist Republicans hoped to preserve voluntarism within a state system that furthered social justice by aiding and protecting the poor and weak; thus most advocates of public maternal and infant welfare maintained that public assistance could not completely replace private charity, even if the state had the necessary financial resources. It was partly through voluntary action on the part of the bourgeoisie that Radical Republicans hoped to gain the loyalty of the working class to the Republic. The feminine nurturing qualities of bourgeois women and their purported ability to sympathize with their poor sisters were called into play: it was their particular task to make the personal contact between the classes.[67]

Legislators had first called upon "lady patrons" to work in co-operation with public authorities in the 1870's as part of the Roussel Law, which created a system of medical supervision of infants placed out to nurse. The participation of two married mothers was essential to the legislators' conception of the local commission.[68] The visits of these "lady inspectors" had an entirely different purpose from those of the medical inspectors; ideally they were to act as friendly patrons of the protected children. The qualifications for these positions were purely moral and social; the minister of the interior doubted that there

67. G. Eustache, *La puériculture, hygiène, et assistance* (Paris: J. B. Baillière, 1903), pp. 255, 287; August Luling, *De la mortalité des nourrissons en rapport avec la modalité de leur alimentation* (Versailles: Imprimerie Aubert, 1901), p. 77; Paul Deschanel and Raphael-Georges Lévy, *L'enfant de la guerre: Sa préservation* (Conférences données à la Salle de la Société de Géographie le 22 novembre 1916), p. 11; Cantine maternelle du XVIIIe arrondissement, *Compte rendu, 1911*, p. 21; *Une expérience sociale: Société maternelle parisienne la pouponnière* (n.d.), p. 62; Melin, *L'assurance maternelle*, pp. 163–64; Jacques Mornet, *Les mutualités maternelles* (Paris: Blond, 1911).

68. J. Jarricot, *Rôle social et pratique du fonctionnement des consultations de nourrissons et des gouttes de lait* (Trévoux: Jeannin, 1909), pp. 84–87; Préfecture de Police, 1re Division, 5e Bureau, *Protection des enfants du premier âge: Historique de la réglementation du service dans le Département de la Seine* (Paris: Imprimerie administrative, 1910), p. 3; Préfet de Police to Maire du 7e arrondissement, January 9, 1878, Archives de la Ville de Paris, V.D.⁶ 1575, No. 4; "Instruction générale du 15 juin, 1877," in Préfecture de Police, *Protection des enfants du premier âge* (Paris, 1909), p. 28.

would be any difficulty in locating appropriate women who were "devoted to good" and familiar with infant care, and he expressed confidence that local opinion, the mayor, and the priest would surely point these women out.[69] The visitors would benefit as well. They would learn to supervise the hygiene and education of young children, and their daughters, accompanying them on these visits, would be initiated into the "august" and "holy" task that awaited them. Legislators also hoped that the contact between indigent and well-off families would make a significant contribution to erasing the "prejudices and biases that cast such evil ferments into society."[70]

In fact, local commissions were organized only in a few places and rarely survived for long. An energetic mayor and the devotion of a few women of leisure were not sufficient to make the local commission system work. The women of the provincial bourgeoisie who volunteered their services did not always possess the necessary qualifications to instruct nurses in scientific hygiene and were not always willing to submit to the local medical inspector's authority. Most medical inspectors testified that where it existed supervision by the "lady patrons" did influence the nurses to keep the children clean, but others complained that those who volunteered had no training in nursing or in child hygiene. Too often, the physicians complained, the visitor was an "honest country woman" who, having raised a large family, believed herself more competent than the medical inspector and did not hesitate to criticize his prescriptions.[71] Local commissions were not always agents of social harmony either. This was especially true in small villages, where a commission member who

69. Chambre des Députés, *Rapport au nom de la commission chargée d'examiner la proposition de Loi Roussel,* June 9, 1874: 118 (Préfecture de Police, DB63).

70. Charles Mercier, *Les Petits-Paris: Etude critique et conseils pratiques sur l'hygiène infantile* (Paris: G. Steinheil, 1898), p. 174; Paterne, "Critique de la Loi Roussel: Ses bienfaits, ses imperfections, modifications qu'il y aurait lieu d'y apporter," *Bericht über den III. Internationalen Kongress für Sauglingsschutz (Gouttes de Lait)* (Berlin: Georg Stilke, 1912), p. 1065; Hélène Moniez, *Les commissions locales du protection du premier age: Rapport présenté au nom de la deuxième section à la Société internationale pour l'étude des questions d'assistance* (Paris: Masson, 1904), p. 3.

71. Moniez, *Les commissions locales,* pp. 13–14, 16–19; A. Chaudet, *Un exemple d'initiative privée: La Commission d'inspection des nourrissons de Sainte-Jamme-sur-Sarthe* (Le Mans: Imprimerie Ch. Blanchet, 1902), pp. 8–13; F. Lédé, "Quelques réflexions sur l'application de la Loi Roussel," *Revue d'hygiène et de police sanitaire* 10 (1888): 456. Paris was an exception; there was a local commission for each arrondissement. Minutes of some survive in the Archives de la Ville de Paris: V.D.[6] 1575, No. 4; V.bis 12Q[7]; V.D.[6] 1393, No. 5.

recommended that a child be removed from a refractory nurse would be threatening a neighbor's livelihood.

A fundamental problem was that the policing mission of the local commission was incompatible with the devotion and maternal solicitude that lady visitors were supposed to embody. Unconvinced, a few members of the Académie de médecine campaigned to bring the local commission back to life in the first decade of the twentieth century. This move was supported by female activists who argued that male physicians were not qualified to oversee the daily care of children. The Conseil national des femmes françaises passed a resolution in favor of keeping the local commissions and even suggested that the commissions also supervise wards of the state and children whose parents received state assistance.[72] Most of the medical inspectors, however, favored increasing physicians' authority in the protective services and reducing that of lay people.

Though women visitors did not ultimately play an important role in the implementation of the Roussel Law, the "lady patron" figured prominently in later programs. As the mortality rate among children placed out to nurse declined, physicians and public welfare officials turned their attention to bringing other groups of children under medical supervision. Men who wanted to win over working-class women to scientific hygiene appealed to wealthy women for assistance as fund raisers and home visitors. "To you," exhorted Henri Bousquet in a lecture to women in Clermont-Ferrand, "belongs the task of bringing us the force of your irresistible apostolat." He quoted Paul Strauss: "As long as women are not, to use the pretty expression of Mme Jeanne Schmahl, the vanguard in the rational protection of mothers and infants, our efforts run the risk of remaining sterile." Bousquet urged his listeners to form a committee to combat infant mortality and, most immediately, to begin to raise funds to start a milk station in Clermont-Ferrand.[73]

Women often constituted a major source of financial support for institutions created and administered by men. This was true, for

---

72. Odette Laguerre and I.-R. Sée, *La protection de l'enfance* (Lyons: Société d'éducation et d'action féministes, 1906), p. 5; Moniez, *Les commissions locales*, p. 2; Chaudet, *Un exemple d'initiative privée*, p. 5.

73. Henri Bousquet, *La dépopulation en France: Moyens de combattre la mortalité infantile: L'oeuvre de la goutte de lait* (Montluçon: Imprimerie du Centre Médical, 1902), p. 15.

example, of the Parisian Association de l'oeuvre sociale du bon lait, founded by a group of men to provide cheap, high-quality milk for working-class mothers and free milk for poor women with young children. In 1909, 343 of the 434 subscribing members were women, though the administrative council and medical committee of the organization were all male.[74] The female patrons organized fund-raising events, distributed free gifts to the poor mothers, and administered the association's material aid program.

Female patrons almost always had the responsibility of distributing the material aid provided by milk stations and infant health consultations. It was common for a crèche, or nursery, to have a committee of "lady patrons" who raised funds and made donations, visited the children's homes, and supervised the use of the assistance they provided. That they were the bearers of gifts of clothing, food, fuel, and money presumably made them more welcome visitors in working-class homes than the inspectors of the protective services. The statutes governing the committees of women patrons usually allowed for gifts to be given at the discretion of the individual visitor or a neighborhood committee, a policy that made the recipients dependent on the generosity of the benefactors and deliberately fostered traditional forms of deference.[75]

The annual reports of milk stations, infant health consultations, and nurseries often included sentimental descriptions and pictures of the activities of the women patrons. At Variot's Goutte de lait in the Belleville section of Paris, for example, the patrons organized an annual Christmas-tree celebration to which they invited the mothers with the largest families, who received clothes, toys, and sweets. In 1911 the fête inspired a painting by Jules Geoffroy which depicts the child of a benefactor giving a symbolic kiss to a poor child under the branches of a Christmas tree.[76] The reports also emphasized the intangible contribution of the women: only women could make their way into the hearts and homes of poor families, and only women

74. *Bulletin de l'Association de l'oeuvre sociale du bon lait,* October 1909: 141–50.
75. Gauchas, "La crèche au point de vue hygiénique et médicale," in Deuxieme Congrès international des oeuvres et institutions féminines (1900), *Compte rendu des travaux,* vol. 2, p. 23; Marie Bazaine, "Crèches et garderies," in ibid., p. 84; Crèche laïque de la Villette, *Notice historique: Comptes rendus,* n.d., p. 29.
76. *Organisation et fonctionnement de la goutte de lait de Belleville, 1892–1911* (Paris: A. Davy, 1911), pp. 4–5.

knew the affectionate and tender words that inspired hope and confidence. They brought "something extra, their affection, their heart, their devotion and the exquisite charm of their unique sensibility, in a word that mysterious force which gives success to all projects they choose to patronize."[77]

Physicians argued that these activities benefited the benefactors as much as the recipients. In theory, contact with children and with working-class women who sacrificed themselves in order to support their families would reawaken the maternal instincts of bourgeois women and stimulate their sense of social responsibility. Physicians often recruited women volunteers to assist them in the consultations, keeping records of the infants' weights, writing down the physicians' observations, and trying to gather information from resistant mothers. Sometimes physicians chose teen-age girls to assist in the examining room, arguing that the consultation provided a sort of apprenticeship in motherhood. Some normal schools and primary schools sent their female students to help at consultations. The latter was an arrangement that ardent supporters of *puériculture* such as Adolphe Pinard and Gaston Variot hoped to make universal.[78]

P. Pecker, a physician in Maule (Seine-et-Oise), found another useful task for "lady patrons" in maternal and infant welfare. Beginning in 1893 poor women were eligible for medical assistance in a hospital at childbirth, but Pecker found that this arrangement still left most pregnant women without the necessary protection. For one thing, medical care was only a small part of what they needed. In addition, he believed, married women with children could not reasonably be expected to leave their children and husband to enter a maternity hospital. Pecker recruited volunteers from among the local bourgeoisie who already had some familiarity with the hygiene of pregnancy and childbirth to distribute material assistance to poor women. He trained the volunteers to recognize the signs of eclampsia and puerperal infection and to understand the advantages of breast-

---

77. *Crèche laïque de la Villette* (Paris: n.p., n.d), p. 10; Rathelot, "L'oeuvre du lait gratuit aux enfants pauvres du 1er âge," *Congrès national d'assistance*, vol. 2, p. 194.

78. Charles Delplanque, *Assistance aux enfants du premier âge privés de ressources (avant et après la naissance): Fonctionnement des consultations du Bureau de bienfaisance de Lille* (Lille: Wilmot-Courtecuisse, 1910), p. 23; Cassoute, *Oeuvre des nourrissons de Marseille: Fonctionnement et résultats* (Marseilles: Imprimerie marseillaise, 1908), p. 3; Marois, *Les Consultations de nourrissons dans l'Yonne en 1910*, pp. 8, 11.

feeding so that they could pass on their knowledge to their clients. The Société des dames mauloises also provided a nurse to do the housework while the patient was in bed.[79] The society attracted a great deal of public attention, and physicians in at least eight other towns followed Pecker's lead and formed similar organizations in their own communities.[80]

Pecker believed that the state should provide generous financial assistance to enable women to take a three- or four-month maternity leave but he also believed that the use of volunteers had an inherent value of its own. Only mothers, he argued, possessed a true understanding of suffering motherhood and the tenderness and compassion that could comfort women in distress. Furthermore, wealthy women would get satisfaction and useful experience through the work and would learn the importance of breast-feeding in fulfilling their patriotic maternal mission. Pecker's term for the Dames mauloises, "*ambulancières maternelles*" (literally, "maternal ambulance nurses"), had military connotations that were not accidental. Women's primary role in developing France's military strength was childbearing, but an understanding of scientific hygiene, Pecker predicted, would be useful when women were called upon to nurse wounded soldiers.[81]

Republican politicians propagated an ideal of the Republican woman, a mother not only to her own children but to the children of the poor as well, inspired by patriotism rather than by religion and guided by physicians rather than by priests. Their gospel was that of scientific hygiene. In Pecker's vision, Louis Pasteur's status approached that of a secular saint. "Rendering grateful homage to PASTEUR with you," he told the Dames mauloises, "we hope to have demonstrated to you that France still possesses the deserved privilege of spreading his benefits to all of humanity through its scientists. . . . But we have above all wanted to sow in your minds the need to know PASTEUR better, for to know him is to dare to save oneself, it is to safeguard children; to know him is not to be a danger to one's

79. Deuxième Congrès international des oeuvres et institutions féminines (1900), *Compte rendu des travaux*, vol. 4, pp. 289–90; P. Pecker, *La puériculture par l'assistance scientifique maternelle à domicile* (Paris: Vigot Frères, 1904).

80. André Jousselin, *Préliminaires de la loi du 27 novembre 1909* (Paris: Librairie de la Société du Recueil Siry, 1910), pp. 110–11; *Association des dames de Briey: Oeuvre d'assistance maternelle à domicile* (Paris: L'emancipatrice, 1902).

81. Pecker, *La puériculture par l'assistance scientifique maternelle à domicile*, p. 133.

neighbor, it is also to love one's country, and finally it is to serve that glorious France, illuminated by its immortal children, in the first rank of whom we see PASTEUR."[82]

These men honored women who gave themselves to charity, just as they glorified history and the masters of thought and science. Marie Béquet de Vienne, founder of the Oeuvre de l'allaitement maternel—essentially a secular version of the Société de charité maternelle—was the embodiment of this ideal. When she died in 1913 a number of prominent politicians spoke in her memory. Paul Strauss, a Radical Republican, employed religious metaphors in his eulogy, describing her "face so proud and fine, her eyes of clarity and of clairvoyance, and her hands, hands of a patrician woman or a sister of charity, hands of gentleness or pardon, hands of a madonna or a stained-glass saint." Georges Martin, a physician and politician, emphasized that Béquet was a "great lay philanthropist," a woman of "purely rationalist philosophy," who also possessed in the highest degree the qualities of solidarity, goodness, fraternity, and charity.[83] She was living proof that such attributes were naturally compatible.

This ideology defined the context in which French women tried to carve out their public niche. As in the United States, Canada, and other western European nations, women in France seeking to expand their professional opportunities, political rights, and a public voice linked these goals with their social reform work. More than women in the United States, French women faced severe institutional and ideological constraints on these efforts. Not only did the government pursue a policy of using private charities to carry out its maternal and child welfare agenda, thereby subjecting these agencies to close supervision, but the population crisis produced antifeminist rhetoric that harshly criticized women's aspirations to any role but a maternal one. In addition, French political philosophy generally—from conservative Catholicism to Social Catholicism to solidarism—condemned liberal individualism as antisocial and ultimately as unpatriotic.[84] Though French women's rights advocates and female so-

82. Ibid., pp. 171–72.

83. Bulletin de l'Oeuvre de l'allaitement maternel et des refuges-ouvroirs pour les femmes enceintes, December 1913.

84. See Offen, "Depopulation, Nationalism, and Feminism in Fin-de-Siècle France," pp. 654, 661–62, 668, 672–74; Karen Offen, "Aspects of the Woman Ques-

cial reformers frequently demanded greater opportunities to participate in the development and administration of maternal and child health policy, they did so in language that emphasized their responsibilities rather than their rights, and they did not reject pronatalist ideology or the notion that maternity was their fundamental duty. In practice they acquiesced in viewing their effective role in social policy in terms of a charitable model rather than an activist one.

French Women's Organizations and Public Policy

In the late nineteenth century, prominent women's rights activists, including the founding members and officers of the Conseil national des femmes françaises, were among the principal benefactors of charitable institutions aiding mothers and infants. Conscious of class differences and the rigidity of class boundaries, wealthy French feminists believed that they had a responsibility to give of their own time and resources to those who were less fortunate. They appealed less to the traditional Catholic ideals of female charity than to the modern philosophy of solidarism, but their work was similar in many ways to that of their Catholic sisters.

The oldest of the non-Catholic maternal and infant welfare institutions was the Oeuvre de l'allaitement maternel, founded in 1876 by Marie Béquet de Vienne to propagate breast-feeding, primarily through the assistance of poor mothers. Breast-feeding women received bread, meat, wine, medicine, fuel, and a complete layette from the organization; women who, according to a physician's certificate, could not breast-feed were given coupons for milk. Frequent and sometimes unannounced visits by the patrons were supposed to preclude fraud.[85] The visitors also gave personal gifts to the most worthy mothers and intervened on their behalf with landlords and employers. In 1892 the society extended its work to include a refuge for pregnant women; it added a second refuge in 1904, and in 1910 opened a

tion during the Third Republic," *Third Republic/ Troisième Republique* 3–4 (1977): 3–6; "Defining Feminism: A Comparative Historical Approach," *Signs* 14 (1988): 145–47; Angus McLaren, *Sexuality and Social Order* (New York: Holmes and Meier, 1983), pp. 165, 154–55.

85. *Actes du Congrès international des oeuvres et institutions féminines* (Paris: Bibliothèque des Annales economiques, 1890), pp. 38–40.

convalescent home. Radical Republican politicians and officials including Paul Strauss considered the Oeuvre to be an ideal private
welfare institution because it was completely secular and nonpolitical.
Hence in 1913 it received state subsidies to the tune of eighteen thousand francs.[86]

Another institution popular with public officials and also generously funded was the Pouponnière of Porchefontaine, a unique institution created by wealthy Mme Charpentier. Maurice Lauzel called
the Pouponnière the realization of Fourier's "Pouponnat" (the section
of the phalanstery where infants were cared for), but in fact it was a
kind of group wet-nursing establishment. Working mothers could
send their infants to the Pouponnière for about the same price they
would pay to a private nurse. The institution housed single mothers,
each of whom nursed her own child and the child of a paying client
and also cared for an older child. To prevent epidemics of contagious
diseases the Pouponnière had rigorous hygienic regulations: the nurses
were quarantined, visiting parents were restricted to specified rooms,
new children underwent a period of isolation before they entered the
general population, and the entire environment was kept as sterile as
possible. These children were probably the most perfectly hygienic
children in France; they were even examined daily by the institution's
physician.[87]

This arrangement met with the approval of public welfare officials
and most physicians because it allowed women to work without
effectively condemning their children to death. It also provided support and protection for single mothers and their children in a more
"moralizing" form than outright charity. The director of the Assistance publique of Paris called upon private associations to create similar institutions throughout the country as a means of keeping from
desperation some of the thousands of women who abandoned their
children each year.[88] The cost of maintaining the institution was quite
high, and financial difficulties almost closed it in 1901. Thanks to the
efforts of Paul Strauss, however, the Pouponnière received a grant

---

86. Ministre de l'intérieur, "Rapport sur l'emploi du crédit ouvert au Ministre de
l'intérieur pour subventionner aux oeuvres d'assistance maternelle et de protection du
premier âge," pp. 447–51; Bulletin de l'Oeuvre de l'allaitement maternel et des refuges-
ouvroirs pour les femmes enceintes, July 1918: 19.
87. Une expérience sociale: Société maternelle parisienne la Pouponnière (n.d.).
88. Ibid., p. 23.

of 31,000 francs from the state lottery funds in addition to its 3,000-franc grant from the minister of the interior and 6,500 francs from the municipal council of Paris. By 1913 the Pouponnière was a favorite of the authorities, and it received a larger grant from the state than did any other private welfare institution except the Société de charité maternelle of Paris.[89]

The *cantines maternelles,* free restaurants for nursing mothers, offered free meals without prior investigation of the recipients' need. Any woman who came to the door and showed that she was lactating was immediately enrolled, under a false name if she chose. M. and Mme Henri Coullet opened the first free restaurants for nursing women in 1904 and 1905, but the bulk of the capital and leadership for most of the *cantines maternelles* in Paris came from women. Supporters of the organization persistently defended it against the charge that it was open to abuse. They wanted to create an atmosphere of dignity and freedom: trusting the beneficiaries degraded them less than would an intrusive home investigation. The patrons purportedly derived great joy from seeing the women feel at home in this healthy atmosphere and open their hearts to the wealthy women who offered them respect and affectionate sympathy.[90] Charging a nominal fee would have *extended* the clientele, supporters argued, since only those who really needed the food would consent to accept it for free and professional beggars stayed away because only food, milk, and medicine were distributed.[91]

The cantines' strict adherence to the principle of trust was remarkable, and probably possible only in a strongly pronatalist context, in which there was a rhetorical consensus that nursing mothers were almost holy. The absence of any investigation, the administrators argued, was a symbolic realization of the absolute equality of all mothers; they paid for their food with the milk they fed their children.[92] Beginning in 1908 the *cantine maternelle* of the 18th arrondissement required all women who came regularly to the meals to attend an infant health consultation; the number of meals served declined

89. Ibid., pp. 28–29; Ministre de l'intérieur, "Rapport sur l'emploi du crédit ouvert au ministre de l'intérieur," p. 447.

90. Cantine maternelle du XVIIIe arrondissement, *Compte rendu,* 1911, p. 14.

91. Ibid., 1909–10, pp. 5–7; Georges Cahen, *L'autre guerre: Essais d'assistance et d'hygiène sociales, 1905–1920* (Nancy: Berger-Levault, 1920), p. 59.

92. Cantine maternelle du XVIIIe arrondissement, *Compte rendu,* 1909–10, p. 7.

drastically, from 23,778 in 1906–7 to 16,433 in 1907–8.[93] As the administrators admitted, women clearly found this requirement to be an unwelcome intrusion. Nonetheless the *cantine* stuck to it; the end goal, after all, was the children's health. In a sense, the mothers were seen as the paid nurses of their own children, but the institution had a moral purpose as well as a material one: the freely given food and respect of the clients' privacy constituted a kind of homage to maternity. Supporters argued that the poor women, many of them single, thus learned self-respect, came to love their children, and underwent a form of social salvation as they found their true place in society.

Essentially these institutions served as a non-Catholic alternative to the Société de charité maternelle. Like the older organization, the new ones provided human and material resources that enabled the state to avoid granting women and children a right to public assistance. The newer institutions, however, served the political aims of Radical Republicans rather than those of conservative aristocratic and church leaders.

Though they emphasized the feminine nature of their benevolence, the organizers of these institutions solicited male leadership. Twenty women and twenty men administered the Oeuvre de l'allaitement maternel; the men dealt with questions of finance and supervised the medical services, and the women directed the distribution of material assistance and operated the refuge.[94] When Béquet died in 1913, none of her women colleagues felt worthy of succeeding her as president. They decided to name two women vice presidents and to ask Paul Bar, a member of the Académie de médecine, to accept the presidency.[95] The Oeuvre nouvelle des crèches parisiennes, an organization that maintained day nurseries for the children of working mothers, had a central committee composed primarily of men and all-male medical and judicial committees, though women made up the vast majority of the patrons.[96]

93. Ibid., 1907–8, pp. 7–8; Cahen, *L'autre guerre*, p. 81.
94. *Actes du Congrès international des oeuvres et institutions féminines,* p. 39.
95. *Bulletin de l'Oeuvre de l'allaitement maternel et des refuges-ouvroirs pour les femmes enceintes,* December 1914: 21.
96. *Oeuvre nouvelle des crèches parisiennes,* March 1904, pp. 10–11.

French Women and Public Policy

Although these women did not reject the idea that France's survival depended on increasing the birthrate, to a certain extent they tried to reframe the pronatalist debate so as to draw attention to the needs and rights of women. They argued, for example, that populationist measures would be more effective if women were allowed a voice in the making and implementation of policies. The Conseil national des femmes françaises, for example, passed a resolution in favor of resurrecting and expanding the local commissions mandated by the Roussel Law, arguing that male physicians were not qualified to oversee the daily care of children. The same organization voted to petition the minister of the interior to retain female inspectors overseeing the care of wards of the state.[97]

Béquet de Vienne, speaking at a general meeting of the Oeuvre de l'allaitment maternel, complained that male policy makers were unwilling to recognize certain causes of depopulation, such as paternal irresponsibility and women's fears of humiliation and poverty. Female juries, she suggested, would understand why single mothers resorted to abortion or infanticide. If the state wanted children, it must see that pregnant women were surrounded with respect and provided with assistance.[98] Gabrielle Chapuis, writing in *Féminisme intégral,* a militant feminist journal, also connected her call for political rights to depopulation. The nation was in danger, she argued, because women were slaves, dependent completely on the whims of men. In the interests of their children, she concluded, women must have the right to manage their finances, administer public funds, and take part in decisions about international affairs and social welfare.[99]

Women could no longer envision childbearing with enthusiasm or even equanimity, the suffragist C. L. de Ferrer observed; because

97. Moniez, *Les commissions locales du protection du premier ĝe,* pp. 1–2; *Action féminine* 10 (1912): 363; Mme Mariceau, "Les femmes administratrices dans établissments publics d'assistance en France," in Deuxième Congrès international des oeuvres et institutions féminines (1900), *Compte rendu des travaux,* vol. 2, pp. 150–54.

98. Quoted in Sicard de Plauzoles, *La maternité et la défense nationale contre la dépopulation* (Paris: V. Giard et E. Brière, 1909), pp. 88–90.

99. Gabrielle Chapuis, "Dépopulation," *Féminisme intégrale,* April 1913.

of unjust laws, maternity brought them only pain. This, she argued, was one of the primary causes of depopulation: "France needs mothers who are happy, protected, aided in their noble duty of maternity."[100] The handful of feminists who openly supported birth control evoked images of suffering motherhood in their condemnations of pronatalism. Writing in the Neo-Malthusian journal *Rénovation,* Mme Membra Jard urged women to leave their cradles empty until they could be certain the children they placed there would not suffer. "Oh pitiful mother!" the radical Nelly Roussel proclaimed, "who would have been queen among bees and who is a slave among men!"[101]

Despite the sympathy they expressed for the plight of working-class mothers, most of the Republican women activists shared the concerns of male bourgeois Republicans about the threat that class conflict and depopulation posed to the nation. In 1900 the section on hygiene of the Congrès international de la condition et les droits de femmes voted in favor of a resolution that a minimum of one month of rest in a maternity hospital or convalescent home be imposed on indigent mothers after childbirth to provide care for the mother and child while preventing possible misuse of the assistance. While some objected that such legislation would be oppressive, especially to women with other children, the view that prevailed was that of Marguerite Durand, who argued that the state had a right to intervene in the family in order to protect the child, just as it had a right to take a young man into the army. There were times, another participant insisted, when it was necessary to force people to take care of themselves.[102]

It was natural, then, for the government to turn to bourgeois

---

100. C. L. de Ferrer, *Pourquoi voteraient-elles? Cahiers exposant quelques-unes des revendications féministes les plus urgentes à solutionner pour le relèvement de la natalité en France* (Paris: Publications encyclopédiques et littéraires, 1910), p. 16; Gabrielle Chapuis, "Epouses et mères," *Féminisme intégral,* April 1913; "Dépopulation."

101. Mme Membra Jard, "Autour des Berceaux," *Rénovation* 1:3 (1911): 2; *Rénovation* 2:1 (1912): 1. See also *Congrès international de la condition et des droits des femmes* (Paris: Imprimerie des arts et manufactures, 1901), pp. 92–93; Deuxième Congrès international des oeuvres et institutions féminines (1900), *Compte rendu des travaux,* vol. 2, p. 62; "Voeux émis par la section d'hygiène du Conseil national des femmes françaises...," n.d. (Archives nationales, F²² 446); Ferrer, *Pourquoi voteraient-elles?* p. 62; Conseil supérieur de l'assistance publique, *Comptes-rendus,* Fascicule No. 37, Sessions de janvier 1892.

102. *Congrès international de la condition et des droits des femmes,* pp. 70, 86–91.

women for assistance in policing the benefits distributed under the maternity-leave legislation, named after Paul Strauss, passed in July 1913. The Strauss Law required all female workers in commerce and industry to take a maternity leave of two months and provided partial compensation for the loss of wages. To receive her benefits a woman had to suspend her usual occupation, rest as much as necessary, and fulfill the hygienic requirements for her own health and that of her child.

The welfare bureau in each commune was responsible for designating someone to make sure that these conditions were fulfilled. It was not necessary, argued the minister of the interior, to create new civil servants for this purpose because the rapidly growing private infant health agencies provided a natural source of volunteers. In towns where such an institution was lacking, visitors could be drawn from among "mothers of families enjoying universal regard for their eminent honesty, their moral value, their spirit of generous liberalism which makes them accept without effort the absolute respect of all political opinions, all religious beliefs as well as all philosophical convictions." The minister referred to the natural sympathy and deep instinct of solidarity between two women: "Taking advantage of that touching instinct, so strong in the hearts of the women of France, it is impossible not to succeed in creating around poor mothers and their newborns a network of enlightened and active affection which will undoubtedly constitute an effective insurance against infant mortality."[103]

To participate in the administration of the law, a private organization had to receive the approval first of the Conseil supérieur de l'assistance publique and then of the ministers of the interior and finance. The group had to show that it could supply the requisite number of volunteers and that it was recognized by all as "completely divorced from any denominational or political concerns."[104] M.-L.

---

103. Ministre de l'intérieur, Circulaire, *Journal official: Bulletin des lois*, August 11, 1913: 7244. On the Strauss Law generally, see Mary Lynn Stewart, *Women, Work, and the French State: Labour Protection and Social Patriarchy, 1879–1919* (Kingston, Ont.: McGill-Queen's University Press, 1989), chap. 8.

104. M.-L. Bérot-Berger, *La dame visiteuse dans la bienfaisance publique ou privée et dans le contrôle de la Loi Strauss, protectrice de la maternité* (Paris: M. Giard et E. Brière, 1914), p. 72. Though the recipients were required to receive the visitors with "deference," the visitors were prohibited from exerting any moral, religious, or political

Bérot-Berger, who had devoted herself to organizing and training visitors for her local *mutualité maternelle,* criticized the application process as unnecessarily long. Considering the time and devotion the visitor's work required, she argued, the government was adding to their burden additional responsibilities and expenses that no government budget offered to pay.[105]

Given this and other obstacles it is doubtful how many communes made use of volunteers for this work. A commission of the municipal council of Paris appointed in 1913 to report on the application of the law recommended limiting the involvement of the Mutualité maternelle for the time being. The Assistance publique of Paris already employed certified nurses and midwives to supervise women who received public maternity care and medical assistance, and these women could easily take on the new tasks.[106] For some communities, however, the new law presented great difficulties. In St.-Etienne, for example, the primary task of the local welfare bureau had been to draw up the list of people eligible for free medical assistance; the bureau did not have the personnel to deal with the twelve hundred or so expected applicants for maternity benefits. Though there was a *mutualité maternelle* in the town, an official of the welfare bureau thought the recruitment of enough visitors would be more difficult than the minister suggested.[107]

In Bérot-Berger's home of St.-Quentin the local *mutualité maternelle* was well prepared to take on the supervisory service. The organization already had a comprehensive system of neighborhood visitors for its members, and Bérot-Berger was eager for her organization to contribute to the implementation of the new law. Though she believed that the government should subsidize the administrative costs of visiting, she also believed that the work was best performed by volunteers, and her vision of the "lady visitor" matched that of the minister. "Let us ask the real French women," she wrote, "devoted wives and mothers, to be the social servants

pressure and were specifically enjoined against persuading the parents to have their children baptized. *Revue philanthropique* 36 (1915): 205.

105. Bérot-Berger, *La dame visiteuse,* p. 14.

106. Conseil municipal de Paris, *Rapport au nom de la 5e commission concernant l'application, à Paris, des lois des 17 juin et 30 juillet 1913, sur l'assistance aux femmes en couches* (Préfecture de Police, D.B. 64).

107. Bureau d'assistance de la ville de St.-Etienne, *La mise en application de deux nouvelles lois sociales* (St.-Etienne: Société de l'imprimerie Théolier, 1913), p. 14.

of wage-earning women in their maternal crisis."[108] They had served their apprenticeship in raising their own children, and the natural sympathy between two women who shared the same suffering and the same noble destiny would see them through. Those who possessed the womanly virtues of tact, simplicity, discretion, vigilance, integrity, and gentle firmness, Bérot-Berger predicted, would have the greatest success.

While many criticized the legislation for limiting the categories of women it covered, few thought to question the supervisory provisions. A leaflet printed by a socialist-feminist organization in Lille, however, warned women that a recipient of maternity benefits must open her home to the visitor appointed by the welfare bureau, even in the absence of her husband. She would find herself "surrendered to the influence—often harmful to the working-class family—of a 'lady of charity,' new model."[109] As the leaflet pointed out, despite all the rhetoric about natural sympathy, comfort, and solidarity, the role of the visitor was to make sure the recipient followed certain rules, and she had the power to have the aid withdrawn. Bérot-Berger warned the prospective visitor, for example, to be friendly with the husband and children and not to give speeches or make complaints, but she emphasized that at least some visits must be unannounced, since only unexpected inspections could be effective. The visitor must also distribute the cash benefits in installments, because the threat of withdrawing them was her most powerful instrument of persuasion.[110] While virtually all those who commented publicly on the law accepted this concept of supervision, it is quite possible that working-class women viewed the visits as an unwanted intrusion.

"Lady patrons" were essential to the policy makers' vision. They were the police of the system, making sure that women actually used their free milk, charitable gifts, and state or private maternity compensation in the manner intended. Unlike American visiting nurses, who claimed authority based on their training, French visitors were deemed qualified to supervise and instruct other women by virtue of their social position. Though ostensibly the personification of the new

---

108. Bérot-Berger, *La dame visiteuse,* p. 14.
109. Secrétariat ouvrier d'hygiène de Lille, *Les droits de la maternité ouvrière (lois des 17 juin et 30 juillet 1913 sur l'assistance aux femmes en couches); conseils aux femmes* (n.d.).
110. Bérot-Berger, *La dame visiteuse,* p. 23.

political theory of social solidarity, they helped to maintain existing class distinctions and deference through the time-honored aristocratic tradition of charitable visiting.

The era of the "lady patron" in maternal and infant welfare was short-lived, however. Charitable visitors, when available, were useful in supervising poor mothers, but as programs to protect infants expanded to cover other social groups, their upper-class aura no longer provided them with sufficient authority. In addition, schools for nurses and in child hygiene began to turn out personnel trained to do the job, especially during and after World War I, when the American Red Cross imported and funded visiting nurses.

Thus in France, as in other western countries, women's voluntary organizations were a critical force in the transition from private charity to public welfare. Bourgeois women's participation in late-nineteenth- and early-twentieth-century social reform movements grew out of domestic ideology and charitable activities rooted in religious impulses, but the institutions created by these movements ultimately produced new professional opportunities for women. In France, however, as in other states with well-established, centralized bureaucracies, women had little opportunity to voice a distinctive female perspective in policy making. The extensive intervention in private charity by the state on the one hand and the Catholic church on the other also inhibited the development of a woman-centered approach to maternal and child welfare. The particular dynamics of French politics further defined women's activism. The anticlerical Republican state and the Catholic church each sought the loyalty of the nation's women, molders of the next generation. Women took sides in this struggle; through their voluntary work they did their duty to God or the Republic. Few were able to transcend the bounds of nationalism and patriotism; for the most part French feminists articulated their demands as good mothers and patriots.

For this reason it was not uncommon to hear women's charity described through military metaphors. Scientists had prepared all the arms necessary to combat infant mortality, Olga Veil-Picard told the members of the Croix blanche, and "these marvelous arms are not too heavy for the shoulders of women! Thus it is for them that it is most fitting to make use of them bravely to support the nation's internal defense." Veil-Picard herself was president of the Pouponnière de Porchefontaine. Women, she proclaimed, should claim the privilege of forming the army of "auxiliaries for the propagation of infant hygiene."[111]

111. Olga J. Veil-Picard, *La puériculture à Porchefontaine* (Conférence faite à la Croix-blanche—Vie heureuse, le 27 janvier 1913), p. 2.

4

American Women and the "Better Baby" Movement

American women did not aspire to be the ladies' auxiliary of the infant health movement; they participated not only as fund raisers and service providers but also as activists who believed they had a mission to arouse the general public to take responsibility for protecting children's lives. The distinctive approach to infant health represented by this popular infant health movement reflected the personal experience of the members of women's clubs and mothers' congresses; in addition, it was a natural outgrowth of their larger mission to improve the moral and physical quality of their communities. Many women government officials, particularly the staff of the U.S. Children's Bureau, saw themselves as the leaders of a grass-roots movement and called upon members of local women's organizations to take initiative in their own communities. At the same time, women physicians and other professionals were in an ambivalent position: they sought to reconcile their dedication to and identification with the voluntary women's organizations on the one hand with their ties to the medical profession and professional institutions on the other. These women served as mediators between the professional and popular infant health movements, working to channel the energy generated by popular campaigns in a direction they saw as constructive.

Though women in many countries sought a voice in politics, particularly in social policy, not all were equally successful. In her work on the reformer Florence Kelley, Kathryn Kish Sklar argues that in the United States the limited nature of the state created opportunities for women. The power of the evangelical religious tradition, the disestablishment of religion, and the inability of the formal polity to address the problems associated with industrialization all worked to empower voluntary associations. Women's access to higher education and the politicization of domestic life through the ideology of republican motherhood helped to empower women's voluntarism in particular.[1] The history of the women's infant health movement illustrates that although women's organizations in the United States rarely enjoyed the benefits of public financial support, the absence of government interference left them with a degree of freedom that French women's organizations did not enjoy. When the U.S. government did intervene in the infant health movement it often had a female face.

In addition, however, the power of the women's infant health movement in the United States derived from the vitality of local organizations in small towns and rural areas as much as from the urban settlement movement. The decentralized nature of public health and welfare in the United States, the scarcity of formal institutions in small towns and rural areas, and the informal nature of local politics all combined to create a political space for women's activism and institution building. Paula Baker has described this phenomenon in terms of the separation that developed in the nineteenth century between the formal male political culture of party politics and office holding and a female political culture that operated informally as a kind of interest-group politics. In the Progressive Era, she argues, women successfully campaigned through their voluntary nonpartisan organizations for legislation to address social problems; in doing so, they "surrendered to government functions that had belonged to the woman's sphere."[2]

---

1. Kathryn Kish Sklar, "Explaining the Power of Women's Political Culture in the Creation of the American Welfare State, 1890–1930," in *Mothers of a New World,* ed. Seth Koven and Sonya Michel (New York: Routledge, 1993); Ellen Fitzpatrick, *Endless Crusade: Women Social Scientists and Progressive Reform* (New York: Oxford University Press, 1990), pp. 79–80; Kathryn Kish Sklar, "Hull House in the 1890s: A Community of Women Reformers," *Signs* 10 (1985): 658–77; Estelle Freedman, "Separatism as Strategy: Female Institution Building, 1870–1930," *Feminist Studies* 5 (1979): 512–29.

2. Paula Baker, "The Domestication of Politics: Women and American Political Society, 1780–1920," *American Historical Review* 89 (1984): 644, 647.

The infant health movement was imbued with the ideology of women's political culture. White women activists perceived indifference, not hostility, as their primary obstacle and believed that the issues they addressed lay outside the bounds of partisan politics. Local women's organizations identified themselves as part of a national movement of women fighting for the recognition of women's needs and concerns, but they did not necessarily see local politics as adversarial. They had faith that the organs of power in their communities would respond if only women spoke out.

The popular infant health movement in the United States therefore reflected the composition and ideology of the organized women's movement. One of the most important goals of the movement was to provide professional medical guidance and care desperately sought by many women, especially those in isolated rural communities. At the same time the movement carried the racism and class bias of the two major white women's organizations of the period, the National Congress of Mothers and Parent-Teacher Associations and the General Federation of Women's Clubs. This perspective was most obvious in the baby health contests, events that first mobilized women's organizations around infant health in large numbers and rewarded mothers whose children approached certain standards of racial, aesthetic, anthropometric, and psychological perfection.

The orientation toward improving the race was also reminiscent of older concerns. Something of the concept of Republican virtue lingered in the efforts to provide the proper environment and necessary resources for the rearing of healthy children and good citizens. The "Better Baby" movement, as the popular infant health movement came to be called, often included activities designed, like patriotic celebrations, to reinforce belief in a mythical harmonious community. The zeal with which women carried out these programs suggest that they took quite seriously their own role in maintaining the Republic, not through formal political institutions but through home, church, and school.

Women's Organizations and Infant Health

The maternal and infant welfare movement united women with diverse political agendas who nonetheless all shared a maternalist ideology. Local suffrage organizations, for example, sometimes employed maternalist rhetoric in their struggle for political rights. Like French feminists they argued that children and the family would be better protected by a government in which women participated; they frequently cited the example of New Zealand, and sometimes western states, pointing out that where women could vote the infant mortality rates were low.[3] The first women's organization to seize on infant mortality as a critical issue, however, was the National Congress of Mothers, which was committed to the preservation of traditional gender roles, did not challenge paternal authority in the home, and avoided taking a stand on suffrage.

This organization, whose early leaders were the wealthy wives of prominent political figures, had a conservative moral agenda from its founding in 1897 and, while it allowed for some participation by African-American women, was very much a white-dominated organization; few of its white affiliates allowed African-American women to participate as equals. One of the foremost agents of the ideology of "scientific motherhood," the congress urged women to employ their professional expertise in the public sphere as well as in the home. Health was an important concern of the congress—five of the twenty-four papers delivered at the first national conference focused on health—but never as an issue distinct from morality. As Helen Gardener of Boston suggested, "We can not hope to have a moral race until we have a mentally and physically sound and sane race. All immorality is a lapse from sound physical and mental health."[4]

Edith Howe introduced the subject of infant mortality at the na-

3. For example, see the following articles in the *Woman's Journal:* "Conserving the Children," February 14, 1914: 53; Alice Stone Blackwell, "Miss Lathrop's Report," February 21, 1914: 60; " 'The Baby Crop,' " August 1, 1914: 226; "Kansas Women Save Babies," January 2, 1915: 7; "Norway Protects Its Mothers," January 2, 1915: 8; "Let Us Save the Babies," May 30, 1914: 172; "Wanted, Better Babies," February 26, 1916: 68; "Free States Take New Steps in Saving Children's Lives," July 15, 1916: 227. Also, letters to Julia Lathrop from Anna DeBaum (3/14/16); Esther Eaton (10/14/14); Celeste Claiborne Garruth (3/30/16) (Records of the U.S. Children's Bureau, National Archives, Washington, D.C., 13–6).

4. Helen H. Gardener, "The Moral Responsibility of Women in Heredity," in National Congress of Mothers, *The Work and Words of the National Congress of Mothers (First Annual Session)* (New York: D. Appleton, 1897), p. 136. See also Mary Madeleine Ladd-Taylor, "Mother-work: Ideology, Public Policy, and the Mothers' Movement, 1890–1930," Ph.D. diss., Yale University, 1986, pp. 72–75, 77–78, 115–16, 118, 135.

tional convention of the National Congress of Mothers in February 1909. She described the horrors of ignorant motherhood and an indifferent community: bad ventilation, open ash cans, milk left in the sun, unwashed milk bottles, soothing syrups, and untrained midwives. "We shall find this flood of evil ever rising to destroy the babies of our land," she warned, "One, and only one, great power can stem the tide—mother's love, informed, organized, militant. Babies could be saved, Howe argued, if mothers knew the causes of infant deaths; if physicians and nurses taught women how to save them; if the schools made children physically fit for education; if health officials understood that "teaching mothers is civic economy"; and if taxpayers voted budgets to provide for the education of mothers in the care of babies.[5]

While in a sense Howe blamed mothers for infant mortality, she saw maternal education as the responsibility of society and called upon women to take leadership in making demands of the community. She asked members of the congress to call local conferences of mothers, women's club members, social workers, health officers, school superintendents, physicians, and nurses and to send delegates to the planned national Conference on the Prevention of Infant Mortality.[6] Like French women who patronized maternal charities, Howe saw women's public activity as a natural outgrowth of their maternal role. She believed, however, that women's power lay not in the individual relationships between wealthy women and poor but in the force of collective action.

Howe was elected national chair of child hygiene work for the National Congress of Mothers. On her return to New York City the philanthropist George W. Wilder donated funds to be placed at her disposal so that she could launch a national campaign to teach mothers about infant hygiene. The Delineator, a New York–based women's magazine, served as the publicity organ for the campaign and published monthly reports of Howe's work. The magazine provided funds for Schools for Mothers in New York City, models that Howe urged women all over the country to emulate. The organizers attracted mothers by taking advantage of the public school as a com-

5. Edith Howe, "Saving the Babies," National Congress of Mothers Magazine 4 (1909): 48.
6. Ibid., p. 49.

munity center. The principal of each school invited mothers to a
"sociable," where they met the physician and nurse who had offered
their services. The physician held weekly classes for mothers where
he or she weighed and examined each child. The nurse was available
at the school for part of every day, made home visits to recent mothers
to show them how to follow the physician's instructions, and held
classes for pregnant women. She also gave attention to the older
children in the families, and she complained to the municipal Tenement House and Health departments and to landlords in an effort to
improve the sanitary conditions of the babies' homes.[7]

The *Delineator* Schools for Mothers basically conformed to the
model provided by the New York Milk Committee stations, and
they were initially most popular in urban areas. By February 1910,
a year after the launching of the campaign, women in New Orleans,
Denver, Providence, Philadelphia, Hackensack, New Jersey, and
Frankford, Pennsylvania, had held *Delineator* Mothers' Conferences.
In these cities, the mothers' clubs generally played an auxiliary role
in infant welfare work. They facilitated the work of public health
officials or provided some of the labor that meager public funds would
not otherwise support. In Philadelphia, for example, mothers' clubs
provided the volunteers for the city's first, abortive, campaign against
infant mortality in the summer of 1908. The following year representatives of the Mothers' Congress attended a meeting in the mayor's
office to address the problem, along with representatives from the
children's hospitals, schools, the Bureau of Health, and private organizations. Mrs. Frederic Schoff, president of the National Congress
of Mothers, was named secretary of the new Philadelphia Alliance
for the Care of Babies.

Physicians already employed by the city held consultations but the
Bureau of Health could not supply visiting nurses. Schoff, as head
of the committee on Ward Organization and Audiences, appointed a
woman in each of the forty-seven wards of the city to chair a neighborhood committee. The 19th Ward committee hired a nurse who
visited 554 mothers to instruct them in infant care and feeding and
met each week to keep records of the babies' weights. At the end of
the summer the committee awarded prizes to the babies who had
been weighed most regularly and to those who had gained the most

7. *Delineator*, December 1909: 522.

weight. Over the next few years, the Bureau of Health was able gradually to replace the volunteers with professional nurses paid out of public funds, and the Mothers' Congress dropped out of the picture.[8]

Members of the Rhode Island Congress of Mothers played a similar role in Providence, making it possible for the health commissioner to carry out his program of leaflet distribution, milk inspection, visiting nurses, and milk stations. The women held open meetings in various languages in schools throughout the city for mothers in the district. The program included entertainment and refreshments to attract an audience, an informal talk on infant care by a physician or nurse, and a question period.[9]

Though mothers' clubs played an auxiliary role on the local level, not unlike that of French "lady patrons," the national leaders of the Mothers' Congress quickly articulated a comprehensive child health program. At the 1911 national meeting, members passed a resolution outlining a national child health policy. The resolution recommended that every board of health include a department of child hygiene to work in cooperation with a committee of mothers to reduce infant mortality; that all boards of health employ skilled nurses to visit new mothers to leave literature and offer additional help if necessary; and that all states adopt the model birth-registration law endorsed by the American Medical Association, the American Health Association and the American Association for the Study and Prevention of Infant Mortality.[10] In 1912 the congress publication *Child-Welfare Magazine* announced that the organization had inaugurated an American Child Welfare Campaign, whose goal was "arousing the whole country to a sense of its duty and responsibility to childhood."[11] Though the congress considered education of mothers the key to reducing infant mortality, it blamed society, not mothers, and called for social action. The new program was consistent with the congress's mission, which was, as Schoff described it, to "battle down the old wall of belief that

8. Edith Howe, "The Delineator Mothers' Conference," *Delineator,* September 1909: 223; "Saving the Babies," *Child-Welfare Magazine* 5 (1910): 73.

9. Sybil Avery Perkins, "Child Hygiene in the Rhode Island Congress of Mothers," *Child-Welfare Magazine* 5 (1911): 164.

10. "Resolutions Adopted by the Second International Congress on Child Welfare, National Congress of Mothers," *Child-Welfare Magazine* 5 (1911): 193.

11. "American Child-Welfare Campaign," *Child-Welfare Magazine* 6 (1912): 172.

mother instinct teaches a woman all she needs to know about child nurture."[12]

The General Federation of Women's Clubs did not take a stand on infant health until 1912, when Mrs. W. W. Hutt proposed a campaign that focused on the health education of children, especially girls. Though the federation did not share the National Congress of Mothers' conservative moral perspective, the two organizations approached infant health in similar ways. "Educate a boy," Hutt suggested, "and you educate a man—educate a girl and you educate a whole generation." Women, she argued, could be the "motive power" in educating public opinion about infant mortality. She urged her audience to work for general sanitary measures, medical inspection of schools, open-air schools for weak children, and the improvement of health conditions in stores, factories, and public buildings.[13] To inspire her audience, Hutt told the story of a woman who learned the hard way that mothers had a responsibility to venture outside their homes. This woman stayed at home with her family, never taking time for church, voluntary societies, clubs, or recreation. Because she was unable to find a sanitary dairy, two of her children died from the impure milk she was forced to buy. Her minister advised her to go to the women's society, which took an interest in the issue and urged her to tell the mayor and the city council. The local newspaper helped to publicize the cause; thanks to her action the town now had the cleanest milk of any town of its size in the state.

Hutt's story reflected the images of the American community and of motherhood which came to characterize the "Better Baby" movement. Childrearing was not an individual activity but was reliant on a well-organized, sanitary community. As Hutt's protagonist concluded, "I found I had to go outside my home to know what was going on inside my baby."[14] Women saw themselves as the only representatives of the interests of children and the family, but they also saw the political system as responsive to their demands. Once

12. Mrs. Frederic Schoff, "Parents' Cooperation in Promotion of Child Hygiene," *Transactions of the Fifteenth International Congress on Hygiene and Demography* (1912), vol. 3, p. 294.

13. Mrs. W. W. Hutt, "The Health Cycle," in General Federation of Women's Clubs, *Eleventh Biennial Convention: Official Report* (n.p.: The Federation, 1912), p. 307.

14. Ibid., p. 309.

aroused, churches, voluntary organizations, public officials, and the press would, Hutt believed, work harmoniously to solve social problems.

From "Better Baby" Contest to
Infant Health Conference

In 1912 and 1913 the popular infant health movement gained momentum, largely as a result of the contest. Invented by two Iowa clubwomen and popularized by the *Woman's Home Companion,* the baby health contest was distinctively American. The contest had no link with the male pediatric establishment; it was entirely the creation of women, and it opened the door for the infant health movement to spread from the cities into small towns and rural areas, where women genuinely became its leaders. In 1911, Mary T. Watts and Margaret Clark, a physician, observing that competitive shows had contributed greatly to the improvement of livestock, wondered whether contests could not do the same for human children. When asked to develop a program for the Woman's Hour at the Iowa State Fair, Clark seized the opportunity to try out the idea. In developing the scorecard she drew both on her observations of hospital and clinic work in Europe and on scorecards used for judging livestock. Parents, preparing their children as if for the more familiar baby beauty show, were surprised and in some cases angry that the physicians who were judging the contest based their decisions not on appearance but on such criteria as weight, height, head circumference, and mental development.[15]

The *Woman's Home Companion* launched its Better Baby Campaign in March 1913. "In two generations," the editors predicted, "it may bring about a social revolution, advance civilization by leaps and bounds, make the men and women of the world happier and better."[16] Like the *Delineator,* the *Woman's Home Companion* looked to women as the natural leaders of this new movement for the improvement of the race. The main vehicle of the campaign was the baby health

15. John J. Biddison, " 'Better Babies,' " *Woman's Home Companion,* March 1913: 96; State Chairmen Reports, General Federation of Women's Clubs, *Eleventh Biennial Convention,* p. 481.
16. "Our Page," *Woman's Home Companion,* March 1913: 27.

contest. The magazine offered to furnish one hundred dollars in gold to the top-scoring city baby and the top-scoring rural baby at state fairs, provided that local authorities set aside two hundred dollars for the contest and a women's organization contributed one hundred dollars. It also offered gold, silver, and bronze medals to the winners and runners-up and a "handsomely engraved certificate" to first-prize winners. All parents would receive their child's scorecard in the mail after the contest along with a personal message from the examiners explaining how the child's condition could be improved.[17]

Women's organizations apparently jumped at the opportunity; by March 1914 the *Woman's Home Companion* claimed that contests had been held in every state except West Virginia, New Hampshire, and Utah and that more than 100,000 children had been examined.[18] The publications of the National Congress of Mothers and the General Federation of Women's Clubs reported scores of contests organized by their local affiliates in all parts of the country, and in some states the contest became an annual event. Physicians examined 220 children in Burlington, Vermont, and 250 in Amarillo, Texas. The Mothers' Circle in Montgomery, Alabama, the Jewish Mothers' Alliance of St. Louis, Missouri, and a group of women physicians in Columbus, Ohio, were just a few of the charitable and public health organizations that held contests.[19]

The baby health contest was peculiarly suited to the resources and ideology of American women's organizations; it represented an approach to infant health that was distinct from that of urban public health officials and very different from that of French women's organizations. The concerns of the "Better Baby" Contest were a far cry from the day-to-day practical concerns of the urban visiting nurse, who dealt primarily with the prevention and treatment of infantile diarrhea among poor children. The "defects" discovered by contest judges were not usually lethal, even potentially. Instead, the contest sought the perfection of American babyhood.

Contest organizers insisted that the event was essentially educa-

17. Ibid.

18. Anna Steese Richardson, "A Year of Better Babies," *Woman's Home Companion*, March 1914: 19–20.

19. "State News," *Child-Welfare Magazine* 8 (1914): 179–93; *Woman's Home Companion*, May 1913: 3, and October 1913: 90. Numerous other examples are documented in the U.S. Children's Bureau Records, 4–14–2–3–0.

tional because it drew the attention of parents to defects in children whose parents believed they were perfect and taught these parents that science could improve the health and mental development of all babies.[20] The contest thus reflected and perpetuated the myth that American society was classless and without inherent political or social conflicts. Education was the great equalizer; parental ignorance rather than poverty was primarily reponsible for children's health problems. Participation was voluntary, so the contest did not violate the sanctity of the home. The expense of a contest was also easily within the means of a local women's group: all they needed were the resources to publicize the event, a few prizes, and the collaboration of a physician or two.

The baby health contest was essentially a eugenic concept, and in fact some women's organizations sponsored what they called "eugenic contests" or "eugenic exhibitions." By definition, "eugenics" refers to efforts to improve the hereditary characteristics of a breed, but to Progressive reformers it meant much more than selective breeding. Though most of those who supported "Better Baby" contests would probably have agreed that "feeble-minded" people and criminals should not be allowed to marry, proponents of "race betterment" or "eugenics" also advocated the education of children and adults to avoid diseases and activities that could cause congenital weakness, diseases, or deformities in their children. To the members of women's organizations, teaching mothers how to care for their children was also a form of eugenics, because it would improve the physical health of future adults. As the president of the National Congress of Mothers wrote, "The Congress of Mothers has for seventeen years worked for race betterment through better opportunities for the prenatal care of babies, baby-saving, and the physical and moral care of children. If that is not 'race betterment,' what is it?"[21]

In theory, baby health contests were designed to reward women for caring intelligently and knowledgeably for their infants, and poor scores were an incentive to improve. One speaker at a baby health contest held at the Race Betterment Congress in 1914 warned the parents of the winners not to rest on their laurels. Those who were

    20. Lydia A. DeVilbiss, "Education for Parenthood," *Proceedings of the First National Conference on Race Betterment* (Battle Creek, Mich.: Gage Printing Co, 1914), p. 266.
    21. "The President's Desk," *Child-Welfare Magazine* 8 (1914): 248–49.

not winners might do better in the end, he suggested, because they would not succumb to overconfidence but would be careful to apply measures for improvement. Even strong advocates of the contest argued that mothers should not come for the prizes but should be motivated only by the desire for information about child care.[22]

Publicity for the contests, however, focused on the search for the "perfect" baby. Anna Steele Richardson's summaries of contests for the *Woman's Home Companion* often boasted that a perfect baby had been discovered in one town or another. In Knoxville, Tennessee, in 1913, physicians were unable to find a single deviation from the standard in one of the competitors, though they put him through the exam twice. "It was hard," wrote Richardson, "for physicians and committee members to keep the secret."[23] In 1917, Mrs. J. E. Howe of Shreveport, Louisiana, herself the mother of a contest winner, bragged to Julia Lathrop that a baby boy had scored 99 percent in the state scientific contest.[24]

An Iowa newspaper printed the story of young Charles O'Toole, who won the title at the first baby health contest at the Iowa State Fair in 1911. He was the one to beat at the 1912 contest, "when the contestants to outmatch the physical perfection of the title holder begin." When the O'Toole family moved to Chicago, a newspaper took advantage of this event to organize a contest; none of the thousands of Chicago babies weighed and scored could match O'Toole.[25] Undoubtedly, the public attention lavished on such wonders as O'Toole discouraged the participation of less healthy children.

Though the contest was supposed to stimulate parents to care better for their children, not only were some of the scoring points clearly aesthetic and not relevant to health, but not all "defects" marked were correctible. In most contests unhealthy babies received little attention. Usually a series of specialists—in small contests, one or two physicians—examined all babies entered. Those who received the highest scores were called back for a more careful examination to determine the winner. A typical scorecard included height, weight, and circum-

22. Walter F. Martin, "Report of the Better Babies Contest," *Proceedings of the First National Conference on Race Betterment*, p. 621.

23. Anna Steese Richardson, "Better Babies in Cities," *Woman's Home Companion*, August 1913: 4.

24. Mrs. J. Howe to Julia Lathrop, 8/1/17 (U.S. Children's Bureau, 4-15-4-3).

25. *Register and Leader*, August 22, 1912 (clipping in ibid., 4-14-2-3-1).

ference of chest and abdomen; quality of skin, fat, and muscles; sitting poise, walking, and running; bones of skull, spine, chest, and limbs; length, width, and circumference of head; shape of eyes and size of forehead; shape and patency of nose; shape and condition of jaw; and number, shape, size, and condition of teeth. The psychological test included scores for facial and ocular expressions, disposition and energy, and attention.[26]

Dr. Clark insisted that these categories had nothing to do with beauty. Facial and ocular expressions, for example, were influenced by "environment, nervous excitability, contention, and training in intelligence, tractability, attention, imitation and disposition."[27] It is true that in the context of contemporary medical understanding, certain apparently aesthetic points were arguably of medical importance. Bad breath or a nose with a broad, flat bridge, a thick base, very small nostrils and a puffy appearance, for example, indicated a chronic respiratory block of some kind. An open mouth, mouth breathing, irregular teeth, a weak or receding lower jaw, and high arched palate were all signs of nasal obstruction, often by tonsils and adenoids.[28] Nevertheless, baby health contests sometimes did degenerate into beauty contests. At the Eugenic Section of the National Western Stock Show in 1913, cash prizes went not only to the top-scoring boy and girl and the "best rural baby," but also to the children with the best hair and skin, the best eyes ("sight not considered"), the best-formed ears, perfect hands and feet, best speech and mentality, and the most perfect teeth.[29]

The sad story of one contestant, published by the *Woman's Home Companion,* illustrates the absurdity such contests could involve. This child, two years old, received perfect scores on most points of the exam, including the shapes and sizes of her lips and forehead and the shape and patency of her nose. A score of 70 percent on "shape, size and position of ears," however, ruined her chances for a prize. The mother poured out her sad tale to the magazine's representative. She

26. Lucia B. Harriman, "Oregon Mothers Conduct Eugenics Department in State Fair," *Child-Welfare Magazine* 7 (1912): 84.

27. Margaret Clark to Julia Lathrop, 4/12/13 (U.S. Children's Bureau, 4–14–2–3–3).

28. Charles Keen Taylor, *The Physical Examination and Training of Children* (Philadelphia: John C. Winston, 1914), p. 27.

29. Mary E. Bates to Julia Lathrop, 2/18/13 (U.S. Children's Bureau, 4–14–2–3–0).

had noticed the prominence of her daughter's ears at birth and bought a ventilated bonnet for her to sleep in but the child did not like the cap, and her physician, father, relatives, and friends all had agreed that the problem was insignificant. Now, the mother mourned, she could never forgive herself: "It is not because she has lost the prize. . . . It is because I realized that I might have corrected and lessened the disfigurement if I had persevered from the day of her birth."[30]

Not surprisingly, all the children pictured in contest publicity were white, though in a few instances urban child health organzations sponsored separate contests for African-American babies.[31] Certainly, no African-American or Asian child could win a contest if competing with white children, because the scorecards, calling for ratings on features such as the shape of the lips or nose, clearly reflected racial stereotypes and racist anthropological theory. Anthropometry treated physical characteristics as intimately related to mental and social qualities and assumed that Nordic Europeans were superior on all counts. Skull shape and size in particular had long been seen as indicators of intelligence. Progressive reformers focused their efforts on improving people through changing their environment, but the notion that intelligence and democratic institutions and virtues were somehow inherent in Teutonic blood lurked underneath.[32]

The frequent analogy to the stock show and the improvement of livestock suggests that selective breeding was indeed in the minds of the creators of the contests. Lydia DeVilbiss, of the Better Babies Bureau of the *Woman's Home Companion,* was an ardent advocate of birth control as a way to reduce the high fertility of "inferior" races. She associated the "Better Babies" movement with education for parenthood, "characterized by its scientific foundation, its clarity, its sacredness, and its holiness." Better Babies, she wrote, meant Better Boys and Girls, Better Men and Women, and Better Parents.[33]

30. Anna Steese Richardson, " 'Better Babies' in Denver," *Woman's Home Companion,* May 1913: 5.

31. Anna Steese Richardson, "Better Babies in the South," *Woman's Home Companion,* July 1913: 5.

32. Kenneth M. Ludmerer, *Genetics and American Society: A Historical Appraisal* (Baltimore: Johns Hopkins University Press, 1972), p. 22; Donald K. Pickens, *Eugenics and the Progressives* (Nashville, Tenn.: Vanderbilt University Press, 1968), pp. 173–75.

33. DeVilbiss, "Education for Parenthood," pp. 270–71; Grace Meigs, "Work of the Division of Child Hygiene, Topeka, Kansas" (U.S. Children's Bureau, 4–15–2–

Mary Bates, a Denver gynecologist active in the American Baby Health Contest Association, wrote to Lathrop, "The sooner we get all of the people to understand the right of the Baby to Better Birth and the right of the community to immunity to degenerate and diseased stock—human,—the better, and every way that carries the lesson will speed the day when we can have scientific elimination before the birth of the unfit, and someday the scientific culture of the fit."[34] Robbins Gilman, head worker at the University Settlement Society in New York City, proposed a contest with a prize for the baby "whose parents have sought to keep and who have kept his environment best, and, maybe the most important, the child with the best selected parental union." This contest, Gilman wrote, would require extensive investigation of the home environment and the parents' heredity—their age at marriage, their defects and vices—as well as their home sanitation and ventilation and their milk supply.[35]

Extreme eugenists advocated far more public intervention in the medical care and economic support of children than most infant health reformers would have countenanced. DeVilbiss argued that producing a child was a service to the state analagous to military service and proposed that mothers should thus be pensioned if in need.[36] Mary E. DeGarmo of St. Louis, author of such publications as the *United States Perfect Baby Monthly* and *How to Classify Normal, Subnormal, and Abnormal Babies, for State Schools,* proposed the creation of a baby census bureau that would provide complete state supervision of children from infancy onward in order to form their character and vocation. "Perfect baby contests" and birth standardization by mental and physical anthropometric tests would be a regular part of the program.[37]

It is not clear how representative such radical proposals were, but eugenics was a logical element of the ideology of the women's clubs and mothers organizations. Both the National Congress of Mothers

1–8). See Regina Markell Morantz-Sanchez, *Sympathy and Science: Women Physicians in American Medicine* (New York: Oxford University Press, 1985), p. 295.

34. Mary E. Bates to Julia Lathrop, 3/30/13 (U.S. Children's Bureau, 4–14–2–3–0).

35. Robbins Gilman, "Better Babies," *Proceedings of the First National Conference on Race Betterment,* p. 272.

36. DeVilbiss, "Education for Parenthood," p. 272.

37. Mary DeGarmo to Julia Lathrop, 3/10/18 (U.S. Children's Bureau, 4–15–4–3).

and the General Federation of Women's Clubs advocated the insti-tutionalization of the "feeble-minded" to prevent them from repro-ducing and legislation to prevent the marriage of other "defective" people. The assumption that social problems had their roots at least partly in the inherently deviant nature of certain people and that American democracy relied on the conformity of the nation's citizens to particular moral and social standards was pervasive among Pro-gressive reformers. Perhaps it derived partly from the concept of Republican virtue or from an evangelical Protestant faith that the purification of society would be achieved through the perfection of individuals. Eugenic measures did not provoke much debate in the women's organizations; their tacit acceptance suggests that the mem-bers assumed their own social distance from the "unfit"; they saw "defects" as the characteristics of outsiders—people of other ethnic groups or of other social classes.

The baby health contest could be a very unpleasant event, and parents and physicians frequently complained. Even Anna Steele Richardson, who had written many articles for the Better Babies Bureau of the *Woman's Home Companion,* admitted in 1914 that when the magazine's representatives could not attend, contest organizers sometimes acted very irresponsibly. Judges carried out the exams carelessly, and several suits were filed over medals and prizes. Frances Sherbon of the U.S. Children's Bureau described a contest in Wausau, Wisconsin, in 1916 in which the only attempt to advise mothers was an "occasional word" dropped by the physicians. The scoring, ac-cording to Sherbon, was worthless, the room hot and overcrowded, and the event generally disorganized.[38]

A woman in Cleveland complained that the judges in a better baby contest held in that city merely glanced at the babies. They scored inconsistently and failed to weigh and measure the contestants as the advertisements had promised. A woman who helped to organize a contest in Washington State described the event as "cruelty to children in the first degree." The children, she wrote, cried and screamed and were forcibly held in the measuring rack and pursued under tables and chairs; two were injured when they fell from a table and a scale:

---

38. Anna Steese Richardson, "Cooperation of National Congress of Mothers and Woman's Home Companion," *Child-Welfare Magazine* 9 (1914): 39; Florence Sherbon to Grace Meigs, 5/24/16 (U.S. Children's Bureau, 4–11–3–5).

"I felt like a criminal when I went home the first night."[39] There was also the danger of commercialism, and not just on the part of the *Woman's Home Companion* or other periodicals that sponsored contests. Milk and infant food companies found baby health contests particularly profitable, sometimes boasting of the contest prizes won by their healthiest customers.[40]

The U.S. Children's Bureau and some physicians also had more fundamental doubts about the value of the contest. Soon after the *Woman's Home Companion* launched its campaign, Lathrop received correspondence from "some of the eastern authorities on infant welfare, much concerned about the proposed baby contest and expressing the view that it is likely to drop to the level of a beauty contest." She wrote in a friendly tone to key figures in the contest movement, asking whether the contest really led to the better care of babies: "I should like to reassure these people from your experience, if I may." Her primary concern was the competitive nature of the contest; she suggested giving all children prizes of some sort.[41] Meanwhile, the Children's Bureau, asked to help plan a child welfare program for the National Conservation Exposition in Knoxville for the fall, proposed a health contest in which each child attaining a certain standard would receive a medal or certificate.[42]

At the same time the women who made up the Committee on Women's and Children's Welfare of the American Medical Association's newly formed Council on Public Health Instruction began to show an interest in the contest. This committee was the successor to the Public Health Education Committee formed by Rosalie Slaughter Morton in 1909. While demonstrating a special commitment to preventive medicine, the members of these committees served as intermediaries between the profession and the female public. One of the goals of the Public Health Education Committee, Morton wrote in

39. Mrs. C. H. Neal to Julia Lathrop, 2/14/16 (U.S. Children's Bureau, 4–14–2–3–1); Julia Lathrop to Mrs. Arthur C. Varney, 7/18/16, and Varney to Lathrop, 8/14/16 (ibid., 4–14–2–4–2).

40. "Indianapolis Baby Week" (ibid., 4–14–2–2–4); Frances Sage Bradley to Anna Louise Strong, 7/7/15 (ibid., 4–11–5–2).

41. Julia Lathrop to Margaret Clarke, 3/27/13 (ibid., 4–14–2–3–3); Mary E. Bates to Lathrop, 3/30/13 (ibid., 4–14–2–3–0).

42. Margaret Clarke to Julia Lathrop, 3/13/13 (ibid., 4–14–2–3–3).

her autobiography, was to restore public confidence in physicians at a time when the profession was under attack.[43]

In the spring and summer of 1913, then, Lathrop and the AMA committee, led by Lenna Meanes, set about redirecting the energy generated by the contest. In June, Meanes's committee called a meeting to coordinate the various elements of the "Better Baby" movement. Those present agreed on three guidelines. First, a standardized scorecard would be developed by a committee in consultation with children's specialists, to be endorsed by the American Medical Association and distributed by the *Woman's Home Companion*. Second, cash prizes would be discouraged; finally, the *Woman's Home Companion* would withdraw all advertising matter from its educational circular.

Gertrude Lane, managing editor of the magazine, wrote of this agreement to Lathrop: "At great cost to ourselves, we have made every concession that we could think of making in order to take away from our connection the stigma of commercialism to which you have objected. . . . The whole matter has become so much bigger than any individual organization or any publication that I trust you will feel that most of your objections to working with us have been met and overcome."[44] In July, however, the magazine agreed to turn over all of its contest correspondence to an independent Baby Health Contest Association after the fall, and by July 1914, Meanes wrote to Lathrop, "So far as we are concerned the *Woman's Home Companion* is entirely out of it."[45]

The bureau and Meanes's committee developed the children's health conference as a noncommercial, noncompetitive replacement for the contest—one that would meet with the approval of the pediatric establishment. Meanes and her colleagues developed a standard scorecard for contests, which it distributed to women's clubs with instructions that discouraged the awarding of prizes of intrinsic value

---

43. Rosalie Slaughter Morton, *A Woman Surgeon* (New York: Frederick A. Stokes, 1937), pp. 165–69; Lenna M. Meanes, "Report of the Committee on Women's and Children's Welfare to the Council on Health and Public Instruction," *Woman's Medical Journal* 26 (1916): 152–56; Morantz-Sanchez, *Sympathy and Science*, p. 285.
44. Gertrude Lane to Julia Lathrop, 6/26/13 (U.S. Children's Bureau, 4–14–2–3–0).
45. Lenna Meanes to Julia Lathrop, 7/16/14 (ibid., 4–14–2–3–0).

and encouraged scoring for improvement over a period of time. The committee also collected ten thousand completed forms from which they compiled anthropometric tables on child development.[46]

Lathrop, too, mediated between the medical establishment and women's organizations. In 1914 she wrote to a number of children's health specialists asking their opinion of the contest. All opposed the awarding of prizes, except perhaps for improvement over time. The only outright condemnations of the contest came from prominent male eastern pediatricians: L. Emmett Holt, Frank Spooner Churchill, and J. S. Abt. Churchill expressed the strongest objections. "I am distinctly and emphatically opposed to them for all reasons," he wrote. "The idea of lining up these human beings as if they were so many pigs or calves is exceedingly repulsive to me."[47]

Children's Health Conferences

The bureau perfected the conference idea, first tried out at the Knoxville Exposition in the fall of 1913. Children were examined carefully (appointments were made for twenty-five-minute sessions), with a special emphasis on nutrition. The physicians used no scorecard but recorded their advice to the parents.[48] They were not supposed to prescribe any medication or particular treatment but only to point out the problem and refer the parents to their family physician. Thus the conference closely resembled the weekly sessions at urban milk stations or infant welfare centers, where physicians examined babies and used the exams to deliver impromptu lectures to the assembled mothers.

By 1914 several of the early leaders of the contest movement, including DeVilbiss, Florence Sherbon, and Meanes, were converted to the conference. "Three cheers for the Babies' Health Conference!" wrote Lydia DeVilbiss. "It is in every way a decided success, and so

46. Meanes, "Report of the Committee on Women's and Children's Welfare," p. 155; Lewis Merriam, "Memo on Baby Health Conferences for Miss Lathrop," 11/22/13 (U.S. Children's Bureau, 4–14–2–4–0).

47. I. A. Abt to Julia Lathrop, 5/9/14; Frank Spooner Churchill to Lathrop, 5/6/14 (U.S. Children's Bureau, 4–14–2–3–3).

48. "Memorandum on Children's Health Conference, Knoxville, Tennessee" (ibid., 4–14–5–1).

great an improvement over the Better Babies' Contest that there is
no comparison."[49] By the end of 1914 the committee was actively
encouraging conferences instead of contests and offered to furnish
scorecards and literature to women's clubs and other organizations.
Meanes hoped that the conference would create a demand for more
permanent stations where babies would be examined every day on a
noncompetitive basis. When the Children's Bureau began to organize
exhibits and a conference for the Panama Pacific Exposition in San
Francisco in 1915, Lathrop asked Meanes to serve on the coordinating
committee.[50]

The bureau took up Meanes's suggestion of using the scorecards
she had developed to examine six babies on certain afternoons
throughout the exposition. Lathrop suggested that because Frances
Sage Bradley, the Children's Bureau physician, would not have time
to handle all the children who came, the reconstituted American Baby
Health Contest Association could add its contribution. Though the
association had never been endorsed by the American Medical Association, the bureau was anxious to avoid a confrontation with the
organization and the contest took place alongside the bureau's conference. As Bradley wrote almost smugly to Lathrop, the contest had
a tragic aftermath. The baby selected as first prize winner died of
tuberculosis a few months later and the parents thought that perhaps
she had caught the disease at the contest. This sad event, Bradley
implied, was the nail in the coffin of the baby health contest.[51]

Meanes expressed the opinion that the AMA committee and the
Children's Bureau would have little trouble converting women's
clubs to accept the conference but thought that state fair boards would
be more difficult to persuade.[52] This seems to have been true; local
women's organizations did look for leadership to these prominent
women, endowed with the authority of the federal government and
the AMA. Furthermore, they soon discovered that the prizes were
not necessary to induce attendance, so eager were mothers for profes-

49. Lydia DeVilbiss to Lenna Meanes, 10/26/14 (ibid., 4–14–2–4–0).
50. Lenna Meanes to Julia Lathrop, 9/21/14 (ibid., 4–11–5–2).
51. Lenna Meanes to Anna Louise Strong, 12/1/14; Frances Sage Bradley to Julia
Lathrop, 7/20/15 (ibid., 4–11–5–2); Lathrop to Hastings H. Hart, 3/19/15 (ibid.,
4–14–2–4–0).
52. Lenna Meanes to Grace Meigs, 11/20/16 (ibid., 4–14–2–3–3).

sional advice. A free medical examination was a valuable gift in itself, especially in rural areas.[53] The bureau also promoted the conference through its rural child welfare studies, carried out by Sherbon and Bradley. The conference was a central component of the Sheppard-Towner programs of the 1920s.

The conference, while it met some of the heartfelt demands of poor and rural women, also suited the needs of the medical profession and did not violate the private system of medical care. The conference helped to instill in parents the idea of regular medical supervision of healthy children; the rule that the conference physician provide no treatment or prescription was designed to avoid arousing the hostility of local practitioners, who sometimes objected that their patients were being taken from them. The conference did not provide regular supervision of children, however, since it was, at least to begin with, a sporadic event—one-time, yearly, or monthly, depending on the available resources. Instead, the conference provided reassurance for mothers, who were probably extremely anxious about their children's health, especially after all the contest publicity. It brought pediatric experts to small towns where the local physicians often had little interest in infant health. The expert was frequently a woman, perhaps a mother herself, whose sympathy and empathy for mothers were much greater than those of the local doctor.

In theory, the conference, like the contest, could serve the purposes of eugenists. Sherbon saw the conference as an important step in the education needed for the establishment of a system of compulsory, periodic examination of every citizen from birth to death and municipal records of the family history of every individual. This system, she thought, would make possible the early detection of subnormal children and children with criminal tendencies in time for treatment and segregation.[54] In practice, however, it seems likely that without scorecards that drew attention to particular characteristics, and without prizes, physicians naturally paid closer attention to each individual and the conference closely resembled a routine physical.

In fact, the baby health contest was not dead, but organizers

53. See *Raising a Baby the Government Way: Mothers' Letters to the Children's Bureau, 1915–1932*, ed. Molly Ladd-Taylor (New Brunswick, N.J.: Rutgers University Press, 1986), pp. 44–45.
54. Florence Sherbon to Julia Lathrop, 5/18/14 (U.S. Children's Bureau, 4–14–2–3–3).

developed several variations on the contest to make it less objectionable: eliminating cash prizes, giving no prizes but publishing the names of the highest scorers, offering both competitive and noncompetitive categories, or giving prizes based on improvement over time. The baby improvement contest was popular among urban milk stations and child welfare centers as an incentive for attendance. At a contest in New York City, for example, prizes were given to those who showed the most improvement over six months and to those whose attendance at the milk station was most regular. The Child Federation in Philadelphia held a similar contest, which also took into account the improvement shown in the cleanliness and general sanitation of the home and the degree of cooperation of the mother, based on observations by the visiting nurse over a four-week period.[55] As Meanes feared, however, commercial bodies and state fair boards were harder to swing away from contests, "for they want the very thing which we are striving to eliminate—namely—competition."[56]

Though its popularity was short-lived, the baby health contest set the scene for the involvement of women's clubs in the infant health movement. It brought the gospel of scientific child rearing into small towns and rural communities and suggested to women's clubs a way in which they could intitiate action on the issue. The invention of the conference also fostered a close relationship among female physicians, the U.S. Children's Bureau, and local and national women's organizations which would shape the American infant health movement over the next several years. The physicians and local and national women's organizations looked to the Children's Bureau for guidance and generally saw its policy as authoritative. In turn, the bureau saw the activism of national and local women's organizations as the key to their success, and consulted prominent clubwomen at every step. But the local organizations were not always tractable or predictable, and the national organizers often found themselves faced with a movement they had inspired but no longer controlled.

55. Lenna Meanes to Julia Lathrop, 7/12/17 (ibid., 4–14–2–3–1), and 7/17/14 (ibid., 4–14–2–3–0); *Baby Week Campaigns,* U.S. Children's Bureau, Miscellaneous Series No. 5 (Bureau Publication No. 15) (Washington, D.C.: Government Printing Office, 1917), pp. 53, 89.

56. Lenna Meanes to Grace Meigs, 11/20/16 (U.S. Children's Bureau, 4–14–2–3–3).

Women's Organizations and the U.S. Children's Bureau

As one-time educational events such as the baby health contest proved successful in directing public attention to child health, local women's organizations began to try to establish permanent institutions. While women in larger cities, especially in the Northeast and the Midwest, worked with well-established public health departments, dispensaries, and hospitals, those in rural areas were starting from scratch. A large proportion of rural counties had almost no public health or welfare institutions at all. In one Kansas county, for example, the county board of health consisted of a health officer paid $250.00 a year to inspect stores, restaurants, slaughterhouses, and schools and to control contagious diseases. In a typical year, however, he actually inspected stores, restaurants and slaughterhouses twice and visited about six of the sixty-seven schools in the county. In 1916 the social service league of the county seat hired a visiting nurse whose work was confined almost entirely to the city. The most significant child health undertaking of 1916 was the "Baby Day" series in the county seat and three of the villages, organized by the visiting nurse.[57]

In 1918 most villages in Wisconsin had still less adequate public health provisions. Each township or village had a local board of health with an officer who might be a farmer or a physician, usually paid ten dollars a year but sometimes nothing. The main work of this officer was to post and remove quarantine notices and fumigate for severe contagious diseases; some did nothing at all.[58] In 1915 the secretary of the newly formed Mothers' Club of Branson, Montana, a small hill town, wrote to Lathrop for advice and literature on Better Babies' work. Her town had no picture shows, dance halls, or "vicious conditions" to combat, only "an utter lack of any attempt at sanitation." The county had no stock law, so cattle ranged through the streets at all times of the year. Thus the club had chosen baby saving as its first project.[59]

The problem was even more severe in the South. In 1909 six of

57. Elizabeth Moore, *Maternity and Infant Care in a Rural County in Kansas,* U.S. Children's Bureau, Rural Child Welfare Series No. 1 (Bureau Publication No. 26) (Washington, D.C.: Government Printing Office, 1917), p. 20.

58. Charles U. Moore to Julia Lathrop, 9/28/16 (U.S. Children's Bureau, 4–15–4–3); Memo attached to letter from Hutchcraft to Moore, 1/9/18 (ibid., 4–11–4–2).

59. Louise R. Cahill to Julia Lathrop, 2/23/15 (ibid., 4–15–3–5–1).

the twelve southeastern states had public health departments more than ten years old, but of these only Florida provided stable funding. The public health department of Arkansas had been created in 1881 but in 1910 still had no office and had yet to receive any money. Between 1910 and 1914 state appropriations for public health work in the South increased by 81 percent, largely as a result of the work undertaken by the Rockefeller Sanitary Commission for the Eradication of Hookworm Disease. Still, by 1915 only seven of one hundred North Carolina counties, three of South Carolina's forty-six counties, and no county in Georgia had full-time health officers.[60]

Even in cities, where public health and medical facilities existed, blacks might not benefit. As historian Edward Beardsley writes, southern health officers and a few white physicians were just "discovering" black health problems in the 1910s.[61] African-American women's clubs and settlements were critical components of the network of African-American institutions that provided basic health and educational services to the African-American community. When Lugenia Burns Hope's Neighborhood Union, an Atlanta settlement, opened its health center, it was the only one in the city that served African Americans.[62] The Neighborhood Union, the Women's Club of Tuskeegee, and the Locust Street Settlement in Hampton, Virginia, held classes on infant care, organized infant health clinics, and lobbied for the hiring of African-American public health nurses as part of much wider health and educational programs for adults as well as children.[63]

African-American women's organizations did not focus on infant health as a separate issue in the way that white women's did, however,

60. See John Ettling, *The Germ of Laziness: Rockefeller Philanthropy and Public Health in the South* (Cambridge, Mass.: Harvard University Press, 1981), pp. 118–21; Edward H. Beardsley, *A History of Neglect: Health Care for Blacks and Mill Workers in the Twentieth-Century South* (Knoxville: University of Tennessee Press, 1987), p. 132.

61. Beardsley, *A History of Neglect*, p. 129; Jacqueline Anne Rouse, *Lugenia Burns Hope, Black Southern Reformer* (Athens: University of Georgia Press, 1989), pp. 59–60.

62. See Cynthia Neverdon-Morton, *Afro-American Women of the South and the Advancement of the Race, 1895–1925* (Knoxville: University of Tennessee Press, 1989), p. 160.

63. Ibid., pp. 108–9; John A. Kenney, "Health Problems of the Negroes," *Journal of the National Medical Association* 3 (1911): 135; Janie Porter Barrett to Julia Lathrop, 10/19/14 (U.S. Children's Bureau, 3–10–1); Rouse, *Lugenia Burns Hope*, pp. 71–72, 80–81; Gerda Lerner, "Early Community Work of Black Club Women," *Journal of Negro History* 59 (1974): 159–60.

perhaps because the health problems among adult African Americans, especially tuberculosis and syphilis, were so severe that infant mortality—though twice as high as for whites—did not stand out as the most urgent public health issue for the community. African-American children also died from these diseases in much larger numbers than white children, so infant health issues may not have been as distinct as for whites. In addition, however, because of the lack of healthcare institutions of all kinds, African-American women did not *specialize* in maternal and infant health to the same extent as white women; their work was essential to all groups.

Thus, to white women in small towns all over the country and African-American women in the South, the newsletters of women's organizations and the U.S. Children's Bureau were more important resources than local physicians or public health officers. The existence of the Children's Bureau staffed by women who had the freedom, though not the money, to do more or less whatever they could dream up in the area of child health gave the local women's organizations a sense of participating in a movement of national scope and importance.

Though the legislation establishing the Children's Bureau limited its mission to research and the dissemination of the information collected, the bureau's staff interpreted the charter liberally. They quite clearly identified themselves as the leaders of the popular infant health movement. In 1912, soon after her appointment as first head of the bureau, Julia Lathrop addressed the Biennial Convention of the General Federation of Women's Clubs. "Where else," she asked, "could the Bureau more reasonably look for cooperation than to this Federation nearly a million strong? . . . These associations . . . represent . . . the most influential and the wisest views in this country on the care and protection of children. If the Bureau can continue to have your aid, it cannot fail of usefulness."[64]

Before 1920 the bureau asked for the cooperation of women's organizations in all its major projects on infant health. In particular, the staff called upon members of the General Federation of Women's Clubs for help, though the National Congress of Mothers had historically demonstrated a greater interest in infant health. The bureau

64. Julia Lathrop, "Children's Bureau," General Federation of Women's Clubs, *Eleventh Biennial Convention*, pp. 447–48.

staff had closer personal ties with the leadership of the General Federation and probably found its philosophy—morally less conservative than the National Congress of Mothers—more congenial. Though the bureau staff responded to African-American women's requests for information and advice, supported their efforts to promote the hiring of black public health nurses, and included African-American communities in its rural child welfare studies, the bureau chose primarily to work with the General Federation of Women's Clubs, an organization that excluded African-American women, in its major national efforts.

Without the female-led Children's Bureau—if, for example, the U.S. Public Health Service had been the federal agency that dealt with infant health—the role of women's organizations would undoubtedly have been less important. Women's organizations worked most closely with state public health officials where those officials were women, such as Dorothy Reed Mendenhall of Wisconsin, Frances Hollingshead of Ohio, and Lydia DeVilbiss of Kansas. Some men—W. A. Davis of Texas, for example—appealed to women's clubs for assistance, but not all male public health officials saw the contribution of women as useful. Frances Sage Bradley, planning a project for the Children's Bureau in North Carolina with a male official of the state department of health, reported that his views on child welfare work in the South coincided with the plan she had suggested except that he excluded the women's clubs altogether. Bradley, herself a southerner, thought the women's clubs represented "the livest activities in many sections of the South," while she described the local medical societies as rather sluggish.[65]

As one of its first projects, the Children's Bureau undertook a campaign for effective legislation to register births in conjunction with the Bureau of Vital Statistics. The inaccurate and spotty vital statistics of the United States were a source of embarrassment to Americans attending international public health conferences. These experts did not even have the resources to calculate a national infant mortality rate. Birthrates and infant death rates were considered accurate only within the "birth registration area," which included only those states in which over 90 percent of births were registered. Birth registration

65. W. A. Davis to Julia Lathrop, 11/5/16 (U.S. Children's Bureau, 4–12–3); Frances Sage Bradley to Grace Meigs, 9/22/15 (ibid., 4–11–2–1).

interested the bureau not only because all reformers considered it a
prerequisite to effective infant health work but because birth certifi-
cates were important in the enforcement of child labor laws, the
bureau's other major concern.[66]

Lathrop came to the biennial convention of the General Federation
of Women's Clubs in 1912 to ask the members' cooperation in the
campaign. Within twelve months, she told them, the federation could
secure effective birth registration for the whole nation, something the
federal government itself could not accomplish. According to the
plan drawn up by Cressy L. Wilbur of the Bureau of Vital Statistics,
committees of women would select names of babies they knew to
have been born in 1913 in small areas with which they were well
acquainted and then check to see if the babies were registered. The
bureau hoped for a nationwide survey that would cover about 5
percent of the reported number of births. In theory, once the women's
organizations had proved the deficiency of current laws and demonstrated the value of accurate vital statistics, legislators would be
convinced to pass more effective laws. The federation's members took
up the call, and by 1914 ten state federations had undertaken birth
registration surveys.[67]

Baby Week, 1916

The Children's Bureau staff also consulted with federation leaders
before making public its plans for an ambitious series of surveys of
maternal and infant health in rural counties.[68] The most impressive
example of the collaboration of the two groups, however, was the
Baby Week campaign of 1916. The first Baby Week had been held
in Chicago in 1914 under the auspices of the Illinois Congress of
Mothers, the Woman's City Club, and the Chicago Medical Woman's
Club and was essentially a publicity campaign to raise funds for the
city's Infant Welfare Association. A lecture series and a baby health

66. See Nancy Pottisham Weiss, "Save the Children: A History of the Children's
Bureau, 1903–1918," Ph.D. diss., University of California, Los Angeles, 1974,
pp. 186–88.
67. Lathrop, "Children's Bureau," p. 456.
68. Anna Louise Strong to Julia Lathrop, 5/19/15 (U.S. Children's Bureau, 4–12–
5–1).

contest in which twelve hundred children competed were the most prominent features, but the program also included streetcar publicity, billboards, theater ads, church sermons, and newspaper cartoons, articles, and editorials.[69] The New York Milk Committee also held a Baby Week in 1914 and other cities followed: Pittsburgh, Indianapolis, Topeka, and Grand Rapids. Baby Week was an urban phenomenon until 1916, when the national Baby Week campaign took advantage of the federation's extensive network in small towns to reach beyond the cities.

In June 1915, Anna Louise Strong, then in charge of the Children's Bureau's child welfare exhibit, drew up a proposal for a nationwide Baby Week which Lathrop sent to the president of the federation. Strong proposed a national event whose goal would be to popularize infant hygiene and to provide publicity for local, state, and national child welfare agencies. The Children's Bureau would furnish exhibits, sample literature, press material, and clerical aid for communicating with local groups. Federation officials approved heartily of the plan.[70] The Baby Week campaign, if carried out, would, suggested Mrs. Max West of the Children's Bureau, "seem to ally the Federation to infant welfare work to some extent at least."[71] In part, the personal links between federation leaders and the bureau staff made such cooperation possible. Ella L. Blair, chair of the Public Health Department of the federation, wrote to Lathrop: "I am also delighted that our own Dr. Bradley is to represent the Bureau in this work and it seems to me that this fact should influence us strongly."[72]

Strong had failed to consider that the National Congress of Mothers was already planning a national Baby Week campaign and that the congress had been involved in child welfare work much longer than the federation had. The links with the federation offended the president of the Mothers' Assembly of the State of New York, who wrote to Mrs. Frederic Schoff, president of the Congress:

> It seems to me that if there is to be a national baby week in March arranged by the Children's Bureau in Washington it should be the

69. Grace Meigs to J. F. Edwards, 5/25/15 (ibid., 4–14–2–1–1); A. L. Lindsay Wynkoop, "Baby Welfare Week," *Woman's Medical Journal* 26 (1916): 123.

70. Julia Lathrop to Mrs. Pennybacker, 7/1/15, and Pennybacker to Lathrop, 7/26/15 (U.S. Children's Bureau, 4–14–2–2–1).

71. Mrs. Max West to Dorothy Reed Mendenhall, 11/3/15 (ibid., 4–15–4–1–1).

72. Ella L. Blair to Julia Lathrop, 8/19/15 (ibid., 4–14–2–2–1).

National Congress of Mothers instead of the National Federation
of Clubs that is called into partnership to work out the details. I
feel that Miss Lathrop is *one* of *us*. . . . The Federation of Clubs is
a general practitioner, the Congress of Mothers is a *child specialist*.
Does it not seem to you that we receive acknowledgement from
the Children's Bureau of our twenty years of preparation for just
such a special task showing the national confidence in us and ap-
preciation of our work and labor of love?

Schoff forwarded a copy of this letter to Lathrop, reminding her that
including the National Congress of Mothers in future statements on
Baby Week would be politically wise.[73] Lathrop agreed that the cooperation of the National Congress of Mothers was very valuable
and in the January issue of *Child-Welfare Magazine* addressed an appeal
to the congress, acknowledging that this organization was already "a
great force in this field."[74]

The form and content of the Baby Week campaigns were typical
of the American child health movement. First, the goal of the campaign was educational—to teach parents and the general public about
the needs of children. Baby Week organizers believed that specific
permanent programs such as those for public health nurses, milk
stations, and child welfare centers would follow a successful educational campaign. The favorite image of Baby Week, however, was
one of a community united in the interests of the child. Much of the
content of Baby Week, however, had little to do with child welfare;
instead, the festivities resembled those of a patriotic holiday. One
Louisiana paper published the following description of the local Baby
Week parade: "In beautiful floats, in push carts, in buggies, on tri-
cycle, on bicycle, in toy automobile, and afoot, each individual holding a tiny flag, a thousand hearts beat happily as they passed through
a street literally lined with admiring and cheering townfolk."[75] It
might have been the Fourth of July, with celebration of the town's
children replacing the commemoration of national independence.
Baby Week thus became a demonstration of the unity of a mythical

73. Mrs. Frederic Schoff to Julia Lathrop, 1/24/16, and Lathrop to Schoff,
1/29/16 (ibid., 4–14–2–2–1); E. E. Routzahn to Grace Meigs, 10/11/15 (ibid.,
4–14–2–2–1).

74. Julia Lathrop, "The Nation-Wide Baby Week," *Child-Welfare Magazine* 10
(1916): 158.

75. Quoted in *Baby Week Campaigns*, p. 38.

classless, morally pure, and democratic community. Women led this mobilization, and their success demonstrated the extent to which they were responsible for the defining of community and for the organization of collective events.

That child health was a good thing was not a controversial assertion, though the means of achieving it might provoke conflict: local physicians, for example, often opposed the hiring of public health nurses, and milk companies might object to an emphasis on breast-feeding. Baby Week, however, was designed to avoid stirring up class conflict or local animosities. Thus the official report of one Baby Week celebration observed that the best feature was the spirit of cooperation among churches, physicians, stores, and private individuals: "This is an unusual feature in this locality, where the general spirit is not always cooperative."[76] Despite this rhetoric of harmony, Jim Crow applied to infants: Baby Week events, like infant health contests, were segregated.[77]

Baby Week organizers could provoke conflict, as did the women of Arena, Wisconsin, when they failed to bring their proposal before the influential male Commercial Club soon enough. One problem was the local prejudice against the state university, whose extension service was promoting Baby Week. Though the Commercial Club rejected the proposal, the women went ahead with the program after representatives of the local Women's Christian Temperance Union and Reading Club, and the Congregational, Methodist-Episcopal, Baptist, and Lutheran ladies' aid societies all met to plan the Baby Week program. Faced with a united front of women, the Commercial Club backed down and promised financial support but no time or leadership.[78] This incident is evidence of potential antagonism, but it is most remarkable for the women's confidence in their united strength and their willingness to confront the town's male leadership.

The typical program had something for everyone. The organizers solicited the active involvement of as many local organizations and interest groups as possible. On Flag Day, for example, every house

76. Quoted in ibid., p. 14.
77. A memo by Grace Meigs about her trip to Norfolk, Va., May 7–8, 1917, describes separate Baby Week celebrations for blacks and whites (U.S. Children's Bureau, 4–14–4–3).
78. Sherbon to Meigs, 5/13/16, and Sherbon to Gillin, 5/2/16 (U.S. Children's Bureau, 4–14–3–5).

with a child was asked to put out a flag and keep it flying throughout
the week. Some committees designed their own flags, while others
used small American flags. In many towns Boy Scouts delivered the
flags, and in one Missouri city the Daughters of the American Revolution shared the expense of distributing American flags to all schoolchildren with infant siblings.[79] Local committees urged churches to
include some mention of Baby Week in their services on Baby Sun-
day. Many ministers chose Baby Week or infant welfare as the subject
of their sermons, and churches often served as centers for the distribution of leaflets or programs for the coming week. Organizers saw
the schools as their most effective advertising tool. School Day was
an essential feature of the campaign, since school programs reached
not only the pupils but their parents as well. In addition to taking
home leaflets, children entered poster contests, heard lectures on infant
care, performed plays, and wrote essays for competitions.

Fathers' Day featured lunchtime lectures to men at work on such
subjects as the "social evil" (prostitution) and its effect on children,
the nature of paternal duty, and social responsibility for children.
Sometimes Welfare Day or Institutions Day focused on the work of
existing child welfare agencies and the support they needed. Many
celebrations featured a parade of babies in carriages pushed by their
mothers or in cars. In Indianapolis in 1915 two bands accompanied
one hundred cars through the main streets, where large crowds were
on hand to cheer them on. State and city officials and officers of child
welfare organizations officially reviewed the parade from the balcony
of a prominent hotel. A St. Louis Baby Week parade included a tour
of inspection of the municipal milk stations, and in a Colorado town
a squad of older children rode on tricycles. The Children's Bureau
stipulated that every Baby Week campaign include a child health
conference, but local organizers often ignored this rule and frequently
made a contest the central event of the program.

Merchants found Baby Week a useful advertising event. The Polk
Sanitary Milk Company of Indianapolis distributed a leaflet attrib-
uting the low infant mortality rate among milk station clients to "the
effective results accomplished in reducing infant mortality by means

79. *Baby Week Campaigns,* p. 35.

of a milk supply of unquestioned purity."[80] In Milwaukee, funds were raised for an elaborate Baby Week by means of a commercial exhibit. An Indianapolis Savings and Trust company advertised: "Government surveys show the death-rate of babies is lowest among people of character who are regular in their habits, simple in their tastes and thrifty. Baby saving and money saving go together."[81]

While infant health in France was associated with military capacity, Baby Week publicity most often suggested that saving babies would contribute to economic prosperity. Favorite slogans included, "Baby health—civic wealth," "Baby health, nation's wealth," "Baby's health means more than wealth," "Arkansas wealth for baby's health," and "Utah's best crop." Official proclamations referred to the loss of infant life as economic waste, and appeals to businessmen pointed out that the infant mortality rate of a city was a useful index to its prosperity.[82] They frequently referred to "baby conservation" as an aspect of the conservation of natural resources. A poem called "They who are about to die" and printed in a public health magazine compared the inadequate steps taken toward saving babies with other conservation efforts:

> O wise, wise world,
> You have learned to guard
> The wealth of your forests from axe and flame;
> On farm, in city, on land and sea,
> 'Conserve, utilize', is your constant cry;
> You save, wise world, where there once was waste—
> But what of the babies about to die?[83]

Religious themes were also common in Baby Week literature, especially in the South. A county home demonstration agent in Jackson, Mississippi, sent Lathrop a copy of a song she had schoolchildren sing and the "Creed and Crusade" they repeated each day at school

80. Polk Sanitary Milk Company, "Baby Week," Indianapolis, October 3–9, 1915 (U.S. Children's Bureau, 4–14–2–2–4).

81. Grace Meigs, "Baby Week in Wisconsin," 4/17/16 (ibid., 4–14–2–2–4); Polk Sanitary Milk Company, "Baby Week."

82. *Baby Week Campaigns*, pp. 27, 58–59.

83. Reprinted in *Wisconsin Baby Week Campaign 1917*, Bulletin of the University of Wisconsin, Extension Division, General Series No. 461, 1917, p. 2.

during Baby Week. The creed suggested an intimate relationship among health, wealth, and social order. It began:

1. That God, our Father, is the Giver of All Life.
2. That health is life as it ought to be.
3. That health is the basis of prosperity and happiness, and therefore our first duty both individually and socially.

It continued:

6. That the Federal Government should establish a Co-ordinate Cabinet Department of Health.
7. That the death of children is a defeat of God's purpose, and their health—physical, mental, and moral—should be a primary function and responsibility of the Church. . . .

The creed concluded with a call for the people of the South to co-operate through the agencies of home and school, medical profession and press, church and government, "for the achievement of health for the individual, for the community, and for the nation."[84]

Baby Week's popularity exceeded the hopes of its organizers and, to a certain extent, dismayed them. The Children's Bureau received inquiries from 4561 of the 14,186 incorporated communities in the United States, and 2193 of these eventually reported celebrations. These communities were sprinkled throughout the country, though 500 were in Kansas alone, probably due to the zeal of Lydia DeVilbiss, head of the state's Division of Child Hygiene. Several southern states reported successful campaigns, as did New Jersey, Vermont, Massachusetts, western Washington, and most of the Midwest. Six hundred eighty-three celebrations were held in communities with fewer than 2500 residents, 488 in towns of 2500 to 10,000, and 210 in unincorporated communities.[85] Lathrop wrote to the correspond-

84. Mrs. J. T. Calhoun to Julia Lathrop, 8/29/16 (U.S. Children's Bureau, 4–14–2–2–1).
85. Julia Lathrop to Elizabeth Hawley Everett, 9/9/16 (ibid., 4–14–2–2–1). *Baby Week Campaigns* reports 2264 celebrations, including 210 in unincorporated communities (p. 108); Lathrop reports Baby Week celebrations in over 4700 communities in a letter to Mrs. Philip N. Moore, 8/10/16 (ibid., 4–14–2–2–1); DeVilbiss to Lathrop, 2/29/16 (ibid., 4–15–2–1–18).

ing secretary of the General Federation of Women's Clubs, "Its success was far beyond our most extravagant anticipation."[86] To Mrs. Philip N. Moore of St. Louis she reported, "At present our reports show Baby Week celebrations in over 4700 communities. Is it not astonishing? It makes me quite solemn." Federation leaders considered Baby Week one of the greatest successes the organization as a whole had ever undertaken.[87]

The Children's Bureau staff had originally intended Baby Week to be a one-time event, but they gave way to popular demand that it be made annual. "I had hoped in the stress of last March," Lathrop wrote, "that there would never be another, but it is inevitable." An Alabama physician wrote to Lathrop that it would be a mistake to allow a discouraging word to go out as to Baby Week in 1917, since people were already planning for the next year.[88] Louella Littlepage of the U.S. Reclamation Service reported that she remembered no movement that had met with such "instant and nationwide enthusiasm" and that it would be foolish to let this new interest go to waste.[89] Grace Meigs, head of the medical division of the Children's Bureau, asked the opinion of Hoyt E. Dearholt, a Michigan public health leader, who responded that "such a thing once started could hardly be stopped." For instance, he wrote, public health officials were unable to stop campaigns against flies, though they now doubted their value.[90] Lydia DeVilbiss wrote, with her usual enthusiasm, "Baby Week I think you will find is going to be a National institution of no little importance."[91]

The Children's Bureau was most interested in the ongoing infant health work stimulated by Baby Week, especially in rural communities. Most local organizers seem to have had at least some ambitions for permanent institutions. The bureau received numerous letters asking for suggestions for follow-up work from Baby Week committees

---

86. Julia Lathrop to Elizabeth Hawley Everett, 8/7/16 (ibid., 4–14–2–2–2).
87. Julia Lathrop to Mrs. Philip N. Moore, 8/10/16, and Moore to Lathrop, 8/14/16 (ibid., 4–14–2–2–2); Elizabeth Hawley Everett to Lathrop, 8/14/16 (ibid., 4–14–2–2–2).
88. Julia Lathrop to Frank Spooner Churchill, 9/25/16 (ibid., 4–14–2–2–1).
89. Louella Littlepage to Julia Lathrop, 4/21/16 (ibid., 4–14–2–2–6).
90. Grace Meigs, "Baby Week in Wisconsin," 4/17/16 (ibid., 4–14–2–2–4).
91. Lydia DeVilbiss to Grace Meigs, 1/15/17 (ibid., 4–3–0–3).

that did not want to disband.[92] An Illinois committee reported that the campaign had finally drawn the interest of the local physicians to the work of the women's organizations. The committee tentatively planned a mothers' institute with sessions on the prevention and care of "bad-air" diseases; cleaning, the fly campaign, and contagious diseases; and infant feeding and the care of foods in summer. In New Jersey the health committee of the state Federation of Women's Clubs asked local organizations to concentrate on the hiring of visiting nurses in every community and the placing of a woman on every local health board and on the state Board of Health. West Hoboken, New Jersey, women successfully campaigned for a municipally funded infant health station, and three nurses and four physicians volunteered their services. Infant welfare stations and mothers' classes or clubs were the most popular form of follow-up work, but some local committees concentrated on school medical inspection and playgrounds, milk inspection, mosquito eradication, or tuberculosis.[93]

Conclusion

Baby Week firmly established the link between the General Federation of Women's Clubs and the Children's Bureau, and put many local women's organizations in touch with the bureau. The bureau provided inspiration, material assistance, literature, and friendly advice by mail and in person. The participation of the federal government also lent an official importance to the work, which made local organizers more confident and endowed them with a greater degree of legitimacy in the eyes of skeptical observers. Thus, the U.S. Children's Bureau assisted women's organizations toward their goal of shaping social institutions conducive to child rearing and an orderly family and community life, and in making child rearing expertise accessible to all women. Skillfully redirecting the contest movement, the Children's Bureau also steered women's organizations away from the most blatant manifestations of eugenics. Over the next several

92. Mrs. Williams to Julia Lathrop, 3/4/16 (ibid., 4–14–1–10); Josephine Pierce to Goodwin, 3/23/16 (ibid., 4–14–2–2–5); Mrs. W. B. Dahl to Goodwin, 3/14/16 (ibid., 4–14–2–5–5).
93. *Baby Week Campaigns,* pp. 64–66; Frank A. Frederick to U.S. Children's Bureau, n.d. (U.S. Children's Bureau, 4–15–2–3).

years the bureau would move further away from these ideas and would focus increasingly on a program emphasizing the rights of women and children to medical care and instruction.

The story of Baby Week and the successful campaigns that followed suggest that women in smaller communities in the United States could effectively wield political influence through the institutions with which they were most familiar: church, home, and school. In organizing Baby Week celebrations, women's organizations agreed to accept the responsibility for human reproduction in its broadest sense, turning their traditional role and traditional institutions to the needs of the modern nation-state. In the process they created new institutions and thereby new professional opportunities, which women often filled.

The access of women to medical training and their appointment to official positions, particularly in the U.S. Children's Bureau, created a channel through which women's voices—particularly those of white women—were heard in the offices of those who made social policy on the state and national level. Furthermore, given the decentralized nature of health and social welfare in the United States and the absence of established public health institutions outside large cities, women's political culture, based in local, informal institutions, proved a sturdy foundation for an effective national infant health movement. For African-American women, autonomy was associated with lack of influence outside the African-American community, while white women were able to define policy at all levels of government. French women, their ability to act independently hindered by the centralized hierarchies of both church and state, struggled to establish a basis for political participation. As a result, it was men's view of women's value to society as childbearers and wage laborers which would determine French maternal and infant health policy.

5

French Public Policy and Motherhood, 1890–1914

During World War I, Dr. Vivia Belle Appleton, dispatched by the Children's Bureau of the American Red Cross to set up a child welfare program in Rennes, a town in Brittany, found much to criticize in French public welfare programs. The poor people of Rennes, she reported, were accustomed to "pauperizing charity"; they knew no other assistance than "material aid given apparently to relieve the giver of the responsibility of thinking whether the recipient was deserving or benefited."[1]

Appleton's disapproval of material assistance was typical of American reformers. American maternal and child welfare programs, based on an ideal of social harmony through individual commitment—analagous to the Protestant concept of conversion—conformed closely to a liberal model of social policy. It is true that financial assistance to poor mothers was an important component of French maternal and child welfare policy. Appleton failed to understand, however, that French welfare programs were far from indiscriminate; they provided public support only under carefully defined conditions. In return for material benefits, the state claimed the right to supervise and control the bearing and care of children.

1. American Red Cross in France, Children's Bureau, *Complete Report, August 1917 to April 1919*, p. 210 (National Archives, Records of the American Red Cross, 942.11, Box 847).

Furthermore, the advocates of French maternal and child welfare programs did not gain their victories easily. Although the Catholic belief that charity generated spiritual benefits for the donor contrasted with the Protestant preference for moral reform of the poor over material gifts, the Catholic doctrine did not necessarily support a generous public welfare policy. Even before the Revolution, advocates of "enlightened" philanthropy criticized traditional charity for its inadequacy and inefficiency as well as for swelling the ranks of the paupers through indiscriminate assistance. Though the Revolution enunciated the principle that everyone had a right to public assistance, a strong work ethic and a fear that generous public assistance programs would promote dependency served to modify this principle in practice.[2] Only the socialist left supported without qualifications the principle enunciated by the Revolution that the state had a responsibility to support the poor.

Employers and liberal politicians in France argued that protective labor legislation violated the basic rights of workers, that unemployment insurance would disrupt the natural economic equilibrium, and that obligatory social-insurance schemes would stifle the traditional French spirit of initiative and transform French citizens into perpetual children.[3] Conservative politicians maintained that protecting single mothers would encourage illegitimacy and that assisting married women would remove men's responsibility to support their wives and children and thereby threaten the family. In the face of such opposition, nationalism and the growing consensus in favor of military preparedness played a critical role in overcoming the objections to public welfare. The French social reforms of the late nineteenth and early twentieth centuries were also part of what Judith Stone has described as an international "search for social peace." As working-class movements became increasingly radical and aggressive, she argues, reformers in the United States, France, Germany, and Great

2. See Alan Forrest, *The French Revolution and the Poor* (New York: St. Martin's Press, 1981), pp. 18, 27–29; Camille Bloch, *L'assistance et l'état en France à la veille de la Révolution* (Geneva: Slatkine-Mégariotis Reprints, 1908), pp. ii, v–vi.
3. See Judith F. Stone, *The Search for Social Peace: Reform Legislation in France, 1890–1914* (Albany: State University of New York Press, 1985), pp. 40–41, 65; Henri Hatzfield, *Du paupérisme à la sécurité sociale: Essai sur les origines de la sécurité sociale en France, 1850–1940* (Paris: Librairie Armand Colin, 1971), p. 90; Sanford Elwitt, *The Third Republic Defended: Bourgeois Reform in France, 1880–1914* (Baton Rouge: Louisiana State University Press, 1986).

Britain called for reforms that would mitigate the economic insecurity that was at the root of workers' discontent.[4] Maternal and child welfare policy thus must be viewed in the context of solidarism, the larger reform philosophy of Radical Republicans.

French solidarism shared much with American Progressivism. Both movements were founded on a world view that denied the existence of inherent social conflict; their proponents sought to prevent class struggle and to defuse working-class rebellion by mitigating the destructive effects of industrial capitalism. Both were based on the notions of social interdependence and organicism and both pursued their goals through state intervention. Motivated equally by anger at the inhumanity of capitalism and fear of the hostility of the working class, both French and American reformers sought personal contact with the working class in order to reassure themselves of their own innocence and the good will of those they saw as victims of oppression.[5]

An important component of solidarism was the belief that the unfortunate, as victims of an unjust social order, had a right to material reparations. Unlike American Progressive reformers, who tended to treat poverty as an environmental and moral issue, French solidarists believed that the wealthy, who benefited from the labor of the working class, had a responsibility to give up some of their wealth in compensation. In seeking to provide workers with access to economic security, solidarism blended on the left with socialism, and independent socialists often were allied with the solidarist Radical Republicans on social issues. Nonetheless, solidarists had no intention of shaking the class structure or challenging the sanctity of private property.[6]

Fearing that establishing a right to public assistance might eliminate all incentives to work and undermine respect for authority, solidarists supported public welfare programs only insofar as these were consistent with their other social and political goals. Protecting and

---

4. Stone, *Search for Social Peace*, pp. 2–4.

5. See Jane Jenson, "Paradigms and Political Discourse: Protective Legislation in France and the United States before 1914," *Canadian Journal of Political Science* 22 (1989): 249; Robert A. Nye, *Crime, Madness, and Politics in Modern France: The Medical Concept of National Decline* (Princeton, N.J.: Princeton University Press, 1984), p. 68; Karen Offen, "Depopulation, Nationalism, and Feminism in Fin-de-Siècle France," *American Historical Review* 89 (1984): 664; Hatzfield, *Du paupérisme à la sécurité sociale*, pp. 271–72.

6. See John A. Scott, *Republican Ideas and the Liberal Tradition in France, 1870–1914* (New York: Octagon, 1966), pp. 176–78; Stone, *Search for Social Peace*, p. 162.

supervising childbearing, the Radical Republicans held, would ultimately contribute to the nation's social stability and military strength. The most effective way to prevent child abandonment and eliminate the nursing business, they argued, was to make working-class mothers the paid nurses of their own children and to make childbearing and child care compatible with wage labor. This was not charity, they maintained, but payment for services to the nation, and therefore did not undermine the recipients' morality and sense of social responsibility. This argument was a powerful one, inasmuch as nationalist pronatalism cut across political divisions.

While solidarists did not see the prerogatives of capital as sacred, and many were hostile to large corporations, corporate leaders who were equally concerned with maintaining social peace but who opposed any move to limit the freedom of employers also made their mark on Republican social policy. Certain groups of reformers, particularly the textile manufacturers and mine owners of the northeast, pursued a strategy of corporate paternalism, often imbued with Social Catholicism, while at the same time mobilizing to defend their autonomy and authority.[7] Like solidarists, corporate paternalists cited the population crisis when they created infant health consultations, crèches, and maternal mutual aid societies, and when they granted their employees maternity leaves and regular breaks to nurse their children in factory nurseries. Their resistance to state intervention consistently frustrated the efforts of Radicals to impose requirements on employers in their quest to enable women to reconcile childbearing with wage labor. While the international political crises of the 1900s and early 1910s made increasingly viable the reformers' arguments that military preparedness depended on the protection of child life, disputes over the legitimacy of state action and the rights of capital defined the debates over maternal and child health policy as the war approached.

Single Mothers and Depopulation

Employers were most politically invested in those aspects of maternal and infant health policy which related directly to women's

7. See Stone, *Search for Social Peace,* pp. 17–19; Elwitt, *The Third Republic Defended,* pp. 10, 295.

employment: maternity leave, compensation for lost income, and day care for the children of wage-earning mothers. Reformers seeking ways to spare single mothers the poverty and shame that often led them to abort, abandon, or kill their offspring encountered a different type of opposition, based on moral grounds. It was in the efforts of Republican politicians to aid single mothers that population concerns most obviously took precedence over traditional moral imperatives.

In the early nineteenth century the state had largely taken over from religious and charitable institutions the responsibility for abandoned children. On the one hand public authorities explained this move as a logical consequence of the Revolutionary ideal that the state had a responsibility to protect the welfare of its citizens.[8] They also recognized, however, that the state had an interest in the survival of these wards, as citizens to populate the colonies, work in agriculture, and serve in the military. A decree issued in 1811 requiring hospices to admit all legitimate and illegitimate unwanted children and making them wards of the state stipulated that male children would be put at the disposition of the minister of the navy at the age of twelve.

The same decree mandated the establishment of *tours*—boxes in the walls of hospices where anyone could abandon a child in complete anonymity, knowing it would be cared for. Mothers or other people could also bring unwanted children to public offices, and women who gave birth in public maternity hospitals were offered the opportunity to send their children directly to a hospice.[9] Proponents of rationalized public assistance objected that by making abandonment too easy the *tours* destroyed families, because women who might have tried to marry could give the children over to the state instead. Women also might take advantage of the system, abandoning their children to the *tours* and then receiving payment as foster mothers for their own children.

By the late 1860s the *tours* had been eliminated and replaced with an open admissions system that required mothers to recognize their children legally but still allowed them to give up their responsibility freely.[10] Beginning in 1869 departments offered a small amount of

8. See Rachel Ginnis Fuchs, *Abandoned Children: Foundlings and Child Welfare in Nineteenth-Century France* (Albany: State University of New York Press, 1984), p. 17.
9. See ibid., pp. 21–24.
10. See R. B. Litchfield and D. Gordon, "Closing the Tour: A Close Look at the

financial assistance to women who, after an interview at the admissions office, chose not to abandon their children. As Jacques Donzelot has argued, this practice grew out of the state's interest in preserving children for the purpose of maximizing the efficiency of national production. In a sense, this system transformed working-class mothers into the paid nurses of their own children, under medical-state supervision.[11]

Such a policy, however, created a dilemma: how could the state save the lives of abandoned children without at least appearing to condone extramarital sex? In fact, the French state did not go very far toward supporting single mothers in the nineteenth century. The aid to prevent abandonment was not standardized and was always far too meager to support a child. The assistance was only temporary; it lasted just long enough to tide a woman over the period of greatest stress. Public and private welfare officials continued to lament the frequently desperate position in which many pregnant women found themselves; rejected by family and employer, often turned out of their homes, and excluded by most charitable societies, it was no wonder they took desperate measures.[12]

Toward the end of the century the declining birthrate directed attention once again toward the plight of single mothers. In 1892, when the Conseil supérieur de l'assistance publique, representing legislators and national and local public welfare officials, heard a report by Loys Bruyère on children under state care, the discussion naturally turned to the subject of how to prevent abandonment, abortion, and infanticide.[13] Dr. Gustave Drouineau, another member of the council, presented a proposal for a law that would require all departments to

Marriage Market, Unwed Mothers, and Abandoned Children in Mid-Nineteenth-Century Amiens," *Journal of Social History* 13 (1980): 458–73.

11. Jacques Donzelot, *The Policing of Families* (New York: Pantheon, 1979), p. 31. For a discussion of the functioning of this system in Paris see Rachel Fuchs, "Morality and Poverty: Public Welfare for Mothers in Paris, 1870–1900," *French History* 2 (1988): 288–311. Fuchs also argues that as concerns about depopulation increased, public policy placed less emphasis on the morality of single mothers.

12. See, for example, comments of Dr. Lugeol, *Congrès international de la protection de l'enfance* (Bordeaux: Bourlange, 1895), pp. 431, 434; R. Felhoen, *Etude statistique sur la mortalité infantile à Roubaix et dans ses cantons comparée avec celle de Lille et Tourcoing, 1871–1905* (Paris: Vigot Frères, 1906), p. 223; Odette Laguerre and I.-R. Sée, *La protection de l'enfance* (Lyons: Société d'éducation et d'action féministes, 1906), p. 8. See Fuchs, "Morality and Poverty," pp. 306–7, on the inadequacy of the assistance.

13. Conseil supérieur de l'assistance publique, *Comptes-rendus,* Fascicule No. 37, Session de janvier 1892, "Création de maternités départementales."

establish maternity hospitals and secret asylums to serve single mothers and to create a system of assistance at home for poor married women.

Providing a haven where single mothers could give birth in complete secrecy was absolutely essential, Drouineau argued, because shame and the fear of discovery frequently led them to commit abortion and infanticide. Aid and shelter would satisfy the majority, however, because poverty and homelessness were the real problems.[14] Drouineau also proposed that all pregnant woman should be treated as sick, pointing out that overwork, poverty, and undernutrition enhanced the dangers of pregnancy.

The issue was an urgent one, he warned, because of the declining birthrate: the country faced a danger so grave that if it failed to take measures to save the lives of all babies born, catastrophe would ensue.[15] Expense should not be an issue, insisted Rochard, a member of the Académie de médecine. Was it not the duty of government, he asked, to prevent through all possible means "the extinction of the population? . . . What does it matter if, each year, we give 28,000 more recruits to France?" Rochard asked his colleagues to excuse him for elaborating at length on the question of national strength, but, he told them, "it is one of those questions that one cannot discuss calmly."[16]

Drouineau's colleagues also invoked the principle of social solidarity, but the needs of the state clearly overshadowed humanitarian and moral considerations in their minds. They admitted that if it were not for the population crisis the council probably would not even be considering the issue. As one member bluntly announced, "The pregnant woman is a national asset. The state is disappointed by the loss of a child. That is why the government has instructed us to draw up a bill on maternal welfare."[17]

Bruyère and a few other members of the commission objected to Drouineau's proposal on the grounds that giving pregnant women the right to secret hospitalization or assistance would remove the incentive for chastity among single women. In addition, Bruyère

14. Ibid., pp. 68–72.
15. Ibid., Fascicule No. 39, Session de juin 1892, "Projet de loi sur l'assistance maternelle," p. 9.
16. Ibid., p. 15.
17. Ibid., p. 17.

maintained, it would undermine men's moral obligation to support the women they impregnated and the duty of husbands to support their wives. Hospitalizing mothers, he added, would also weaken family ties because it left older children unattended. In any case, he did not think that the proposed bill would stimulate many births because it did not address what he saw as the cause of the declining birthrate: the enrichment and selfishness of the bourgeoisie, who were unwilling to sacrifice their own well-being for any reason and reluctant to divide their fortunes among many children.

Bruyère's moral vision was similar to that of conservative Catholics; both believed that economic pressures enforced morality and strengthened the family. Both right and left mythologized the family as the basis of the social structure and of the nation's moral strength, and both wanted to encourage large families. Conservative Catholics, however, believed that the nation's crisis was essentially a spiritual one. They resisted the notion that economic changes were the cause of the declining rate of marital fertility and tended to deny that maternal and child welfare programs could significantly affect the demographic crisis.

It was within marriage, wrote conservative author Alcide Leroux, for example, that the nation's hope lay. Leroux admitted that women's shame was the cause of much infant mortality among illegitimate children but stressed that the rising rate of illegitimate births was a source of social decay and disorganization. He did not comment publicly on the maternity-assistance law, but he represented an attitude toward illegitimacy opposed to that of Drouineau: saving all children born regardless of the moral consequences, he argued, would not contribute to the nation's salvation.[18] These conservatives believed not only that piety was a source of social order but that economic hardships enforced morality. Assistance from outside, unless accompanied by a spiritual influence, could remove single women's fear of pregnancy and men's responsibility to support their families.

Those who favored the maternal welfare bill were not unaware of the potentially harmful moral consequences of their proposal, but they were convinced that state support and supervision of single

18. Alcide Leroux, "La question de la dépopulation devant l'Académie de médecine," *Société académique de Nantes et du département de la Loire-Inférieure, Annales,* 7th ser. 2 (1891): 354–59.

mothers would ultimately serve the nation better than traditional moral controls. They suggested several measures to prevent abuse of the programs by those not strictly eligible for aid. Drouineau's committee proposed, for example, that a medical examination determine the urgency of each applicant's need for rest and the most suitable form of aid.[19] One of the most difficult problems facing the council was that in order to maintain complete secrecy maternity hospitals had to admit women without first investigating their means and morals. How, then, could they discourage applications from women who did not really need the secrecy? The council's solution was twofold: first, to create *asiles-ouvroirs* (asylum-workshops) that would provide shelter, material aid, and medical care without secrecy; and second, to require strict isolation of the women in the secret maternity hospitals. It was important, argued Marcel Briand, not to make the secret maternity hospital an Eden; instead, it should be a workshop where women rehabilitated themselves through work.[20]

In effect, the advocates of comprehensive maternity assistance proposed that the state make a bargain with women. If women knew that society would offer them protection and rehabilitation, they would have everything to gain by completing their pregnancies and nursing their children. Not only would the children thus saved serve the nation, Drouineau argued, but the state would benefit in other ways as well. *Asiles-ouvroirs,* for example, could work positive moral benefits; not only did they discourage abortion and infanticide but they also made more likely reconciliation of the mothers with their families, their placement in domestic service, and their marriage to the children's fathers. Protecting maternity would also make possible the severe punishment of those who committed infanticide and abortion—something that was not morally defensible so long as society offered no shelter to women driven to crime by shame and despair. In fact, Drouineau argued, turning the critics' arguments on their heads, laissez-faire social policy increased illegitimacy by leaving all responsibility to the mother. It was the fear of having children which disorganized the family, provoked men's extramarital sexual activity, and encouraged birth control.[21]

19. Conseil supérieur de l'assistance publique, *Comptes-rendus,* Fascicule No. 39, p. 5.
20. Ibid., p. 37.
21. Ibid., p. 119; Gustave Drouineau, "Maternités départementales," in *Congrès national d'assistance* (Lyons: Ancienne imprimerie A. Waltener, 1894), vol. 2, p. 237.

The majority of the members of the council agreed with Drouineau and voted in favor of a proposal for legislation to provide maternity assistance to all poor women. The bill would give all indigent married women the right to aid at home in the last few months of pregnancy, the type of aid and its duration to be determined by a physician. Women without homes would be cared for in maternity hospitals, asylums, and secret maternity institutions, the selection depending on how long they needed aid and whether or not they required secrecy. The law would require all departments to establish *asiles-ouvroirs* where indigent pregnant women could work and live during pregnancy. Finally, secret maternity hospitals would care for women in complete isolation.[22]

The report of the council remained buried in the files of the Ministry of the Interior, but some of its components were included in measures implemented over the next fifteen years. A law passed in 1893 to provide medical assistance for the indigent sick stipulated that women who became destitute as a result of pregnancy were entitled to receive medical care at childbirth and hospitalization if necessary. In many communes the necessary facilities were not available, however, and aid at home was useless if a woman had no place to go or wanted her secrecy protected. Besides, medical care was only a small part of what pregnant women needed. A few municipalities or departments offered financial assistance to fill the gap.[23] The assistance to prevent abandonment mandated by the law of 1869 was very inconsistent; in many departments it was too small to be of real help and in most places a woman could receive her first allocation only after she had nursed her child for three months.[24] A law passed in 1904, however,

22. Conseil supérieur de l'assistance publique, *Comptes-rendus*, Fascicule No. 39, pp. 5–8.
23. On communal and departmental assistance see A. Vallin, *La femme salariée et la maternité* (Paris: Arthur Rousseau, 1911), pp. 117–19; J. Fauconnet, *L'assistance aux filles-mères et aux enfants illégitimes du premier âge, en France* (Paris: V. Giard et E. Brière, 1907), p. 123; G. Eustache, *La puériculture, hygiène, et assistance* (Paris: J.-B. Ballière, 1903), pp. 262–64; P. Pecker, *La puériculture par l'assistance scientifique et maternelle à domicile* (Paris: Vigot Frères, 1904), pp. 119–20, 283–85; F. Merlin, "L'assistance aux femmes en couches" (unlabeled clipping in Bibliothèque Marguerite Durand, Dos. 614 MAT); "Un exemple à suivre: Le moyen ingénieux de corriger une loi défectueuse," *L'Action féminine* 6 (1914): 603–4. In Paris in the 1890s aid was available to married as well as single mothers, though in 1895 records show that 94 percent of the beneficiaries were single, widowed, or abandoned married women. Fuchs, "Morality and Poverty," pp. 299–301.
24. Delage, "Contribution à l'étude des questions d'assistance: Notes succinctes

expanded the definition of eligibility for this type of aid to include destitute legitimate as well as illegitimate children and specified minimum levels for the allocations. In 1906 the parliament further extended the legislation to cover all those whose parents did not have sufficient resources to care for them.

Women's Wage Labor and the Protection of Maternity

Although the desperate position of single mothers continued to pose concerns for policy makers, as the turn of the century approached physicians and legislators became increasingly concerned about married working-class women. Having had some success in reducing infant mortality from gastrointestinal diseases in the late nineteenth century, physicians in both France and the United States began to argue that the 17 to 20 percent of infant deaths resulting from "congenital debility"—prematurity, low birth weight, and congenital illnesses or malformations—could also be prevented. Deaths in the first month of life, the most treacherous, were clearly due more often to the mothers' condition during pregnancy and childbirth than to the care the children received. American physicians and public health authorities addressed this problem through prenatal care and education but French legislators and physicians focused their attention on women's wage labor.

In the 1890s physicians throughout Europe began to accumulate evidence that hard work during pregnancy could damage the fetus. In 1895, Pinard presented the results of a study of the birth weights of children born in the Baudelocque Clinic in Paris in a report to the Académie de médecine. He concluded that women who worked up until the time of birth had smaller children than those who rested in a refuge or hospital for ten days or more. Under Pinard's direction other researchers duplicated his results and also found that women who rested had, on an average, longer pregnancies than women who worked throughout pregnancy. Pinard, reporting these results to members of the commission on depopulation, concluded that aside from genetic diseases and diseases in the mother, the most common

---

sur le service des enfants assistés de la Gironde," *Congrès international de la protection de l'enfance*, p. 271.

cause of premature births was overwork.[25] Other researchers began to develop a long list of industrial toxins that endangered the children of women employed in certain industries.[26]

Resting for a month or two after childbirth was equally important not only for the mother's complete recovery and future reproductive health but also because it allowed her to care properly for her infant and to breast-feed during the child's most vulnerable months. In support of this claim one French author cited a study by a physician in Dresden, where legislation prohibited the employment of women who had given birth within the previous month. Studying a group of working-class mothers, this researcher found a distinctive pattern: the infant mortality rate was lowest in the first month, usually the most fatal month, but almost doubled in the second month when women were legally allowed to return to work.[27]

This evidence had alarming implications for France, inasmuch as many French mothers worked outside the home. Almost all of the women who gave birth in Pinard's clinic stayed in the hospital less than the twelve days physicians considered adequate in normal cases. Of about four hundred women Pinard surveyed, one hundred and thirty said they left to go back to work—forty-one because they feared losing their positions and eighty-nine in order to pay for their children's care.[28] A government study of women in various industries in Paris revealed that, though they generally did not fear losing their jobs if they took a maternity leave, the workers rarely stopped more than two or three days before their due date and usually returned within nine days.[29]

This information on the relationship between infant mortality and women's wage labor had alarming implications for France and lent support to the widely expressed view of politicians, moralists, sociologists, working-class leaders, and members of the Catholic hierarchy that women should not have to labor outside the home. The notion that tranquil and happy maternity should be honored as "one

25. Commission de la dépopulation, Sous-commission de la mortalité, *Séances, 1902–3,* Séances des 5 et 19 mars, p. 16.
26. See Deborah Bernson, *Nécessité d'une loi protectrice pour la femme ouvrière avant et après ses couches* (Paris: Société d'éditions scientifiques, 1899), pp. 30–48.
27. Ibid., p. 78.
28. Ibid., p. 115.
29. "Note sur la situation des femmes en couches dans l'industrie privée à Paris," n.d. (Archives nationales, F²² 445).

of the best elements in social peace and economic prosperity" was voiced by the left as well as the right, yet despite the prevalence of a gender ideology that asserted the primacy of women's maternal and domestic role, women played a vital and recognized role in the French economy.[30] The percentage of French women active in the labor force increased from 40 percent in 1866 to 59 percent in 1906. In 1905 this included 20 percent of married women, the highest percentage in the western world.[31] Many of these women had small children. In 1872, 14.3 percent of families in Roubaix with the youngest child under five years and 19.3 percent of those in Anzin relied at least partly on the mother's income.[32] In 1906 nearly one-third of the women active in the nonagricultural labor force worked in their homes, assisting their artisan husbands, working in the family business, or taking in home work. Their long hours were often not compatible with the care of young children, and families could not spare their economic contribution; many of the children sent out to nurse were the offspring of artisans and shopkeepers.[33]

This pattern of female employment was quite different from that of England and the United States; industrialization was slower in France, and into the late nineteenth century manufacturing was based in small, often family-owned firms, while agriculture remained a much more important part of the economy. In 1911, 69 percent of single women in England were employed, but only 9.6 percent of married women. In 1900 the U.S. Census showed that only 5.6 percent of all married women in the United States were engaged in "gainful occupations" in the home or outside. Married women worked outside the home in the United States only in the poorest

30. Quotation in Chambre des Députes, Annexe au procès-verbal de la séance du 30 juin 1910, *Proposition de loi tendant à améliorer et à égaliser les conditions des congés de maternité accordés aux femmes employées dans les services de l'état et dans les établissements industrielles, présentée par Louis Marin et Betoulle;* Marie-Hélène Zylberberg-Hocquard, *Féminisme et syndicalisme en France* (Paris: Editions Anthropos, 1978), pp. 91, 139–40, 185–90; Offen, "Depopulation, Nationalism, and Feminism in Fin-de-Siècle France," p. 660.

31. Zylberberg-Hocquard, *Féminisme et syndicalisme en France,* p. 17; Fernand Braudel and Ernest Labrousse, eds., *Histoire économique et sociale de la France* (Paris: Presses Universitaires de France, 1979), vol. 4:1, p. 458.

32. See Louise A. Tilly, "Structure de l'emploi, travail des femmes, et changement démographique dans deux villes industrielles: Anzin et Roubaix, 1872–1906," *Le mouvement social,* no. 105 (October–December 1978): 45.

33. Département de la Seine, Protection des enfants du premier âge, *Rapport annuel,* 1906, p. 72.

families; of these, few sent their children away to a nurse. Thus working mothers were not invisible in France as they were in the United States and Britain. As Mary Lynn Stewart writes, the "deep-seated belief that women belonged in the home was usually tempered by economic calculations that the secondary labor market needed cheap labor."[34]

At the heart of French maternal and child welfare policy, therefore, was the effort to reconcile women's two roles: mother and worker. Enabling women to take time off from work to give birth, recuperate, and care for their newborns was an important aspect of this reconciliation. Eventually, France would see the development of a system of mandatory, government-compensated maternity leaves. This system evolved within the context of larger debates about the proper role of employers and public powers in social insurance generally.

In the provision of maternal welfare, corporate efforts preceded legislation. In 1909 government investigators found that at least 151 employers voluntarily offered some kind of protection for their workers during maternity.[35] This figure included employers who offered direct cash benefits, free medical care, or aid in kind; employers who contributed to a mutual aid fund on behalf of their workers; and those who allowed or required women to take maternity leaves. In most cases the workers also had to make some contribution to a maternity fund. A few employers offered relatively comprehensive benefits, but these were exceptional. More typical were A. Badin and Son in Barentin, near Rouen, who offered a bonus to those workers who breast-fed and maintained a crèche and facilities for nursing. In Wasquehal, an industrial city in the Nord, departmental health authorities persuaded industrialists to pay one franc for each day one of

34. Mary Lynn Stewart, *Women, Work, and the French State: Labour Protection and Social Patriarchy, 1879–1919* (Kingston, Ont.: McGill-Queen's University Press, 1989), p. 57; Mary Lynn McDougall, "Working-Class Women during the Industrial Revolution," in *Becoming Visible: Women in European History,* ed. Renate Bridenthal and Claudia Koonz (Boston: Houghton Mifflin, 1977), p. 268; Leslie Tentler, *Wage-Earning Women: Industrial Work and Family Life in the United States, 1900–1930* (New York: Oxford University Press, 1979), p. 154; Jane Jenson, "Gender and Reproduction; or, Babies and the State," *Studies in Political Economy* 20 (1986): 29, 35; Jenson, "Paradigms and Political Discourse," pp. 240–41, 244.

35. "Enquête du service de l'inspection du travail sur la protection actuellement assurée aux femmes en état de grossesse ou récemment accouchées occupées dans le commerce ou l'industrie," October–November 1909 (Archives nationales, F^{22} 445).

their employees spent at the local maternity hospital.[36] A factory
in Noisel-sur-Marne provided medical care, free medication, a
layette, and twenty francs to cover the costs of childbirth. The benefits did not amount to nearly enough, however, to make up for
the wages the mother lost if she took the month-long maternity
leave required by the company.[37]

Employers also created the *mutualité maternelle,* or maternal mutual
aid society, destined to become one of the most popular maternal
and child welfare institutions. The *mutualité maternelle* offered the
benefits of charity, including a committee of female patrons who
exercised their personal moral influence with the beneficiaries. It had
none of the disadvantages of traditional benevolence, however, because it required the beneficiaries to contribute to the fund. To many
legislators mutual aid seemed to provide the solution to France's
maternal and infant welfare dilemma; by subsidizing the *mutualité
maternelle,* it seemed, the government could provide comprehensive
coverage without imposing on employers or public funds and without
undermining the incentives for moral independence among the working class.

Until the middle of the nineteenth century, mutual aid societies
were a working-class tradition in France. Some were descended from
old trade and craft brotherhoods and others were fronts for illegal
labor-organizing activities. In the late nineteenth century, however,
liberal philanthropists, Social Catholics, and St. Simonians became
attracted to the concept as a substitute for traditional charity because
it could teach thrift (*prévoyance*).[38] Contributing from their own pock-
ets, these philanthropists diverted mutualism away from its original
purposes, which included freeing members of the working class from
dependence on charity in times of need. The new generation of mutual
aid societies were enlightened charitable organizations, distributing
aid not at random but only to the deserving poor—the thrifty—and
in theory thus fostering sobriety and other related virtues. By 1900

36. J. Hideux, *Crèche des etablissements A. Badin et Fils: Prime à l'allaitement maternel*
(Barentin: n.p., 1908).
37. Elie Decherf, "Etude critique des oeuvres françaises de protection de l'enfance,"
Bericht über den III. Internationalen Kongress für Sauglingsschutz (Gouttes de Lait) (Berlin:
Georg Stilke, 1912), vol. 1, p. 388.
38. See Zylberberg-Hocquard, *Féminisme et syndicalisme en France,* p. 11; Jacques
Léonard, *La médecine entre les savoirs et les pouvoirs: Histoire intellectuelle et politique de
la médecine française au XIXe siècle* (Paris: Aubier Montaigne, 1981), p. 306.

mutualism was the favorite form of insurance among liberals, because it constituted an alternative to obligatory insurance legislation. In 1898 the national legislature passed a law facilitating the establishment of mutual aid societies and provided subsidies for them.[39]

The first mutual aid society designed specifically to protect women against the hazards of maternity was founded in 1862 by an industrialist, Jean Dollfus of Mulhouse. Dollfus required each of his female employees aged eighteen to forty-five to pay twenty centimes into a maternity fund every two weeks. In return she was entitled to her full wages during six weeks of maternity leave.[40] In 1891 a group of Parisian merchants and manufacturers organized a *mutualité maternelle* in Paris with the funds from a charity fête and with the aid of three syndical chambers (sewing and clothing manufacture; lace and embroidery; trimming, buttons, and haberdashery).[41] At first the society admitted only women working in the fashion and clothing industries, but in 1904 it expanded to admit all working women in the department.

Though the *mutualité maternelle* was designed as an alternative to charity, it had many charitable characteristics. Members' subscriptions supplied only about one-sixth of the organization's funds; the subscriptions of honorary members, donations, and public subsidies furnished the rest. A group of female patrons, sometimes the wives, sisters, and daughters of the employer, made the rules. These women also administered each section, distributed the cash benefits in person, made sure that the recipients followed their physicians' instructions and rested according to the society's regulations, and distributed additional items of clothing or cradles at their own discretion.

Despite the key role of women in maintaining these organizations, men and employers dominated the movement. Most *mutualités maternelles* were founded by syndical chambers or by individual employers, though general mutual aid societies in several departments formed branches to cover the maternity needs of the members and their families. At the first national congress of *mutualités maternelles* all the honorary presidents and all the officers of the organizing com-

39. See Léonard, *La médecine entre les savoirs et les pouvoirs*, p. 307; Stone, *Search for Social Peace*, pp. 64–65; Hatzfield, *Du paupérisme à la sécurité sociale*, pp. 202–8.
40. Vallin, *La femme salariée et la maternité*, p. 147.
41. Félix Poussineau, "Rapport sur la mutualité maternelle," *Bericht über den III. Internationalen Kongress für Sauglingsschutz*, p. 890.

mission were men; only four members of the commission were female presidents of local sections. Four hundred and twenty-four of the 540 members were men.[42]

Initially the *mutualités maternelles* limited their activities to the provision of financial support for women who took time off, but they soon became comprehensive maternal and infant health institutions. In addition to cash benefits of twelve to twenty-five francs a week for four weeks after childbirth, most distributed additional benefits to women who nursed for two months and additional items such as layettes, cradles, linen, and medications as needed. They also maintained milk stations and infant health consultations and provided prenatal care and a home assistant while the mother was in bed.[43] Following the typical pattern of French maternal and infant welfare programs, financial assistance and medical supervision were inseparable aspects of the *mutualité maternelle*.

In 1913 the Mutualité maternelle of Paris had twenty sections in the city and forty-one in the suburbs; there were fifty-one similar institutions in other departments. An additional 352 general mutual aid societies received government funds to subsidize their maternity benefit provisions.[44] In early 1913 the municipal council of Paris demonstrated its faith in mutualism through a subsidy of eighty thousand francs, enabling the society to extend its benefits and services to poor pregnant women. As a result, the *mutualité* took over the administration of much of the city's maternal welfare program.[45] To aid in this work the Mutualité maternelle of Paris received a larger public subsidy than did any other private maternal and child welfare agency in the country.

To many, mutualism seemed to offer a creative new vision of social organization. The Alliance d'hygiène social, a "social hygiene" association focusing on tuberculosis, alcoholism, and infant mortality,

42. *Premier Congrès national de la mutualité maternelle,* 1908, pp. 4–5.

43. Félix Poussineau, *La maternité chez l'ouvrière en 1910* (Paris: La Mutualité maternelle, 1910), p. 4; Jacques Mornet, *Les mutualités maternelles* (Paris: Blond, 1911), pp. 18, 28; Alliance d'hygiène sociale, *La lutte sociale contre la mortalité infantile dans le Pas-de-Calais et le Nord: Extraits du compte-rendu du Congrès d'hygiène sociale d'Arras* (Bordeaux: Librairie de la Mutualité, 1904), pp. 323–25.

44. Ministre de l'intérieur, "Rapport sur l'emploi du crédit ouvert au Ministre de l'intérieur pour subvenir aux oeuvres d'assistance maternelle et de protection du premier âge," *Journal officiel,* January 16, 1913: 454–56.

45. *Bulletin trimestrielle de la Ligue contre la mortalité infantile,* 2d ser., 12 (1913): 5.

emphasized mutual aid as the solution to some of French society's most distressing problems. At a meeting of the alliance in 1904, Paul Foubert claimed that when mutual aid enabled them to stay at home and clean their homes, women chased away germs, saved their children's lives, and kept their husbands and sons away from the bar.[46] Mutualism, argued another leader of the movement, was a moralizing force; as a school of social responsibility it taught people to accept the idea of the universal equality of all and the right of all to social justice.[47] In theory, mutual aid societies also promoted class harmony because they facilitated personal contact between the bourgeoisie and the working class. This new relationship would be different from the traditional benevolent one, however, because mutual aid societies, by requiring the members to contribute to the fund, provided aid that was not humiliating.

Mutual aid also reached women not usually touched by private charity: working-class women who were too proud to ask for charity or public assistance. These women had the praiseworthy "self-respect" that public welfare officials were anxious to instill in the working class as a whole. They were the heroines of the infant health movement—"these valiant creatures, often as needy as they are brave"—because they bore children for the nation at the expense of their health and though exhausted by work. They faithfully fulfilled their social role, undaunted by poverty, overwork, and humiliation, and without asking for assistance.[48] This group was the key to France's future, because they were the women who would bear the nation's next generation's work force. Félix Poussineau, founder of the Mutualité maternelle of Paris and the institution's most active advocate, wrote, referring to the benefits of his favorite institution: "Women, having less fear of the crisis of maternity, restored each time by a refreshing rest, sure of assistance that is not humiliating, no longer see the coming of a new child as an increased burden and a direct cause of poverty."[49]

Voluntary corporate welfare plans, including *mutualités maternelles,*

---

46. Alliance d'hygiène sociale, *La lutte sociale contre la mortalité infantile,* pp. 321–22.

47. Ibid., p. 6.

48. Ibid., p. 146.

49. Félix Poussineau, *La mutualité maternelle: Rapport fait à la Commission de la dépopulation* (Melun: Emile Legrand, 1903), p. 13.

however, covered only a small percentage of workers; in the 1890s politicians, welfare officials, and physicians began to press for legislation making maternity leaves mandatory for all wage-earning women. Not only would such legislation save the lives of many children, its advocates argued, but it would preserve the mothers' health and consequently their future reproductive capacity. Maternity leaves might even address the depopulation crisis directly, because women who were protected from overwork, anxiety, and injury during pregnancy and childbirth would be less likely to practice birth control than those whose experience of childbearing was one of pain, emotional stress, financial worry, and isolation. While private charities and most categories of public assistance benefited mostly indigent women and children, these new proposals, like *mutualités maternelles,* were designed the reach "respectable" working-class families. For those who believed that the declining birthrate was a function of economic hardship, maternity benefits seemed to be a significant step toward resolving the population crisis, because they would eliminate some of the financial stress associated with childbearing.

The Debate over Maternity Leave

Most of the controversy over maternity-leave legislation concerned the issue of compensation for the wages lost; the question of whether the state could or should establish the principle of a right to public assistance was one that divided politicians along ideological lines. While socialists argued that the poor had an absolute right to unconditional assistance, the Republican majority sought ways to overcome the objections posed by liberal economic theory and by their own fears that financial assistance fostered dependency and moral irresponsibility. In part, they evaded the question by defining maternity benefits not as assistance but as payment for the services women rendered to the state through motherhood. They also proposed that recipients be required to meet certain conditions, such as submission to medical supervision and home visits; maternity benefits could thus be described as the price paid by the state for controlling women's performance of their maternal duties.

At an international congress on labor legislation in 1890 a French delegate, the moderate Republican political leader Jules Simon, introduced a resolution asking governments to prohibit the employment of women for a month after childbirth. The resolution passed unanimously, and within fifteen years all the European nations except France, Russia, and Turkey had legislation to this effect.[50] This legislation was of questionable value, however: although in several countries the women affected benefited from compulsory sickness- or maternity-insurance provisions, in most countries they were entitled to no compensation for the wages they lost.[51]

Most French advocates of maternal welfare legislation recognized the flaws in these provisions and insisted that women be compensated for their lost wages. In Belgium and England, they pointed out, where the laws prohibited women from working but did not provide for compensation, women did their best to get around the law. Deborah Bernson, one of the few female French physicians visible in the campaign for maternity-protection legislation, wrote angrily that the existing laws were "cruelly ironic." How dare the legislators, she asked, claim that such legislation was in the workers' interest? In fact, she argued, workers suffered from such measures because capitalists, with no interest in employing a woman weakened by pregnancy, cared not at all how she would find the means to live. "The human being," Bernson concluded, "is completely obliterated before their fury for profit."[52] Maternity leave without compensation, wrote Louis Marin, representing the Association nationale française pour la protection légale des travailleurs, was not only antidemocratic and prevented repopulation but also "opposed to all improvements in family life."[53]

In part it was the insistence of socialists and Republicans that maternity leave legislation include financial provisions which held up the French parliament on this issue for so long. The future of the nation was at stake, argued Marin and others, and supporting preg-

50. Felhoen, *Etude statistique sur la mortalité infantile à Roubaix*, p. 227; Gemähling, "La femme ouvrière et la maternité," *L'Action populaire* 98 (1905–6): 20. On French maternity-leave debates in the context of wider debates over the regulation of women's work, see Stewart, *Women, Work, and the French State*, chap. 8.

51. See Vallin, *La femme salariée et la maternité*, pp. 43–69; Mrs. Max West, "The Development of Prenatal Care in the United States," *Transactions of the American Association for the Study and Prevention of Infant Mortality* 5 (1914): 76–79.

52. Bernson, *Nécessité d'une loi protectrice*, p. 111.

53. Louis Marin and Paul Strauss, rapporteurs, Association nationale française pour la protection légale des travailleurs, "La protection de la maternité ouvrière," *Compte rendu des discussions.—Voeux Adoptés*, 7th ser., no. 2 (1912): 14.

nant women would help to save it. Considering that the nation spent about one billion francs a year for national defense, Maurice Berteaux, deputy from the Seine-et-Oise, pointed out, it was completely reasonable to expect the government to come up with the twenty-five million necessary to defend mothers and children from sickness and death, the greatest enemies of humanity.[54] In 1901 the members of the national obstetrical and pediatric association resolved that all pregnant women should have the right to the assistance necessary to live under the appropriate conditions during the last three months of pregnancy and the month after childbirth. This statement served as a model for other bodies, including the Commission on Depopulation, which approved a similar resolution introduced by Pinard in 1902.[55]

In the parliament the issue of maternity leaves did not divide legislators clearly along ideological lines.[56] While a few staunch liberals insisted that prohibiting the employment of women after childbirth violated their right to work, by the early 1890s the parliamentary debates reflected a remarkable consensus that such regulation was appropriate and even that it was necessary to compensate women in some fashion for the loss of their wages. The continuing disagreement concerned the source of the funds and the extension of the legislation to farmers' wives, to women employed at home, and to housewives.

To many writers and legislators, mutual aid seemed to promise a solution to France's maternity-leave problem. Because it offered optional insurance it answered the objections of the ardent defenders of individualism. It also partly answered the problem of public expense. The Ministry of Labor estimated that of the 880,000 women over

54. Maurice Berteaux, Preface to Pecker, *La puériculture par l'assistance scientifique*, p. 29.

55. Eustache, *La puériculture, hygiène, et assistance*, p. 39; Commission de la dépopulation, Sous-commission de la mortalité, *Rapport général sur les causes de la mortalité* (Présenté par M. Paul Strauss), 1911, p. 64; Commission de la dépopulation, Sous-commission de la mortalité, *Séances, 1902–3*, Séance du 2 juillet 1902, p. 19.

56. For an account of the legislative debate over maternity leaves see Stewart, *Women, Work, and the French State,* chap. 8, and Mary Lynn McDougall, "Protecting Infants: The French Campaign for Maternity Leaves, 1890s–1913," *French Historical Studies* 13 (1983): 79–105. Stewart also argues that in the early debates arguments based on humanitarian appeals failed, while in the later debates, after the turn of the century, the utilitarian concern with depopulation provided the most powerful argument for maternity-leave legislation.

eighteen employed in industry and commerce forty to fifty thousand gave birth each year. If all women working outside their homes were included, the figure came to about 140,000.[57] A. Vallin calculated that providing benefits for all working women would thus cost the government sixteen to seventeen million francs a year.[58] Requiring women to pay one or two francs a year into existing societies subsidized by the state—"a contribution so small that it is rather a sign of goodwill than a financial sacrifice"—would prevent all appearance of charity, Poussineau argued, and would save the government money in the administration of the program.[59]

In 1886 the Social Catholic and monarchist deputy Count Albert de Mun proposed, as part of a bill regulating women's working hours, that all women should be required to take four weeks' rest after birth. Few of his colleagues voiced their support for the measure. The reporting committee withdrew the proposal without argument after Yves Guyot, a liberal deputy, objected to the idea of requiring workers to furnish a certificate from a physician or midwife. Employers had no right, Guyot argued, to look into the details of workers' private lives.[60]

The Chamber of Deputies debated de Mun's proposal several times over the next six years.[61] In 1891, when the liberal deputy François Deloncle argued that the adoption of de Mun's proposal would mean abandoning women to asylums and the street by taking away their means of support, Emile Brousse, a reform socialist, took up his suggestion. Unless women were compensated for their loss of wages, Brousse maintained, they would try to avoid pregnancy and single women would resort increasingly to abortion and infanticide. The only solution, he concluded, was to provide compensation. He proposed allocations of one franc a day from a fund fed by the state, the departments, and private donations. Brousse admitted that the measure would be expensive, but, "What is that to save the health of so

57. "Note sur la proposition de loi de M. Strauss sur la protection et l'assistance des mères et des nourrices," October 19, 1911 (Archives nationales, F^{22} 445).

58. Vallin, La femme salariée et la maternité, p. 192.

59. Félix Poussineau, La mutualité maternelle: Rapport complémentaire adressé à la Commission de la dépopulation (Melun: Emile Legrand, 1903), pp. 11–12.

60. Annales de la Chambre des Députés (hereafter ACD), June 18, 1888, p. 1807.

61. ACD, July 8, 1890, February 5, 1891, October 29, 1892, November 3–4, 1892; Stewart, Women, Work, and the French State, pp. 173–78.

many children who, one day, will be entrusted with defending our frontiers?"[62]

Brousse's amendment convinced de Mun to withdraw his proposal altogether; the issue had proven far more complex and controversial than he had imagined. Liberals repeatedly objected that the measure would violate women's right to work and that the state had no business interfering in such private matters. The deputies' embarrassment at any allusion to sexuality and childbirth also hampered the debates.[63] The Chamber continued to discuss the question, however, and by 1892, with the population crisis much in the public eye, the debate centered not on the principle of compensation but on who should be covered, to what extent, and through what means. A few liberals maintained their position, but members on both the right and the left supported some kind of compulsory maternity-insurance system. Some liberals were even willing to modify or put aside their principles to accommodate measures to protect maternal and infant health. The best known of these, Paul Leroy-Beaulieu, opposed all legislation to regulate the work of adults, but he made an exception in the case of maternity leaves because the life of another person—the child—was at stake.[64]

Counterproposals from the left and the right defined the terms of the debate. Paul Lafargue and other socialists argued that employers, who profited from the exploitation of women's labor, should support some of the financial burden and that all working women, including those employed at home, should benefit. De Mun, on the other hand, objected to direct public assistance on the grounds that it would discourage individual thrift and stifle private initiative. The only proper role of government in public assistance, he argued, was to subsidize and encourage the work of private organizations.[65] Other conservative deputies maintained that farm wives were equally hard working and thus should be included.[66]

In 1892 the Chamber adopted Brousse's proposal that the national government and the departments share the costs of providing benefits

62. ACD, February 5, 1891, p. 232.
63. ACD, July 8, 1890, pp. 1877–78.
64. André Jousselin, Préliminaires de la loi du 27 novembre 1909 (Paris: Librairie de la Société du Recueil Sirey, 1910), p. 69.
65. ACD, October 29, 1892, p. 1381.
66. Ibid., p. 1382.

of one franc a day.[67] Though the proposal made no further progress
in the legislature, the general idea was accepted by the majority of
deputies. Few took seriously Lafargue's proposal that all working
women be paid three to six francs a day from the fourth month of
pregnancy through the entire nursing period, but Deloncle's staunch
liberal position was equally unpopular.[68] Beginning in 1892, the minister of finance posed a major obstacle to maternity benefit legislation,
however. The minister opposed all proposals to extend the coverage
to nonindustrial workers on the grounds that the financial burden
would be too great, and in 1892 he proposed that the communes take
on most of the responsibility with some aid from the departments.[69]

Paul Strauss introduced a new paid maternity-leave bill into the
more conservative Senate in 1899.[70] When Strauss's bill first came up
for debate in 1903 the Senate voted to send it to a second reading,
but it moved very slowly after that. Strauss held the middle ground
between those, both right and left, who would extend the bill to
cover all women habitually doing paid work and the minister of
finance, who threatened to withdraw the government's support of
the bill if such an amendment were accepted.[71] Strauss and the government's representatives were determined to avoid establishing a
right to assistance. Instead, they argued that the bill was essentially
a measure to regulate industrial labor and the compensation a logical
corollary designed to meet the needs thus generated. Though agricultural workers and women who worked at home were deserving,
no regulatory structure existed which would make it possible to include them in this bill. The emphasis on industrialization as a cause
of infant mortality and depopulation made this a plausible position.

In 1906, Senator Engerand introduced a more moderate measure
that would prohibit employers from firing workers for taking a
maternity leave of up to eight weeks.[72] In their debates on this bill

67. ACD, November 4, 1892.
68. ACD, November 3, 1892, pp. 1389–90.
69. ACD, October 29, 1892, p. 1382.
70. This proposal initially included mandatory maternity leaves with state-funded
compensation, measures for regulating the dairy industry, and certain of the proposals
of the Conseil supérieur de l'assistance publique for maternity hospitals, but by the
second reading was limited to maternity leaves alone. Sénat, Documents parlementaires,
No. 235, Nov. 14, 1899.
71. Annales du Sénat (hereafter AS), December 3, 1903.
72. Chambre des Députés, Documents parlementaires, No. 199, July 5, 1906.

the senators explicitly supported the inclusion of single women. Whether the mothers were single or married, Strauss argued, ("They are all mothers," interjected a voice from the right), they were all "holy and august for this reason," and the legislature had a responsibility to protect them all.[73] The law also substantially increased state subsidies to private maternal and infant welfare institutions. The Engerand bill became law in 1909. The government's support of this bill reflected its stated policy, which was that it preferred to subsidize and encourage mutual aid societies rather than to pay direct benefits.[74]

Finally approved by the Senate in 1912, Strauss's bill passed to the Chamber of Deputies, where the members of that body blamed the conservatives in the Senate for the slow progress of the legislation. Engerand and the minister of labor, defending the bill against more radical proposals to cover all poor women, also cited the conservative tendencies of the Senate as a reason for moderation. Socialist deputies such as Henri Schmidt wanted to include housewives; in a sense, Schmidt argued, the bill discriminated against the most needy inasmuch as women who already had several children usually stayed home to care for their families.[75] The minister of labor insisted that the government support all maternal and child health measures but that it was necessary to proceed in stages. Leftist deputies finally withdrew their amendments and the Chamber voted to pass the bill, adding the following resolution: "The Chamber, resolved to assure maternity assistance to all women without adequate resources, asks the Government to provide, in the Finance Law of 1913, the ways and means necessary to give immediately to women working at home the consideration accorded to workers, employees, and domestic servants working away from home."[76] Less than a year later the Chamber adopted Schmidt's proposal to extend benefits to all women without adequate resources.[77]

The progress of the debate over twenty-five years indicates a growing consensus in favor of obligatory compensated maternity leaves. The population crisis provided the most common and persuasive

73. AS, October 30, 1908, p. 429.
74. Vallin, La femme salariée et la maternité, p. 193.
75. ACD, June 12, 1913, p. 1735.
76. Ibid., p. 1876.
77. ACD, March 17, 1914, p. 1672.

arguments for maternity benefits. By 1913 the resurgence of French nationalism and a growing consensus in support of military preparedness in response to the resurgence of the German threat made the depopulation crisis all the more compelling.[78] Politicians did not agree, however, on which form of insurance would best serve the social and economic interests of the nation. The legislation attempted to answer many of the objections to direct compensation by the government: women would receive the benefits, for example, only on the condition that they rested and followed the instructions of a home visitor designated by the local welfare bureau. The law also allowed municipalities to arrange for private organizations to take over the distribution of benefits and the supervision of recipients, thus leaving room for private charity to work its moral influence.[79]

The Strauss Law, combining financial benefits with close hygienic supervision, was a major victory for the Radical Republican vision of maternal and child welfare; the call for urgent measures to counteract depopulation had prevailed over the liberal and conservative opposition to public welfare. At the same time the socialist proposal that benefits be distributed to all poor women, rather than just to those who worked outside the home, failed. The measure was, as the government had hoped, one designed not so much to alleviate poverty as to encourage childbearing among working-class women.

Whether the law functioned as its proponents hoped is not clear, because flaws in the legislation made enforcement difficult. To a limited extent, the imperatives created by the population crisis prevailed over the prerogatives of capital, because it was now illegal to hire a woman who had recently given birth. To protect workers from intrusive and embarrassing questions by their employers, however, the law stipulated that an employer could be penalized only if the government could prove that he or she had *knowingly* violated the law.

---

78. On nationalism and military preparedness in French politics and social policy in the prewar years, see Nye, *Crime, Madness, and Politics*, p. 314; Stewart, *Women, Work, and the French State*, p. 185; John C. Hunter, "The Problem of the French Birth Rate on the Eve of World War I," *French Historical Studies* 2 (1962): 491–92; Eugen Weber, *The Nationalist Revival in France, 1905–1914* (Berkeley: University of California Press, 1968), p. 10.

79. Ministre de l'intérieur, "Circulaire relative à l'assistance aux femmes en couches (loi du 17 juin 1913 et loi de finances du 30 juillet 1913, articles 68–75)," *Journal officiel*, August 11, 1913: 7242–45; Ministre du travail et de la prévoyance sociale, Circulaire du 13 août 1913, "Repos des femmes en couches" (Archives nationales, F²² 445).

The minister of labor thus encouraged voluntary compliance; he instructed inspectors to appeal to the employers' patriotism, emphasizing that the measure would help to counteract depopulation and that employers themselves would benefit in the long run as a result of the growth in the supply of labor. At the same time, inspectors had to convince workers that it was in their best interests to take advantage of the law and that the benefits were theirs by right and not out of charity.[80] The problem was that the benefits compensated women only partially for the wages they lost. There is some evidence that women took advantage of the law but that they understood their own interests differently from the legislators. During World War I, for example, visiting nurses in Lyons observed that women often did not believe that the benefits carried the obligation to rest; some worked until the last minute while collecting wages, state benefits, and private assistance.[81]

Eight-week maternity leaves, even if compensated, went only part of the way toward solving the problems of women workers with young children; providing infants with care after their mothers returned to their jobs was another major challenge of French maternal and child welfare policy. By the late nineteenth century, physicians and politicians began to see the crèche as a replacement for the nursing industry and as an essential part of the solution to depopulation, not only because it relieved some of the stress faced by working mothers but because it made a positive contribution to children's health. As a result, reformers in France, unlike their American colleagues, viewed the funding of child care as an obligation of the employer or the public.

Crèches and the Protection of Infant Health

In 1844, Firmin Marbeau proposed to the welfare bureau in a poor Parisian neighborhood that it establish a child care facility, or crèche, as an alternative to the reputedly dirty, careless and ignorant baby

---

80. Ministre du travail et de la prévoyance sociale, Circulaire du 13 août 1913 (Archives nationales, F^{22} 445).

81. Emmanuel Perret, *Les visiteuses de l'enfance: Le "District Nursing"; Un essai d'hygiène sociale par la Croix-rouge américaine à Lyon* (Trévoux: Imprimerie J. Jeannin, 1919), p. 123.

sitters with whom poor mothers left their children. Marbeau hoped that the crèche would benefit destitute children, often kept alive only by their mothers' begging. He thus arranged for fourteen women to be freed from the almshouse to demonstrate that the crèche enabled them to earn their living without begging.[82]

Though he had originally conceived the crèche as an institution to prevent begging, Marbeau came to see it as an essential service for working mothers; in the 1870s he advocated the establishment of a crèche in every commune or neighborhood where at least one hundred women were employed outside the home. Members of the committee appointed by the Chamber of Deputies to consider the Roussel Law in 1874 agreed that crèches could enable women to avoid sending their children to nurse in the country.[83] Crèches gained popularity among both secular and religious charitable agencies; by 1868 there were eighty-five crèches in the country, including twenty-two in the Seine. By 1888 there were more than 150.[84]

The crèche mirrored one of the fundamental paradoxes of French maternal and child welfare policy. While on the one hand legislators hoped to encourage women to care for their infants at home on the premise that a mother's care was the best, on the other hand they undermined the independence of women by supervising their activities and regulating their conditions. Although the crèche was designed to allow mothers to work without being separated from their children, the literature in favor of crèches clearly illustrates the mistrust French legislators and physicians felt toward the abilities of French women, and the willingness of these men to take responsibility out of mothers' hands. Critics frequently blamed crèches for spreading contagious diseases, but defenders of the institution ultimately claimed that children were better off in the crèche than at home. Although the goal of the crèche was to maintain the integrity of the family and enable women to fulfill their natural female role of motherhood, proponents of crèches often implied that it was morally

82. Firmin Marbeau, "Réglementation des crèches publiques et privées," *Deuxième Congrès national d'assistance* (Rouen: Imprimerie Cagniard, 1898), vol. 1, p. 68.

83. Chambre des Députés, Annexe au procès-verbal de la séance du 9 juin 1874, *Rapport au nom de la commission chargée d'examiner la proposition de Loi Roussel*, p. 99.

84. Delpech, "Rapport sur l'hygiène des crèches," *Bulletin de l'Académie de médecine*, 34 (1869): 874; Conseil supérieur de l'assistance publique, *Comptes-rendus*, Fascicule No. 6, 1888, "Crèches, sociétés de charité maternelles."

healthier for mothers to work than to be dependent upon charity. As the administrators of one crèche described its role: "Compare two mothers: one, in order not to leave her newborn, extends her hand to passers-by, she begs in snow and rain; the other gets up at five o'clock in the morning, brings her child to the crèche, and runs to work; she comes back to nurse and returns to the crèche at least twice during the day; when evening comes, she takes the child with her. Which one does the most good for her child?"[85]

Though in theory one purpose of the crèche was to enable mothers to spend more time with their children, most crèches required regular attendance even when the parents took a day off from work. Some physicians complained that children were sometimes kept at home because of the parents' "laziness" and that mothers with irregular employment brought their children irregularly.[86] Henri Bouquet argued that parents should become accustomed to being prompt. Those who persisted in their irregular behavior—those whose attendance depended on the season, the work they had, and their personal convenience—should be permanently excluded. Consistent attendance and promptness were necessary, Bouquet insisted, both to facilitate the crèche's routine and to enable children to benefit from the crèche's regime, a key point of which was regularity.[87] A report on crèches in the Seine proposed offering rewards for regular attendance or for the best-kept children to stimulate attendance.[88]

Crèches, like most charitable and public welfare institutions, were not purely practical services. Their advocates frequently claimed they exerted a "moralizing" influence. Many crèches run by religious orders or under clerical patronage were designed to introduce children to Catholic practices and beliefs at an early age in the hopes that the children would spread the word to their parents. The Catholic crèches of Rouen, reported one writer, "contribute much to raising the level of familial feelings in popular households." Under their healthy influence many free unions had been consecrated by marriage and blessed by the church, and many children thus legitimized. This writer

---

85. Crèche de la Bastide, *Rapport annuel*, 1909, p. 5.

86. Felhoen, *Etude statistique sur la mortalité infantile à Roubaix*, p. 194; Henri Bouquet, *La puériculture sociale* (Paris: Blond, 1911), p. 204.

87. Bouquet, *La puériculture sociale*, p. 123.

88. Département de la Seine, Protection des enfants du premier âge, *Rapport annuel*, 1890, p. 100.

cited the example of a young child who, on returning from the crèche in the evening, took his father's hand, showed him how to make the sign of the cross, and asked him, "Papa, prayer like at the crèche."[89]

To the secular Republican authorities such prosyletizing was anathema, but they too believed that the crèche could be a powerful social influence. Some argued that the crèche benefited the whole family inasmuch as parents, gratified to see their children healthy and happy, were moved to strengthen their commitment to the family.[90] The crèche was not a form of charity, its advocates were quick to point out, because in most cases the parents paid a small fee. Like the *mutualité maternelle* an institution of *prévoyance* (literally, "foresight"), it established the principle that parents should undergo some sacrifices for their children's benefit.

Just as important were the hygienic benefits of creches. Most crèches admitted only children of women forced by poverty to work, in order to prevent the separation of mother and child when not absolutely necessary. Not only was motherhood women's sacred duty, but statistics showed that children cared for by their mothers were far healthier than those cared for by paid caretakers. Advocates of crèches, however, believed that they were more than simply a necessary evil: they were actually a positive force and provided better care and a healthier environment for children than working-class mothers did.

Marbeau reported that the only criticism of his first crèche was that the contrast between the excellent conditions in the crèche and those at home could be fatal.[91] Crèches should be spread as widely as possible, one of the leaders in the child health movement in Bordeaux wrote, in order "to ensure to the child that which is indispensable to him from the point of view of health, food, and good hygiene, and which he most often lacks in the households of the indigent and even of the working class."[92] Because the staff bathed the children each day and often sent home sterilized milk for their night feedings, mothers had little to do. As the annual report of the Oeuvre nouvelle

89. Victor Duval, *La charité à Rouen: Les oeuvres catholiques* (Rouen: Ancienne imprimerie Lapierre, 1895), pp. 33–34.

90. Boluquet, "Rapport sur l'oeuvre des crèches dans la Gironde," *Congrès international de la protection de l'enfance*, p. 129.

91. Marbeau, "Réglementation des crèches publiques et privées," p. 67.

92. Boluquet, "Rapport sur l'oeuvre des crèches dans la Gironde," p. 129.

des crèches parisiennes bragged, during the whole of the baby's stay at the crèche—until the age of three years—the child cost the family nothing.[93] In some ways, however, crèches actually tried to protect children from their mothers. The crèche's sanitary measures, for example, included daily sterilization of the clothes in which the children came from home, and parents were never permitted inside the crèche itself. A special antechamber was provided for mothers who came to nurse their children during the day, and they were often required to put on a blouse belonging to the crèche and wash their hands and breasts.[94]

The fear that bringing infants together would create the perfect conditions for the spread of contagious diseases was genuine, and even those crèches that were run according to accepted standards sometimes suffered epidemics. Among the critics of crèches were numbered some of the most prominent physicians in the infant health movement. Adolphe Pinard stood alone in his insistence that no infant health measure was appropriate if it recognized that women's employment was necessary, even temporarily. He was naturally among the staunchest opponents of crèches. When the issue of crèches came up in the debates of the Commission on Depopulation in 1902, Gaston Variot, founder of one of the first milk stations, pointed out that the children in Parisian crèches were in an appalling state of health and frequently exhibited signs of malnutrition. Variot was glad, he said later, to have provoked the discussion on crèches, because it proved the superiority of the milk station.[95] At all times eager to promote his own institution, he ignored the obvious fact that, as Paul Strauss pointed out, the milk station did not solve the problems of mothers who had to work outside the home.

Despite these objections, support and regulation of crèches had been an early and important aspect of French child welfare policy. In 1862 an imperial decree had established government subsidies for crèches and placed them under the protection of the empress. A ministerial decree issued later that year established sanitary regulations

93. *Oeuvre nouvelle des crèches parisiennes,* March 1904, p. 6.
94. For example, see Mme Philippe Dussaud, "La crèche du VIe arrondissement," in Deuxième Congrès international des oeuvres et institutions féminines (1900), *Compte rendu des travaux* (Paris: Imprimerie typographique Charles Blot, 1902), vol. 2, p. 35.
95. Commission de dépopulation, Sous-commission de la mortalité, *Séances, 1902–3,* Séance du 17 décembre 1902, p. 14.

for all crèches, including daily medical visits and the vaccination of all the children. To receive government funds a crèche had to report each year to the prefect and submit to public supervision. Crèches receiving public funds were required to exclude all mothers who did not breast-feed to the extent they were able and those whose behavior was subject to "serious reproach."[96]

In the 1890s, as the population crisis reared its head, physicians and public and private welfare officials debated the role crèches could play in the battle against infant mortality. In 1897, Henri Monod, director of the national government's public health and welfare agency, urged the Conseil supérieur de l'assistance publique to approve new regulations. "It is unnecessary to stress the absolutely urgent nature presented by the reform of the regulation of crèches," he told the council's members, "at a time when we worry so rightly about the constant excess of deaths over French births, given that infant mortality forms one of the principal elements of general mortality."[97] The policy of the government was to regulate crèches closely but not so strictly as to force them out of existence. A ministerial circular of 1898 urged prefects to encourage the creation of crèches and to seek departmental and municipal subsidies for them. The minister instructed the prefects not to judge new crèches too harshly. It was far more useful, he argued, to get the crèches to make improvements than to close them, since the existing crèches were not sufficient to meet the needs of the population and many of their defects were simply a function of a lack of money.[98]

The nation's crèches were not overcrowded, however. In 1898, a total of 350 crèches, including ninety-two in Paris, had a total of about fourteen thousand places, while well over one hundred thousand workers gave birth each year. Nevertheless, Parisian statistics showed that in the 1890s only about two-thirds of the available places were filled.[99] The committee reporting these numbers attributed

96. Conseil supérieur de l'assistance publique, *Comptes-rendus*, Fascicule No. 6, 1888, pp. 5–10.

97. Quoted in Henri Napias, "Réglementation des crèches publiques et privées," *Deuxième Congrès national de l'assistance*, vol. 1, p. 37.

98. Préfecture de Police, *Protection des enfants du premier âge: Historique de la réglementation du service dans le département de la Seine* (Paris: Imprimerie Administrative, 1910), p. 134; Département de la Seine, Protection des enfants du premier âge, Rapport annuel, 1903, pp. 96, 108.

99. H. Napias, "De l'organisation des crèches," *Deuxième Congrès national d'assis-*

mothers' hesitation to trust the crèches solely to ignorance and prejudice. Administrators of crèches expected mothers to trust blindly in
the superiority of the care they offered; they frequently did not even
allow mothers inside to inspect the facilities. It did not occur to them
that working-class mothers had the right or the ability to evaluate a
charitable institution; the administrators assumed that such mothers
did not care where their children were.

Many women, however, did care; they chose to spend extra money
for a baby sitter rather than take advantage of the crèche. In 1919 the
Conseil national des femmes françaises reported that crèches definitely
had a bad reputation among mothers; even during the war some good
crèches remained partly empty.[100] Crèches were not designed to meet
the needs of working mothers. They were not open at night or on
Sundays though many women worked at those times; they were often
too far from the mother's place of work to allow her to travel back
and forth to nurse; some refused admission to illegitimate children;
and the Assistance publique refused aid to single mothers who placed
their children in a crèche.

One innovation designed to remedy some of these deficiencies was
the *garderie,* a place on the premises of a commercial or manufacturing
establishment where workers could nurse their children, or a full-
fledged crèche a few steps from the mother's work station. Physicians
writing about infant health praised such "industrial crèches" as ideal,
because they enabled women to nurse as often as every three hours
if their employers granted them permission to take the time off. Thus
the supposedly inevitable association between women's employment
and the abandonment of breast-feeding would be broken. The Association pour la protection légale des travailleurs, a national labor-
reform organization, resolved that all women should be allowed time
off to nurse their infants during working hours and that every establishment employing fifty or more women should be required to maintain a crèche.[101] As early as the late 1860s, a few employers had

tance, vol. 1, p. 35; Jacques Bonzon, *Cent ans de lutte sociale: La législation de l'enfance,
1789–1894* (Paris: Librairie Guillaumin, 1894), p. 63; Département de la Seine, Protection des enfants du premier âge, *Rapport annuel,* 1890, p. 90.

100. Conseil national des femmes françaises, *Rapport annuel,* 1918–19, p. 29.

101. Gemähling, "La femme ouvrière et la maternité," p. 32; Joseph Mercier, "De
l'utilité des crèches industrielles pour obtenir et encourager l'allaitement maternel,"
Bericht über den III. Internationalen Kongress für Sauglingsschutz (Gouttes de Lait), p. 763;
Bouquet, *La puériculture sociale,* pp. 197–200; B. Roussy, *Education domestique de la*

established crèches as part of their industrial welfare programs, which sometimes included nursing bonuses or maternity benefits as well.[102]

The proposal that employers bear the financial and administrative burdens of providing child care, however, enountered opposition from those representing business interests. In the legislative debates on the issue, disagreement arose primarily over the question of whether or not employers would respond to encouragement or whether they would resist all moral pressure unless threatened with material penalties. The debate naturally broke down along ideological lines, with those on the left insisting that coercive measures were essential.

The majority of legislators were unwilling to ignore the desires of industrialists. A bill that would have required employers to allow nursing mothers two half-hour breaks each day to breast-feed their infants in a room designed specifically for this purpose passed the Chamber of Deputies as an amendment to an appropriations bill in 1913 but never emerged from committee in the Senate.[103] Though Paris was usually far ahead of other cities and the nation as a whole, in 1914 a Parisian commission investigating women's and children's industrial labor failed to recommend decisive official action in this area. The commission resolved only to encourage employers to do their best to make available a place suitable for breast-feeding, and it urged local governments and the state to aid generously in efforts to create crèches, milk stations, and infant health consultations convenient to the places where women worked. In 1914, Paul Strauss suggested that the government offer special benefits to those employers who voluntarily created crèches or nursing rooms, but he admitted the impossibility of imposing upon employers the obligation to provide them.[104]

femme et rénovation sociale (Paris: Delagrave, 1914), p. 199; Vallin, La femme salariée et la maternité, p. 144. These physicians all supported legislation requiring employers to maintain nursing rooms.

102. Decherf, "Etude critique des oeuvres françaises de protection de l'enfance," p. 400; Charles Delplanque, Assistance aux enfants du premier âge privés de ressources (avant et après la naissance) (Lille: Wilmot-Courtecuisse, 1910), p. 35; Hideux, Crèche des établissements A. Badin et Fils; Paul Lederlin, Les oeuvres sociales de la Blanchisserie de Thaon (Thaon-les-Vosges: n.p., 1914); note on "Allaitement," by M. Séguin, Inspecteur du travail, December 3, 1913 (Archives nationales, F²² 446).

103. Archives nationales, C7340, Dos. 107.

104. Département de la Seine, Compte-rendu de la Commission départementale du travail des enfants, des filles mineures, et des femmes dans l'industrie, Procès-verbal de la séance

Conclusion

As the history of the industrial crèche suggests, the interests of employers and the dominance of liberal economic theory constituted the greatest challenge to maternal and child welfare legislation in France. In their efforts to reconcile wage labor and childbearing, legislators were reluctant to place any burdens on employers. Those opposed to legislation that would force employers to institute child welfare provisions pointed to employers who had created infant health consultations, crèches, and maternity-leave systems on their own inititiative. In some cases, such measures were part of a broad corporate welfare plan designed to attract and retain a stable and contented labor force. Some employers responded to specific requests by government officials while still others took voluntary measures in order to forestall coercive legislation. Coal-mining companies in the northeast—generally leaders of corporate paternalism—developed perhaps the most extensive maternal and infant health programs: one survey counted thirteen companies in the Pas-de-Calais with infant health consultations. Employers were not blind to the advantages to the nation and the economy of a healthy and growing population but they were opposed to measures that would limit their control over their employees or threaten their supply of labor.[105]

More than ever, as the war approached, depopulation formed the rhetorical basis for debates about the protection of maternal and infant health. Radical Republicans increasingly advocated state intervention as the solution to this and other social problems; though pronatalism cut across political lines and made possible the passage of the Strauss Law, the extent to which the Radicals were able to carry out their programs was limited by the resistance of employers to challenges to their authority.[106] When World War I arrived, the long-foreseen catastrophe, women poured into war factories and the birthrate plummeted. The population question loomed larger than ever as a national

---

du vendredi, 19 juin 1914 (Archives nationales, F²² 446); Abel Craissac, *Allaitement maternel au magasin et à l'atelier* (Paris: Imprimerie nationale, 1916), p. 9.

105. "Les compagnies houillères françaises et la lutte contre la mortalité infantile," (Archives nationales, 40.AS.65); Alliance d'hygiène sociale, *La lutte sociale contre la mortalité infantile*, pp. 12–13; Hatzfield, *Du paupérisme à la sécurité sociale*, p. 104. See Archives nationales, F²² 445, for a series of letters from chambers of commerce supporting, with qualifications, the Engerand and Strauss laws.

106. See Stone, *Search for Social Peace*, pp. 158, 170–80.

emergency, and the parliament debated a new wave of pronatalist bills. At the same time, the value of women's labor to the nation was explicitly recognized; how to protect children without threatening the labor supply became an urgent problem. American political leaders agreed that France's future depended on the survival of its children, and the American Red Cross came to the aid of France with a new agenda for French maternal and child welfare. The American Red Cross came armed with the educational programs developed in American cities and towns, and it introduced public health nursing to France.

Though Vivia Appleton found French public assistance programs disturbing, French public welfare authorities willingly accepted the American innovations, and by 1920 the professional medical-social home visitor was an important feature of French maternal and child welfare policy. In a sense, the visiting nurse was simply a professional visiting lady; as such, she was a natural agent in the French system of supervised child care. Radicals supported social insurance and public assistance with the ultimate goal of controlling rather than liberating workers; they shared these objectives with corporate reformers.[107] They saw the population crisis as both cause and symptom of widespread physical, social, and moral degeneration; the visiting nurse, as the embodiment of the intimate relationship between physical and social health, was well-armed as a warrior in the battle against depopulation.

107. Elwitt, *Third Republic Defended*, pp. 295–96.

6

"Baby's Health—Civic Wealth": The Work of the U.S. Children's Bureau

By 1913 it was clear that the men who controlled political and economic power in France—the national administration, legislators, industrialists, and professionals—saw the welfare of France's children as a critical factor in the nation's future. Convinced that population growth, military power, and national survival were intimately linked, the government and legislators acted in the belief that the state had an interest in expending resources to protect mothers and infants. In contrast, before the U.S. entry into World War I, reformers in the United States did not employ military metaphors in their discussions of child health. Not only was there no pervasive national sense of military urgency to exploit, but those most interested in maternal and child health did not believe that the nation's strength resided in military might or that its greatest threats came from foreign enemies. American infant health workers often wrote that healthy citizens made a nation great in some unspecified way—"The Children of Today Are the Citizens of Tomorrow" was a popular slogan—but more often they described the value of child health in purely economic terms. "The greatest asset of any nation is the health and efficiency of the people," proclaimed the letterhead of the National Women's Christian Temperance Union's Department of Health.[1]

In appealing to the economic interests of individuals and com-

1. Frances Lerther to "Friends," 9/20/16 (U.S. Children's Bureau, 4–12–4).

munities, reformers hoped to tap the motivating force of American society. For the most part, they failed. Until 1917 maternal and infant health was never the subject of debate in the U.S. Congress; private organizations continued to bear most of the costs of local maternal and infant health programs; and public agencies constantly struggled for the funds they needed to fulfill their goals.[2] Historians have cited a "heightened concern over the state of natural resources" and a sense that children were the nation's greatest resource as the sources of Progressive child welfare reforms.[3] The reformers' writings and activities are evidence that such an interest existed, but their pleas that the public recognize the value of child life did not have the political resonance that such arguments had in France.

At first the campaigns of medical specialists to improve and standardize medical education through new clinical and research institutions influenced maternal and infant health care primarily in large cities, which had the necessary resources and population. Relatively few communities provided public funding for milk stations and visiting nurses, and in 1915 43 percent of the nation's 551 infant welfare stations and 49 percent of visiting nurses were located in just eight large cities. Only four states and eighteen cities had bureaus of child hygiene. When the U.S. Children's Bureau was created in 1912 no other agency dealt to any significant extent with infant health and no agency had a broad conception of child welfare policy.[4]

Thus President Taft's decision to place the U.S. Children's Bureau in the hands of women and to appoint Julia Lathrop as its first chief in effect empowered women to shape American maternal and child welfare policy. The absence of a public health and welfare bureaucracy in the United States worked to the advantage of the bureau; its staff had no obligation to work through or rely on existing federal, state,

2. Richard A. Meckel, *Save the Babies: American Public Health Reform and the Prevention of Infant Mortality, 1850–1929* (Baltimore: Johns Hopkins University Press, 1990), pp. 133–34, 142–43.
3. Quote from Nancy Pottishman Weiss, "Save the Children: A History of the Children's Bureau, 1903–1918," Ph.D. diss., University of California, Los Angeles, 1974, pp. 23–24. See also Manfred J. Waserman, "The Emergence of Modern Health Care: Pediatrics, Public Health, and the Federal Government," Ph.D. diss., Catholic University, 1982, p. 77.
4. See Meckel, *Save the Babies,* pp. 134, 142: Jacqueline K. Parker and Edward M. Carpenter, "Julia Lathrop and the Children's Bureau: The Emergence of an Institution," *Social Service Review* 55 (1981): 64.

or local agencies. Even within the limits defined by its funds and official mandate, the bureau staff had considerable freedom to pursue their visions, and they made the most of it. Interpreting broadly their assigned task of initiating research and disseminating the results, the bureau, along with leaders of the public health nursing profession and of women's voluntary organizations, developed and propagated a distinctive vision of maternal and child welfare. This vision owed more to the settlement philosophy, female physicians' sense of social mission, and maternalist activism than to the new specialties of pediatrics and obstetrics or to male Progressive leaders' dedication to economic efficiency.

Focused on rural areas and small towns, where the grass-roots strength of the women's infant health movement was concentrated and where the bureau did not come into conflict with institutional pediatrics, obstetrics, and public health, the bureau's work increasingly emphasized the health of mothers for their own sake and not just because it affected their children. The bureau staff saw the mobilization of women to demand assistance and protection during pregnancy and childbearing as an essential feminist goal of women's political activism, since it required society to recognize the value of women's lives and labor. The bureau was also unusual in articulating a conception of human potential which did not emphasize the utilitarian value of human life. In the words of Julia Lathrop, the Children's Bureau was "an aid in securing for every child the life and liberty, which the fundamental law of the republic has promised— life and liberty interpreted in terms of to-day and tomorrow, life full and healthful—education free and public, opening and training the mind and the heart and the hand—occupation in due order, in brief, a fair start for the pursuit of happiness."[5]

5. Julia C. Lathrop, "The Children's Bureau," *Thirty-ninth National Conference of Charities and Corrections,* 1912, p. 30. See also Lillian Wald, *The House on Henry Street* (New York: Henry Holt, 1915), pp. 68, 167–68. On the Children's Bureau's approach to child welfare see Robyn Muncy, *Creating a Female Dominion in American Reform, 1890–1935* (New York: Oxford University Press, 1991), chap. 2. Molly Ladd-Taylor distinguishes two views of infant mortality: clubwomen and social settlement workers saw baby-saving as part of a larger campaign for women's dignity, the rights of mothers, and the recognition of the value of children's lives; conservatives saw infant mortality as a waste of national resources and associated child health with the eugenic goal of the perfection of the race. Mary Madeleine Ladd-Taylor, "Mother-work: Ideology, Public Policy, and the Mothers' Movement, 1890–1930," Ph.D. diss., Yale

The bureau operated, however, within the limits posed by American political culture. Though fighting for government action in areas previously considered outside the proper realm of federal activity, its staff struggled to create a maternal and infant health policy that would not appear to impose government will on communities or individuals and that would not stifle their independent initiative. Unlike French maternal and child welfare agencies, the U.S. Children's Bureau sought primarily to foster, inspire, and guide an independent infant health movement by providing models, information, and limited material assistance.

This conception of maternal and infant welfare arose alongside the medical model of pediatric and obstetrical care. While the bureau treated infant mortality as a social and economic problem, male obstetricians and pediatricians tended to see it essentially as a medical problem to be solved through improving the training of physicians, increasing research opportunities, and building hospitals. These two models did not come into direct conflict before World War I, partly because much of their vision was a shared one and partly because the Children's Bureau chose to concentrate its efforts in small towns and rural areas where few medical specialists chose to work. When the U.S. Congress began to consider major federal allocations for maternal and infant welfare after World War I, however, the two groups struggled for control over national policy.

The Children's Bureau Infant Mortality Studies

Though the Children's Bureau had been conceived by reformers involved primarily in the movement against child labor, the staff deliberately selected infant health as its initial focus, because child labor was politically volatile. Infant health work, they thought, could establish the bureau's credibility without inviting attacks.[6] As its first project the bureau undertook a series of studies of infant mortality in representative medium-sized cities: Johnstown, Pennsylvania; Brockton, Massachusetts; Manchester, New Hampshire; Montclair,

---

University, 1986, p. 295. I would argue that the line dividing the two perspectives was not always clear.

6. Weiss, "Save the Children," p. 185; Parker and Carpenter, "Julia Lathrop and the Children's Bureau," p. 64; Muncy, *Creating a Female Dominion*, pp. 38–46.

New Jersey; and Saginaw, Michigan. The bureau chose to avoid larger cities where infant health work was relatively well established and where the staff would inevitably have competed with the male physicians, long-established charitable organizations, and public health officials who dominated public health work. The smaller cities welcomed the bureau's resources and allowed them considerable freedom in which to operate.

Through these studies, which absorbed most of the bureau's energy for two years, the staff began to articulate its conception of maternal and child welfare.[7] From the first, the bureau's researchers treated infant mortality as a social problem. In part, this was a decision based on the fact that the bureau had no medical staff, but this approach was entirely compatible with the researchers' convictions that health problems had a social basis.[8] Thus they surveyed the sanitary conditions of the neighborhoods they visited and studied the relationship between infant mortality rates and housing conditions, men's wages, women's employment, nativity, literacy, and methods of infant feeding.

The researchers decided that the best way to obtain the information they needed was to interview in their homes all the women who had borne children within the past year. This effort to come into contact with individual mothers was to become a characteristic feature of the bureau's work; it reflected the staff's belief that infant welfare was properly a concern of women and that women's own stories constituted more reliable evidence than aggregate statistics. Over the next eight years they became increasingly certain that their mission would be accomplished through the awakening, education, and mobilization of women.

The staff sought the cooperation of community organizations and leaders in publicizing the survey in an effort to gain the confidence of the women they wanted to interview: "The greatest care was taken to make clear that the Government does not desire to intrude upon the privacy of family life, but that it asks the cooperation of American mothers in an effort to safeguard the lives of babies."[9] It was important

7. Parker and Carpenter, "Julia Lathrop and the Children's Bureau," p. 66.
8. *First Annual Report of the Chief, U.S. Children's Bureau to the Secretary of Labor* (Washington, D.C.: Government Printing Office, 1913), p. 8.
9. Ibid.

to the bureau that it avoid any suggestion of coercion; even more than in France, the family was sacred territory.

The bureau's administrators insisted that the national government had no right to force a program on any community, but they also argued that each community had the responsibility to develop its own programs. When they referred to "civic responsibility" they did not mean that the local government should intitiate action; instead they suggested that voluntary organizations take on the task of raising funds and arousing the public, with public programs as their ultimate goal. On one level, this intent reflected a faith that American local governments functioned democratically as an organic expression of the community's will.[10] At the same time, the bureau staff translated the moral ideal of self-reliance and responsibility from the individual to the community level, so that in the bureau's correspondence and publicity community initiative resembled a moral imperative.

The consensus among historians of the Children's Bureau is that the urban studies, in concluding that poverty was the single most important factor in infant mortality, challenged the assumption of early infant health programs that maternal ignorance was the primary cause of infant mortality.[11] It is true that the researchers repeatedly pointed out the close correlation between poverty and infant mortality, sometimes antagonizing local elites. Angry that the bureau's report on their city seemed to blame infant mortality on low wages, mill owners in Manchester, New Hampshire, tried to fight the bureau by taking their complaints to Congress.[12] The authors of the reports qualified this emphasis on poverty, however, admitting their inability to separate the effects of poverty on infant health from those of ignorance, illiteracy, inadequate housing, and poor sanitation. Ultimately, while they sympathized with the plight of the poor, they proposed education and environmental improvements rather than financial assistance as solutions to the problem of infant mortality. The solutions the bureau staff recommended included educational pro-

10. On settlement leaders' ideals of democracy and community see Rivka Shpak Lissak, *Pluralism and Progressives: Hull House and the New Immigrant, 1890–1919* (Chicago: University of Chicago Press, 1989), pp. 13–20.

11. See Weiss, "Save the Children," p. 197; Meckel, *Save the Babies*, pp. 180–83; Janet Pacht Brickman, "Mother Love—Mother Death: Maternal and Infant Care, Social Class and the Role of Government," Ph.D. diss., City University of New York, 1978, pp. 287–90; Ladd-Taylor, "Mother-work," pp. 313–17.

12. See Parker and Carpenter, "Julia Lathrop and the Children's Bureau," p. 66.

grams along the lines of existing urban public health programs: infant health consultations, follow-up home visits by public health nurses, municipal sanitation measures, and tenement inspection.[13]

It is not clear that economic assistance would have been the most effective immediate infant health measure. After all, Ireland, one of the poorest countries in Europe, had the third lowest infant mortality rate, probably because breast-feeding was almost universal there.[14] In a comparative perspective, however, it is important to note that the bureau even chose to consider such characteristics as literacy and ethnicity. French researchers also believed the correlation between housing conditions and alcoholism and infant mortality to be an important one; they too argued that maternal ignorance of hygiene was one of the primary causes of infant mortality, especially among the poor. They did not focus so closely, however, on defining the behavioral characteristics of the poor and they were certain that economic hardship in itself contributed directly to infant mortality because it deprived infants of their mothers' care.

Perhaps with the aid of a computer and multiple regression analysis the bureau's researchers would have felt confident in ranking their variables in order of the importance of their influence on infant health. As it was, they found only a tangle of social pathology with poverty at the center. In attempting to explain, for example, why infant mortality rates were highest in the most crowded neighborhoods, a bureau writer suggested that a mother was often tempted to overfeed her baby or feed it irregularly if it slept with her and disturbed her rest. Ignorance was also partly responsible because mothers often kept the windows closed even when the means for good ventilation existed. If, however, the rooms were badly heated and opening the

13. See Mary V. Dempsey, *Infant Mortality: Results of a Field Study in Brockton, Massachusetts*, U.S. Children's Bureau, Infant Mortality Series No. 8 (Bureau Publication No. 37) (Washington, D.C.: Government Printing Office, 1919), p. 56; Nila F. Allen, *Infant Mortality: Results of a Field Study in Saginaw, Michigan*, U.S. Children's Bureau, Infant Mortality Series No. 9 (Bureau Publication No. 52) (Washington, D.C.: Government Printing Office, 1919), p. 62; *Infant Mortality, Montclair, New Jersey: A Study of Infant Mortality in a Suburban Community*, U.S. Children's Bureau, Infant Mortality Series No. 4 (Bureau Publication No. 11) (Washington, D.C.: Government Printing Office, 1915), p. 13.

14. Carlo M. Cipolla, *The Economic History of World Population*, 7th ed. (Middlesex, England: Penguin, 1978), p. 98. Among European countries, only Sweden and Norway had lower rates of infant mortality than Ireland.

windows would make it too cold or would let in soot, ashes, and dirt, they had no choice. The reporter concluded with an indictment of conditions beyond the parents' control: "The foreigners, who generally have the most miserable homes, are not dirty people who select bad living conditions through innate poor judgment, low standards and lack of taste." It was the only housing they could afford.[15]

The researchers also found that wealthy mothers could often overcome the disadvantages of artificial feeding, while poverty partly nullified the benefits of breast-feeding. Perhaps, the authors of the Manchester study concluded, "poverty usually means low standards and ignorance on the part of the mother," while well-off mothers had better medical attention and more knowledge of infant hygiene.[16] They also concluded that literacy was an independent factor in infant mortality—though highly correlated with poverty—since literate women had access to written sources of information on the care of infants.[17] In Saginaw the survey showed that children of foreign-born parents who did not speak English had a higher mortality rate than those whose parents were immigrants but spoke English. In this case the reporter suggested that, since they were more likely to be recent immigrants, "poverty and its attendant evils are factors probably more important than the inability of the mother to speak English."[18]

On the other hand, the researchers puzzled over why the French-Canadians in Manchester had a higher infant mortality rate than other immigrant groups had, even though they had a higher income, the women were employed less in the lower income categories, they spoke English more often, had been in the country longer, and were more likely to be literate. Perhaps, the researchers concluded, it was because the French-Canadians were not "Americanized": they retained their foreign language and distinct "channels of expression" such as separate schools, churches, orphanages, political and pleasure

15. Emma Duke, *Infant Mortality; Results of a Field Study in Johnstown, Pennsylvania*, U.S. Children's Bureau, Infant Mortality Series No. 3 (Bureau Publication No. 9) (Washington, D.C.: Government Printing Office, 1915), p. 26.
16. Beatrice Sheets Duncan and Emma Duke, *Infant Mortality: Results of a Field Study in Manchester, New Hampshire*, U.S. Children's Bureau, Infant Mortality Series No. 6 (Bureau Publication No. 20) (Washington, D.C.: Government Printing Office, 1917), p. 71.
17. Dempsey, *Infant Mortality . . . Brockton*, p. 28.
18. Allen, *Infant Mortality . . . Saginaw*, p. 25.

clubs, and their own daily French newspaper. They also were more likely than other groups to feed their children artificially.[19]

The bureau staff, like others in the social settlement tradition, represented a strain of social reform which deemphasized the responsibility of the poor for their own plight and in particular tended not to blame their immorality and lack of self-control.[20] The researchers chose not to consider venereal disease and alcoholism in their study, for example, though physicians treated these as important factors in infant mortality, because it would not have beeen "fair or practicable" to enter the home and ask questions regarding issues that could be considered "personally humiliating."[21] In this respect the bureau stood out against others who entirely discounted poverty as a factor in infant mortality. "[In] the last analysis," wrote Helen Putnam, a Boston reformer, "it is the individual mother herself who must assume the largest responsibilities for the prevention of infant mortality."[22] A matron in a factory in East St. Louis, Illinois, concerned about tuberculosis, also blamed working-class women for their ill health and that of their children. She wrote to the National Americanization Committee asking, "Isn't there some medium through which we can teach these girls the dangers and fatal results of the crowded way they live? . . . Swift and Company bear the expenses and try so hard to care for the babies, but they don't understand the meaning of the disease, its dangers, etc."[23]

In contrast, consistent with their belief in social democracy, the bureau staff sympathized strongly with the poor as the victims of industrial capitalism and were aware that poverty sometimes made it impossible for people to observe the rules of hygiene. Nonetheless, they expressed an understanding of social pathology which clearly had some relation to traditional moral concepts of virtue. Thus on

19. Duncan and Duke, *Infant Mortality . . . Manchester,* p. 63.

20. See Mina Carson, *Settlement Folk: Social Thought and the American Settlement Movement, 1885–1930* (Chicago: University of Chicago Press, 1990), pp. 122–29.

21. *Second Annual Report of the Chief, Children's Bureau to the Secretary of Labor* (Washington, D.C.: Government Printing Office, 1914), p. 7.

22. Helen C. Putnam, "Dr. Snedden on Public Schools and Infant Mortality," *Child-Welfare Magazine* 9 (1914): 121. See also Sonya Michel and Robyn Rose, "The Paradox of Maternalism: Elizabeth Lowell Putnam and the American Welfare State," *Gender and History* (forthcoming).

23. Alice B. Woodring to "Madam," n.d. (U.S. Children's Bureau, 4–12–1–4–10).

the one hand they pointed to economic injustice as a critical factor in infant health: they noted "a coincidence of underpaid fathers, over-worked and ignorant mothers, and those hazards to the life of off-spring which individual parents can not avoid or control. This points toward the imperative need of ascertaining a standard of life for the American family."[24] At the same time, in answer to the question of whether Brockton's liquor-control law was a factor in that city's relatively low infant mortality rate (as many inhabitants believed), they answered: "Any influence which tends to make healthier parents, better homes, and more contented families will tend to reduce the number of infant deaths. . . . In a city having excellent sanitation fa-cilities, a strong sense of civic pride, good wages, and intelligent workers, the abolition of saloons might be considered either as cause or effect."[25]

"Education, not charity," could have been the motto of the Amer-ican infant health movement. Though French politicians, physicians, and feminists rejected traditional forms of charity, they did not exhibit the same antipathy as Americans did toward public assistance or the principle of charity. Even Radical Republican politicians in France saw private charity, particularly female benevolence, as a potential solution to some of the spiritual problems of the bourgeoisie and as a way of mediating class conflict. In particular, financial assistance of mothers seemed justified to French policy makers because it could prevent the separation of mother and child. In the United States neither women's failure to fulfill their maternal duties nor the em-ployment of mothers carried the emotional or political force apparent in French studies.

Children's Bureau and other researchers in the United States who studied the relationship between women's employment and infant health concluded that women's wage labor contributed little to the infant mortality rate in the United States. From their reading of re-ports of European studies the Children's Bureau staff were aware that high rates of women's industrial employment were generally assumed to be associated with high infant mortality rates. They were reluctant to draw definitive conclusions from the results of their own research, however.

24. *Second Annual Report of the Chief, Children's Bureau*, p. 8.
25. Dempsey, *Infant Mortality . . . Brockton*, p. 55.

Every Child a Lion

In Montclair the researchers found that infant mortality was closely related to the mothers' employment, but because they counted women who took in laundry or had lodgers in their homes as employed, they did not single out the separation of children from their mothers as the central issue. Instead they argued that hard work of any kind during pregnancy could weaken a woman's health and decrease her chances of bearing a healthy child. If she kept working after birth she was likely to stop breast-feeding.[26] In Manchester the researchers found, not unexpectedly, that the number of stillbirths and the infant mortality rate were higher among children of women who worked outside the home in all income groups.[27] In Brockton, however, the infant mortality rate was actually slightly higher among children of women who were *not* gainfully employed than for mothers earning wages either at home or outside the home. The researchers concluded that little difference existed between the two groups because mothers who were "not gainfully employed" actually did as much hard physical labor as those who worked for wages.[28]

This sympathy for the hard work that women did at home was typical of the Children's Bureau staff and became even more evident in their later studies of rural maternal welfare. The bureau researchers may have been deliberately avoiding an outright condemnation of women's industrial work so as not to supply evidence for attacks on women's right to work. Lathrop, commenting to the press on the results of the studies, emphasized that women worked in order to supplement their husbands' low wages and not for their amusement or personal satisfaction. "And we must not forget," she wrote, "that there can be a standard of life so low that the mother who is without a job and sits at home hungry can do less for her child's life than the mother who works for wages and can feed it and herself." Thus, she noted, while the death rate among infants of wage-earning mothers was higher than among non-wage-earning, the reverse was true in the group in which fathers had the lowest income.[29]

26. *Infant Mortality, Montclair, New Jersey*, p. 21.
27. Duncan and Duke, *Infant Mortality . . . Manchester*, pp. 53–54.
28. Dempsey, *Infant Mortality . . . Brockton*, p. 37.
29. Julia C. Lathrop, "The Relation of the Father's Wage to Infant Mortality," 11/5/15 (U.S. Children's Bureau, 8–2–1–5).

Women's Employment and Infant Mortality

Suffragists commenting on infant mortality also seemed at pains to deny that women's employment directly threatened child welfare. Eva Ward, for example, writing in support of maternity benefits in the *Woman's Journal* in 1916, argued that poverty, not women's work, was the worst enemy of child welfare. Similarly, Harriot Stanton Blatch cited a study by Clara Collett for the British government which showed no clear relationship between the employment of married women and infant mortality.[30]

Advocates of women's rights were not the only ones to come to this conclusion. A U.S. Senate commission appointed to study the employment of women and children devoted a volume of its report to a study of the relationship between women's employment and infant mortality in Massachusetts.[31] Though the state's most important industries employed women in large numbers, the researchers concluded that women's wage labor had very little influence at all on the infant mortality rate in Massachusetts.

Edward Bunnell Phelps, writing for the commission, analyzed aggregate statistics for twelve Massachusetts cities; he argued that the birthrate in a community and the percentage of foreign-born and illiterate women were more closely associated with mortality than was the employment of women. Waltham, Lynn, and North Adams, for example, were among the ten cities in Massachusetts with the highest rates of female employment but among the fifteen with the lowest infant mortality. Conversely, Boston, Cambridge, and Chelsea had relatively few employed women but high infant mortality rates.[32] Immigrants, Phelps wrote, lived in the worst of the social and economic conditions that fostered infant mortality: they were usually poor and ignorant; they tended to marry early and have large families; they preferred to employ midwives; they lived in the worst

30. Eva Ward, "In Defense of the Maternity Benefit," *Woman's Journal*, April 29, 1916: 138; Harriot Stanton Blatch, *Mobilizing Woman-Power* (New York: Woman's Press, 1918), p. 113.

31. U.S. Cong., Senate, 61st Cong., 2d Sess., Document No. 645, *Infant Mortality and Its Relation to the Employment of Mothers*, vol. 13 of *Report on Condition of Woman and Child Wage-Earners in the United States*, 1912.

32. Ibid., p. 38.

housing; and the women were not equipped to cope with their new, unfamiliar environment.[33]

The Senate's researchers also conducted an intensive study of infant mortality in Fall River. After interviewing the mothers of all the infants who had died over the past year they concluded that women's employment actually contributed little to infant mortality in that city. First, they found no significant difference in the age or cause of death between the children of women who had worked during pregnancy and those of women who had not worked outside the home.[34] The most striking finding was that the percentage of deaths in the first year from diarrhea, enteritis, and gastritis was 62.7 percent for children whose mothers worked and only 34.6 percent for those whose mothers did not work; the researchers concluded, however, that maternal employment raised the city's overall infant mortality rate only slightly, inasmuch as the percentage of infant deaths due to these diseases was only 38.6 percent for the city as a whole because relatively few mothers of infants were employed.[35]

Thus, though there was evidence that the employment of women deprived children of proper care, Charles H. Verrill, reporting the results of the Senate study, concluded that even in New England's textile cities the employment of women presented no urgent threat to infant life. Instead, he placed the blame solely on maternal incompetence: "The causes of excessive infant mortality in Fall River may be summed up in a sentence as the mother's ignorance of proper feeding, of proper care, and of the simplest requirements of hygiene. To this all the other causes must be regarded as secondary."[36]

Though the Senate commission report focused far more on ignorance than the Children's Bureau reports would, both furnish evidence that mothers who worked outside the home were all but invisible to policy makers. To a certain extent the difference between the United States and France in this respect can be attributed to a difference in objective conditions: relatively few married women in the United States worked outside the home, especially if they had young children. Nonetheless, French researchers were predisposed to focus on women's work outside the home. The separation of children

33. Ibid., p. 53.
34. Ibid., p. 119.
35. Ibid., p. 74.
36. Ibid.

from their mothers had tremendous political and symbolic significance in France and was associated with doubts about the maternal instincts of French women and fears about the degeneration of the family. Had physical labor really been their primary concern they might, like the U.S. Children's Bureau, have taken seriously the work women did in their homes and on family farms. Despite the extensive debates about women's work in France, public and private agencies in that country acknowledged the fact of women's employment, recognized many of the needs of working women, and did far more to assist them than did reformers in the United States.[37]

In the United States, there were efforts on the state level to regulate new mothers' employment. In 1912, Massachusetts and Vermont passed laws prohibiting employers from knowingly employing women within two weeks before or four weeks after childbirth; New York passed a similar law that applied only to the period *after* childbirth.[38] None of these laws included provisions to compensate women for the wages lost, and critics argued that the laws were essentially unenforceable because it was virtually impossible to prove that an employer had "knowingly" hired a woman who had recently given birth.[39] Testimony before the New York State Factory Investigating Commission suggests that even among advocates of regulation there was no consensus that maternity benefits were a necessary corollary of a prohibition of women's work.

Several of those who testified, including Melinda Scott of the Wom-

37. See Jane Jenson, "Representations of Gender: Policies to 'Protect' Women Workers and Infants in France and the United States before 1914," in *Women, the State, and Welfare,* ed. Linda Gordon (Madison: University of Wisconsin Press, 1990), p. 71. Jenson argues that in the United States "women's citizenship rights were claimed almost exclusively because of their supposed maternal qualities." Thus they were invisible, as workers and welfare programs addressed them only as mothers. In contrast, in France, there was widespread social acceptance of women's participation in the labor force, and women claimed the identity of "citizen-producer."

38. Connecticut passed legislation similar to that of Massachusetts and Vermont in 1913, but extended the period of prenatal rest to four weeks. Mrs. Max West, "The Development of Prenatal Care in the United States," *Transactions of the American Association for the Study and Prevention of Infant Mortality* 5 (1914): 74.

39. Edward Bunnell Phelps, "The World-Wide Effort to Diminish Infant Mortality—Its Present Status and Its Possibilities," *Transactions of the Fifteenth International Congress on Hygiene and Demography* (1912) (Washington, D.C.: Government Printing Office, 1913), vol. 6, p. 171. The French Strauss Law also stipulated that employers could not be penalized unless they knowingly violated the law, but because women who took leaves were entitled to cash benefits there was some incentive for them to do so.

en's Trade Union League, E. B. Phelps, Frances Perkins, director of
investigations for the commission, and George Goler of the Rochester
Public Health Department insisted that compensation was essential—
otherwise, as Phelps pointed out, women would be faced with a
choice between breaking the law and starving.[40] Others who testified
in favor of the bill either ignored the issue of compensation or suggested that the only real solution was to pay men wages high enough
to enable them to support their families. "I think it a monstrous
outrage that a woman should be employed in that condition," labor
reformer Florence Kelley testified; she did not believe, however, that
it was necessary for women to work under existing economic conditions. Women did it, she argued, "largely through a mistaken idea
of thrift on the part of the family, or by the shiftlessness and selfishness
of the husband drinking up the family earnings, and largely encouraged by the manufacturers or employers for the purpose of reducing
the wages by having both heads of the family and all the children
contributing to the family purse."[41] Woods Hutchinson, a New York
City physician, agreed that the wisest way of preventing the employment of women before and after childbirth was to give men a
decent living wage.[42]

Because American reformers did not consider the employment of
married women to be essential to the family or the economy—and
in fact actively opposed it—they did not make a great effort to reconcile childbearing and wage labor.[43] If they saw the employment of
pregnant women as exploitative their solution was simply to prohibit
it. Similarly, the few employers in the United States who tried to
provide maternity assistance seemed more concerned with keeping
pregnant women out of the factory than with providing material
benefits or care. Mary Barrett Gilson of the Clothcraft Shops of
the Joseph and Feiss Company in Cleveland, for example, wrote to
Mrs. Max West of the Children's Bureau boasting that her company

40. New York State Factory Investigating Commission, *Preliminary Report* (Albany: Argus, 1912), pp. 331–32, 964, 1280, 1804.
41. Ibid., p. 1599.
42. Ibid., p. 154.
43. Jane Jenson, "Paradigms and Political Discourse: Protective Legislation in
France and the United States before 1914," *Canadian Journal of Political Science* 22
(1989): 235–58. Deborah Dwork makes a similar argument about Britain in *War Is
Good for Babies and Other Young Children: A History of the Infant and Child Welfare
Movement in England, 1898–1918* (London: Tavistock, 1987), pp. 35–36.

had largely solved its problem with pregnant women by trying to eliminate young married women from its work force "in cases where no hardships result from this policy."[44]

The Medical Model of Maternal and Infant Care

Having successfully reduced infant deaths from diarrhea, members of the American Association for the Study and Prevention of Infant Mortality and urban public health officials turned their attention to early infant deaths, those presumably the result of prenatal factors. While French physicians focused primarily on women's wage labor as the prime villain, medical specialists in the United States paid little attention to women's work and did not emphasize harmful environmental and economic conditions at all. Instead they initiated programs to instruct women and provide them with medical supervision. Their work was closely linked with the development of a medical model of maternal welfare, one that would come into conflict with the Children's Bureau's broader social vision.

Central to this medical model was the assumption that childbearing was a pathological condition. If only the public would believe this, argued Joseph B. DeLee, a Chicago obstetrician, midwives would be eliminated, women would naturally give birth in hospitals, a "better class of men" would choose to practice obstetrics, physicians would be better educated to care for women in existing surroundings, and women would routinely seek prenatal care.[45] Another obstetrician, Edward P. Davis, believed that outpatient obstetric services should be eliminated altogether. "Why," he asked, "should students of obstetrics be sent into filthy tenements to learn how to practice obstetrics properly?"[46]

The midwife controversy, the subject of debate year after year at the meetings of the American Association for the Study and Prevention of Infant Mortality, provides fascinating evidence of the often

44. Mary Barrett Gilson to Mrs. Max West, 4/28/15 (U.S. Children's Bureau, 4-2-0-3).
45. Quoted in Edward P. Davis, "The Springs of a Nation's Life," *Transactions of the American Association for the Study and Prevention of Infant Mortality* 9 (1918): 114–16.
46. Ibid., p. 111.

blatantly self-serving motives of obstetricians and their exploitation of infant mortality in creating propaganda for the profession.[47] In the late nineteenth century, midwives in cities in the United States served primarily immigrant and black women; native-born white women employed physicians. Many immigrant midwives had been trained in European schools, but American obstetricians considered them all incompatible with their vision of modern scientific medicine. The obstetricians' own studies showed that general practitioners were responsible for more maternal and infant deaths than were midwives, but outspoken obstetricians such as J. Whitridge Williams of Baltimore obstinately insisted that it was ridiculous to believe that illiterate immigrant women could learn to do competent obstetrics. The only solution, Williams insisted, was to improve the obstetrical training of physicians.[48]

Most who agreed with Williams on this point also believed that some training and regulation of midwives was necessary until alternative institutions were available and women were convinced of the superiority of physicians. Some public health officials, including S. Josephine Baker, hoped to establish an extensive training system for midwives and envisioned the incorporation of midwives into maternity-care programs. Under Baker's leadership, New York City established the first municipally supported school for midwives in the United States in 1911; most physicians and public health officials considered the Bellevue School to be the only institution in the United States that provided adequate training.[49]

Those who called for the immediate abolition of midwives, however, had enough influence in Massachusetts that in 1907 all practitioners other than licensed physicians were prohibited from attending births. Though midwives continued to practice, the law prevented any training or regulation of their work, because theoretically they did not exist. That midwives attended 40 to 90 percent of all births in many large cities was galling to obstetricians, because medical

47. For detailed discussions of the midwife controversy, see Judy Barrett Litoff, *American Midwives, 1860 to the Present* (Westport, Conn.: Greenwood Press, 1978), chap. 5; Frances E. Kobrin, "The American Midwife Controversy: A Crisis in Professionalization," *Bulletin of the History of Medicine* 40 (1966): 350–63.

48. J. Whitridge Williams, "The Midwife Problem and Medical Education in the United States," *Transactions of the American Association for the Study and Prevention of Infant Mortality* 2 (1911): 183.

49. Litoff, *American Midwives*, p. 48.

schools coveted the midwives' patients for training purposes. Midwives, Charles Ziegler protested, had charge of 50 percent of all the obstetrical "material" in the country without contributing anything to the knowledge of the subject.[50]

"Prenatal care is plainly the coming thing in infant work, and all the cities are beginning to talk about it," wrote Mrs. Max West to Lathrop in 1914 from Springfield, Massachussetts, where she was on a trip to study prenatal care in New England.[51] The discussions at the meetings of the American Association for the Study and Prevention of Infant Mortality, the reports of affiliated societies, and correspondence with the Children's Bureau staff provide ample evidence that prenatal care represented the most important trend in infant health work in the mid–1910s. The new prenatal programs conformed to the same pattern as the programs to prevent deaths from diarrheal diseases, with an emphasis on instruction in the home and medical supervision. Public health authorities and private health and charitable agencies hired nurses to visit mothers and instruct them in nutrition, hygiene, and the need for medical examinations and helped them to make preparations for childbirth.

Some public health officials and obstetricians hoped to use these prenatal services, sometimes combined with free maternity care, to undermine midwives' practices. Free clinics could be used, suggested Charles V. Chapin of Providence, Rhode Island, to draw patients away from midwives. Though he admitted that he knew of no evidence that midwives hindered public health work, he thought it was important that the clinic patients could be used for teaching purposes.[52] Some agencies provided prenatal care or nursing care at the time of delivery only to women under the care of a physician; women who chose to employ a midwife were denied access to these services.[53]

50. Charles Edward Ziegler, "The Elimination of the Midwife," *Transactions of the American Association for the Study and Prevention of Infant Mortality* 3 (1912): 224–25. On midwives in Massachusetts see Eugene R. Declerq, "The Nature and Style of Practice of Immigrant Midwives in Early Twentieth Century Massachusetts," *Journal of Social History* 18 (1985): 113–29.

51. Mrs. Max West to Julia Lathrop, 11/16/14 (U.S. Children's Bureau, 4–15–4–1–1); Meckel, *Save the Babies,* pp. 165–68.

52. Charles V. Chapin, "The Control of Midwifery," in U.S. Children's Bureau, *Standards of Child Welfare: A Report of the Children's Bureau Conferences, May and June 1919,* Conference Series No. 1 (Bureau Publication No. 62) (Washington, D.C.: Government Printing Office, 1919), p. 162.

53. Physicians at the New York Midwifery Dispensary refused to allow midwives

The Maternity Center Association of New York City provides a good example of the way in which prenatal care programs could lead women to abandon midwives for physicians and hospital delivery. Founded by a group of male physicians working with the city's Health Commissioner and with the financial aid of the Women's City Club, the Maternity Center Association had as its goal the provision of supervision and scientific care for every expectant mother, "so that every child born in the city of New York shall have proper care before birth, at birth, and during the days immediately following birth." By 1920 the association had nineteen centers and subcenters, each serving a particular geographical zone. Each center tried to keep a record of every pregnancy in its district. Nurses canvased for pregnant women and impressed on them the importance of medical supervision and of good medical care at childbirth. The nurses made regular and frequent home visits, instructed the mothers in the hygiene of pregnancy and in child care and the importance of breastfeeding, and helped them to make the necessary arrangements for the birth. At the clinics women received medical exams and were persuaded to engage a private physician or register at a hospital. Whenever possible, the workers encouraged the women to accept medical aid for confinement rather than employ a midwife.[54]

The medical model acquired new legitimacy during World War I, when in 1917, the Child Welfare Committee of the General Medical Board of the Council for National Defense created a subcommittee on midwife practice. The report of this committee, made up of three men, including J. Whitridge Williams, articulated the views of obstetricians. The committee concluded that founding or extending schools to teach midwifery was neither possible nor desirable. No midwife, the committee argued, should be allowed to attend a birth

to participate at all in their patients' care. Nancy Schrom Dye, "Modern Obstetrics and Working-class Women: New York Midwifery Dispensary, 1890–1920," *Journal of Social History* 20 (1987): 558.

54. Anne Stevens, "A Program for Maternity Care," *Public Health Nursing Quarterly* 10 (1918): 95–99; quote in Anne A. Stevens, "The Work of the Maternity Center Association," *Transactions of the American Child Health Association*, 1919: 53; Reports of Affiliated Societies, *Transactions of the American Association for the Study and Prevention of Infant Mortality* 9 (1918): 303; Brickman, "Mother Love—Mother Death," p. 305; Anne Shannon Monroe, "Adventuring in Motherhood," *Good Housekeeping*, May 1920: 129–30.

unless a physician had examined the patient, supervised her prenatal care, and certified that she was likely to have a normal delivery.[55]

The U.S. Children's Bureau Model of
Maternal and Infant Care

Grace Meigs, head of the Medical Division of the Children's Bureau, found the implications of the General Medical Board's report disturbing. The object of the proposed regulations, she pointed out in a memo to Julia Lathrop, was clearly to hasten the abolition of midwives. In any case, she argued, the plan was not practicable inasmuch as a woman who preferred a midwife would hardly be willing to submit to an examination by a male physician first. Instead, Meigs proposed that public health nurses with obstetrical training be responsible for supervising midwives without supplanting them.[56] It was this rejection of the primacy of the physician and hospitals in maternity care which characterized the bureau's model of maternal and infant welfare, one which was shared by some other women physicians and leaders of the nursing profession.[57]

Like obstetricians, these women advocated prenatal instruction and saw the provision of professional maternity care to all women as an urgent priority. The bureau staff, public health nursing leaders, and the leaders of national women's organizations, however, struggled to avert the increasing hegemony of male obstetricians and the pathological conception of childbirth. They defined the public health nurse as the primary agent of instruction and the primary caregiver, particularly in rural areas, and warned that the trend toward the hospitalization of childbirth was a dangerous one. They believed that nurses with obstetrical training could supervise most aspects of ma-

55. "Report of the Sub-Committee on Midwife Practice of the General Medical Board of the Council for National Defense," n.d. (c. 1918) (U.S. Children's Bureau, 10,333).

56. Grace Meigs, "On the Report of the Sub-Committee on Midwife Practice of the General Medical Board of the Council for National Defense," 9/12/18 (Ibid., 10,333).

57. For example, see S. Josephine Baker, "Schools for Midwives," *Transactions of the American Association for the Study and Prevention of Infant Mortality* 2 (1911): 232; Carolyn Van Blarcom's comments in ibid., p. 247; Wald, *House on Henry Street*, pp. 57–58.

ternity care and rarely mentioned physicians in their plans for rural programs for maternity care.[58]

Small towns and rural areas provided the greatest opportunities for the bureau staff to realize their ideals; where medical institutions and public health agencies were rudimentary the bureau did not have to worry about competing with the medical establishment. Local women's organizations were a vital political force in small towns; in these the bureau hoped to find grass-roots support for their work. The success of the baby health contests was proof that rural women were eager for help in child rearing. Letters to the U.S. Department of Agriculture and the U.S. Children's Bureau indicated that isolation and poverty made themselves felt most severely during pregnancy and childbirth. In the sparsely settled prairie and mountain states many women had no access to either traditional or modern health care.[59]

In 1915, Congress increased the bureau's funding to more than five times its previous level, enabling the agency to hire Grace Meigs as its first medical expert. The greatly expanded staff began planning a series of investigations of rural counties, beginning in Indiana and North Carolina in the fall of 1915. Broadly interpreting the bureau's charter, they incorporated direct educational work into their plans and hoped to stimulate permanent local child health institutions. They chose the child health conference—at which physicians examined infants and instructed their mothers—as an ideal way of gathering information and at the same time advising individual mothers. They hoped too that their work would stimulate ongoing programs; the conference was also a model that small communities could easily duplicate. By January 1916, Florence Sherbon, former secretary of the American Baby Health Contest Association, was holding child health conferences in Indiana in conjunction with a series of talks, demonstrations, slide show programs, and a child welfare exhibit.[60]

58. Carolyn Van Blarcom, "Visiting Obstetrical Nurses," *Transactions of the American Association for the Study and Prevention of Infant Mortality* 2 (1911): 343.

59. Elizabeth Moore, *Maternity and Infant Care in a Rural County in Kansas,* U.S. Children's Bureau, Rural Child Welfare Series No. 1 (Bureau Publication No. 26) (Washington, D.C.: Government Printing Office, 1917), p. 8; Grace L. Meigs, "Rural Obstetrics," *Transactions of the American Association for the Study and Prevention of Infant Mortality* 7 (1916): 46.

60. A. L. Strong, "Plan for Cooperation in County Work between the Children's Bureau and Any University Extension Division or Any State Federation of Clubs," 1915 (U.S. Children's Bureau, 4–12–5–1); memorandum on interview about Chil-

Sherbon stayed in each community for about a week after the conference to organize a committee of local residents interested in planning follow-up work, helping them to draw up plans for the
employment of a visiting nurse or for the creation of a child welfare
center.[61]

The North Carolina study, carried out by Frances Sage Bradley,
was a far more ambitious project. Bradley had been one of the first
women to graduate from Cornell Medical School and in her practice
in Atlanta had established a reputation as a pioneer in child hygiene.[62]
Working for the Children's Bureau, she held a conference and child
welfare exhibit in each township in two counties, one representative
of the lowland region, the other the most remote mountain county
she could find. She also undertook an intensive, detailed house-to-
house study of one township in the lowland county and three town-
ships in the mountain county. She visited every midwife who had
attended a case within the past five years, studied the effectiveness of
birth-registration laws and conducted a brief survey of the hygienic
conditions in the local schools. The study covered nearly all aspects
of the social and economic conditions that affected child welfare; its
goal, as Bradley stated it, was to reveal if possible the "relation of
early home life to later health and efficiency."[63] In none of its subsequent studies did the bureau undertake such a complete survey of
social and economic conditions; the later studies, in Wisconsin, Montana, Wyoming, and Mississippi, reflect an increasing interest in prenatal care and childbirth.

Unlike most public health officials and urban medical specialists,
the Children's Bureau focused on women's experience of maternity.
While French public policy protected women as childbearers and
American urban programs for infant health emphasized prenatal care
as an essential aspect of infant welfare, the bureau staff assumed that

---

dren's Health Conference, Indiana, 11/1/15 (ibid., 4–11–1–1); Grace Meigs to Bittner,
12/31/15 (ibid., 4–11–1–1); Parker and Carpenter, "Julia Lathrop and the Children's
Bureau," pp. 65–66.

61. Grace Meigs, Memorandum on Indiana Conferences, 2/21/16 (U.S. Children's
Bureau, 4–11–1–0).

62. See Lloyd C. Taylor, The Medical Profession and Social Reform, 1885–1945 (New
York: St. Martin's Press, 1974), p. 63.

63. Frances Sage Bradley, "Suggested Plan for an Investigation of Conditions
Concerning Mothers and Babies in a Rural County," 2/16 (U.S. Children's Bureau,
4–11–2–2).

women's lives had inherent value separate from the lives of their children and argued that maternal suffering and death was in itself intolerable. As the rural studies progressed, improving the quality of women's lives and encouraging communities and families to recognize the importance of women's work and existence became as important to the researchers as saving infant lives.[64]

It may not be accidental that the bureau staff's sense of female solidarity emerges most clearly through the rural studies. As native-born white women they could probably more easily empathize with rural and small-town women, most of whom were native-born or northern European, than with southern and eastern European urban immigrants. For the most part the rural studies suggest little of the ambivalence about the relationship between poverty and maternal and infant mortality that characterized the urban studies, except where the researchers worked in a black community in the North Carolina lowland county. Suspicious of the corrupting influence of the urban environment, the bureau staff also inherited the belief characteristic of American reformers that farm living fostered a wholesome independence, pride, and moral fortitude. To the French bourgeoise, rural life was synonymous with backwardness, ignorance, and superstition. Urban Progressives in the United States believed that the inefficiency of agricultural production was a hindrance to progress but they also believed that rural life was the source of the moral strength that supported the nation's democracy. Improving the quality of rural life, they thought, might help to stem the tide of urban migration.[65]

To the bureau staff and to the agricultural and home economics extension agents with whom they worked, a sense of community was a critical aspect of the ideal small town. When they entered a small town or rural township, they looked for community spirit— an eagerness of individuals to mobilize their resources to address the community's problems. The bureau insisted that its job lay in stimulating permanent local work and not in imposing programs on pas-

---

64. See, for example, Grace Meigs, memorandum to Lathrop, Sumner, and Bradley on plans for rural investigations, 6/17 (ibid., 4–12–5–1).

65. See David D. Danbom, *The Resisted Revolution* (Ames: Iowa State University Press, 1979), pp. 24–36; William L. Bowers, *The Country Life Movement in America* (Port Washington, N.Y.: Kennikat Press, 1974), p. 15; Carson, *Settlement Folk*, pp. 112–13.

sive or unwilling communities. The staff sometimes even implied that it was better to have no infant health institution than to have one that the "community" did not initiate or at least welcome. "We feel very sorry," Grace Meigs wrote to Sherbon, who was struggling with an apathetic Wisconsin county, "that you and the Bureau should be put in the position of urging upon a community something which they are not anxious to receive."[66]

In part this attitude reflected the staff's understanding of the proper role of the national government in social policy. As one of the few federal social welfare agencies—one whose very existence was controversial—the bureau was anxious not to imitate "autocratic" European government agencies in any way. The bureau staff also placed a moral value on community responsibility and initiative analagous to the value they placed on individual thrift and independence. Thus they argued that child welfare programs that relied on wealthy philanthropists were dangerous because they hindered the collective taking of responsibility by the community. In the eyes of the bureau staff, "Work for infant welfare is coming to be regarded as more than a philanthropy or an expression of good will. It is a profoundly important public concern which tests the public spirit and the democracy of a community."[67]

As chief of the Division of Child Hygiene of the Kansas State Board of Health, Lydia DeVilbiss put this principle to work when she organized a child welfare contest for the counties of Kansas in 1916. She convinced the governor to offer a trophy to the county with the best health record for the year, based on both public and voluntary activities.[68] DeVilbiss reported to Lathrop on the moral benefits of such a program: "Instead of going into the country districts and trying to persuade the farmer folk to do what we want them to do, this plan proposes to put them on their mettle and let them do for them-

66. Grace Meigs to Florence Sherbon, 5/19/16 (U.S. Children's Bureau, 4–11–3–5).

67. *Second Annual Report of the Chief, Children's Bureau,* p. 8. On settlement leaders' ideas of community responsibility see Lissak, *Pluralism and Progressives,* pp. 13–14, and Carson, *Settlement Folk,* p. 112.

68. *Baby Week Campaigns,* U.S. Children's Bureau, Miscellaneous Series No. 5 (Bureau Publication No. 15) (Washington, D.C.: Government Printing Office, 1917), pp. 51–52.

selves what we want them to do and what we should have difficulty in getting them to do in any other way."[69]

Thus, when the Children's Bureau researchers began to consider working in a particular county, they first sought the cooperation of influential and representative local organizations, focusing especially on the informal power structures. Before beginning work in any community they obtained the assurance of cooperation from the state board of health, the county medical society, and the local women's organizations. As soon as they arrived they contacted physicians and ministers, the city and county superintendants of schools, any visiting or school nurses or county extension agents, and sometimes leading businessmen.

The members of local women's organizations were essential contacts. If they could get the interest and active cooperation of the local club women, Bradley wrote, other women would surely follow.[70] The bureau viewed women's clubs as the manifestation of female solidarity and also believed that they had genuine power and importance in local politics. Never did Sherbon, Bradley, or their assistants complain that men did not listen to the women's organizations; nor did they mention women's inability to vote as a disadvantage in local politics. On occasion, their confidence that a united group of women could overcome the inertia or opposition of male-dominated bodies was indeed borne out. Thus their concept of democracy seems to have hinged not so much on the existence of formal political structures but rather on an environment and social life that fostered a spirit of cooperation and responsibility. This concept in turn rested on the assumption that a consensus was possible because social relations were fundamentally harmonious.[71]

The bureau staff had great faith in the schools as a potential base for community cooperation. They saw public schools as the most important of democratic institutions, since they believed that literate and well-informed citizens constituted the essence of democracy. Un-

69. Lydia Allen DeVilbiss to Julia Lathrop, 11/23/15 (U.S. Children's Bureau, 4–15–2–1–8).

70. Frances Sage Bradley to Grace Meigs, 11/11/15 (ibid., 4–11–1–1).

71. See Lissak, *Pluralism and Progressives,* pp. 13–15, on democracy and consensus in Hull House philosophy. On women's political culture, see Paula Baker, "The Domestication of Politics: Women and American Political Society, 1780–1920," *American Historical Review* 89 (1984): 620–47.

fortunately, schools were not always important in rural communities. Bradley wrote of her disappointment that in many country districts parents paid little attention to the school; many parents did not know the teacher and never even entered the building. "The place of the meeting," she concluded reluctantly, "should be left to the parents, notwithstanding our desire to establish the school as a community center."[72]

The bureau sought the cooperation of local physicians not as potential allies but as an obstacle to be overcome before the real work could proceed. When Arthur B. Emmons, a prominent eastern pediatrician, responded to West's request for suggestions as to how to proceed with the rural investigations, he suggested that the people could be reached through the "community physician," but the bureau's researchers expected little help from the local physicians in the rural counties they studied.[73] More often than not they found physicians either overtly hostile to their work or so ignorant of child hygiene as to be of little assistance.

Many physicians feared that any form of free medical care would undermine their practices.[74] Sometimes an unfortunate public health nurse had to contend with a local physician like the "sick old man who calls births registration 'damn nonsense.' "[75] Some physicians changed their minds, however, when they found out that the conference physician actually encouraged people to see their family doctors. Others were pleased to discover that a public health nurse could take over time-consuming bedside care. Many other physicians were simply apathetic, and Sherbon and Bradley frequently reported that professional jealousy or personal conflicts among the local physicians prevented them from cooperating.[76] Of course, hostility and indif-

72. Frances Sage Bradley, "Lessons Learned in Making Rural Studies" (U.S. Children's Bureau, 4–12–5–1).

73. Arthur B. Emmons to Mrs. Max West, 4/25/16 (ibid., 4–3–0–4).

74. "A Trip to Lexington, Virginia, May 10 and 11, 1915" (ibid., 4–15–0).

75. Mary Bartlett Dixon to Miss Rose, 5/22/18 (ibid., 4–12–1).

76. "Question Corner," *National Organization of Public Health Nursing*, 1917, p. 197; Grace Meigs, memorandum on visit to Boston, November 15–16, 1917 (U.S. Children's Bureau, 4–15–4–3); Florence Sherbon to Grace Meigs, 3/31/17 (ibid., 4–11–1–10); 3/24/16 (ibid., 4–11–1–1); 6/12/16 (ibid., 4–11–3–5); Meigs, Report on Indiana Conferences, 2/21/16 (ibid., 4–11–1–0); E. J. Huenekens, "The Minnesota Plan for the Establishment of Infant Welfare Clinics in Smaller Towns," *Transactions of the American Association for the Study and Prevention of Infant Mortality* 9 (1918): 189.

ference among physicians were not universal, and public health officials and the bureau staff sometimes found unexpected allies among
physicians eager to help. Bradley, attending the meetings of the North
Carolina State Medical Association, initially "heard the same old gags
about the stupid obstinate women who are determined to die in spite
of the Med. Profession etc. etc." To her astonishment, however, the
membership voted almost unanimously to interrupt the meeting to
hear her speak and each delegate wanted the bureau to study his
community.[77] In Indiana, Sherbon found a physician who had been
unfriendly and sarcastic before her program, but afterward called it
a "revolutionary thing" and claimed that he could see the results in
the attitude of his patients toward their children and in the conduct
of pregnant women.[78]

Even if physicians were interested in helping with the conferences,
however, the bureau's workers frequently found them embarassingly
ignorant. Sherbon wrote to Meigs from Indiana suggesting that local
doctors and nurses always be asked to participate in the bureau's
conferences—"not that they are any real help (sometimes quite the
contrary!) but it does educate them amazingly."[79] Sherbon commented on the need for a detailed manual of private instructions for
the examiners at health conferences, "as these men are embarassed
by their helplessness, and often feel like boys on the dunce block, in
spite of my attempts to put them at ease." A separate pamphlet, she
thought, "would spare exposing them to the laity!"[80]

Male physicians, Sherbon and Bradley concluded, were apparently
too arrogant to consider practical details; trained exclusively to deal
with disease rather than health, they were ill suited to child health
work. Bradley scorned the "thoroughly scientific" doctors she came
across, none of whom had "common *horse sense*."[81] "It seems quite
impossible," she wrote, "to find a man doctor who will fill out a
record, with simple constructive suggestions. I think they minimize
the importance of the home care, and the hygiene of the mother, or

---

77. Frances Sage Bradley to Julia Lathrop, 4/20/16 (U.S. Children's Bureau, 4–
11-2–5).
78. Florence Sherbon to West, 7/15/16 (ibid., 4–11-3–5).
79. Florence Sherbon to Grace Meigs, 11/9/15 (ibid., 4–11-1–1).
80. Florence Sherbon to Grace Meigs, 3/17/17 (ibid., 4–14-2–4–0).
81. Frances Sage Bradley to Julia Lathrop, 7/29/16 (ibid., 4–11-2–5).

else assume that the mother knows more than she does."[82] She criticized one physician who was "evidently accustomed to working with a nurse who relieves him of all those details which mean the success or failure of a doctor's advice." She found especially frustrating a doctor who threw the stool samples of babies with diarrhea into a neighbor's yard. "And we have been trying so hard," Bradley complained, "to have them [the mothers] protect their children from flies and stools of sick children."[83]

Sherbon and Bradley began their rural studies already predisposed to mistrust male members of the medical profession, but the studies proved to be a personally and intellectually liberating experience; they returned home to challenge the emerging medical model of maternal and child health. Traditional methods of child care and health care, they discovered, often produced results as good as those of "scientific" hygiene; childbearing was, under the right conditions, a perfectly normal physiological process, and midwives, who knew enough to let nature take its course in most cases, were not nearly as dangerous as the average physician.

Rarely, if ever, had any women traveled freely throughout the country at the expense of the government, undertaking a project of their own design under the direction of women and with their government authority as a badge of legitimacy. The letters Sherbon and Bradley wrote to the Washington staff vividly convey their sense of adventure. Bradley, traveling in North Carolina in the spring of 1916, found a warm welcome nearly everywhere she went. She was exhilirated at the response: "And when we find farmers and their wives, stopping their ploughing and planting in the middle of April and driving 10 and 15 miles to learn how to raise children, it makes one feel that the work is worthwhile."[84] She was thrilled at the contact she was able to have with the most "backward," "primitive," elements of American society. "They're the people we're after," she wrote of a committee of schoolteachers, "One teacher schools, moonlight schools and all the rest of it . . . deaf children, dull children, lazy children and weakly, and nobody knows why."[85] In Green's Creek

82. Frances Sage Bradley to Grace Meigs, 3/17/16 (ibid., 4–11–2–5).
83. Frances Sage Bradley to Julia Lathrop, 7/29/16 (ibid., 4–11–2–5).
84. Frances Sage Bradley to Grace Meigs, 4/21/16 (ibid., 4–11–2–5).
85. Frances Sage Bradley to Julia Lathrop, 2/25/16 (ibid., 4–11–2–3).

she was disappointed that the village was too near the little towns of Dillsboro and Sylva "to find any very interesting obstetrical data most of the women having doctors." She had found the black midwives in Cumberland most interesting, though, since they used herbs, roots, and magic.[86]

Bradley and her assistant, Margaretta Williamson, approached the experience with something like a pioneer spirit.[87] As they climbed deep into the mountains in search of remote backwoods communities, Bradley wrote to Meigs that the people were very happy; she and Williamson were almost ready to become mountaineers themselves.[88] She described one community as a kind of primitive paradise, untainted by the material temptations of modern urban society. "Their contentment and rather stubborn assurance of well-being are of course the result of their limited horizon," she wrote, "and one almost doubts the wisdom or kindness of helping them see what is beyond. They are happy as long as they have no standard of comparison, much happier than the same class of people in cities." Divorce and discontent were almost unknown. If only they could be taught to cook bread and vegetables instead of half-cooked hog and hominy, Bradley concluded, "I should be inclined to build a dyke or a barbed wire fence around Grays Creek Township and keep government employees and would-be educators out."[89]

Bradley came to sympathize with the rural people's mistrust of physicians. Few able physicians located in their small communities; the only doctors who came their way were traveling quacks or "accidental medical students." Women relied on midwives, who, though ignorant, were "a fairly clean, decent sort, and with a wholesome horror of interfering with nature." Though they took no asceptic precautions, Bradley had heard of very few cases of infection. "Obstetrics," she reported, "is considered a strictly normal process, often not even a midwife being considered necessary."[90]

Equally inspired by her own rural experience, Florence Sherbon wrote, "This Wisconsin work has been like opening a door to the

86. Frances Sage Bradley to Grace Meigs, 11/12/16 (ibid., 4–11–2–5).
87. Margaretta Williamson to Emma Duke, 3/5/16 (ibid., 4–11–2–5).
88. Frances Sage Bradley to Grace Meigs, 12–3–16 (ibid., 4–11–2–5).
89. Frances Sage Bradley to Grace Meigs, 6/12/16 (ibid., 4–11–2–5).
90. "Report on Rural Work in North Carolina 11/15 to 12/15, 1916" (ibid., 4–11–2–7).

thing which I have felt urging me in a groping, blind way ever since the child welfare work 'got me.' "[91] Sitting on a culvert waiting for a chauffeur and watching a woman and man put up hay together while two toddlers sat and watched, she described to Viola Paradise in the Washington office the German families she had recently visited. None of these families, she wrote, ever called a physician for anything and yet all had healthy children. One woman worked up until delivery and made bread the third day after and yet, to Sherbon's surprise, had a happy, healthy baby. "Its awfully disconcerting to have one's preconceived ideas get such jolts," she wrote. "I am not nearly so sure about some things as I used to be!"[92] Two weeks later she wrote to Meigs with an urgent request for information on the midwife question: "We are meeting it fair and square here and its a big problem. Another of my preconceived ideas getting a big jolt!"[93]

The example of these healthy country women, most of whom had never had a doctor in the house, Sherbon later wrote in the *Woman's Medical Journal*, proved that expert medical service was not a basic requirement for normal maternity. Many of these women "violate every canon set by modern obstetricians as to pre-natal conduct." Country women had fewer complications than urban women, she concluded, because they had so much exercise and fresh air.[94] So enamored of the country life was Sherbon that West teased her, "Dear Doctor Lady: . . . I am most particularly interested in your researches into the pregnant state. . . . If, as I said before, the country life and all that pertains to it really are a panacea for the pain and sorrow of childbirth, it is awfully worthwhile to find that out."[95]

Before beginning her study, Sherbon later recounted, she had been committed to the extermination of the midwife. She thought pregnancy was pathological and was convinced that every time a woman gave birth she took her life in her hands. Her Wisconsin experience, she reported to the American Association for the Study and Prevention of Infant Mortality, convinced her not only that the German or

91. Florence Sherbon to Julia Lathrop, 6/22/16 (ibid., 4–12–4).
92. Florence Sherbon to Viola Paradise, 7/4/16 (ibid., 4–11–3–5).
93. Florence Sherbon to Grace Meigs, 7/18/16 (ibid., 4–11–3–5).
94. Florence Sherbon, "Maternal Efficiency—a Field for Research," *Woman's Medical Journal* 27 (1917): 35; Sherbon to West, 7/15/16 (U.S. Children's Bureau, 4–11–3–5).
95. Mrs. Max West to Florence Sherbon, 7/18/16 (U.S. Children's Bureau, 4–11–3–5).

Polish midwife was far better than the country doctor but that the entire direction of maternal welfare was wrong. "I believe we are in danger," she warned, "of placidly accepting the increasing pathologicity . . . and of institutionalizing maternity, and that about the time we get this elaborate system of maternity hospitals established and going, by state and municipal appropriations, just about that time we will wake up to the fact that after all an institution is not the best place to have a baby."[96]

Though some other female physicians agreed with Sherbon that pregnancy could be a normal physiological function, the conclusion to be drawn from the Children's Bureau's rural studies was not that farm women lived in an earthly paradise.[97] Instead, the studies revealed that isolation, back-breaking work, and lack of assistance in the home were reflected in a high maternal mortality rate and a high rate of early infant deaths, especially in the mountains and the high plains. Country women, argued Dorothy Reed Mendenhall, a lecturer for the Extension Service in Wisconsin who also worked for the Children's Bureau at times, suffered "infinitely more hardship and privation than would be tolerated in a city of any size."[98]

Women in the mountain states had a particularly hard time. There were only three registered physicians in the 5,500 square miles of a Montana county studied by the bureau, so women frequently left the area for childbirth. Of those who stayed, more than half had only a neighboring woman—often a practical nurse—to help, while one-eighth had only their husbands. The maternal mortality rate in the area was 12.7 per thousand, five times higher than that of Italy.[99] Though the women surveyed in the bureau's Kansas study were much better off—their work was not too hard and most could afford medical care if they needed it (95 percent had a physician at childbirth)—

96. Quoted in Grace L. Meigs, "Rural Obstetrics," *Transactions of the American Association for the Study and Prevention of Infant Mortality* 7 (1916): 65.

97. See Dorothy Reed Mendenhall, "Work of the Extension Department in Educating the Mother along the Lines of Prenatal Care and Infant Hygiene," *Transactions of the American Association for the Study and Prevention of Infant Mortality* 7 (1916): 217.

98. Comments by Dorothy Reed Mendenhall, Discussion, Session on Continuation Schools, *Transactions of the American Association for the Study and Prevention of Infant Mortality* 5 (1914): 250.

99. Viola I. Paradise, *Maternity Care and the Welfare of Young Children in a Homesteading County in Montana*, U.S. Children's Bureau, Rural Child Welfare Series No. 3 (Bureau Publication No. 34) (Washington, D.C.: Government Printing Office, 1919), pp. 27, 42.

few had any kind of prenatal care. In Wyoming, the bureau found women more than fifty miles from the nearest physician or nurse.[100]

The bureau staff were eager to hear these women's stories. They corresponded with nursing leaders in Wyoming to arrange medical and nursing care for one woman who had written to the bureau of her trouble with a complicated pregnancy.[101] Caroline Hedger, traveling in Wyoming for the bureau, made a trip to give Mrs. Phelps, the suffering woman, a physical exam and later sent her five pounds of dried fruit.[102] Phelps reported that two women and two babies in her community had died within a year. She wrote bitterly, "If the woman had been a thoroughbred cow worth 3 or 4 hundred dollars Wyoming's State veterinary would have been rushed out here to save her and the calf, but it doesn't seem worthwhile to save babies and mothers in general. That's what hurts me so."[103] The bureau staff proposed to make a collection of letters from farm women telling of the hardships they suffered during pregnancy and childbirth and the difficulty they had getting help. They envisioned a book similar to *Maternity,* a collection of stories by working-class women about the pain and poverty associated with childbearing, published by the Women's Cooperative Guild in England.[104]

This attention to the suffering of women was central to the bureau's approach to maternity care. The isolation of women in childbirth, a high maternal mortality rate, an inadequate health care system—the bureau interpreted all of these as evidence of women's oppression. The struggle for public maternity care, they believed, meant educating and organizing women to demand attention to their interests and

100. Elizabeth Moore, *Maternity and Infant Care in a Rural County in Kansas,* U.S. Children's Bureau, Rural Child Welfare Series No. 1 (Washington, D.C.: Government Printing Office, 1917), pp. 47–48; Mrs. James E. Mills to Caroline Hedger, 4/14/17 (U.S. Children's Bureau, 4–3–0–3).

101. Mrs. Max West to Ella P. Crandall, 10/26/16; U.S. Children's Bureau to Mrs. Phelps, 10/27/16; Ysabelle Waters to West, 11/3/16 (U.S. Children's Bureau, 4–3–0–3). The empathy of the bureau staff with the maternity experiences of women who wrote to the bureau for advice is illustrated in Molly Ladd-Taylor, *Raising a Baby the Government Way: Mothers' Letters to the Children's Bureau, 1915–1932* (New Brunswick, N.J.: Rutgers University Press, 1986).

102. Caroline Hedger to Julia Lathrop, 11/20/16 and 11/23/16 (U.S. Children's Bureau, 4–3–0–3).

103. Mrs. Phelps to Julia Lathrop, 12/13/16 (ibid., 4–3–0–3).

104. Viola Paradise to Florence Sherbon and Elizabeth Moore, 5/16/16 (ibid., 4–11–3–5); Grace Meigs, "Interview with Mrs. W. N. Hutt and Leonarda Goss," 5/31/16 (ibid., 4–12–1).

needs. West wrote to Arthur B. Emmons complaining of the tone of "patronage, and something like condescension toward women who must accept free medical service of this sort, if they have any at all." Doctors should be "fighting for the establishment of this right," she argued, "rather than preaching to the women as to what their duty is."[105]

West, like other members of the bureau staff, advocated a comprehensive system of county nurses who would carry out their work primarily in the home but would also be in charge of small cottage hospitals equipped with surgical facilities to handle complicated cases.[106] Mary Sewall Gardner and Ella Phillips Crandall, leaders in public health nursing, argued that rural visiting nurses should also be midwives; despite physicians' opposition to midwives in the United States, Gardner and Crandall pointed out that European statistics showed that trained midwives were effective.[107] Gardner and Crandall proposed that maternal and infant health care be placed primarily in the hands of female professionals rather than in the hands of male general practitioners and obstetricians. The training of physicians in modern obstetrics, using poor women as clinical "material"—an important factor in the medical model of maternity care—was of little importance in their program.

When the Section on Nursing and Social Work of the American Association for the Study and Prevention of Infant Mortality passed a resolution urging the training of obstetric nurses to supervise normal maternity cases, physicians objected.[108] It was the issue of national medical insurance for maternity and infant care, however, that brought the bureau into direct conflict with the medical profession. The isolation of rural women from all forms of health care convinced

105. Mrs. Max West to Arthur B. Emmons, 12/18/15 (ibid., 4-2-0-4).

106. The proposal for a system of cottage hospitals staffed by nurses was based on the Canadian example. See Suzann Buckley, "Ladies or Midwives? Efforts to Reduce Infant and Maternal Mortality," in *A Not Unreasonable Claim: Women and Reform in Canada, 1880–1920's,* ed. Linda Kealey (Toronto: Women's Press, 1979), p. 137.

107. Mary Sewall Gardner and Ella Phillips Crandall, "Recommendations Concerning Rural Maternity Nursing Service in Wyoming," 4/30/17 (U.S. Children's Bureau, 4-12-5-2).

108. Discussion, Section on Nursing and Social Work with Section on Midwifery, *Transactions of the American Association for the Study and Prevention of Infant Mortality* 2 (1911): 284-85.

the bureau staff that the provision of maternity care was a proper function of government. "Certainly a woman who gives a child to the country," wrote West, "has an inherent right to the best care that can be given to her."[109] Economic hardship, she argued, prevented many women from obtaining good care at childbirth and from taking rest they needed; some form of maternity insurance was clearly essential. Thus, when Lathrop and her staff began to develop a proposal for a national maternal and infant health policy in 1916 and 1917, they envisioned a program that would pay for certain kinds of medical care.

In its campaigns for maternity insurance the bureau had allies among both male and female labor reformers and advocates of social insurance legislation. The American Association for Labor Legislation, for example, drafted a health insurance bill including maternity benefits that would cover medical care for insured women and the wives of insured men, and a weekly benefit for insured women on the condition they refrain from gainful employment.[110] The bureau did not couch its argument in favor of maternity benefits primarily in terms of the dangers of women's industrial labor, however. Instead, they cited the acute shortage of medical care, especially in rural areas. Unlike the American Association for Labor Legislation bill and French maternity-benefit proposals, Lathrop's was not designed primarily to enable wage-earning women to take time off but rather to make professional health care universally available. Under the proposal Lathrop supported, a very large percentage of the rural population would fall into the income category (earning under twelve hundred dollars) eligible for benefits.[111]

Advocates of maternity insurance were well aware that they supported a controversial measure and that their opponents inevitably associated compulsory insurance proposals with tyranny and socialism. Eva Ward, writing in the feminist *Woman's Journal,* attributed this opposition to a misconception of the principles of insurance;

---

109. Mrs. Max West to Arthur B. Emmons, 12/18/15 (U.S. Children's Bureau, 4-2-0-4).

110. Julia Lathrop, "Public Protection of Maternity," *American Labor Legislation Review* 7 (1917): 28.

111. Ibid., p. 31. Lathrop saw the urban-industrial emphasis of the AALL's bill as too narrow. Meckel, *Save the Babies,* pp. 189-95.

Americans did not realize, she thought, that only those who paid into the fund for a certain period were eligible to receive benefits.[112] In his study of the movement for social security in the United States, Roy Lubove argues that social insurance came into conflict not only with the ideology of voluntarism but with various private vested interests. Private health insurance companies lobbied vigorously against compulsory health insurance bills. The medical profession did not hide its economic interests in its fight against maternity insurance.[113]

Proposed maternity-assistance legislation in Massachusetts, submitted to the state legislature in 1916, 1917, and 1919, failed each time in the face of organized opposition from the medical profession. When the subject of maternity insurance came up in 1915 in the American Association for the Study and Prevention of Infant Mortality, some physicians expressed their fears that the government would regulate their fees in connection with compulsory insurance.[114] An official of the Wisconsin Department of Health scorned the claim that poverty and hardship were the cause of high rural maternal and infant death rates. He argued that farm families, presumably out of stubborn miserliness, simply refused to pay for a physician's services or to employ trained nurses, though these were readily available. If they did not receive prenatal care it was simply because they wanted to avoid the expense; if they did not have help in the house it was because they were unwilling to pay a reasonable wage.[115]

The pediatrician Arthur B. Emmons of Boston, on the other hand, thought that Boston had too many free prenatal care services, catering to those who were simply hunting for cheap obstetrical care; he suspected that rural people had a spirit of independence and eagerness to learn.[116] In comparison, it is significant that the French medical profession did not see maternity insurance as a threat to itself. The American medical profession had to defend its hegemony in a way

112. Ward, "In Defense of the Maternity Benefit," p. 138.
113. Lubove, The Struggle for Social Security, p. 9.
114. Session on Economic Aspects of Infant Welfare: Maternity Insurance, Transactions of the American Association for the Study and Prevention of Infant Mortality 6 (1915): 206; Meigs, "Rural Obstetrics," p. 72.
115. Dr. Heinike to Elizabeth Moore, 2/15/18 (U.S. Children's Bureau, 4–11–3–5).
116. Arthur B. Emmons to Mrs. Max West, 3/1/17 (ibid., 4–15–4–1–1); West, "Boston, Mass.—Prenatal Care," 11/9/14 (ibid., 4–15–4–1–1).

the French medical profession did not. French medical organizations were among the most vocal supporters of public maternal and infant welfare programs.

Though Lathrop openly advocated maternity insurance, she was pessimistic about its prospects in the United States. Social insurance, she privately admitted in 1916, was years away.[117] Her pessimism was justified: the bureau's campaign for a national maternal and infant health program culminated in the Sheppard-Towner Act, which provided for maternal education but did not pay for medical care, and women in the United States have yet to win the right to compensated maternity leave. World War I, however, created the conditions that enabled women activists' model of maternal and child welfare to triumph briefly. The loss of adult male lives on the battlefield made it possible for American supporters of child welfare programs to argue that child health was a patriotic issue. As women mobilized as part of the war effort, the popular child health movement became a truly national one. After the war, women's organizations and the Children's Bureau drew on this movement to drum up massive popular support for a federal maternal and infant health program.

117. Julia Lathrop to Mrs. Frederick A. Halsing, 6/3/16 (ibid., 4–15–4–1).

7

"Bread, Bullets, and Babies": Saving the Next Generation in France and the United States

As head of the New York City Bureau of Child Hygiene, S. Josephine Baker greeted foreign dignitaries from all over Europe who came to observe the work of her agency. In 1918 her guests also included Theodore Roosevelt, who had, as his secretary described it, recently "developed a lively interest in the Bureau's work."[1] Baker found all this attention "extraordinarily flattering," but she also found it disturbing, in the context of the patriotic emphasis on preserving the next generation. Indeed, a speaker at the meeting of the American Association for the Study and Prevention of Infant Mortality in 1917 had argued, "This war is going to depend not only on bread and bullets, but on bread, bullets and babies."[2] "It had taken the sinister stimulus of mass-murder," Baker wrote, "to make the fighting nations see the necessity for saving children."[3]

As the United States mobilized its forces to fight the war, the argument that child welfare programs would help to ensure a supply of healthy army recruits in the future was heard for the first time. Child welfare workers warned that if the United States did not take appropriate steps it too could someday find itself in the same predic-

1. S. Josephine Baker, *Fighting for Life* (New York: Macmillan, 1939), p. 177.
2. Discussion on Propaganda, *Transactions of the American Association for the Study and Prevention of Infant Mortality* 8 (1917): 269.
3. Baker, *Fighting for Life*, pp. 171–72.

ament as France.[4] Journalists and politicians in the United States began to employ military metaphors when they spoke about child welfare, and child welfare workers called on the public to save infant lives as a patriotic measure, just as their French colleagues had been doing for forty years. In 1918 the U.S. Children's Bureau and the Council for National Defense mobilized women in unprecedented numbers to organize Children's Year activities. Children's Year, promoted by the bureau as part of the war effort, reached several times more children than had the wildly successful national Baby Week campaign of 1916.

In France the war, which brought a sharp decline in births as well as devastating mortality rates, seemed to fulfill the most dire predictions of social scientists. A military officer representing the conservative Alliance nationale pour l'accroissement de la population française warned an audience of soldiers that Neo-Malthusian propaganda was a German plot to depopulate France. Sadly, he continued, the enemy's secret agents had found the French people only too willing either through blindness or guilt to spread the word.[5] The protection of the health of working mothers and their infants became a burning issue in the Académie de médecine, and charitable organizations intensified their efforts to meet the special needs of working women and soldiers' wives. The Chamber of Deputies debated and passed more comprehensive maternal and infant health measures than ever before. Americans hastened to the aid of their ally; the introduction of visiting nurses by the American Red Cross was perhaps the most important and lasting wartime innovation in French maternal and infant health programs.

Though some feminist goals such as suffrage and expanded employment opportunities seem to have been furthered by the war, these apparent victories were often only temporary. Likewise, only in a very limited sense can wartime maternal and child health programs

4. "Conserving the Babies," *Johnstown Democrat,* October 5, 1917 (clipping in U.S. Children's Bureau 12–7); Jacob Sobel, "Conservation of Baby Life in the Tenement," *Medical Record* 93 (1918): 676; Eugene R. Kelley, "What the Divisions of Child Hygiene of the State Departments of Health Are Doing," *Transactions of the American Association for the Study and Prevention of Infant Mortality* 9 (1918): 84; Charles H. Miner, "The Influence of Prenatal Care on Infant Mortality," *Pennsylvania Medical Journal* 21 (1918): 502.

5. [Capitaine] DeBlic, *Nous les aurons. Mais après . . . ?* (Paris: L'Alliance nationale pour l'accroissement de la population française, 1916), pp. 22–23.

be seen as gains for women and children. As Margaret and Patrice Higonnet write, war leads to the symbolic politicization of women's reproductive functions; the consequent developments in paternalistic state policy are not designed to protect or aid women but rather are intended to protect the state's own need for a healthy and growing population and a productive work force.[6] World War I lent legitimacy to government intervention and centralization in all areas of social and economic activity. As Baker so bitterly pointed out, in maternal and child welfare policy a heightened attention to the supply of human resources led governments to take decisive action where before they had hesitated. In addition, the effect of the war was to enhance the role of the more repressive elements of maternal and child welfare policies.

The obvious importance of human reproduction to nations at war tended to stimulate renewed efforts to control women's childbearing, and the extension of political repression—which, in the United States, lasted well beyond the end of the war—legitimized measures that sacrificed individual rights to the needs of society. In France, postwar pronatalist legislation included measures to repress birth control propaganda and a punitive antiabortion policy. In the United States, eugenics took on greater prominence, and campaigns for the mass weighing and measuring of infants, mimicking the physical and mental examination of army recruits, reflected a growing zeal for the classification of children on the basis of intelligence and potential deviance. Wartime pronatalism and xenophobia in the United States gave new life to the concept of race suicide and inspired a new wave of programs and propaganda designed to inspire or shame native-born middle- and upper-class women into bearing children to carry on the "race." These new forces in maternal and infant health campaigns lent renewed vigor to the prewar movement but at the same time constituted a rival to the U.S. Children's Bureau's maternalist vision. The postwar period produced the Sheppard-Towner Act—the product of the bureau's campaign for a federal maternal and infant health program—which would define federal and state-level policy

6. Margaret R. Higonnet and Patrice L.-R. Higonnet, "The Double Helix," in *Behind the Lines: Gender and the Two World Wars,* ed. Margaret Randolph et al. (New Haven: Yale University Press, 1987), pp. 36–37.

through the 1920s. Wartime and postwar politics, however, also generated new opposition to Progressive social programs.

French Infant Health Policy and the War

In the tumult of the crisis created by the war, French officials at first had little time to think about the future of the race. Local authorities and private agencies hastened to try to meet the needs of mothers and children affected by wartime conditions. The war interrupted the milk supply and the transportation of foundlings to wet-nurses in the country and multiplied the number of widows and orphans. At first the sudden collapse of industry brought general unemployment for women, but by 1915 the industrial mobilization of women had increased the demand for child-care facilities.[7]

Local government agencies distributed milk, helped poor mothers pay the cost of wet-nurses, and, in at least one city, created a system of cantines to feed pregnant women, nursing mothers, and young children.[8] In Paris a central bureau of maternal and child welfare coordinated an intensive, centralized maternity-care system, coordinating the work of private agencies—including the Oeuvre nouvelle des crèches parisiennes, the Pouponnière of Porchefontaine, the Oeuvre de l'allaitement maternel, and the Fédération des cantines maternelles—that expanded their services to meet the increased demand.[9] The central bureau also mobilized women volunteers in an effort to organize the care of all pregnant women within the juris-

7. Clothilde Mulon, "French Experience," in *Standards of Child Welfare: A Report of the Children's Bureau Conferences, May and June 1919*, U.S. Children's Bureau, Conference Series No. 1 (Bureau Publication No. 60) (Washington, D.C: Government Printing Office, 1919), pp. 211–12; G. Variot, *La puériculture et la guerre* (Paris: O. Doin, 1918), pp. 19–24.
8. Alliance d'hygiène sociale, *La guerre et la vie de demain*, vol. 1, pp. 104, 119; Département de la Seine, *Protection des enfants du premier âge: Rapport annuel, 1914*, p. 41; Variot, *La puériculture et la guerre*, p. 123.
9. Oeuvre nouvelle des crèches parisiennes, *Oeuvres d'hospitalisation de guerre: Rapport sur le fonctionnement de l'oeuvre depuis le 8 août 1914 au 31 décembre 1915*, p. 2; *Bulletin de l'Oeuvre de l'allaitement maternel et des refuges-ouvroirs pour les femmes enceintes*, No. 198, Supplément (December 1914); Georges Cahen, *L'autre guerre: Essais d'assistance et d'hygiène sociales, 1905–1920* (Nancy: Berger-Levault, 1920), p. 89; Alliance d'hygiène sociale, *La guerre et la vie de demain*, vol. 1, pp. 89–90.

diction of the city's military government. The volunteers sought out poor women in maternity hospitals and in the municipal buildings where they came to claim medical assistance or to declare their children's births, and made sure that they obtained food, medical care, and public assistance. In the first year of the war all existing agencies serving mothers and children in Paris doubled or tripled the number of beds they provided. Altogether they aided 12,300 women between August 1 and December 31, 1914.[10]

The most significant development related to maternal and infant health during the war was the increase in the industrial employment of women, especially in the production of arms and munitions.[11] The wartime debate over the effect of the employment of women in industry on childbearing and infant health highlighted the conflicting nature of the state's demands on women. In April 1916 the government established a Comité du travail féminin to deal with questions relating to the employment of women in arms and munitions factories under government control. Senator Paul Strauss presided over the committee; its members included representatives of the medical profession, labor unions, and feminist organizations as well as administrators of the agency responsible for overseeing labor regulations and the war industry. At the top of the committee's agenda, Strauss announced at the first meeting, was a campaign to increase the employment of women in war factories in order to free men for mobilization into the army. The ultimate goal of the committee, however, was to see that women were employed in the manner best suited to their aptitudes, their interests, and their physical and moral health, "in order to safeguard the race and prepare for the future."[12] With these two objectives in mind the committee designated members to investigate the suitability of various jobs for women, wages, hy-

---

10. Alliance d'hygiène social, *La guerre et la vie de demain,* vol. 1, pp. 92–101.

11. In March 1916 women made up 18 percent of the labor force in war factories. In the Seine, the largest center of war industry, women were about one-third of the war labor force in 1918. "Travaux du Comité du travail féminin, séance d'ouverture, 5 mai 1916," in Ministre de l'armement et des fabrications de guerre, Direction de la main d'oeuvre, *Protection et utilisation de la main d'oeuvre féminine dans les usines de guerre,* 1917, p. 105 (Archives nationales, F²² 439); Mathilde Dubesset, Françoise Thébaud, and Catherine Vincent, "Les munitionnettes de la Seine," in *1914–1918, l'autre front,* ed. Patrick Fridenson (Paris: Editions ouvrières, 1977), p. 190.

12. "Travaux du Comité du travail féminine, séance d'ouverture, 5 mai 1916," p. 105.

giene and safety, housing, transportation, and child-care facilities. In August, as its first action, the committee issued a circular recommending the creation of breast-feeding rooms and crèches in war factories.[13]

On December 3, 1916, Adolphe Pinard presented a report to the Académie de médecine on wartime child welfare in Paris in which he attacked the committee's efforts to increase the employment of women in war factories. The report precipitated a hot controversy within the academy, for Pinard forced the members to confront the government's basic dilemma: how to reconcile the employment of women in war industry with the nation's urgent need for children. Pinard claimed that the entrance of pregnant women and nursing mothers into war factories was responsible for an increase in the rates of infant mortality and prematurity. He proposed legislation that would go beyond the Strauss Law to prohibit the employment of women throughout pregnancy and for six months after childbirth, with compensation of five francs a day.[14]

Pinard's assault on the committee's work focused attention on the government's decision to emphasize war production over maternal and infant health. Almost no one who spoke in the ensuing debate agreed completely with Pinard; as usual Pinard, a zealous pronatalist, took an extreme position. The question was a thorny one, however, and the members of the academy wrestled uneasily with it, aware that supporting the recruitment of women workers would conflict at least to some extent with prevailing medical opinion. They agreed that the nation urgently needed women in the war factories but also conceded that it badly needed their children. At issue were such questions as whether or not keeping pregnant women out of war factories altogether would have an appreciable effect on production; to what extent women's employment in war factories rather than other conditions associated with the war was responsible for the increase in infant mortality; and whether employers should be required or merely urged to institute protective measures.[15]

13. Direction de la main d'oeuvre, 5e section, Note pour le Ministre, March 20, 1917 (Archives nationales, F^{22} 448).

14. "Rapport de M. le Docteur Pinard," (Archives nationales, F^{22} 448); "Veillons sur la mère, protégeons l'enfant" (clipping, Archives nationales, F^{22} 448).

15. J.-A. Doléris, "La protection des femmes et des enfants dans l'usine" (Archives nationales, F^{22} 444); Bulletin de l'Académie de médecine, October 5, 1916, December 3,

The government's reaction to Pinard's report suggests that in the eyes of the administration war production was the more immediate priority. Officials at the ministries of war and labor were concerned that Pinard's report might hamper their effort to recruit women workers. One official, who doubted the validity of Pinard's statistics, asked that another physician study the report.[16] Dr. Erasme Bonnaire—a member of the government committee, chief of obstetrics at the Maternité, and a member of the Conseil supérieur de l'assistance publique—drew up a report supporting the government's position. Citing statistics of his own to refute Pinard's claim that work in war industry was harmful to women's reproductive capacities, Bonnaire concluded that the absolute needs of national defense outweighed the risks to the population of employing women in factories.[17]

After hearing Bonnaire's report the Comité du travail féminin issued a series of resolutions recognizing that an increase in the employment of women in war factories was potentially dangerous but urging protective measures that would interfere only slightly with the employment of women. The committee proposed that pregnant women be excluded from physically strenuous tasks and night work and isolated from toxic substances, with compensation for any reduction in wages which resulted from such changes; that four weeks of rest before birth be made obligatory; and that maternal and infant health consultations be established in factories.[18] In January 1917 the Ministre de l'armement et des fabrications de guerre, which was in charge of munitions production, issued a circular to factory inspectors, calling the attention of industrialists to the committee's resolutions and urging them to establish breast-feeding rooms, crèches, and bonuses to compensate women for the time they took off to nurse.[19]

Paul Strauss, representing the government's position in the Aca-

---

1916, January 2, 1917, February 27, 1917, March 6, 1917, March 13, 1917; Dubesset, Thébaud, and Vincente discuss the debate in detail in "Les munitionettes de la Seine."

16. M. Simiad to M. [G]oineau, November 5, 1916, Note No. 4,656; Ministre du travail et de la prévoyance sociale to Sous-Secrétariat d'Etat de l'artillerie et des munitions, n.d. (Archives nationales, F^{22} 448).

17. E. Bonnaire, "Rapport sur le travail féminin dans les fabriques de munitions," Bulletin des usines de guerre, no. 35 (December 25, 1916): 276.

18. Ibid., p. 279.

19. Ministre de l'armement et des fabrications de guerre to MM. les Contrôleurs de la main d'ouevre, January 4, 1917 (Archives nationales F^{22} 444).

démie de médecine, minimized the effect of the employment of women in war factories on depopulation. First, he argued, women's factory work had been increasing throughout the century and was only partly a result of the war. He also pointed out that the nation's most "industrious" families were also the most prolific, thus moderating his prewar position on the ill effects of women's employment.[20] In March, after a series of drawn-out debates, the academy adopted resolutions almost identical to those of the government committee, citing the potential demographic danger posed by the increase in female industrial workers.

Maternal and child health continued to concern the committee throughout the war.[21] One of its major efforts was a campaign to generalize breast-feeding rooms and crèches within factories. In 1917 parliament passed a law requiring all industrial and commercial employers to enable women to nurse during working hours. The new law was introduced into the Chamber of Deputies in February 1917 as a populationist measure. It specified that for a year after giving birth all women employed in the establishments covered by the law had the right to an hour a day to breast-feed in the establishment, in an appropriate environment. Employers of more than one hundred women aged fifteen or over could be required to install a breast-feeding room in or near the factory.[22] Before the war legislators had hesitated to *require* employers to provide accommodations for breast-feeding; the wartime crisis had made coercive action more acceptable. In September the Ministre de l'armement issued a memorandum stating, "It is important that state establishments provide an example of rapid realization of the legislative prescriptions and that measures

20. *Bulletin de l'Académie de médecine,* February 27, 1917: 274–75.
21. Service ouvrier, Ministre de l'armement et des fabrications de guerre, Cabinet du Ministre, Note, March 8, 1917; Ministre de l'armement et des fabrications de guerre to MM. les Directeurs des établissements de l'artillerie et des poudreries, May 1, 1917; Chef de Cabinet chargé de la direction du service ouvrier to M. le Sous-Secrétariat d'Etat, Ministère de guerre, November 7, 1917; E. Bonnaire to Paul Strauss, November 26, 1916; "Note pour le ministre," December 17, 1916 (Archives nationales, F[22] 448); "Circulaire générale du 1er juillet 1917," in Ministre de l'armement, *Protection et utilisation de la main d'oeuvre féminine,* 1917. See also various documents in Archives nationales, F[22] 532.
22. Chambre des Députés, Annexe au procès-verbal de la séance du 16 fevrier 1917, *Proposition de loi tendant à assurer aux femmes occupées dans les établissements industriels ou commerciaux la possibilité d'allaiter leurs enfants;* "Loi du 5 août 1917, concernant l'allaitement maternel dans les établissements industriels et commerciaux," *Journal officiel,* August 6, 1917.

already taken be completed as soon as possible." By March 1918 the Comité du travail féminin counted nineteen state munitions factories that had taken steps to establish breast-feeding rooms and crèches.[23]

Despite this apparent commitment to providing child-care facilities, many planned crèches never materialized. In an arsenal in Rennes employing six thousand women, for example, the breast-feeding room did not begin functioning until three weeks before the armistice; the crèche, in planning for fifteen months, never opened at all. A government survey of 175 factories employing more than one hundred women showed that only 53 had breast-feeding rooms, 27 had crèches, and 39 had *garderies* for older children.[24] Some employers claimed that women were not interested in taking advantage of these facilities; others made attendance obligatory for all their employees' children in order to ensure that the money spent was not wasted.[25]

Employers often objected to the pressure to establish breast-feeding rooms; they preferred to contribute to insurance funds that enabled women to stay home and nurse.[26] After the war, as the state's interest in women's industrial labor waned, employers found that much of the pressure to create child-care facilities had disappeared, and many crèches and breast-feeding rooms closed. While today feminists favor the idea of state-supported child care facilities as a way of making possible women's economic independence and full social participation, in early-twentieth-century France crèches were seen only as a means of preventing depopulation without threatening the labor supply. Even the Conseil national des femmes françaises, which had lobbied during the war for legislation to require employers to institute breast-feeding rooms, saw the heart of the matter as one of reconciling two urgent needs—the need of modern society for women's industrial

23. Memo (signed, "Loucheur"), September 30, 1917 (Archives nationales, F[22] 446); Comité du travail féminin, "Rapport sur les oeuvres de protection de l'enfance dans les établissements de l'état," *Bulletin des usines de guerre,* March 18, 1918: 375–76.

24. Detailed results of the survey of infant-care facilities in war factories are in Archives nationales, F[22] 534; Alice LaMazière, *Sauvons les bébés* (Niort: Imprimerie A. Chiron, 1920), p. 5.

25. Berthrot (Inspecteur divisionnaire) to Ministre du travail et de la prévoyance sociale, April 17, 1917 (Archives nationales, F[22] 446).

26. Paul Winckler to M. le Directeur du travail, n.d.; "Notice concernant l'allaitement maternel dans les établissements industriels et commerciaux," September 25, 1920 (Archives nationales, F[22] 446); Dubesset, Thébaud, and Vincent, "Les munitionnettes de la Seine," p. 208.

labor and the country's need for children.[27] As Denise Riley argues in her study of British women workers during World War II, child welfare institutions designed to meet the needs of the state or of industry are frequently temporary in nature and do not necessarily meet the needs of women.[28]

The War and the American Infant Health Movement

Even before the United States entered the war, American child welfare advocates began to point out the impetus given by the war to maternal and child welfare work in other countries. They noted that in Britain, for example, the infant mortality rate in the second year of the war was lower than before 1914, despite all the hardships associated with the war.[29] Some pointed out the irony of European superiority in child welfare, an irony heightened by Americans' enthusiasm for donating money to save Belgian and French children.[30]

In her autobiography S. Josephine Baker describes her meeting with a woman wearing a new khaki uniform, about to leave for London to supervise the feeding of school lunches to schoolchildren. When the woman expressed her horror that 12 percent of these children were undernourished as a result of the war, Baker coldly informed her that 21 percent of New York schoolchildren were also undernourished, largely on account of the same war. "Perhaps," Baker wrote, "it was my own lack of uniform that made me so sharp about it." Baker also liked to point out that it was "seven times safer to be

27. *L'Action féminine* 9 (1917): 168. Also see Mary Lynn McDougall, "Protecting Infants: The French Campaign for Maternity Leaves, 1890s–1913," *French Historical Studies* 13 (1983): 104.

28. Denise Riley, "The Free Mothers: Pronatalism and Working Mothers in Industry at the End of the Last War in Britain," *History Workshop Journal* 11 (Spring 1981): 100–101. Also see Riley's *War in the Nursery: Theories of the Child and Mother* (London: Virago, 1983), her article in Higonnet et al., *Behind the Lines,* pp. 260–71; and Sonya Michel, "American Women and the Discourse of the Democratic Family in World War II," in ibid., pp. 160–67.

29. R. H. Bishop, Jr., "Your Health and Its Care" (U.S. Children's Bureau, 4–15–4–3); "Mrs. Thompson of Eureka Arkansas in Talk" (ibid., 8–2–1–11); "Children in War Time; Fourth Article: Babies and War," (press release) 9/17/17 (ibid., 8–2–1–10).

30. Maria Montalvo, "We Are Saving French Babies—Why Not Our Own as Well?" *New York Tribune,* June 9, 1918: 4 (clipping in U.S. Children's Bureau, 4–15–4–2).

a soldier in the trenches of France than to be born a baby in the United States."[31]

Still, child health was one of many social issues that local governments took up, often for the first time, as part of the war effort; the Children's Bureau and most of the activists with whom they spoke agreed that the war generated increased support for child welfare programs on the part of the government and the general public.[32] The U.S. Public Health Service, whose appropriations were increased more than sixteenfold between 1917 and 1918 to enable it to deal with various civic health activities connected with the war, established the Section of Child and Mental Hygiene.[33] For the first time the service, a male-dominated agency, began to compete seriously with the Children's Bureau.

Though the war stayed overseas, child welfare workers argued that it indirectly affected American children in several ways. The high price of milk, for example, concerned public welfare officials.[34] Some agencies also found that private donations to the Red Cross diverted money from local child welfare programs.[35] Another problem was that the war precipitated a severe shortage of nurses and physicians in the United States; in 1920 public and private child health agencies were still complaining that even if they could obtain the necessary funds it was nearly impossible to find medical personnel to staff their programs.[36] The employment of women in war factories attracted little attention in the United States, however; only the Children's Bureau staff and a few other public and private welfare officials ex-

31. Baker, *Fighting for Life,* pp. 168–69.

32. "War Time Measures of Economic Preparedness and Social Welfare" (U.S. Children's Bureau, 8–2–1–10); Maurice MacDonald Seymour, "Rural Work for Infant Welfare in Canada and Other Countries," *Transactions of the American Association for the Study and Prevention of Infant Mortality* 9 (1918): 223–29.

33. See Manfred J. Waserman, "The Emergence of Modern Health Care: Pediatrics, Public Health, and the Federal Government," Ph.D. diss., Catholic University, 1982, pp. 124, 126–27.

34. Estelle B. Hunter to Julia Lathrop, 11/16/17 (U.S. Children's Bureau, 4–15–4–3); Janet Geister, interview with Edwin Baetger and Asa Gardiner, 2/11/18 (ibid., 4–16–4–2); Geister, interview with Thomas J. Stranch, 1/21/18 (ibid., 4–15–4–3).

35. Elizabeth G. Baurhyte to Julia Lathrop, 5/19/17 (ibid., 4–15–4–1); Charles Edward Ziegler to Mrs. Max West, 1/27/18 (ibid., 4–15–4–1).

36. Agnes Morris to Anna Rude, 4/9/20 (ibid., 4–15–1–20); Harriet L. Hartley, "The City Nurse as an Agent for the Prevention of Infant Mortality," *Transactions of the American Association for the Study and Prevention of Infant Mortality* 9 (1918): 122; *Transactions of the American Child Hygiene Association,* 1919: 296.

pressed concern that the increasing employment of mothers would cause increases in infant mortality and juvenile delinquency.[37] A few agencies opened day nurseries to cope with the increased need for child care, but there was no general movement or indication of general interest among public health and welfare officials.[38]

The major wartime infant health campaigns in the United States thus did not respond to needs created directly by the war, as they did in France. Instead they grew out of a generalized interest in human resources and the creation of a patriotic citizenry. "We must profit by the experience of France," one physician cautioned a group of South Dakota doctors. "We must awaken to the fact that the preservation and perpetuation of our national life depends upon the saving of babies in the years to come."[39]

Even women who rejected the idea that the nation's strength lay in its military power exploited wartime patriotism in an effort to gain support for their programs. In 1918 Baker wrote that, all humanitarian reasons aside, feeding children was "a war measure second in importance only to the fighting itself."[40] One picture in a Children's Bureau child welfare exhibit showed General Pershing at the age of six, accompanied by the caption: "Was it worthwhile saving this baby? He is helping to save the world. You may learn how to save your baby."[41]

37. "Children in War Time" (press release), April 10, 1917 (U.S. Children's Bureau, 8–2–1–0); Irene Kaufmann Settlement House, *Yearbook* (Pittsburgh, 1918); Julia C. Lathrop, "The Federal Children's Bureau and the Children's Year," *Fifth National Conference of Catholic Charities, 1918*, p. 152; Lois Lindsey Wynekoop, "The Woman Physician and Child Welfare in War Time," *Woman's Medical Journal* 28 (1918): 195; Pansy V. Besom, "How to Conduct a Survey in the Interest of Child Welfare Work," *Transactions of the American Association for the Study and Prevention of Infant Mortality* 9 (1918): 203; S. Josephine Baker, "Lessons from the Draft," *Transactions of the American Association for the Study and Prevention of Infant Mortality* 9 (1918): 183.

38. See Reports of Affiliated Societies in *Transactions of the American Association for the Study and Prevention of Infant Mortality* 9 (1918): 295, 322.

39. Quote in F. C. Rodda, "Infant Mortality," *Journal—Lancet* 38 (1918): 504; Anne A. Stevens, "The Work of the Maternity Center Association," *Transactions of the American Child Hygiene Association*, 1919: 54; H. S. Nelson to Julia Lathrop, 1/3/18 (U.S. Children's Bureau, 4–5–4–3); Edward P. Davis, "The Springs of a Nation's Life," *Transactions of the American Association for the Study and Prevention of Infant Mortality* 9 (1918): 106.

40. S. Josephine Baker, "The Relation of War to the Nourishment of Children," *Woman's Medical Journal* 28 (1918): 52.

41. *Child Welfare Memorandum*, 11/25/18 (records of the Council for National Defense, National Archives, 15-B16).

The Children's Bureau staff did not feel entirely comfortable, however, with an emphasis on "the question of the numbers of lives to replace those killed in battle" but preferred to point out "the importance of training for efficiency and the industrial future of the nation"[42] Perhaps more than saving lives for the army of the future, "Saving the Race for Democracy" meant ensuring the nation's future economic and political soundness: "The health and the efficiency, and the enthusiasm that springs from health and efficiency on the part of the munitions worker, the food producer, the shipbuilder, and the railroad employee—these are the sinews of this war."[43] As Homer Folks, a social worker and national leader in child welfare, wrote, "no form of preparedness is more vital than the conservation of human lives, on whom in the last analysis must depend the safety of the nation from foes within as well as from foes without."[44] This belief that the physical, mental, and moral molding of citizens would preserve the political and social structure of the United States was to influence child welfare work strongly after the war.

Baker attributed the new popularity of child welfare programs to an unquestioning acceptance of "the paternalistic character of government"—she referred, of course, to citizens' toleration of the suspension of some civil liberties and some of the principles of free enterprise for the war effort.[45] Baker personally experienced the effects of the government's new authoritarianism as well as its new interest in child welfare. Soon after the United States declared war, she recalled in her autobiography, a large international organization (probably the American Red Cross) asked her to go to France to take charge of all its work with refugee and homeless children—a "huge and important and intoxicatingly useful job." Baker accepted with joy,

42. A. Rochester to Curtice Hitchcock, 3/16/18 (U.S. Children's Bureau, 8-2-1-11).

43. C. E.-A. Winslow, *The Public Health Nurse: How She Helps to Keep Babies Well,* U.S. Children's Bureau, Children's Year Leaflet No. 6 (Bureau Publication No. 47) (Washington, D.C.: Government Printing Office, 1918), p. 7; Marie de Montalvo, "Saving the Race for Democracy Is War Work," *New York Tribune,* May 26, 1918 (clipping in U.S. Children's Bureau, 4-15-4-2).

44. Homer Folks, "Are Babies Worth Saving?" *Transactions of the American Association for the Study and Prevention of Infant Mortality* 6 (1915): 42.

45. Baker, "The Relation of War to the Nourishment of Children," p. 49. Huntington Wilson makes a similar point in his letter to Lathrop of 2/21/18 (U.S. Children's Bureau, 4-1). See also Grace Meigs, interview with Miss Peabody, 5/9/18 (ibid., 4-15-4-3).

only to receive within a day a telegram from Washington informing her that "the powers there" wanted her to refuse the job because she was needed more at home. Though, as she later put it, this made her look "both impolite and yellow," she complied with the request and soon received an elaborately engraved certificate announcing her appointment as an assistant surgeon-general with the rank of major.[46]

Children's Year, 1918–1919

Like the earlier national Baby Week campaigns, Children's Year, a joint effort of the Children's Bureau and the Woman's Committee of the Council for National Defense, depended for its success on the mobilization of local women's organizations through the national and state structures of the National Congress of Mothers and the General Federation of Women's Clubs. Drawing on the enthusiasm for organizing generated by the war, Children's Year mobilized more women in more communities than ever before in support of the Children's Bureau's maternal and child health program.

The bureau presented Children's Year—scheduled to begin in April 1918, the anniversary of American entrance into the war—as a contribution to the war effort, citing the experience of other warring countries that "civilians must promptly understand that they have new responsibilities for a nation's children when its young men have gone to war."[47] President Woodrow Wilson endorsed the program, writing, "Next to the duty of doing everything possible for the soldiers at the front, there could be, it seems to me, no more patriotic duty than that of protecting the children, who constitute one-third of our population."[48] The bureau received funds from the president's War Emergency Fund for this campaign and a conference on child

46. Baker, *Fighting for Life*, pp. 168–69.
47. *Sixth Annual Report of the Chief, Children's Bureau to the Secretary of Labor* (Washington, D.C.: Government Printing Office, 1918), p. 21; *Seventh Annual Report of the Chief, Children's Bureau to the Secretary of Labor* (Washington, D.C.: Government Printing Office, 1919), p. 7; *Child Welfare Circular*, no. 6 (February 18, 1918); press release, 2/25/18 (Council for National Defense, 13G-B1); C.-E. A. Winslow, *The Public Health Nurse*, p. 3.
48. Quoted in *Sixth Annual Report of the Chief, Children's Bureau*, p. 24.

welfare standards to be held in 1919, more than equal to the agency's congressional appropriations for 1919.[49]

One of the major goals of the campaign was to preserve the family and existing standards of child welfare under the economic and social pressures created by the war. The bureau stressed the increased employment of mothers in factories. "When Mothers Go Out to Work," a proposed poster proclaimed, "The Country Pays in Dead Babies, Sickly Children, Wild Youth."[50] Thus the bureau advocated measures to enable mothers to care for their own children at home. This position was consistent with the results of the bureau's studies in urban infant mortality. Lathrop summarized: "It was perfectly clear that as wages went up, the women stayed home and took care of the children and did not go out to help earn the living, and that as income went up, the infant mortality rate went down."[51] Therefore she supported a family wage for male workers, supplementary income for families without fathers, and an eight-hour day and a prohibition on night work for women with small children.

Another part of the Children's Year program was a campaign to maintain existing restrictions on child labor despite the increased demand for workers.[52] A third component was Patriotic Play Week, designed to publicize the need for "wholesome" recreation. Finally, the bureau and the Council for National Defense launched a campaign to have all the children in the country below school age weighed and measured. This campaign was designed to assess the physical condition of the next generation—local committees were asked to send the results of the tests to the bureau for tabulation—and to draw attention to the need for proper care to prevent defects.

The weighing and measuring test proved to be an excellent organizing tool. "The *door* to the *greatest* problem of rural nursing," argued one speaker at the 1918 meeting of the American Association for the Study and Prevention of Infant Mortality, "has been opened by the spirit of patriotism that has flashed up in the tired bodies and heroic

49. Waserman, "The Emergence of Modern Health Care," pp. 119–20.

50. U.S. Children's Bureau, 8–2–1–11; *Sixth Annual Report of the Chief, Children's Bureau,* pp. 15–16; Lathrop, "The Federal Children's Bureau and the Children's Year," p. 150.

51. Lathrop, "The Federal Children's Bureau and the Children's Year," p. 150.

52. Julia Lathrop to W. B. Wilson, 3/31/17 (U.S. Children's Bureau, 12–7).

minds of our rural women."[53] The Woman's Committee of the Council for National Defense had about 17,000 local units with an estimated total membership of 11 million. These local committees deluged the country with publicity and, by May 1919, 16,811 communities had conducted weighing and measuring tests.[54] Wisconsin workers returned record cards for about 65 percent of the state's children under five years of age; three other states reported measurements for about half their preschool population; seven more weighed and measured more than one-third.[55]

More important in the eyes of the Children's Bureau, the campaign was successful in arousing public support for permanent maternal and child health programs. The secretary of the California State Board of Health attributed the success of the campaign for a State Bureau of Child Hygiene to the Children's Year program.[56] In New Orleans the Children's Year campaign raised $45,000 that was used to hire a trained supervisor for the city's public health nurses and to increase the nursing staff from eight to thirty-three, making possible the establishment of twenty-nine new health centers.[57] From Delaware the Children's Year committee reported that it had opened a "considerable number" of health centers; at the end of the campaign the state legislature created the Child Welfare Reconstruction Committee to develop a comprehensive state child welfare program.[58] Partly as a result of the Children's Year campaign, South Carolina improved its system of birth registration so that it met the national standard in 1919.[59] Other states reported more modest results—a few child health

53. Katherine Olmsted, "Problems of Maternal Welfare Work in Rural Communities," *Transactions of the American Association for the Study and Prevention of Infant Mortality* 9 (1918): 214.

54. *Sixth Annual Report of the Chief, Children's Bureau*, p. 22; *Seventh Annual Report of the Chief, Children's Bureau*, p. 8. This compares with about 2,200 reported Baby Week celebrations in 1916. *Baby Week Campaigns*, U.S. Children's Bureau, Miscellaneous Series No. 5 (Bureau Publication No. 15) (Washington, D.C.: Government Printing Office, 1917), p. 108; Julia Lathrop to Elizabeth Hawley Everett, 9/9/16 (U.S. Children's Bureau, 4–14–22–1).

55. Press release, 2/11/19 (U.S. Children's Bureau, 8–2–1–11).

56. W. H. Kellogg to Julia Lathrop, 9/30/18 (ibid., 4–15–2–1–6).

57. *Seventh Annual Report of the Chief, U.S. Children's Bureau*, p. 11.

58. "Reports of Affiliated Societies," *Transactions of the American Child Hygiene Association*, 1919: 264.

59. Ruth A. Dodd, "Opportunities of the Rural Public Health Nurse to Develop Child Hygiene," ibid., p. 242.

centers here, a few new county nurses there—but in 1919 and 1920 the consensus of child welfare workers everywhere was that public interest had been aroused in areas not previously touched by the movement. Women in many states began to think in terms of comprehensive policies where before they had thought in terms of one-time events or programs.

The American Red Cross in France

The focus of most of these child health efforts was the public health nurse. Toward the end of the war, the United States began to export its concept of public health nursing, first to France and later to central and eastern Europe. In carrying out this campaign, the Rockefeller Commission and the American Red Cross acted as agents of the American mission to carry liberalism throughout the world. They also facilitated the professionalization of women's maternal and infant health work.

The role of the "visiting lady," a familiar figure in French maternal and child welfare programs, resembled that of the visiting nurse in some respects, but "visiting ladies" tended to be inspectors and supervisors rather than teachers. They had no professional training or authority; insofar as they instructed mothers in hygiene and infant care they worked only under the direct supervision of a physician.[60] A few women had attempted to found schools to train visiting nurses before the war. In 1914 two women organized the Association des infirmières-visiteuses as part of an effort to establish public health nursing as a recognized profession.[61] These efforts went largely unnoticed, however, though a few French physicians advocated the employment of professionally trained female home visitors to supervise infant care and instruct mothers in child hygiene. For example,

60. *Bulletin de l'Oeuvre de l'allaitement maternel et des refuges-ouvroirs pour les femmes enceintes*, July 1918: 10; Emmanuel Perret, *Les visiteuses de l'enfance* (Trévoux: Imprimerie J. Jeannin, 1919), pp. 19–21; Institut de puériculture de l'hospice des enfants assistés, *L'oeuvre des dames assistantes de la goutte de lait*, 1916–1917, p. 4.
61. Berthe Milliard, "Les écoles d'hygiène sociale," in *Exposition nationale de la maternité et de l'enfance, Congrès des institutions d'assistance et d'hygiène sociales*, 1921, p. 38; Yvonne Knibiehler, "Vocations sans voile, les métiers sociaux," in *Madame ou Mademoiselle? Itinéraires de la solitude féminine, XVIIIe–XXe siècle*, ed. Arlette Farge and Christiane Klapisch-Zuber (n.p.: Montalba, 1984), p. 170.

Gaston Variot, a pediatrician and leading advocate for national infant health programs, envisioned mandatory home visits to all children by professionals. Voluntary "lady visitors," he argued, were welcomed by poor women because they brought material assistance as well as advice, but they had no authority with which to gain entrance into the home of the bourgeoisie.[62]

Wartime health programs would provide the impetus for the transformation of French public health. In 1916, in an effort to control tuberculosis, the parliament passed a law facilitating the creation of social hygiene dispensaries and making their establishment mandatory in communes with high rates of tuberculosis. The Rockefeller Commission's campaign to prevent tuberculosis helped to define the role of the visiting nurse in public health work and made her acceptable to the medical profession.[63]

Recognizing that France's population crisis was a political problem with international implications, the Red Cross undertook a maternal and child welfare campaign in that country in conjunction with its work with refugees. American public health and political leaders warned that the future of the French nation was in danger and that France's plight was an example of what lay in store for their own nation; they also argued that strengthening France was important for international politics. If France's population problem was not solved, the physician Theodore Merrill predicted at a meeting of the American Association for the Study and Prevention of Infant Mortality, in fifty years France would be about as influential in Europe as Portugal was at the time.[64] "Perhaps no greater misfortune could befall the world," another speaker at the meeting warned, "than to suffer Gallic mentality to be submerged in a twilight of the Gods."[65]

62. Variot, La puériculture et la guerre, pp. 132–33.
63. See Yvonne Knibiehler, "La 'Lutte antituberculeuse' instrument de la médicalisation des classes populaires (1870–1930)," Annales de Bretagne et des pays de l'ouest 86 (1979): 327–28.
64. Theodore C. Merrill, "Some Economic Hints from France," American Journal of Obstetrics 76 (1917): 406; William Palmer Lucas, "Report of the First Month's Activities of the Children's Bureau" (Archives of the American Red Cross, 942.11/08 (Box 847)); American Red Cross in France, Children's Bureau, Complete Report, August 1917 to April 1919 (Archives of the American Red Cross, 942.11 (Box 847)); "Infant Welfare Commission to Safeguard Child Life in France," Red Cross Bulletin, August 25, 1917: 3.
65. Quoted in F. V. Beitler, "Reduction of Infant Mortality due to Prenatal and

In 1917 the Children's Bureau of the Red Cross dispatched a team of physicians and nurses to France under the leadership of William Palmer Lucas, a professor of pediatrics at the University of California. The bureau initially focused on relief work for refugee children, but its ultimate goal was to establish the foundations for a permanent national child welfare program. Lucas' wife reported to the American Association for the Study and Prevention of Infant Mortality that the bureau would make a constant effort to involve French people in the work as much as possible so that when the Red Cross left "the plans for the children's work will have been so thoroughly received by French thought that a national program for child welfare will become an essential part of their government work."[66] It is surprising that the American Red Cross apparently failed to recognize that child welfare already assumed much more importance in French thought than in U.S. politics. This is perhaps testimony to the significant differences in the two approaches to infant welfare: maternity leaves, assistance to prevent abandonment, and crèches seemed unimportant to Americans in light of the absence of campaigns of public health education and programs of public health nurses.

The Red Cross undertook its most important child welfare work in Lyons, where its Children's Bureau had established a large center for refugees. The bureau's plan for Lyons had three elements: an educational baby show similar to those popular in American cities; a training program for visiting nurses to be employed by existing agencies and in a model district nursing program; and an organization to centralize all child welfare work in the city.[67]

The Baby Show opened in Lyons in April 1918 and then moved on to Marseilles, St. Etienne, and Toulouse. The show included the standard features of baby shows in Philadelphia, San Francisco, and Chicago: booths highlighting the work of local agencies and showing ideal foods, furnishings, and activities for children; live demonstrations of infant feeding and bathing; free physical and dental examinations; and a model playground. The exhibit was successful in

Obstetrical Conditions by Public Health Authorities," *Transactions of the American Association for the Study and Prevention of Infant Mortality* 8 (1917): 81.

66. Mrs. William Palmer Lucas, "The Work of the Children's Bureau of the American Red Cross in France," *Transactions of the American Association for the Study and Prevention of Infant Mortality* 9 (1918): 39.

67. American Red Cross in France, Children's Bureau, *Complete Report,* p. 3.

drawing large crowds; in Lyons attendance averaged nine thousand a day.[68]

The organizers also succeeded in creating a display of community cooperation. In the United States, child welfare workers and women's organizations, arguing that child welfare should be a nonpolitical issue, treated infant health events—the Baby Show, Baby Day, and Baby Week—as demonstrations of community harmony. To these observers, French child welfare agencies, divided by religion and political affiliation, appeared petty and contentious.[69] One American reporter commented that continued social service action was much more difficult than in the United States, "whose citizens have the habit of public expression and cooperation. Social, political and religious interests in America are not such bars to team-work as they are among the French."[70]

The Red Cross boasted of its success in St.-Etienne, "the center of a large, radical, restless, laboring population, conspicuous for strikes, pacifism propaganda, and anti-American feeling."[71] Red Cross representatives succeeded in convincing labor leaders of "the idealism and the unselfish strength of purpose" of their work. At the exhibit's opening session the inhabitants of St.-Etienne were astonished to see clergymen and leaders of the Socialist party, along with the mayor and the prefect, all on the same platform in an unprecedented display of political harmony.[72]

Behind the "practical idealism" the American Red Cross tried so hard to convey to the French lay the desire to ignore or gloss over conflicts in order to create an image of harmony and the appearance of consensus. Red Cross workers often had only a vague sense of the values they were trying to communicate. One wrote, referring to the schoolchildren who had their teeth cleaned at the exhibit: "Their glittering, snowy teeth, when they emerged from [the dentist's] hands were advertisements of American ideals in themselves."[73] American

68. Ibid., pp. 16, 169; Clifford G. Grulee, "The Lyons Baby Show," *Transactions of the American Association for the Study and Prevention of Infant Mortality* 9 (1918): 46; Fisher Ames, Jr., *American Red Cross Work among the French People* (New York: Macmillan, 1921), p. 144.
69. American Red Cross in France, Children's Bureau, *Complete Report*, p. 19.
70. Ames, *American Red Cross Work among the French People*, p. 146.
71. American Red Cross in France, Children's Bureau, *Complete Report*, p. 164.
72. Ames, *American Red Cross Work among the French People*, p. 143.
73. American Red Cross in France, Children's Bureau, *Complete Report*, p. 17.

educators who worked with schoolchildren, however, knew that part
of their goal was to develop, through American games, "leadership,
team play, initiative, and cooperation, qualities so rarely found in
French games."[74] These qualities—the same that Progressive reformers tried to develop in immigrant children in the United States—
constituted the essence of good Republican citzenship, American-
style.

The Red Cross hoped to demonstrate that child welfare agents in
Lyons could overcome their political differences in an effort to centralize and coordinate their efforts. In March 1918, Lucas arranged
for a meeting of representatives of all of Lyons' child welfare agencies
and presented his plan. He proposed that the Red Cross, with the
cooperation of French physicians, train French women as visiting
nurses and place them at the disposal of hospital maternity or children's services and private child welfare agencies. The nurses would
also be used to create a model district nursing system in one of the
city's poor neighborhoods under the direction of a committee representing the American Red Cross and local agencies.[75]

The committee opened a central office in the chosen neighborhood
and hired three visiting nurses and two social workers to initiate a
public health and social program that conformed to the ideals of
American Progressive reformers. With the aid of birth records and
other agencies operating in the district a secretary maintained a card
file with medical and social information on each child. The visiting
nurses helped women plan for childbirth, instructed them in child
hygiene, assisted them in obtaining the public assistance to which
they were entitled, and put them into contact with private agencies.
Twice a month the visiting nurses met with representatives of the
American Red Cross and other cooperating agencies and local public
welfare officials to discuss each family's situation and progress and
to allocate discretionary funds.[76]

Lyons' public welfare officials were reportedly pleased with the
success of this work; by the time the Red Cross withdrew, the city

74. Ibid., p. 160.
75. Perret, *Les visiteuses de l'enfance*, pp. 23–30; Marcel Hervier, *Les oeuvres de
l'enfance à Lyon* (Paris: Editions de la Nouvelle Revue, 1921), p. 7; Sophie C. Nelson,
"Work with Children in Lyon, France," *Public Health Nurse* 11 (1919): 726–27.
76. Perret, *Les visiteuses de l'enfance*, p. 100.

had planned a district nursing program that would cover the entire city. In his preface to a book on child welfare in Lyons, the mayor thanked the Red Cross for the aid it had offered to his city in centralizing infant welfare work.[77] The private agencies also found the trained visiting nurses a useful addition to their staff; their training in medico-social supervision and instruction in child hygiene were entirely compatible with the work of all these agencies. Physicians— the potential opposition—were pleased to have someone who would make sure that patients followed their directions.[78]

In Paris the Red Cross opened twelve children's dispensaries designed, like the Lyons experiment, to demonstrate the value of home visiting and coordinated child welfare work. In the 19th arrondissement, a dispensary operated by the Red Cross in cooperation with the Rockefeller Commission became a "genuine social settlement" with resident personnel, kindergarten, playground, clubs for women, men, and boys, and classes in English.[79] The Red Cross Children's Bureau also took over the Pouponnière of Porchefontaine as a training facility. In other cities and towns all over France, Red Cross workers introduced American child welfare methods on a smaller scale.[80]

When the American Red Cross withdrew from France in July 1919 it left funds sufficient to ensure that French infant health programs would continue to follow the path it had laid out. The Red Cross offered to give 500,000 to one million francs to Lyon on the condition that an equal amount be donated by local residents, and an additional 200,000 francs to put the new system into operation.[81] The Americans left a total of 100,000 francs to Bordeaux for the training of visiting nurses, the foundation of a federation of child welfare agencies, and

77. Hervier, Les oeuvres de l'enfance à Lyon, p. 2; Nelson, "Work with Children in Lyon, France," p. 725.

78. Perret quotes from the reports of physicians attached to these agencies in Les visiteuses de l'enfance, pp. 35–36, 44, 47–49, 53–54, 58.

79. Ames, American Red Cross Work among the French People, p. 121; American Red Cross in France, Report on Paris Dispensaries, May 1, 1918, pp. 3–7; Daniel Halévy, Pour l'enfance et la famille par l'aide sociale: Historique de l'oeuvre (Paris: n.p, n.d.), p. 5.

80. American Red Cross in France, Children's Bureau, Complete Report, pp. 61–66; Ames, American Red Cross Work among the French People, p. 125; "France Adopts American Child Welfare Methods," Public Health Nurse 11 (1918): 686; American Red Cross in France, Department of Civil Affairs, Report of the Director, April 1, 1918, pp. 5–8.

81. Perret, Les visiteuses de l'enfance, p. 134.

the organization of milk committees. The dispensary and social center in the 19th arrondissement in Paris received thirty thousand francs.[82] Most generous was a gift of one million francs to establish a central school of *puériculture* in Paris. This school, placed under the Faculté de Médecine at the University of Paris, would train physicians, midwives, and visiting nurses, offer preventive health services for infants, pregnant women, and nursing mothers, and eventually sponsor scientific research in obstetrics and pediatrics.[83]

French physicians and child welfare officials seemed to welcome the visiting nurse wholeheartedly. In Bordeaux the new federation of child welfare agencies planned a district nursing program after the Red Cross model in Lyons.[84] In addition to the Ecole de puériculture in Paris, other nursing schools began to train students for the new visiting nurse diploma.[85] In 1919 the Ligue contre la mortalité infantile published an appeal to maternal and child welfare agencies urging the training of infant health visitors to carry out the Strauss Law.[86] Maternal and child health programs including visiting nurses were an important aspect of the populationist proposals that proliferated during and immediately following the war.

After the War in France

With the end of the war and the return of men to the factories, women found themselves surrounded more than ever before by propaganda urging them to stay home and bear children.[87] The pronatalist movement had celebrated its first legislative victories in the year be-

82. Halévy, *Pour l'enfance et la famille par l'aide sociale,* p. 9; American Red Cross in France, Children's Bureau, *Complete Report,* p. 56.

83. Ames, *American Red Cross Work among the French People,* p. 123; "Convention entre la Croix rouge américaine et le Comité d'organisation de l'Ecole de puériculture," in American Red Cross in France, Children's Bureau, *Complete Report.* See also *Ecole de puériculture de la Faculté de médecine de Paris* (Paris: L'Emancipatrice, 1921).

84. Archives nationales, F⁴ 2908, Dos. No.1197.

85. Jules Renault and B. Labeaume, "L'évolution de la protection de l'enfance," *Bulletin de l'Académie de médecine* 3d ser. 117 (1937): 769.

86. Ligue contre la mortalité infantile, "Appel aux oeuvres d'assistance maternelle et infantile en France," *Revue philanthropique* 40 (1919): 213–14. Also printed in *L'Enfant* 26 (1919): 163.

87. See Yvonne Knibiehler and Catherine Fouquet, *Histoire des mères du Moyen Age à nos jours* (n.p.: Editions Montalba, 1977), pp. 305–8.

fore the war: assistance to poor families with several children; family allowances for men in the military; and income tax deductions for dependents. Prominent among the new pronatalist organizations after the war was the Congrès de natalité, first proposed by the president of the Nancy Chamber of Commerce and supported by other business organizations. The wide-ranging program of this organization included support for *mutualités maternelles* and asylums for indigent mothers, family allowances and a tax on all childless adults over the age of twenty-eight, and a public campaign against divorce and for the teaching of moral and sexual discipline in schools. In 1920 one of the members of the congress's executive commission, J.-L. Breton, a member of the Republican-Socialist party, was named to head the new Ministry of Social Hygiene and Welfare. He organized a council on the birthrate; among the thirty members he appointed were Adolphe Pinard and Charles Richet.

Conservative Catholics objected to the economic and hygienic focus of this council. They still preferred to describe depopulation (*dénatalité* was the new term) not as the effect of defective legislation but as a disease of the will and of the soul. One of their members complained that the hygienists were ever-present at meetings on depopulation. The increasing importance given to *puériculture* in particular, he argued, was dangerous, for it lent credence to the idea that decreasing the infant mortality rate would resolve the problem.[88]

In the immediate postwar period the Chamber of Deputies considered at least eleven bills designed to increase the rate of population growth, most of which included more or less comprehensive measures to protect maternal and infant health.[89] In general the proposals were not new; they included breast-feeding bonuses, the extension and improvement of the Roussel Law, the creation of departmental maternity hospitals and asylums for single pregnant women, antiabortion legislation, the reestablishment of the *tours,* and increasing the benefits allocated under the Strauss Law. Of the many legislative

88. See Robert Talmy, *Histoire du mouvement familial en France 1896–1939* (Aubenas: Union nationale des caisses d'allocations familiales, 1962), vol. 1, pp. 259–63, 212–15, 245. Talmy's history is written from the perspective of the conservative Catholic profamily movement.

89. These proposals are described and analyzed in Chambre des Députés, Annexe au procès-verbal de la 2e séance du 21 mars 1919, *Rapport fait au nom de la Commission d'assurance et de prévoyance sociales.*

proposals designed specifically to save infant lives the only one actually enacted was a law granting a monthly bonus of fifteen francs to women covered under the Strauss Law if they breast-fed for twelve months.[90] Over the next fifteen years, however, measures initiated by the administration and the legislature gradually defined a pronatalist family policy that had an important repressive component but benefited maternal and infant health indirectly.

A 1920 law punished abortion severely and prohibited all birth control propaganda. In 1923 two decrees mandated the teaching of *puériculture* in girls' schools.[91] A decree issued in 1920 also created bonuses for families on the birth of any child after the second; in 1923 pronatalists won their long campaign for legislation granting monthly benefits to families for each child after the second and providing other bonuses for large families, such as reductions on railroad fares and direct taxes. Family allowances, originally designed by employers to ease the financial hardships of their workers without raising the general wage level, became more and more common through the 1920s and were increasingly encouraged by the government as a means of increasing the birthrate. In 1939 legislation standardized and generalized this institution as part of a series of financial measures designed to provide incentives to childbearing.[92]

The Communist and Socialist parties opposed the most repressive measures against birth control. They maintained instead that financial assistance to families, maternity insurance, and child care were the most effective and humane ways to promote population growth. Maternity benefits were included in the social insurance system created in 1928, an important victory for the left.[93] Though it had initially condemned the repressive law of 1920, in the 1930s the Communist party moved closer to the position that Malthusianism was a bour-

90. Ministre de l'intérieur, Circular to MM les Préfets, November 3, 1919, and December 1, 1919 (Archives nationales, F² 2088).

91. Francis Ronsin, *La Grève des ventres: Propagande Néo-Malthusienne et baisse de la natalité française, XIXe–XXe siècles* (n.p.: Editions Aubier Montaigne, 1980), pp. 146–47; Thébaud, "Donner la vie," p. 305.

92. Jane Jenson, "The Liberation and New Rights for French Women," in Higonnet et al., *Behind the Lines,* pp. 280–83. Jenson points out that family allowances remained a pronatalist policy during and after World War II separate from social insurance, which supplemented family income only when it fell below a certain level.

93. Thébaud, "Donner la vie," pp. 86–91, 96–100; David Glass, *Population Policies and Movements in Europe* (Oxford: Clarendon Press, 1940), p. 104.

geois reflex and that all women wanted to be mothers but were prevented from fulfilling their desires by social and economic conditions.[94] When in power in 1936–37, the Popular Front did not try to repeal the repressive law of 1920 but pushed instead for more generous family allowances. Politicians on the right and left still disputed the proper means of increasing the population, as they disagreed on the nature of French society and in particular on whether moral decadence or economic oppression was responsible for the decline in the birthrate. Nonetheless, all the major political parties continued to see depopulation as a significant problem, and pronatalism continued to be one of the primary concerns of family policy and of social insurance programs that affected women and children.

After the War in the United States

As France, like other countries throughout Europe, committed itself to a family policy whose primary goal was to promote population growth, the United States moved in a different direction. In 1928—the year the French parliament voted to establish obligatory maternity insurance—the U.S. Congress refused to approve the continued funding of the federal maternal and infant health program created in 1921. The war stimulated nationwide interest in infant health and inspired the mobilization of women which made possible the passage of the Sheppard-Towner Act in 1921, providing federal funding for maternal and infant health programs. At the same time, out of the war grew a new form of political reaction and repression; the greatest achievement of the women's maternal and infant health movement was only temporary. The failure of one-third of the nation's young men to live up to the army's physical and mental standards provided good publicity for child welfare advocates, but the increasing emphasis on human resources also brought the racist and nativist tendencies in the child health movement to the forefront.

Julia Lathrop first proposed federal aid to state maternal and infant health programs in 1917, and the next year Jeannette Rankin introduced into Congress a bill, predecessor to the Sheppard-Towner Act, to provide federal funds for infant health centers, medical and nursing

94. Thébaud, "Donner la vie," pp. 113–17.

care for mothers and infants at home or in hospitals, instruction of women in prenatal and infant hygiene, and visiting nurses. Congress failed to act on Rankin's proposal, but in 1919 Senator Morris Sheppard of Texas and Representative Horace Towner of Iowa introduced a similar measure. Their proposal, in its final version, provided federal matching funds to the states for instruction in maternal and child hygiene. It did not provide medical care or financial assistance to mothers but allocated funds only for visiting nurses, infant health conferences (essentially well-baby clinics), and the distribution of literature. A state had the right to refuse aid, and had to create a bureau of child hygiene or child welfare to be eligible for funds.[95]

The Sheppard-Towner bill encountered opposition from several sources; its passage is testimony to the extent and effectiveness of the campaign to mobilize women on its behalf launched by the Children's Bureau, the General Federation of Women's Clubs, the National Congress of Mothers, and women's magazines. The most concerted opposition to the bill came from the U.S. Public Health Service, which objected to the provision that the Children's Bureau administer the program. At issue were the questions of whether women or men should control child welfare policy and whether maternal and infant health was a social question as well as a medical one.

In 1918, Caroline Fleming of the U.S. Children's Bureau attended a meeting at the office of the surgeon general to discuss a proposed child-conservation program to be undertaken by the Public Health Service. The proposal was, in effect, a direct assault on the territory of the bureau. The plan included federal cooperation with state and local authorities to make prenatal care and infant welfare stations available and to promote the training of midwives or obstetrical attendants and the supervision of child welfare institutions, schools, and child labor conditions.[96] At the hearings on the Sheppard-Towner bill in 1920, J. W. Schereschewsky, assistant surgeon-general, made

95. See J. Stanley Lemons, *The Woman Citizen: Social Feminism in the 1920's* (Urbana: University of Illinois Press, 1973), p. 154; *Seventh Annual Report of the Chief, Children's Bureau,* p. 25; U.S. Cong., House, Committee on Labor, *Hygiene of Maternity and Infancy: Hearings before the Committee on H.R. 12634,* 1919, pp. 3–4; Waserman, "The Emergence of Modern Health Care," pp. 131–32.

96. Taliaferro Clark, "Report on Conference on Child Conservation at Office of Surgeon-General of the United States Public Health Service," 12/2/18 (U.S. Children's Bureau, 4–15–4–3); Rupert Blue to Lathrop, 11/22/19 (ibid., 4–12–4); Waserman, "The Emergence of Modern Health Care," pp. 106–9.

explicit his agency's designs on the bureau's domain when he testified that he would feel better if the bureau were actually part of the Public Health Service.[97]

Public Health Service officials argued before Congress that infant mortality was almost exclusively a medical issue rather than a social one and that infant health work should therefore be integrated into general public health work.[98] Concerned to counteract the hegemony of male physicians who ignored the needs of women and children, the bureau's defenders insisted that the medical aspects of maternal and infant welfare programs were useless without efforts to improve or counteract social and economic conditions. "We are aware," Lathrop stated, "that there are aspects of life which require the services of physicians, but they are a small part of child welfare and must be considered in relation to the social field." Florence Kelley expressed even more bluntly the feeling of women activists that child welfare should rest in their hands. "The achievements of the Public Health Service," she testified, "do not satisfy the women of this country."[99]

The major opponent to the Sheppard-Towner bill itself was the American Medical Association.[100] The bill, argued the association's representatives, would be an entering wedge for state health insurance and thereby contribute to undermining the principle of free enterprise in the medical profession. The pediatric section of the organization, however, passed a resolution supporting the legislation. Ironically, antivivisectionists and the American Medical Liberty League also campaigned against the legislation because they thought it would destroy people's freedom to choose their own physician and thus force allopathic medicine on the public.[101] These groups were joined

97. U.S. Cong., House, Committee on Interstate and Foreign Commerce, *Public Protection of Maternity and Infancy: Hearings before the Committee on H.R. 10925*, December 21–29, 1920, p. 165. For a discussion of the conflicts between the Children's Bureau and the Public Health Service, see Robyn Muncy, *Creating a Female Dominion in American Reform, 1890–1935* (New York: Oxford University Press, 1991), pp. 142–48.

98. U.S. Cong., House, Committee on Interstate and Foreign Commerce, *Public Protection of Maternity and Infancy*, pp. 136, 138–39; Lottie Bigler, "Expectant Mothers in Rural Regions," *Transactions of the American Child Hygiene Association*, 1920, p. 51.

99. U.S. Cong., House, Committee on Interstate and Foreign Commerce, *Public Protection of Maternity and Infancy*, pp. 20–21, 27, 51–53, 68–77.

100. The Council on Health and Public Instruction of the American Medical Association did support the bill, however. Lemons, *The Woman Citizen*, p. 164.

101. U.S. Cong., House, Committee on Interstate and Foreign Commerce, *Public Protection of Maternity and Infancy*, pp. 100–101, 111, 127–29.

by several conservative organizations: the National Association Opposed to Woman Suffrage, the Woman Patriots, the Daughters of
the American Revolution, and the Sentinels of the Republic. Members
of these organizations objected to the "paternalism" of federal social
welfare measures and warned that such legislation could lead to "socialism, bolshevism, and sovietism."[102] The real problems, they argued, were moral. The most effective way to improve the race,
according to an article on the Sheppard-Towner bill in the *Fitchburg*
(Massachusetts) *Sentinel,* was through "more religion, better morals,
better habits, better protection by right dressing, better living and
working conditions, less dancing, less theaters, more fresh air, less
burning of the midnight oil."[103]

The combined efforts of these groups failed to defeat the bill. The
Children's Bureau had some support from male politicians, physicians, and public health officials. Representative Towner, whose name
appeared on the bill, argued, "The Children's Bureau, after all, is a
women's bureau. It affects their interests more than it affects any
other interests because the women are intimately connected both in
knowledge and in sympathy with child welfare."[104] The state health
officer of Wisconsin reported to Dorothy Reed Mendenhall of the
Children's Bureau that he much preferred to have help from the
bureau, since the Public Health Service tried to control state health
work. The American Child Health Association (formerly the American Association for the Study and Prevention of Infant Mortality)
lobbied for the bill, and the American Federation of Labor also lent
its support.[105]

The passage of the bill, however, must be attributed to the campaign launched by women's organizations. Mrs. Henry W. Keyes,
the wife of a New Hampshire senator and a woman's club member
and former antisuffragist, predicted a "sex war" if the government

102. Ibid., p. 158; Janet Pacht Brickman, "Mother Love—Mother Death: Maternal and Infant Care, Social Class and the Role of Government," Ph.D. diss., City
University of New York, 1978, p. 558.
103. U.S. Cong., House, Committee on Interstate and Foreign Commerce, *Public
Protection of Maternity and Infancy,* p. 186.
104. Ibid., p. 176.
105. Dorothy Reed Mendenhall to Julia Lathrop, 6/3/19 (U.S. Children's Bureau,
4–12–3); U.S. Cong., House, Committee on Interstate and Foreign Commerce, *Public
Protection of Maternity and Infancy,* p. 37; U.S. Cong., House, Committee on Labor,
Hygiene of Maternity and Infancy, p. 17.

took no steps to protect maternity. "Women are saying all over the rural districts," she reported, that " 'if there was something that was killing that number of men every year, how long would it take Congress to pass a law to try to stop it?' "[106] Women's organizations supporting the bill included the Women's Christian Temperance Union, the National League of Women Voters, the General Federation of Women's Clubs, the National Congress of Mothers, the National Council of Jewish Women, the Young Women's Christian Association, the National Women's Trade Union League, the Medical Women's National Organization, and the General Federation of Business and Professional Women. *Good Housekeeping* magazine and the publications of the National Congress of Mothers and the General Federation of Women's Clubs printed repeated appeals asking their readers to write to their congressmen.[107] Local and state leaders of the drive for the Sheppard-Towner Act called directly on the women mobilized for the Children's Year campaign. In all, a writer for *Good Housekeeping* estimated that nearly fifteen million women endorsed the bill directly or through the officers of organizations to which they belonged.[108]

This movement undoubtedly benefited from the publicity surrounding military subscription. In an article in *Good Housekeeping* supporting the bill, Mary Stewart wrote, "If you tell a mother that too many of our boys reach manhood with flat feet, crooked backs or weak lungs and that camp life helps correct these ills she will answer that this is no argument for universal military training but for the Maternal and Infant Welfare Bill."[109] The women who organized Children's Year and who campaigned for the Sheppard-Towner Act frequently reminded their audience that the army had rejected one-

106. U.S. Cong., House, Committee on Interstate and Foreign Commerce, *Public Protection of Maternity and Infancy*, p. 46. Molly Ladd-Taylor has described the role of women activists in the passage of the Sheppard-Towner Act, the functioning of the act, and its demise in "Protecting Mothers and Infants: The Rise and Fall of the Sheppard-Towner Act," paper presented at the Berkshire Conference on the History of Women, June 19, 1987.

107. Anne Martin, " 'We Couldn't Afford a Doctor,' " *Good Housekeeping*, April 1920: 19; Anne Shannon Monroe, "Adventuring in Motherhood," *Good Housekeeping*, May 1920: 28; Rose Wilder Lane, "Mother No. 22,999," *Good Housekeeping*, March 1920: 22; *Child-Welfare Magazine* 14 (1920): 165; Lemons, *The Woman Citizen*, p. 169.

108. Martin, " 'We Couldn't Afford a Doctor,' " p. 138. On the campaign for the Sheppard-Towner Act, see Muncy, *Creating a Female Dominion*, pp. 116–20.

109. Mary Stewart, "The New Politics," *Good Housekeeping*, July 1920: 49.

third of its potential recruits as physically unsound.[110] Though this
military dimension did not necessarily reflect the perspective of the
organizers, they did not hesitate to exploit the nationalism aroused
by the war. A cartoon, uncannily titled "A scene on 1940" and drawn
by a sixth-grader in Springfield, Illinois, suggests that child welfare
advocates successfully conveyed to the public the importance of child
health to military preparedness. The cartoon depicts a tall soldier
saying, "I was a Better Baby in 1918"; facing him is a much shorter
man who says, "I'm sorry I wasn't, I'm too small to get in the
army."[111]

The passage of the Sheppard-Towner Act in 1921, which authorized
over one million dollars per year to be distributed in matching funds
to the states, seemed to signify a definitive national commitment to
maternal and infant health. It made possible the creation of almost
3,000 permanent prenatal centers and 2,600 rural child health centers;
Sheppard-Towner agents made over three million home visits. In
1929 the Children's Bureau estimated that its programs reached over
one-half of the children born that year.[112] The program also facilitated
the development of public health in rural areas, and the founding of
urban child health centers peaked in the 1920s.

During the period preceding the passage of the bill, the Children's
Bureau hoped that if it drew public attention to the large number of

110. *Child-Welfare Magazine* 12 (1918): 193 and 13 (1919): 160; S. Josephine Baker,
"Lessons from the Draft," *Transactions of the American Association for the Study and
Prevention of Infant Mortality* 9 (1918): 186; Anna E. Rude, "The Progress of Children's
Year," ibid., p. 64; Margaret Hughes, "After-War Work for Children," *Public Health*
(Publication of the Michigan State Board of Health), April 1919, p. 168; Mrs. Andrew
Wilson, "Child Welfare Work in Wheeling, West Virginia," *Public Health Nurse* 11
(1919): 142; "Children's Centers Suggested as Memorials to Soldiers," 2/10/19 (U.S.
Children's Bureau, 8–2–1–11); Mrs. Max West (first in a series of twenty-three articles
to be released as press material for Children's Year), Childrens Bureau suggestions
for posters, 2/28/18 (ibid., 8–2–1–11).
111. *Springfield Open Air Crusader,* May 1918: 3.
112. See Mary Madeleine Ladd-Taylor, "Mother-work: Ideology, Public Policy,
and the Mothers' Movement, 1890–1930," Ph.D. diss., Yale University, 1986,
pp. 358–60; Sydney A. Halpern, *American Pediatrics: The Social Dynamics of Professionalism, 1880–1980* (Berkeley: University of California Press, 1988), p. 86; Richard
A. Meckel, *Save the Babies: American Public Health Reform and the Prevention of Infant
Mortality, 1850–1929* (Baltimore: Johns Hopkins University Press, 1990), pp. 211–13;
Muncy, *Creating a Female Dominion,* chap. 4; Sheila Rothman, *Woman's Proper Place*
(New York: Basic Books, 1978), pp. 136–42. On the implementation of the Sheppard-
Towner Act also see Molly Ladd-Taylor, " 'Grannies' and 'Spinsters': Midwife Ed-
ucation under the Sheppard-Towner Act," *Journal of Social History* 22 (1988): 255–77.

children with physical defects the weighing and measuring tests would serve as a publicity campaign for public health nurses and child welfare centers.[113] Following the bureau's guidelines many local organizations used the results of the tests to educate parents and urged them to take their children to a physician for treatment; others employed nurses to follow all children found to be below the standards for their age or turned the records over to the local visiting nurse society.[114]

The weighing and measuring tests, like baby health contests, were also susceptible to a different interpretation, however; some organizers saw routine examinations of children as a means of seeking out defective children for the purpose of segregating them. A Rhode Island group, for example, reported that its house-to-house canvassers made "tactful inquiries" about blind, "defective," and retarded children and noted the answers on the record card.[115] Some state leaders proposed that the weighing and measuring be made compulsory; some local organizers actually advertised their tests as mandatory. "Nothing in the spirit of the American people," countered the Children's Bureau, "nor of these times in which we fight autocracy invites the use of anything but moral suasion."[116]

Referring to the poor health of army recruits as inspiration reinforced that tendency of the infant health movement—most explicit in the Baby Health Contest movement—which sought to perfect American babyhood and defined its goals as "race betterment." The weighing and measuring tests imitated the large-scale medical examination of young men for the army, and the language of Children's Year publicity suggested a clear parallel with military recruitment. A Michigan public health magazine reported that "Uncle Sam has asked the American parents to weigh and measure their children for him. He desires to get acquainted with the little children of the nation."[117]

113. *April and May Weighing and Measuring Test,* Part 3, Follow-Up Work, U.S. Children's Bureau, Children's Year Leaflet No. 2 (Bureau Publication No. 38) (Washington, D.C.: Government Printing Office, 1919), p. 3.

114. *Child-Welfare Magazine* 13 (1919): 243; Newsletter for Directors of State Divisions of Child Hygiene, April 1920: 13 (U.S. Children's Bureau, 4–15–1–3–0); Mary Evelyn Bryden to Julia Lathrop, 2/5/20 (ibid., 4–14–2–4–0).

115. *Child Welfare Memorandum,* No. 4 (December 12, 1918): 5 (Council for National Defense, 15-B6).

116. Ibid., No. 23 (July 15, 1918); Julia Lathrop to Woman's Committee, 7/15/18 (Council for National Defense, 13G-B1).

117. Hughes, "After-War Work for Children," p. 168.

The introduction of mental and psychological testing as part of infant health campaigns suggests a further parallel with army recruitment.[118] The increasing popularity of mental testing as part of child health campaigns reflected the preoccupation among social scientists and educators with identifying and isolating the "feeble-minded," frequently blamed as the group responsible for most crime and social deviance. The interest in "mental defectives" found its way into the meetings of the American Association for the Study and Prevention of Infant Mortality. In a paper on the care of preschool children presented in 1917, for example, Lawrence Royster emphasized the importance of locating those deformed by tuberculosis and polio—most of whom he thought could be made into useful citizens through orthopedic surgery—and the more threatening and ever-increasing feeble-minded, who, according to the author, should be segregated in places where they could not harm the community.[119]

The infant health movement thus contributed to and was transformed by new definitions of deviance. Some writers even went so far as to claim an association between infant health and political subversion or labor radicalism, implying that physically healthy infants would grow naturally into upstanding citizens. Popular publicity for child health measures during the war exploited the environment of crisis and appealed to fears of political subversion. Articles advertising the *Delineator* magazine's "Seventh Baby Campaign," referring to the estimated one of every seven babies born who died before their first birthday, and inspired by the polio epidemic of 1916, were written in terms that implied impending disaster. For example, Honoré Willsie, writer for the *Delineator,* wrote of the "Doomed Seventh Baby."[120] Constant vigilance was necessary, the articles suggested, to prevent deaths from such diseases as typhoid—the result of unsanitary

118. For discussions of the army mental testing and its impact see Stephen Jay Gould, *The Mismeasure of Man* (New York: Norton, 1981), pp. 192–226, and Franz Samelson, "Was Early Mental Testing (a) Racist Inspired, (b) Objective Science, (c) A Technology for Democracy, (d) The Origin of Multiple-Choice Exams, (e) None of the Above?" in *Psychological Testing and American Society, 1890–1930,* ed. Michael M. Sokal (New Brunswick, N.J.: Rutgers University Press, 1987), pp. 119–20.

119. Lawrence T. Royster, "Care of Children of Pre-School Age," *Transactions of the American Association for the Study and Prevention of Infant Mortality* 8 (1917): 48; *Reports from the Field* (Newsletter of the Woman's Committee, New Jersey Division of the Council for National Defense), May 1919; Peter L. Tyor and Leland V. Bell, *Caring for the Retarded in America* (Westport, Conn.: Greenwood Press, 1984), p. 97.

120. Honoré Willsie, "Save the Seventh Baby," *Delineator,* April 1917: 6.

dairy practices, which all the scrubbing and scalding of bottles could do nothing to counteract—and ultimately to maintain the internal strength of the nation against subversion so that it could fight the Germans, "that more obvious menace across the sea."[121]

Child health workers explicitly linked infant health with juvenile delinquency and other forms of social deviance. The Children's Bureau and the Council for National Defense were just as concerned to preserve family morality as to conserve human resources. The bureau feared that women's work in war industry would have a ruinous effect on family life and on the health and morals of older children left without supervision. "The home and family should be preserved at all costs," cautioned one issue of the *Child Welfare Circular* of the Council for National Defense.[122] In particular, child welfare workers began to emphasize juvenile delinquency; by measuring the mental health and intelligence of children along with physical health they attempted to classify potential deviants at a young age. In the reactionary political climate of the postwar period it was not unusual for public health authorities to claim that public health was a "remedy for Bolshevism" and other forms of political or social unrest.[123] Herbert Hoover, recently returned from coordinating American contributions to the relief and reconstruction of Europe after the war, expressed the conviction, for example, that community nurses would in the long run decrease the need for police.[124]

Postwar political reaction, xenophobia, and racism intensified "race suicide" fears, and these were in turn reflected in the child health movement. In 1918, S. Josephine Baker warned members of the American Association for the Study and Prevention of Infant Mortality, "We can no longer look at the question calmly and say we can continue to build our population up by immigration and let the native-born die."[125] Child welfare advocates, like others concerned with what they saw as moral and social degeneration, pointed to the genetic or

121. Charles E. Terry, "The Story of a Baby Boy," *Delineator*, May 1917: 7; Honoré Willsie, "Whose Business Is It?" ibid., April 1918: 18.

122. *Child Welfare Circular*, No. 10 (April 3, 1918): 3 (Council for National Defense, 13G-B1).

123. "Round Table Conference on Rural Health," comments of James A. Hayne, *Transactions of the American Child Hygiene Association*, 1920, p. 237.

124. Herbert Hoover, "A Program for American Children," *Transactions of the American Child Hygiene Association*, 1920, p. 24.

125. Baker, "Lessons from the Draft," p. 181.

cultural inferiority of the southern and eastern European immigrants as the source of the evil. While some focused on the "Americanization" of immigrants, including the teaching of "those standards of living and ideals of service which we proudly call American," others focused their efforts on increasing the birth rate among the upstanding white native-born.[126]

With race suicide in mind, maternal and infant health campaigns in this period were frequently directed toward the native-born white middle class rather than to the poor. Several maternal and child health reformers lamented the neglect on the part of maternal and child health programs of the people of "moderate means," "the Americans, the native women, the old stock people, who are living a rural life."[127] In Boston, Chicago, and Baltimore, child health institutions announced special maternity-care programs and classes in prenatal and child care for "the better class women and the wives of men of moderate means."[128] In part, these programs may have been designed to lure paying patients to give birth in the hospital, but the motivations of J. Whitridge Williams, a prominent Baltimore obstetrician who offered a series of lectures to women, were clear. Women with fewer than three children, he told an overflow crowd at one of these lectures, could not claim to be patriotic Americans. "What we need—what we must have—if the country is to be preserved," he announced, "is more children from the God-fearing Anglo-Saxon men and women, with traditions."[129] One state health commissioner supported the Sheppard-Towner bill as "the only prospect of maintaining a leav-

126. Quote from Harriet Anderson, "Child Welfare and Americanization," 2/13/19, p. 3 (U.S. Children's Bureau, 8–2–1–11). See also Mrs. William Lowell Putnam, "President's Address," *Transactions of the American Association for the Study and Prevention of Infant Mortality* 9 (1918): 17, 21; "Round Table Discussion on Americanization," *Transactions of the American Association for the Study and Prevention of Infant Mortality* 9 (1918): 230–41; Gertrude Vaile to Lathrop, 6/17/19 (U.S. Children's Bureau, 4–12–1).

127. Testimony of Florence Kelley, U.S. Cong., House, Committee on Labor, *Hygiene of Maternity and Infancy*, pp. 37–38.

128. Jessie F. Choistee Ree to Lathrop, 10/27/19 (U.S. Children's Bureau, 14–1–9–2); Putnam, "President's Address," pp. 21–23; Monroe, "Adventuring in Motherhood," p. 130; R. W. Lobenstine, "Maternity Centers in New York City," in U.S. Children's Bureau, *Standards of Child Welfare*, p. 185.

129. Quoted in "Scores U.S. Women for Race Suicide," *Evening Sun* (Baltimore), April 4, 1919 (clipping in U.S. Children's Bureau, 1–4–1–9–2).

ening of the native-born," because rural women would benefit most.[130]

As in France, postwar maternal and infant health programs in the United States were part of the pronatalist repertoire. They served as a vehicle for propaganda designed to rekindle women's maternal instincts. As in France, the advocates of such programs also hoped that providing medical and social services would alleviate some of the economic pressures that supposedly lay behind birth control. The pattern is a familiar one: the belief that a declining birth rate imperiled national security brought with it an idealization of motherhood and efforts to intimidate or cajole women into devoting their lives to bearing and raising children.

Thus, while World War I made possible the realization of a good part of the Children's Bureau's vision, maternal and child welfare policy in the 1920s would be shaped by other social and political forces as well: antifeminism and the political reaction against Progressive social reform; the maturation of the obstetrical and pediatric specialties; and the hardening of medical opposition to social insurance. A fragmented women's movement would lack the force to save Sheppard-Towner at the end of the decade.

Despite many physicians' fears that public clinics would deprive private practitioners of patients, Sheppard-Towner programs actually helped to create a growing market for medical services, because they taught parents that regular medical supervision of children's health was valuable. Students and young specialists also gained precious clinical experience at the centers.[131] Nonetheless, medical opposition to the program intensified over the course of the decade; when the program came up for renewal, the American Academy of Pediatrics endorsed the measure only on the condition that it include a provision forbidding government clinics from competing with fee-for-service practice. The waning of medical support for child health centers was in large part the result of the gradual decline of dispensaries and public clinics more generally, as medical training and elite practice moved into hospitals. Furthermore, as many pediatricians now based their

130. Quoted in U.S. Cong., House, Committee on Interstate and Foreign Commerce, *Protection of Maternity and Infancy*, p. 57.
131. See Halpern, *American Pediatrics*, pp. 20, 99; Rothman, *Woman's Proper Place*, pp. 143–44.

practices on preventive care and supervision of healthy children, the health centers constituted direct competition.[132]

The American Medical Association led the campaign to defeat renewal of the Sheppard-Towner Act in 1927, along with such conservative organizations as the Sentinels of the Republic and the Woman Patriots.[133] Though the Children's Bureau struggled to save the program, it was not supported as it had been in the first campaign by a powerful women's movement; though women in the 1920s were organized in even larger numbers than in the previous decade, they were not joined into a distinct voting bloc. They joined groups whose members were linked less by their common womanhood than by other aspects of their identity. Often they worked closely with male-dominated organizations, and women professionals and activists were more likely to pursue the new opportunities open to them outside women's institutions.[134] The programs and institutions that women built in the 1910s and 1920s did create the framework for maternal and infant health programs created under the Social Security Act of 1935, but by the end of the 1930s, as S. Josephine Baker lamented, women had lost their preeminence in the field.[135]

Like the women's infant health movement, the Progressive rhetoric that described children as a valuable national resource was a passing phenomenon in the United States. As these two forces declined, maternal and child health care in the United States were shaped by physicians' struggles to protect their professional interests and the principle that welfare was a dangerous and degrading institution. Ironically, just as public health nursing declined in the United States,

132. Rothman, *Woman's Proper Place*, pp. 150–51; Halpern, *American Pediatrics*, pp. 99–101.

133. See Lemons, *Woman Citizen*, pp. 171–73; Ladd-Taylor, "Mother-work," pp. 370–74; Rothman, *Woman's Proper Place*, p. 152; Muncy, *Creating a Female Dominion*, pp. 128–29.

134. See Nancy F. Cott, *The Grounding of Modern Feminism* (New Haven: Yale University Press, 1987), pp. 87, 95–97; Susan Ware, *Partner and I: Molly Dewson, Feminism, and New Deal Politics* (New Haven: Yale University Press, 1987), pp. 90–92; Muncy, *Creating a Female Dominion*, pp. 127–28. Muncy argues that female reformers, in eschewing partisan politics, denied themselves the only possible path to power.

135. Baker, *Fighting for Life*, p. 201. See Regina Markell Morantz-Sanchez, *Sympathy and Science: Women Physicians in American Medicine* (New York: Oxford University Press, 1985), pp. 314–15; Muncy, *Creating a Female Dominion*, chap. 5. Muncy argues that the female "child welfare dominion" retained sufficient vitality and respect in the 1930s that it influenced New Deal programs.

as medical care moved increasingly into hospitals and interest in health care for the poor diminished, the new French approach to public health, introduced by Americans, created new professional opportunities for French women.[136] The commitment of the French to protecting child health, based on a combination of national military and economic interests and embedded in a national social insurance system, would prove the more enduring one.

136. On the decline of public health nursing in the United States in the 1920s see Karen Buhler-Wilkerson, *False Dawn: The Rise and Fall of Public Health Nursing, 1900–1930* (New York: Garland, 1989), chap. 5. On the rise of public health nursing in infant health and antituberculosis work in France see Yvonne Knibiehler et al., *Cornettes et blouses blanches: Les infirmières dans la société française (1880–1980)* (Paris: Hachette, 1984), chap. 4.

Conclusion: Comparative Issues in Maternal and Infant Health Policy

Between 1880 and 1920, when the foundation for welfare-state institutions was laid in the industrial world, efforts to prevent infant mortality provided much of the impetus for maternal and child welfare programs. To a certain extent, the history of maternal and child welfare policy in the United States and France, as in other western nations, is a shared one. The provision of clean milk, an emphasis on the education of mothers in infant care, the promotion of breast-feeding, and the routine medical supervision of all infants were elements common to campaigns to prevent infant mortality in many countries.

The larger ideological and political framework for these campaigns was provided by bourgeois reform movements based on a philosophy of social organicism and the essential harmony among social classes, which sought to expand the social role of the state to protect the working class from some of the worst abuses of capitalism. In attempting to come to terms with the social problems associated with industrialization and urbanization, reformers turned to a medical model of national physical and moral degeneration, drawing on new scientific theories about the bacterial and genetic transmission of diseases.[1] Thus they argued that the state had an interest in making an investment in child life for economic, social, or military reasons.

1. See Robert A. Nye, *Crime, Madness, and Politics in Modern France: The Medical*

The nature of this discourse depended on the political circumstances specific to each nation. While in the United States it centered on ethnicity and economic efficiency and in France on military weakness and population growth, in Britain infant health was associated with the nation's ability to maintain its international economic and political preeminence.[2] These political differences were significant; they help to explain, for example, the greater urgency of French concerns about saving infant lives in comparison with the United States, and the willingness of the French state to invest significant resources in maternal and child health care. The important place of racial and moral purity in American nationalism is also important to an understanding of why eugenics was so prominent in infant health campaigns in the United States.

In addition, however, there were structural differences between French and American infant health programs which also require explanation. Women were prominent and influential in maternal and infant health policy in the United States but were relegated to a subordinate voluntary and symbolic role in France; ironically, however, French policy treated mothers more generously.[3] Compensated maternity leave would form the keystone of French maternity policy but was rejected by legislators in the United States and was never an important goal of American reformers. The organized medical profession in France was one of the most consistent advocates of maternal and infant health programs, while in the United States it was perhaps the most potent opponent.

Much of the recent scholarship on the history of the welfare state suggests that an understanding of welfare institutions must be based on the comparative history of the formation of national state structures; the goals, ideologies, and achievements of reform groups must be studied in their institutional context. Looking at the United States,

---

Concept of National Decline (Princeton, N.J.: Princeton University Press, 1984), pp. 330–35.

2. On Britain see Deborah Dwork, *War Is Good for Babies and Other Young Children: A History of the Infant and Child Welfare Movement in England, 1898–1918* (London: Tavistock, 1987); Anna Davin, "Imperialism and Motherhood," *History Workshop Journal* 5 (Spring 1978): 9–66; Jane Lewis, *The Politics of Motherhood: Child and Maternal Welfare in England, 1900–1939* (London: Croom Helm, 1980).

3. See Seth Koven and Sonya Michel, "Womanly Duties: Maternalist Politics and the Origins of Welfare States in France, Germany, Great Britain, and the United States, 1880–1920," *American Historical Review* 95 (1990): 1076–1108.

scholars have argued that the late development of bureaucracies, the decentralization of government decision making, the detachment of political parties from class-based agendas, and the disproportionate influence on legislation of southern white agricultural elites and other interest groups were among the factors that retarded the development of core social welfare institutions, including the social security and national health insurance systems that provided important components of maternal and infant health care in European nations.[4]

The history of the medical profession and its relationship to the welfare state must also be understood in this context. Like representatives of other professional groups that participated in the maternal and infant health movement, physicians pursued their own professional agenda within the larger reform organizations. French medicine was shaped by the early development of a centralized system of medical education and licensing and the important place of large hospitals within a national public welfare structure. Furthermore, because the state repeatedly called upon physicians' expertise in its efforts to combat epidemics, the identity and ethos of the organized medical profession was based as much on its role in public hygiene as on therapeutics and the private physician–patient relationship.[5] French physicians, like other French professionals, therefore depended heavily on the state for their professional legitimacy. They derived much of their authority in maternal and child health through public institutions, as they were called upon to certify, inspect, and supervise in the name of the state; the granting or refusal of a license or assistance often depended on a physician's word.

Free enterprise and the decentralization of medical education and licensing in the United States allowed practitioners of alternative schools of healing to compete effectively with "regular" doctors until the late nineteenth century. In the Progressive Era, physicians in the United States were still seeking to establish the clinical institutions and educational standards that would solidify their professional authority. One segment of the medical profession, including many

4. For a discussion of this view see the introduction to *The Politics of Social Policy in the United States,* ed. Margaret Weir, Ann Shola Orloff, and Theda Skocpol (Princeton, N.J.: Princeton University Press, 1988), especially pp. 16–27.

5. Particularly useful on this subject are the articles in *Professions and the French State, 1700–1900,* ed. Gerald L. Geison (Philadelphia: University of Pennsylvania Press, 1984).

women physicians, pediatricians, and public health officials, did actively support public health programs and social insurance. Obstetricians and pediatricians were also able to use campaigns to prevent infant mortality to achieve professional goals such as eliminating midwives and teaching mothers the value of routine examinations for healthy children. Much of the medical support for public funding of medical care evaporated by the late 1920s, however, as American physicians' mistrust of state intervention hardened and they came to believe that their interests were best served by self-regulation and a free market.[6]

The history of political institutions, education, and social welfare bureaucracies is also important for an explanation of the relationship of women's organizations to emerging welfare states. One of the most significant developments in the history of the welfare state in recent years has been feminist historians' recognition of the central role of "maternalist" movements in the creation of social institutions in the late nineteenth and early twentieth centuries.[7] Bourgeois women's movements carried into the reform enterprise the humanitarian and moralistic rhetoric of their traditional charity work, a special interest in maternal and child welfare, and a claim to understand the needs of poor women based on a belief in the universal sisterhood of shared female experience, particularly motherhood. The ideology of women's activism grew out of the domestic sphere, but women used it as they moved into the public realm, where they helped to build new social and health institutions through which the state intervened in private life, especially in reproduction. Women thus figured prominently among the social service professionals who were the agents of intervention; in the case of maternal and infant health, these included physicians, public health nurses, social workers, and *assistantes*

6. A comparison of the French and American medical professions is found in Matthew Ramsey, "The Politics of Professional Monopoly in Nineteenth-Century Medicine: The French Model and Its Rivals," in *Professions and the French State,* pp. 250–53, 274–76. On the medical profession, social insurance, and medical institutions in the United States in the Progressive Era see James G. Burrow, *Organized Medicine in the Progressive Era: The Move toward Monopoly* (Baltimore: Johns Hopkins University Press, 1977); Charles Rosenberg, *The Care of Strangers: The Rise of America's Hospital System* (New York: Basic Books, 1987), pp. 178–85, 199–201.

7. See *Mothers of a New World: Maternalist Politics and the Origins of Welfare States,* ed. Seth Koven and Sonya Michel (London: Routledge, forthcoming). For a summary of some of this work see Koven and Michel, "Womanly Duties."

sociales. For middle-class women, then, reform movements helped to create the jobs they held as they entered the world of work.

While this phenomenon was an international one, women in different countries were not equally successful in their efforts to achieve professional status and to influence policy. As Kathryn Kish Sklar points out, in the United States the inability of the formal, male polity to deal with the social problems of industrial society created a political space in which women were able to to pursue a gender-based agenda. Other historians suggest that in countries with strong bureaucracies women were precluded from participating.[8] The success of the American women's maternal and infant health movement and the visibility of female professionals within the new institutions illustrates the tremendous potential power of women's political culture in the American context. Organized women's influence was greatest where bureaucracies were least developed. This influence is apparent on the local level in small towns, where public health institutions were rudimentary or nonexistent in the early twentieth century, and often at the state level, where women were appointed to direct newly created bureaus of child hygiene.

In addition, because social welfare, with few exceptions, was not a concern of the federal government until the Progressive Era, women were able to serve in influential positions in new agencies and were able to shape federal maternal and infant welfare policy until after World War I. The comparison with France also illustrates the significance of women's ability to form autonomous educational and social welfare institutions. The late development of uniform medical licensing and educational standards allowed women access to professional careers in medicine.[9] Furthermore, the evangelical Protestant tradition not only stimulated the formation of women's charity and reform associations, but it also granted them more freedom than did

8. Kathryn Kish Sklar, "Explaining the Power of Women's Political Culture in the Creation of the American Welfare State," in *Mothers of a New World*. On women in German social welfare bureaucracy, see Jean Quataert, "A Source Analysis in German Women's History: Factory Inspectors' Reports and the Shaping of Working Class Lives, 1878–1914," *Central European History* 16 (June 1983): 99–121.

9. On the history of female physicians in the United States see Regina Markell Morantz-Sanchez, *Sympathy and Science: Women Physicians in American Medicine* (New York: Oxford University Press, 1985); Mary Roth Walsh, *"Doctors Wanted: No Women Need Apply": Sexual Barriers in the Medical Profession, 1835–1975* (New Haven: Yale University Press, 1977).

the hierarchical and centralized structures of the Catholic church in France.

In France, major women's educational and charitable institutions were traditionally subject to direct church authority. By the early twentieth century, Catholic women as well as women in the the anticlerical camp had developed organizations that were structurally independent of the church, but in the context of major political struggles over the institutional and cultural power of the church, Catholic women did not separate themselves politically from the church's position. Furthermore, from at least the late eighteenth century, French women's charities were never free of state intervention. Throughout the nineteenth century the government regulated private charities and provided a favored few with financial support. In the early twentieth century Republican leaders increasingly encouraged, subsidized, and supervised private agencies, utilizing them as an instrument of public policy. Both Republicans and Social Catholics explicitly sought to exploit bourgeois women's energy and their supposed links with working-class women; the home was a crucial battleground for reformers intent on shaping families in which women cheerfully bore children for the Republic and kept comfortable homes for their sober, hard-working husbands.

In the United States, bourgeois women reformers were more independent of male control. The staff of the U.S. Children's Bureau and other professional women along with female government officials identified themselves as leaders of a women's movement and developed policies that responded to what they saw as the expressed needs of the nation's women. The Children's Bureau staff made consistent efforts to solicit the needs of diverse women; they took individual women's requests for information and advice seriously, and their research methodology was one that maximized researchers' face-to-face contact with mothers. The bureau also persisted in seeing infant mortality as a social issue rather than as just a medical problem, and female physicians associated with the agency came to reject key elements of the obstetricians' pathological model of childbirth. It is also significant that the bureau staff were pioneers in maternal health; they asserted the inherent value of women's lives and saw the suffering of women in itself as a proper concern of policy.

While these reformers' sympathy for the plight of poor women, their recognition of the constraints imposed on motherhood by poverty, and their commitment to reaching African-American children as well as white cannot be questioned, they did not in fact respond equally to all women. They treated the General Federation of Women's Clubs and, to a lesser extent, the National Congress of Mothers as representative of all of American womanhood. Both, however, were middle- and upper-class white organizations with obvious racist and nativist tendencies that were clearly reflected, for example, in the baby health contest movement. As Nancy Cott's work suggests, one important reason that the remarkably broad coalition that fought for the Sheppard-Towner Act did not survive the 1920s is that only in a very limited sense did American women share the experience of motherhood; what they did have in common was not enough to provide the basis for ongoing gender-based political struggles. Cott also argues that in the 1920s professional women tended to see their vocational success as independent of the interests of women as a group.[10] Even in the 1910s, female physicians who clearly expressed a sense of identity with the voluntary women's movement had served as mediators between the medical profession as a whole and women's organizations. The U.S. Children's Bureau and the American Medical Association Committee on Women's and Children's Welfare, for example, had worked to channel the energy generated by the baby health contests in a direction consistent with physicians' professional goals. Baby health conferences ultimately taught women to rely on physicians as authorities on well-child care, without at the same time establishing a right to medical care.

The 1910s and 1920s constituted a transitional period for the women's movement in the United States, one that saw the organizational flowering of equal-rights individualist feminism and its split from the "maternalist" movement whose goals were rooted in a belief in inherent differences between women and men and which persisted in treating motherhood as woman's essential social identity. The question of whether these categories, developed to describe the history of Anglo-American feminism, can be applied to other countries has stimulated some debate among women's historians in the past few

10. On the consciousness of female professionals see Nancy F. Cott, *The Grounding of Modern Feminism* (New Haven: Yale University Press, 1987), pp. 225–39. In Chapter 3, on female voluntarist politics in the 1920s, Cott argues that women tended to join organizations that had female-only membership but were focused on aspects of identity and interest that were not related only to women.

years. Karen Offen suggests that individualistic feminism did not develop in France in the 1910s and 1920s partly because the family remained the unit of production for peasants and craftsmen. Instead, twentieth-century French feminism continued to emphasize social interdependence and responsibility.[11] As this study suggests, maternal ideology was far more difficult to challenge in France than in the United States, given the overwhelming nature of French pronatalism, the symbolic place of motherhood in the ideology of the Republic and of Catholic religion, and a nationalist ideology that kept returning to the question of population growth and military preparedness. The continued insecurity of the Republic and of the French nation in the twentieth century meant that French feminists who made claims based on a philosophy of individual rights and a rejection of maternity could be accused of unpatriotic behavior.

The irony, of course, is that although women seem to have wielded greater power in the United States, in many ways the French state treated motherhood with much greater respect. While women in the the United States won property and political rights much earlier than French women, American women have yet to achieve a public commitment to motherhood in the form of publicly funded child care, universal access to medical services, maternity insurance, or even the right to get their jobs back if they take maternity leaves.

An American woman who gave birth in France in the 1970s recalls the little ways in which the French state made known the value it placed on maternity: the card identifying her as a pregnant woman entitling her to priority seating on buses and subways, for example, and the "pittance" she automatically received each month because she breast-fed her child.[12] In contrast, childbirth in the United States is a private affair for most; benefits and rights depend for the most part on individual employers, labor unions, and insurance companies, except in the case of poor women who qualify for highly stigmatized Aid to Families with Dependent Children and Medicaid benefits and for nutritional supplement programs.

11. See Karen Offen, "Defining Feminism: A Comparative Historical Approach," *Signs* 14 (1988): 119–57; Nancy F. Cott, "Comment on Karen Offen's 'Defining Feminism: A Comparative Historical Approach,' " ibid. 15 (1990): 203–5. Also see Offen's earlier discussion of French feminism in "Depopulation, Nationalism, and Feminism in Fin-de-Siècle France," *American Historical Review* 89 (1984): 648–76.
12. Conversation with Carolyn Burke, September 10, 1990.

French women's entitlement to benefits originated in the years before and after World War I, and was derived from their service to the nation. (It is revealing that in Parisian subway cars first priority seating, according the posted notices, goes to disabled military veterans). Similarly, as the breast-feeding bonus illustrates, many of the benefits were intended to shape behavior. Thus French Republican politicians attempted to remove the social stigma from single motherhood, made indigent mothers eligible for medical assistance, guaranteed a woman her job back after a maternity leave, provided compensation for maternity leaves, and subsidized crèches. In return, the state demanded the right to supervise and inspect the performance of mothers. On the other hand, the French government also made it hard for women to avoid motherhood, through repressive birth control and abortion legislation. The fact that a larger percentage of French women continued to work for their living did not change this image of women as essentially mothers: mother and worker were not separate categories in French policy, while until recently in the United States the working mother remained invisible.[13]

It would be a mistake to glorify French maternal and infant health policy; the material commitment to children's lives did not match its rhetoric. The benefits provided by the state to women required to take maternity leaves, for example, did not nearly compensate them for the wages they lost. As Denise Riley writes, "There is a crucial difference between invoking 'the mother' and speaking about the practical needs of women with children."[14] In the United States today the difference between rhetoric and reality is still extreme. In *Pricing the Priceless Child,* Viviana Zelizer traces the emergence of the economically "worthless" but emotionally "priceless" child in the United States in the twentieth century. As child labor laws and compulsory education transformed children from economic assets into economic

13. On the effects on women's work of the assumption that women with children should not work, see Alice Kessler-Harris, *Out to Work: A History of Wage-Earning Women in the United States* (Oxford: Oxford University Press, 1982), pp. 213, 295–97.

14. Denise Riley, " 'The Free Mothers': Pronatalism and Working Women in Industry at the End of the Last War in Britain," *History Workshop Journal* 11 (Spring 1981): 101. For a discussion of the implementation of protective legislation in France and its effects on women see Mary Lynn Stewart, *Women, Work, and the French State: Labour Protection and Social Patriarchy, 1879–1919* (Kingston, Ont.: McGill-Queen's University Press, 1989), pp. 199–202.

burdens, she argues, child life was invested instead with religious or sentimental meaning.[15] Despite the sentimental value of children, the nation's indifference to child life is reflected in the great disparity between the infant mortality rates of white children and those of nonwhite children; despite the tremendous scientific and technological advances of the past decades, the vision of Progressive reformers has yet to be fulfilled.[16]

15. Viviana A. Zelizer, *Pricing the Priceless Child: The Changing Social Value of Children* (New York: Basic Books, 1985).

16. On trends in infant mortality rates since the 1930s see Sam Shapiro, Edward Schlesinger, and Robert E. L. Nesbitt, Jr., *Infant, Perinatal, Maternal, and Childhood Mortality in the United States* (Cambridge, Mass.: Harvard University Press, 1968), chap. 1; *Improvement in Infant and Perinatal Mortality in the United States, 1965–1973*, U.S. Department of Health and Human Services, Department of Health, Education, and Welfare Publication No. (HSA) 78–5743; Food Research and Action Center, *The Widening Gap: The Incidence and Distribution of Infant Mortality and Low Birthweight in the United States, 1978–1982* (Washington, D.C.: Food Research and Action Center, 1984).

Index

Library of Congress Cataloging-in-Publication Data

Klaus, Alisa, 1956-
    Every child a lion : the origins of maternal and infant health
  policy in the United States and France, 1890-1920 / Alisa Klaus.
        p.   cm.
    Includes bibliographical references and index.
    ISBN 0-8014-2447-X (alk. paper)
      1. Infant health services—Government policy—United States—History.   2. Infant health
  services—Government policy—France—History.   3. Maternal health services—Government
  policy—United States—History.   4. Maternal health services—Government policy—France—
  History.   I. Title.
  RJ102.K5   1993
  362.1'9892'010973—dc20   92-34682